# Early Shakespeare
# Authorship Doubts

*For Richard Whalen
Oxfordian Extraordinaire!*

*Bry W. Willhd*

# Early Shakespeare
# Authorship Doubts

Bryan H. Wildenthal

Zindabad Press
2019

First Edition (hardcover version), June 2019 (with minor corrections and revisions, not affecting pagination, August 2019)

ISBN 978-1-73271-660-5


Published by:

Zindabad Press
P.O. Box 81026
San Diego, CA 92138


Printed by Lulu (https://www.lulu.com)

By the same author:

*Native American Sovereignty on Trial: A Handbook With Cases, Laws, and Documents* (ABC-CLIO, 2003)

for my ever-loving husband
Ashish

"O know, sweet love, I always write of you ..."

*Shake-speare's Sonnet 76*


and

respectfully dedicated to Sir George Greenwood (1850–1928)
brilliant scholar, lawyer, author, Shakespeare lover,
doubter, liberal politician, advocate of freedom
for India (far ahead of his time), and
all-around inspiration

"*Adon* deafly masking through
... in purple robes distained ...
One whose power floweth far,
That should have been of our rhyme
The only object and the star."

Thomas Edwards, *L'Envoy* to *Narcissus* (1593)

"*Adon*" referring to the unnamed author
of Shakespeare's *Venus and Adonis*

"My name be buried where my body is ..."

*Shake-speare's Sonnet* 72

"Your name [beloved] from hence immortal life shall have,
Though I, once gone, to all the world must die."

*Shake-speare's Sonnet* 81

by an "ever-living poet"

"ever-living" in the dedication indicating, in 1609, a deceased author, seven years before
Shakspere of Stratford died; an author identified only in the title, with a blank space
between two lines on the title page where the author's name should appear; the
name of Henry Wriothesley, Earl of Southampton, widely believed to be the
beloved youth of the *Sonnets*, having been given "immortal life" by the
dedications of *Venus and Adonis* in 1593 and *Lucrece* in 1594

"Let thy beams shine as far as farthest Ind[ia],
... [and] verses live supported by a spear."

*Envy's Scourge, and Virtue's Honour* (c. 1605–15)
sole surviving copy of a poem by an unknown author

# TABLE OF CONTENTS

See pages 66-67 for the table of contents of Part IV, including
an overview in Part IV.30 of five indications that the author
"Shakespeare" died years before 1616.

PREFACE

Why write another book about who wrote Shakespeare? It's a good question. Certainly nobody paid me. Friends, colleagues, even my mother-in-law—while cheerfully supportive—have, I think, wondered what motivated me. My ever-patient husband, on the other hand, never doubted the project for a moment—yet another reason he's the perfect spouse.

Motivation is an endlessly fascinating mystery of human behavior. It is a large part of what draws me to the Shakespeare Authorship Question (SAQ)—that and the inherent interest of a rich body of literature and vivid period in human history. What really motivated that author to produce these passionate, surpassingly beautiful, often obsessive and tortured expressions of the human condition? And to even begin to answer that question, don't we need to figure out who the author really was?

That it was only to make money is quite unbelievable, though many authors do (also) want to make money from writing and there's absolutely nothing wrong with that. I hope to myself. To quote the *First Folio*'s preface, I say to the great variety of my own readers, "whatever you do, *Buy*"[1] this book!

---

[1] *First Folio*, p. 7 (letter "To the great Variety of Readers") (emphasis added; capitalization in original). We have, in fact, ample evidence that the person I think was the author frantically pursued, to the end of his life, various schemes to restore and improve his financial condition. But for various reasons quite understandable in light of his social background and circumstances, he didn't seem to view writing as the best way to do that—though his writing may have

(footnote continued on next page)

Defenders of the conventional "Stratfordian" theory about the author "William Shakespeare" often claim that nobody had any doubts about the authorship for hundreds of years after his death. But this book explores *dozens* of expressions of authorship doubt *during Shakespeare's own lifetime,* going back at least *thirty years before* the Stratfordian attribution was first suggested in the posthumous First Folio of 1623.

This remarkable documentary evidence includes five separate items independently corroborating that the true author died many years before the death of William Shakspere of Stratford-upon-Avon in 1616—an event which received no public or literary notice at the time. I use the spelling "Shakspere" for convenience, to distinguish between the Stratford man and the author (whoever that was), for reasons more fully explained later.[2]

The evidence of early doubts has been largely ignored—its very existence mostly denied—by the complacent guardians of academic orthodoxy in the field of Shakespeare studies. Many writers in Elizabethan and Jacobean times raised questions about the authorship of the works of "Shakespeare" *even as they were first published.* Yet a leading Shakespeare "expert" recently declared he would flunk any student who dared to raise such questions. Some prominent professors have gone so far as to viciously slander those who entertain authorship doubts as comparable to Holocaust deniers.[3] Do they protest too much? This book explores what *they don't want you to know—or even ask questions about.*

---

(footnote continued from previous page)

had something to do with a secretive and very generous stipend that Queen Elizabeth began giving him in 1586. If that gets your curiosity going, see Part I, note 4; Part IV.19 & note 459; Cutting, "Sufficient Warrant" (2017); Cutting, "Tin Letters" (2017).

　　[2] See Part IV.30 on indications of death before 1616; see also Part III.A on the spelling of "Shakespeare" and "Shakspere," Part I & note 34 on the Great Silence of 1616, and Part III.B & note 49 on who *really* has a "1604 problem."

　　[3] See below in this Preface (text related to note 12), and Part V.D & note 56, for more on the outrageous comparisons to Holocaust denial. On Professor James

(footnote continued on next page)

This is the most sensational literary mystery of all time—and an academic and intellectual scandal of the first order. In my own long career as a professor, I have had more than ample exposure to academic humbug and how spectacularly mistaken the prevailing conventional wisdom may sometimes be. My most important articles on American constitutional history, one cited by the U.S. Supreme Court, helped overturn a suffocatingly dominant conventional view about the central meaning of the Fourteenth Amendment in relation to the Bill of Rights—an orthodoxy that reigned supreme at leading American law schools for half a century but which turned out to be profoundly mistaken.[4]

I will always be baffled by the oft-heard suggestion that it doesn't matter who the author Shakespeare was because we have the works and that's enough. Should not the extraordinary (perhaps unique) character of the works *heighten* (not *reduce*) our interest in whoever wrote them? This suggestion most often comes from those who simply prefer the traditional authorship attribution. Yet it sits very uneasily next to the obvious passion (which we doubters understand and respect) that many traditionalists bring to their view of the author.

I will return to these issues in the Conclusion (Part V). For now, it suffices to quote Katherine Chiljan: "If the true biography of one of the greatest minds of Western civilization does not matter, then whose does?"[5]

The main rationale for this book is that amazingly little has been written, from any *systematic* or *comprehensive* perspective,

---

(footnote continued from previous page)
Shapiro's threat (possibly humorous but still bullying even if so) to fail any of his students who persisted in asking him authorship questions, see Part V.D.

[4] See, *e.g.*, Wildenthal, "Nationalizing the Bill of Rights" (2007), cited in *McDonald v. Chicago*, 561 U.S. 742, 763 n. 10, 829 n. 10, 830 n. 12, 841 (2010) (opinion of the Court and concurring opinion), and *Timbs v. Indiana*, 586 U.S. ___, 139 S. Ct. 682, 691 (2019) (concurring opinion).

[5] Chiljan, p. 340.

on the subject of Shakespeare authorship doubts during this crucial early time period. Yet such doubts have great importance for the broader modern SAQ. The evidence explored in this book has until now remained buried for the most part, unknown and difficult to access for most readers. It has appeared in countless obscure newsletter and journal articles and in various passages in books by different writers. Most of these books and articles have never achieved wide notice or circulation. This book, citing and building with gratitude on the work of all these writers, seeks to present the key evidence—as much as I could feasibly locate and assemble—in an organized, coherent, and accessible way.

Diana Price's and Katherine Chiljan's superb books, *Shakespeare's Unorthodox Biography* (2001) and *Shakespeare Suppressed* (2011), contain the most extensive prior surveys of some of these early indications of authorship doubt. This book engages in an extended dialogue with theirs and is in some ways a sequel. Not only could I not have written it without theirs, the very idea of writing it would never even have occurred to me.

It may sound trite to say I wrote this book for the sheer love of doing so, but that's also true. Part II comments on the fact that so many "amateur" independent scholars have devoted so much unpaid effort to all sides of the SAQ. Recall that the true and literal meaning of "amateur" is one who pursues an endeavor purely out of love. In that light, no one could question the love we all have for these literary works and their author (or authors)—whoever he, she, or they were. We just can't agree who it was.

This book relies mostly on secondary sources and is largely a critical analysis and synthesis of modern published scholarship, both orthodox and skeptical, dealing with the SAQ. It also engages directly with some primary Elizabethan and Jacobean sources, but only to a more limited extent. I am a law professor, not a scholar of English literature, and fully cognizant of my relative lack of background and expertise in this field, in which I am most certainly an amateur.

I have, however, been a professional scholar and writer for decades, the author of a textbook from a major publisher as well as numerous widely cited articles in leading scholarly law journals. I am familiar with rigorous standards of scholarly ethics, historical research, and textual analysis. In particular, my studies of legal history have involved challenges closely analogous to studying Shakespeare or any archaic literature: how to carefully interpret and contextualize such writings and figure out how they were read and understood by their contemporaries.

As noted above, my scholarly work has been deemed important enough to be relied upon by the U.S. Supreme Court. It was cited by briefs filed on both sides in one deeply divided case.[6] My academic peers and generations of students, from very diverse philosophical and ideological perspectives, have come to trust and respect me as a fair and reliable teacher and scholar.

Reasonable scholars have interpreted and evaluated the evidence discussed in this book—and will continue to do so—in many different ways. I do not claim any unique insights into the truth. Much work remains to be done. I welcome constructive comments and criticism.[7] I hope the issues explored here will be taken up and pursued by scholars with more expertise than me.

---

[6] See note 1 (referring to *McDonald*; the *Timbs* decision was unanimous)

[7] I have researched the issues and the relevant past literature to the best of my ability within the limits of my available time and resources, consistent with the need to get the book published promptly to advance the discussion of this important subject. I do worry, however, that I may have reinvented the wheel on some points, perhaps missing some published discussions anticipating, supporting, or undermining certain points, which I should have cited (and would have, had I known). My sincere apologies, if so, to any such previous writers. I would be most grateful for any additional citations that readers may provide (please contact me directly at bryanw@gmail.com). Despite my efforts, this book doubtless contains errors. Mistakes are inevitable even in the best scholarly work and I am not so arrogant as to think mine is the "best."

In the foregoing spirit, I will maintain a free updated memorandum at the site where I first posted preview excerpts of the manuscript, where I will acknowledge and discuss relevant corrections, updates, and supplemental citations. This Preface, and Parts I, II, and V, will also remain freely available at that site

(footnote continued on next page)

I presented a preliminary outline of this project at the Annual Conference of the Shakespeare Oxford Fellowship (SOF) on October 14, 2017 (available on YouTube). See listings under Wildenthal in the Bibliography.

This book is deeply in debt, as my citations throughout reveal, to a vast number of studies by past and present scholars. A very selective list would have to include, most notably, works by Sir George Greenwood, J. Thomas Looney, Charlton Ogburn Jr., Diana Price, Katherine Chiljan, Professor Roger Stritmatter, Mark Anderson, John Hamill, Stephanie Hopkins Hughes, Richard Malim, and Robert Detobel (who passed away as this book was completed[8]), as well as the 2013 anthology edited by John Shahan and Alexander Waugh, a 1998 article by Professor Lukas Erne (an orthodox scholar based in Geneva), and a remarkable series of articles during 2013–18 by Alexander Waugh, Julia Cleave, Jan Cole, and Patrick O'Brien.

Several of the latter articles appeared in the newsletter of Britain's De Vere Society (DVS). Many other articles cited extensively herein have been published in the SOF's peer-reviewed scholarly journal, *The Oxfordian*, and in the SOF *Newsletter*. (See the Bibliography for the DVS and SOF websites.) I have also consulted and cite frequently a large number of orthodox Stratfordian studies.

Alexander Waugh, in particular, has produced a stunning flood of articles and presentations in the last six years on Shakespeare's Stratford Monument, the *Sonnets*, the 1623 *First Folio*,

---

(footnote continued from previous page)

(https://ssrn.com/abstract=3007393), as a teaser which I hope will induce more people to buy the full book. Also included in that free posting is the complete Bibliography (with numerous hotlinks embedded in the pdf), which should itself be a valuable resource for other researchers.

[8] Detobel, a scholar of Belgian (Flemish) origin who settled in Germany and worked there most of his life, died in September 2018 at age 79. He was one of our most rigorous, admired, and productive Oxfordian scholars. See "Detobel: In Memoriam" (2018).

and related issues. His work has not yet received the respectful attention it deserves. I think Waugh has achieved a decisive and historic breakthrough in the SAQ. This book frequently cites his work where it bears on the issue of early authorship doubts, and it merits careful further study beyond my capacity here. Waugh & Stritmatter's forthcoming *New Shakespeare Allusion Book* will greatly enhance the accessibility of all early references to Shakespeare, including early expressions of authorship doubt.

The foregoing is far from an exhaustive list. I am obviously indebted to all the scholars and works cited in the following pages (please see the Bibliography). But the foregoing scholars are mentioned here because they specifically sparked my interest in the subject of early Shakespeare authorship doubts.

I would add a special thanks to Stephanie Hopkins Hughes, founding editor of *The Oxfordian* (1998–2007), whose gracious and welcoming outreach in 2009 played no small part in getting me actively involved in the SAQ and SOF. I am grateful to Jim Warren for his encouraging comments on the overall project; and also to Bob Meyers, Katherine Chiljan, Chris Pannell, and the late W. Ron Hess,[9] for very helpful comments on Part IV.2 (discussing *Groats-Worth of Wit*), first written as a freestanding article.

Indeed, I am grateful to all my friends and colleagues in the SOF and DVS (both named and unnamed here)—as well as to my loving extended family and friends—for all their support and camaraderie. For reading parts of the manuscript and offering helpful comments, I am also thankful to Martin Hyatt, Tom Owen-Towle, Bill Glaser, Catherine Hatinguais, Jan Scheffer, my husband Ashish Agrawal, my sister Becky Wildenthal, my nephew Raghav Agarwal (who also gave cogent advice on marketing), and my mother-in-law Pushpa Lala.

---

[9] Hess (age 70) and his wife died in May 2019 as this book went to press, victims of a shocking double homicide. He was a respected scholar of the SAQ. I will always be grateful for his kind and selfless assistance.

Needless to say, I bear exclusive blame for any mistakes and shortcomings in this book, which would probably have been reduced had I been more willing to follow advice. None of the people mentioned above should be assumed to endorse any views or arguments stated herein.

I myself am an Oxfordian. My view is that William Shakspere of Stratford-upon-Avon (1564–1616) was almost certainly not the primary author of the "Shakespeare" canon and that Edward de Vere, 17th Earl of Oxford (1550–1604), very probably was.[10]

This book, however, is not primarily an Oxfordian tract. Nor, strictly speaking, does it aim to provide yet another refutation of the orthodox Stratfordian view. Rather, as the title indicates, it is about the historical reality of early Shakespeare authorship *doubts*. Quite naturally, however, I do not shy away from noting when the evidence does in fact undermine the conventional authorship attribution and support the Oxfordian theory.

In quotations of primary Elizabethan and Jacobean sources (both text and titles), I silently modernize most spellings, while remaining a stickler about preserving italics, capitalization, and other emphases in the originals, at least upon first quotation (unless indicated otherwise). I generally indicate with brackets any alteration of punctuation (always, certainly, any change in

---

[10] See Wildenthal, "How I Became an Oxfordian," and sources cited in Part I, note 4; see also Part III.A on the spelling of "Shakespeare" and "Shakspere." Stylistically, I find it preferable and convenient to refer to Edward de Vere most often by the simple shorthand "Vere," his family name. The "de" was and is a prefix commonly used in aristocratic names (and modern names with such origins), analogous to *"von"* in German or *"of"* in English. Vere was Edward *"of"* the family Vere, just as he became Earl *"of"* Oxford. Just as he is often referred to simply by his title, "Oxford," it makes equal sense to refer to him simply by his family name, "Vere." There is evidence that he himself was quite comfortable with that simple appellation. See Prechter (2002). As Prechter suggested, it may not have been appropriate to use "de" at all when referring to *other* members of the Vere family who did not hold the title of earl. In any event, it seems to me needlessly clunky and awkward to constantly use "de Vere" when referring to Edward de Vere simply by his surname. We do not go around calling him "of Oxford"!

word choice), but not where apostrophes are inserted to conform with modern style (I guess I have a thing about those, or view them as part of "spelling"). Brackets indicate my own alterations, explanations, or commentary, unless otherwise noted.

As my extensive Bibliography and footnotes illustrate, I have tried to be very thorough in providing source citations. I use footnotes (not endnotes or parenthetical citations in the text) for reasons of convenience, transparency, smooth textual flow, and obstinate personal preference. Within the footnotes and in the Bibliography, citations follow my own modified version of Modern Language Association (MLA) format.[11] This book does not, however, provide footnotes or citations for dates, events, and other basic facts which are or may be common knowledge for those well-informed about history and literature in general or Shakespeare in particular. One may easily verify and explore such points in

---

[11] In-line parenthetical citations are the preferred MLA style but are clunky at best, even if merely providing a concise citation of authority. They interrupt distractingly the flow of text, more so than a footnote or endnote call. And they do not accommodate digressions, which are often useful. Endnotes resolve some of those problems and avoid the arguable distraction and consumption of space of footnotes at the bottom of each page of text. But endnotes create worse problems of their own. It is very difficult to find endnote calls, or even to tell if any exist on a given page, without careful scanning of the text. I have often found that very annoying. It is much easier when the notes themselves appear at the bottom of the same page. Footnotes also promote transparency in citations and sourcing. I often find it valuable to check as I read along what sources and scholars (if any) an author is relying upon, and footnotes allow that to be done at a glance.

Digressions are almost pointless if one has to flip back and forth to and from the end of a book or article. And it is very inconvenient to be forced to do so even to determine what sources the author is relying upon. Keeping all citations and digressions at the bottom of each page to which they relate—*i.e.,* using traditional footnotes—is concededly an imperfect compromise, but in my view by far the best solution on balance (using, of course, short-form citations in the notes with full source information in the Bibliography).

Furthermore, I find traditional footnotes have the salutary effect of forcing me constantly to consider whether any digression (or anything I want to say) really belongs in the text, or is best relegated to a footnote, or perhaps should be omitted altogether—and if it is retained (in text or footnote), to keep it as concise as possible. Endnotes can become an all-too-easy dumping ground (which few readers ever look at anyway) for undisciplined writers.

standard reference works, including *Wikipedia*—preferably making cautious and appropriate use of the latter convenient online resource (see discussion in Part II). This book cites the latter types of sources only when they may be of particular interest.

Since the third word in Part I—repeated often throughout the book—is "Stratfordian," I must address the proper naming of the disputants in the Shakespeare Authorship Question. This naming issue has become as bitterly contested as everything else about the debate. "Stratfordian" is obviously the simplest, most neutrally descriptive and informative, and thus fairest way to describe those who adhere to and defend the traditional proposition that the author of the works of "Shakespeare" was Shakspere of Stratford. For many decades, this perfectly useful label (and its logical opposite, "anti-Stratfordian") found general acceptance among Stratfordians themselves as well as skeptics.

This nomenclature is not in any way biased against those who adhere to the orthodox view of authorship. It highlights the name of the town they themselves have turned into a veritable shrine to which many Shakespeare lovers make pilgrimages. If anything, it frames the issue unfavorably to authorship doubters, since "anti" has connotations of negativity and contrariness.

In recent years, however—perhaps sensing the debate shifting against them?—many leading Stratfordians have made an ostentatious effort to reject this useful terminology. They have sought to claim the smugly circular, vague, and uninformative term "Shakespearean" for their side, while trying to impose the nonsensical and offensive epithet "anti-Shakespearean" on those who doubt or reject the Stratfordian theory.

"Non-Stratfordian" is perhaps the most neutral and inclusive term for the highly diverse camp of doubters, though "anti-Stratfordian" does not bother me at all and still seems very convenient. "Post-Stratfordian" is a clever alternative which may gain in popularity. "Skeptic" and "doubter" are also perfectly fair and accurate synonyms for non- (or anti- or post-) Stratfordians, as are "orthodox," "conventional," or "traditional" to describe Stratfordians and their views.

Some of us skeptics are actually not in great doubt and do in fact reject—at least as a matter of strong probability, based on all our reading and study to date and our best analysis of available evidence—the idea that Shakspere of Stratford was the true author of the works of Shakespeare. But to label us "Shakespeare deniers" as some Stratfordians do—trying to compare us, on some occasions, to Holocaust deniers—is even more nonsensical and outrageous than calling us "anti-Shakespearean."[12]

Authorship skeptics do not oppose or "deny" Shakespeare. We revere the works, the author, and the name too (even though it is most likely a pseudonym). Nor are we anti-*Shakspere of Stratford* for that matter. We have nothing against *him* or his *town*. Both seem to have played an important role in this entire fascinating mystery. People will always visit Stratford itself for that reason and for its fine theatres. I am eagerly looking forward to doing so myself. We certainly would not want anyone in the tourism or entertainment industries to lose their jobs.

We merely doubt (or think highly implausible) the Stratfordian *theory* that Shakspere was the great writer "Shakespeare." If he was not, then *his* identity has been stolen and disrespected *as much as the author's*.[13]

It is modern Stratfordian academics who disrespect the author (whoever that was), when they show so little interest in the authorship puzzle staring us all in the face. This is a mystery

---

[12] For more on these terminology wars, and why the comparison to Holocaust denial in particular (offered even by some prominent and respected academics, like Professors Stephen Greenblatt and Gary Taylor), is especially outrageous and irresponsible—and disrespectful to Holocaust victims themselves—see Part V.D & note 56; Wildenthal, "Rollett and Shapiro," pp. 7-9.

[13] See generally Pointon (2011). Playing up the inherent fascination of the authorship mystery, instead of just hawking the chintzy traditional myth, might actually be a way for Stratford to *enhance* its appeal to tourists and Shakespeare fans. The authorship mystery is the main reason I plan to visit.

that deeply interested more than a few people during Elizabethan and Jacobean times, as this book demonstrates.

I prefer to avoid pejorative labels like "denier" or "denialist," but if Stratfordians insist on tossing such terms about, then the irresistible and ironic fact must be noted that they live in glass houses. Stratfordian academics are the real denialists to the extent they deny the documented reality of authorship doubts expressed by Shakespeare's own contemporaries.

Bryan H. Wildenthal
San Diego, California
May 2019

# I. INTRODUCTION:
## THE STRATFORDIAN THEORY OF SHAKESPEARE AUTHORSHIP AND THE DENIAL OF EARLY DOUBTS AS THE CENTRAL STRATFORDIAN CLAIM

The dominant "Stratfordian" theory concerning the Shakespeare Authorship Question (SAQ) is that the literary works credited to "William Shakespeare" (some published under that name, some first published anonymously) were written (at least mainly) by William Shakspere of Stratford-upon-Avon (1564–1616).[1] In defense of that proposition, Stratfordians make various supporting arguments, of which the two most important may be summarized as the "ample early evidence" claim and the "no early doubts" claim.

The first of these is the claim that plenty of evidence dating back to Shakspere of Stratford's lifetime affirmatively documents and proves that he personally was (and was known as) the author of the "Shakespeare" plays and poems. The second is the claim that nobody doubted or questioned the authorship of the works of Shakespeare during his lifetime or for a long time afterward.

Orthodox scholars have asserted these claims many times in various ways, and they have found an echo chamber among the general public. If you spend any time reading online comments to

---

[1] See Part III.A for a discussion of why it is eminently reasonable to render his surname with that spelling, and for a general discussion of spelling issues. The Preface discusses the term "Stratfordian" and the fraught issue of how to label those who debate the SAQ.

news articles or blog postings about the SAQ—or Amazon reader reviews of books on the subject (especially if the book expresses authorship doubt), or reviews by those *claiming* to have read the book or in some cases brazenly boasting *not* to have read it—you will see many repetitions of these two basic themes. You will also see a lot of name-calling directed at doubters, alleging snobbery, mental illness, and even comparisons to Holocaust denial.[2]

This book argues that the central and most important Stratfordian claim is the second one: that no authorship doubts or questions arose during Shakespeare's own time nor for centuries afterward. It challenges that claim.

Not nearly enough has been written about this "no early doubts" claim, nor about the fascinating evidence whose very existence it denies. Julia Cleave aptly described "this all-too-familiar claim" as a "stock Stratfordian meme."[3] It is often the most emphatic and reflexive response to those who propose other authorship candidates, like the leading one: Edward de Vere, 17th Earl of Oxford (1550–1604).[4] Cleave noted, as my experience

---

[2] See, *e.g.*, Part V.C-D; Wildenthal, "Rollett and Shapiro," pp. 7-9. On the comparison to Holocaust denial—an especially outrageous and reckless argumentative card played all too often by some Stratfordian advocates, one deeply disrespectful to Holocaust victims themselves—see especially Part V.D, note 56.

[3] Cleave, p. 32. Cleave's valuable article focused on doubts from 1645 to 1852, in contrast to this book's focus on doubts predating 1616.

[4] The Oxfordian theory was launched by John Thomas Looney (1870–1944) in his 1920 book, republished with added commentaries by Ruth Loyd Miller (1975) and in an excellent new annotated edition by James Warren (2018). The most important follow-up studies to date are the books by Charlton Ogburn Jr. (1984, rev. 1992) and Mark Anderson (2005)—and Professor Roger Stritmatter's dissertation (2001, 4th ed. 2015), showing striking linkages between marked verses in Vere's Geneva Bible and biblical allusions in the Shakespeare canon (see Anderson, app. A, pp. 381-92, for a useful summary).

Warren's *Index* (4th ed. 2017) provides a useful guide to the vast Oxfordian scholarship of the past century, including many articles by Stephanie Hopkins Hughes (founding editor, *The Oxfordian*, 1998–2007; see *Politicworm* website and her forthcoming *Shakespeare and the Birth of the London Stage*); see also, *e.g.*, Nina Green, *Oxford Authorship* website; Whalen (1994); Sobran (1997); Malim (2004, 2012); Farina (2006); Moore (2009); Fox (2012); Magri (2014); Goldstein (2016); Whittemore (2016); Cutting (2018); Jiménez (2018); Cheryl

(footnote continued on next page)

confirms, that "the meme in its starkest form has gone viral ... and needs to be robustly challenged."[5]

A great deal has been written, by contrast, about the "ample early evidence" claim. It too has obvious importance and merits some review here. But if you read the works of orthodox scholars carefully, you will see they are actually ambivalent about that claim. They occasionally concede, in moments of candor, that essentially *no* documentary evidence *contemporary to Shakspere of Stratford's lifetime* clearly and specifically links him to the works of "Shakespeare."

Surprisingly, one may cite for this point the 2013 Cambridge University Press anthology co-edited by those high priests of

---

(footnote continued from previous page)
Eagan-Donovan's documentary (2018); Alexander Waugh, "My Shakespeare Rise!" (2018); "Twenty Poems of Edward de Vere" (2018); Stritmatter, *Poems of Edward de Vere* (2019). The latter studies show extensive parallels to the Shake-speare canon, also seen in Vere's letters. See, *e.g.*, Fowler (1986); Sobran, pp. 106-08, 231-86; Cutting, "Tin Letters" (2017).

The parallels in Vere's life with themes, incidents, and knowledge in the canon are also stunning. See, *e.g.*, Jiménez (2009); note 33 below. The biograph-ical and poetic-epistolary parallels, along with the biblical linkages explored by Stritmatter, constitute three independent bodies of mutually corroborating and reinforcing circumstantial evidence—each rich and powerful in itself and to-gether going well beyond anything that could plausibly be dismissed as coincid-ental. Most people who have rejected the Oxfordian theory have never carefully examined this mass of evidence, most who do find it compelling. During 1986–2016, five Justices of the U.S. Supreme Court—Harry A. Blackmun, Sandra Day O'Connor, Lewis F. Powell Jr., Antonin Scalia, and John Paul Stevens—rejected the Stratfordian theory, of whom three (Blackmun, Scalia, and Stevens) declared themselves Oxfordians. See Bravin; Wildenthal, "Oxfordian Era." Another useful source, though deeply biased, is Professor Alan Nelson's 2003 biography of Vere, which displays tendentious hostility to its own subject and does not seriously address the Oxfordian theory. Anderson (2005) is a far better biography. See also Green's concisely documented biography (on her website) and Ward (1928).

There are other authorship candidates (none as strong as Vere), but a full discussion is beyond the scope of this book. See comments in text below and notes 42 and 44 (on the Baconian theory); Parts III.B & note 43, and V & note 37 (on the Marlovian theory); Part IV.12 & note 298 (on the Sackvillean theory); and Part IV.30 (providing some overall discussion of alternative candidates); see also, *e.g.*, Hope & Holston; Hughes, "Oxfordian Response" (2009); Leahy (2018).

[5] Cleave, p. 32.

Stratfordian orthodoxy, the Rev. Paul Edmondson (an actual Anglican priest) and Sir Stanley Wells, in an essay by Wells himself. Wells is Professor Emeritus, University of Birmingham, Honorary President of the Shakespeare Birthplace Trust, and is considered one of the two or three top living experts on Shakespeare. The Edmondson-Wells anthology is the most ambitious attempt yet to lay authorship doubts to rest. But Wells's essay in this volume acknowledged that "despite the mass of evidence" available from Shakspere's lifetime, "there is *none* that explicitly and incontrovertibly identifies [the author 'Shakespeare'] with Stratford-upon-Avon."[6]

John Shahan has noted that Wells's 2013 essay omitted two early allusions undercutting that identification and raising significant authorship doubts, despite Wells's stated "aim to list all explicit references [to Shakespeare] surviving up to ... 1642."[7]

The references ignored by Wells were: (1) a strange allusion strongly implying the name was a pseudonym, in a list of poets in the 1628 edition of a book by Thomas Vicars, following the odd omission of Shakespeare from the same list in the 1624 edition of the same book; and (2) references to "Shakspere" and "Shakspeare" as merely a theatrical company shareholder and one of several "men players" (actors; he was listed third among them) in a 1635 answer by his fellow shareholder Cuthbert Burbage, submitted to Lord Chamberlain Philip Herbert (Earl of Pembroke and Montgomery), in response to a petition concerning a theatre business dispute. The 1635 answer contained no hint that Shak-

---

[6] Wells, "Allusions," in Edmondson & Wells (2013), p. 81 (emphasis added). For earlier efforts to defend the Stratfordian theory against doubters, see, *e.g.*, Matus (1994) and McCrea's optimistically titled *The Case for Shakespeare: The End of the Authorship Question* (2005). Professor James Shapiro, in his book *Contested Will* (2010), p. 281, endorsed Matus and McCrea as offering "the strongest arguments" for the Stratfordian theory.

[7] Wells, "Allusions," p. 74; see also Shahan, "Beyond Reasonable Doubt, Part 1," pp. 3-5 (points 12 and 16).

spere was any kind of writer, much less Britain's most celebrated poet-playwright.[8]

Orthodox scholars often try to have it both ways by making broad assertions that seem to imply there is ample early evidence for the Stratfordian theory. But they frequently also, without blushing too much at the inconsistency, deploy an alternative fallback claim: Even if the early evidence for Shakspere's authorship is very sparse, well, it was a long time ago, that's typical for surviving records of the time, and we have even less contemporaneous evidence documenting the careers of other writers of that era.

The latter fallback claim is a blatantly false diversionary tactic. It has been resoundingly disproven. As Diana Price demonstrated in her 2001 book, we have *far less* contemporaneous and *personally identifying* evidence of Shakspere's supposed literary career than for other Elizabethan or Jacobean writers, most of whom were much less important yet somehow much better documented.[9] In fact, we have almost none before 1623. It is not even remotely a close call. The discrepancy is gaping and undeniable.

---

[8] As Shahan noted, it seems this "would have greatly strengthened" the answer. Shahan, "Beyond Reasonable Doubt, Part 1," p. 4 (point 16). Likewise devoid of any hint that Shakspere was a writer are the writings left by many of his family members and associates, including his own son-in-law. Some of his *presumed* associates, like Ben Jonson, did of course leave writings dating after Shakspere's death in 1616 that indicate (or hint in curiously ambiguous fashion) that he was a writer, but that is another matter, and many of those writings in themselves raise doubts. See, *e.g.*, discussion in text below and notes 35-37 & 40; Part III.B & note 38. The point is that many of his *known* associates and family members did *not* betray to posterity any awareness whatsoever that he was any kind of writer at all, much less England's greatest. See Part II & note 2.

Philip Herbert was one of the two noblemen to whom the 1623 *First Folio* of Shakespeare plays was dedicated (see note 41)—supposedly authored by actor-shareholder "Shakspere." The *Folio* was republished in 1632, just three years before Burbage's 1635 answer. For more on the Vicars and Burbage references, see Chambers (1930), v. 2, app. A, pp. 65-66 (Burbage); Ogburn, pp. 113-14 (Burbage); Chiljan, pp. 28, 103-04, 193 (both); Shahan & Waugh, pp. xiii, 198-99 (both); Schurink (2006) (Vicars); D. Nelson (2008) (Vicars).

[9] Price, ch. 8, pp. 112-58; ch. 17, pp. 296-307; and pp. 309-22 ("Appendix: Chart of Literary Paper Trails"); see also Shahan & Waugh, ch. 3, pp. 41-45 (providing a useful graphic of Price's findings).

But many Stratfordians keep right on robotically repeating this debunked canard anyway.

Wells, for example, in his 2013 essay, began and ended with sweeping assertions of ample early evidence. He declared at the outset that he would "demonstrate ... an abundance of such evidence"[10] and concluded 14 pages later: "The evidence that Shakespeare wrote Shakespeare is overwhelming, and to dispute it is to challenge the entire validity of historical research."[11] But just before that conclusion, perhaps recognizing that some readers might not swallow the full party line, Wells deployed the fallback maneuver: "Gaps in the record ... make people uneasy. There are certainly gaps in the records of Shakespeare's life, *but there is nothing unusual about them. We know more about him than about many of his contemporaries* ...."[12]

No, we do not, and Wells knows it—not with regard to relevant *literary* evidence. After all, buried in the middle of that very same essay (as quoted above), Wells blurted out his confession that the ample early evidence claim is a myth. Given the degree of cognitive dissonance suggested by these intellectual contortions, it seems a bit rich that Wells has had the gall to accuse anti-Stratfordians of lacking mental stability.[13]

Professor Lukas Erne, an unusually candid and thoughtful Stratfordian scholar, anticipated and supported Price's argument in 1998: "With possibly no other English author [than Shakespeare] is there a greater discrepancy between the scarcity of extant historical documents that reliably deal with the author's life"—much less, Erne might have added, his *literary* career—"and the precision with which biographers have tried to trace his life."

---

[10] Wells, "Allusions," p. 73.
[11] Wells, "Allusions," p. 87.
[12] Wells, "Allusions," p. 87 (emphasis added).
[13] See, *e.g.*, Edmondson & Wells (2011); Shahan, "SAC Letters to SBT and RSC re: Wells' False and Libelous Claims About Authorship Doubters" (2010, 2014, and 2015).

Erne admitted "this has created a gap between how much" we really know about Shakespeare "and the inferences that can be drawn ... with a reasonable degree of certainty .... Apocryphal stories have contributed their share ...."[14]

By contrast, Professor James Shapiro, in his 2010 book *Contested Will*, offered a drive-by critique of Price that demonstrated either Shapiro's intellectual dishonesty or at best (implausibly) that he somehow missed Price's point. For example, Shapiro scolded Price for daring to point out the lack of evidence that Shakspere "had a *direct relationship* with a patron."[15] But Shapiro failed to note any evidence of *literary* patronage because he knows perfectly well there is none.[16]

---

[14] Erne, "Mythography," pp. 438-39.

[15] Shapiro (2010), p. 243 (Shapiro's emphasis); see also Price, p. 310.

[16] Shapiro asserted that Shakspere "wore the livery of the Lord Chamberlain, served King James both as a King's Man and as a Groom of the Chamber, and directly addressed a patron, the Earl of Southampton, in the [dedication] letters prefacing both *Venus and Adonis* [1593] and *[The Rape of] Lucrece* [1594]." Shapiro (2010), p. 243. But Shakspere's work *as an actor* in the Lord Chamberlain's or King's Men (scantily documented as it is) obviously does not suggest *literary* patronage, nor any writing career whatsoever. See Wildenthal, "Rollett and Shapiro," pp. 1-2 (responding to a more recent and similarly unconvincing claim by Shapiro and others); compare Schuessler (2016) and Wolfe & Witmore (2017) (straining to parlay references to "Shakespeare the player" in the context of the Stratford man's coat-of-arms, and separate impersonal references to the author "Shakespeare," into a refutation of authorship doubts)

While *the author "Shakespeare"* did address Southampton in a way that *could be read* as an appeal for patronage, there is no evidence of any actual patronage by Southampton of that author, nor any evidence whatsoever connecting Southampton (or any *literary patron*) with *Shakspere the actor*—precisely Price's point, ignored by Shapiro. If, hypothetically, "Shakespeare" was a pseudonym for an aristocrat, then obviously the Southampton dedications were *pretending to be something they were not*—to be written (perhaps as a polite fiction many saw through) by one of lower social status. There was obviously no aristocrat by the name of "William Shakespeare," as everyone in the small world of the Elizabethan elite would have known perfectly well. This renders quite silly the oftheard Stratfordian objection (repeated, for example, by Sir Jonathan Bate in 2017; see Waugh & Bate, at minutes 23-24), that a senior nobleman would never have addressed the much younger Southampton so obsequiously. Of course he would not have (and did not), *openly using his true name*. But if he used the pseudonym of a commoner, he would have *had* to make the dedications plausibly

(footnote continued on next page)

Shapiro also mocked Price, again failing to rebut her findings, for daring to note the lack of evidence that Shakspere—in contrast to many writers of the time—received any "[n]otice at death as a writer"[17] or was ever "paid to write."[18] Attentive readers will note that while Shapiro cited Shakspere's shareholding in a theatrical company and that he may have played some role in preparing an *impresa* (a heraldic device), he did not even try to rebut what he snidely dismissed as Price's "assur[ance] ... that there is no evidence of his 'having been paid to write.' Readers are invited to make up their own minds."[19] Indeed they are. Did Shapiro seriously mean to suggest that actors or theatre investors were also, necessarily, "paid to write"?

---

(footnote continued from previous page)
obsequious. Anything else would have defeated the point of the pseudonym—and might have been viewed as a public insult to Southampton.

[17] Price, p. 310, quoted in Shapiro (2010), p. 243. Shapiro sarcastically stated: "I'm not sure how those who wrote memorial tributes to him, or paid for or carved his monument, or labored to create the Pavier editions or the First Folio, might feel about that. ... [T]ime had apparently expired before all these memorial efforts were realized." Shapiro (2010), pp. 243-44. Well, yes, that was (again) exactly Price's point—years went by before alleged "memorials" appeared, with almost complete and deafening silence in the meantime about the supposed passing of Britain's greatest writer. See note 34. As for the obviously fishy and peculiar Stratford monument, see note 35.

The 1623 *First Folio* (far less the 1619 Pavier editions) offered only vague and scattered hints about the author's identity or biography. Neither had any clear linkage to Shakspere's death in 1616, though it may have cleared the way for the *Folio*'s curiously elliptical suggestions of some connection to him. See note 36. There are several vague lamentational references in the *Folio* prefatory materials to the author having died some time in the past. But the only specific reference offering any concrete clue is the comment in the letter "To the great Variety of Readers," p. 7, that the author was "by death" deprived of the opportunity "to have set forth, and overseen his own writings." That fits very well with Edward de Vere's death in 1604 (see note 4), when "Shakespeare" seems to have been in the midst of producing new or revised works, but is oddly inconsistent with Shakspere's retirement to Stratford for years during which he would have had ample leisure to collect and edit his writings. See also Part III.B & notes 49-53 (discussing Shakspere's 1604 and 1616 problems, in contrast to Vere's alleged, actually nonexistent, "1604 problem").

[18] Price, p. 310, quoted in Shapiro (2010), p. 244.
[19] Shapiro (2010), p. 244.

Please note, dear readers, that a "relationship with a patron," "notice at death as a writer," and being "paid to write" are only *three of ten* categories of literary evidence discussed by Price. Shapiro was free to target whatever he felt were Price's weakest points, so please note, given his failed rebuttal on the three categories he chose to address, that he simply ignored the other seven. Shakspere, unlike any of the 24 known writers surveyed by Price, *is a complete blank in all ten categories.* All 24, even the famously mysterious Christopher Marlowe (who died at 29 before most of his works were published), have evidence in at least three categories; 19 have evidence in at least five. Twelve writers score in at least *seven*. Shakspere sticks out like a sore thumb.[20]

There are, as it happens, at least two contemporaneous references that do arguably suggest (at least indirectly) some connection between the works of Shakespeare and an actor—presumably from Stratford, though that was not stated—with the same (or similar) name. Both are familiar staples of the Stratfordian theory and discussed by Wells—although (as noted) he conceded that no such references "explicitly and incontrovertibly identif[y] [the author] with Stratford-upon-Avon."[21] What Wells ignored, or was oblivious to, was the irony that *both* items *also* indicate significant early authorship doubts, as discussed in Part IV along with much additional evidence of such doubts.[22]

---

[20] See Price, pp. 310-13.

[21] Wells, "Allusions," p. 81.

[22] The two references are in Greene, *Groats-Worth of Wit* (1592) (see Part IV.2), and the third anonymous *Parnassus* play (c. 1601) (see Part IV.16). See Wells, "Allusions," pp. 73-74 (discussing *Groats-Worth*), pp. 77-78 (discussing the *Parnassus* plays). Ironically, as discussed in Part IV.2.f, the author of another essay in the Edmondson-Wells anthology acknowledged that *Groats-Worth* expresses authorship doubts. See Jowett (2013), pp. 89-91. A third connection (between "poesy" and a "player" called "W.S.") is suggested by Davies of Hereford's *Microcosmos* (1603) (see Part IV.20), which raises still more early doubts. Parts IV.20 and 26 discuss additional writings by Davies of Hereford (see, *e.g.*, Part IV.20, note 464), as well as the 1613 "Rutland *impresa*."

Wells was quite correct to argue, more broadly, that post-humous materials are a perfectly valid and legitimate form of evidence, entitled to whatever weight they may fairly deserve. When Stratfordians dismiss as "circumstantial" the compelling evidence pointing to Edward de Vere as author of the works of Shakespeare, Oxfordians have correctly responded that circumstantial evidence is likewise—as any lawyer knows—perfectly valid, legitimate, and entitled to whatever weight it may have under, well, the circumstances. Indeed, circumstantial evidence, even though "indirect," may often be superior in force and reliability to eyewitness and other "direct" forms of evidence.[23]

But while posthumous or *post hoc* evidence has legitimate weight, it is also materially different. It has long been treated by historians and lawyers, and properly so, as generally entitled to less weight than contemporaneous evidence. At the same time, while it is certainly significant that the Stratfordian theory is mainly supported only by posthumous (not contemporaneous) evidence, the main problem with the posthumous Stratfordian evidence is not its posthumous nature but rather its specifically suspicious content.[24]

The British duo of Wells and Edmondson are matched by Professor Shapiro of Columbia University—an adamant Stratford-ian who seems to have become the most prominent Shakespeare expert in North America. In a *New York Times* op-ed, Shapiro claimed the "testimony of contemporary writers, court records and much else ... confirms that [Shakspere of Stratford] wrote the works attributed to him."[25] It is not entirely clear what Shapiro meant by "court records," but this was deeply misleading even if

---

[23] For Wells's argument in defense of posthumous evidence, see "Allusions," p. 81. On the circumstantial evidence for the Oxfordian theory, see note 4.

[24] See, *e.g.*, notes 33-37. For an excellent overview of evidentiary principles as applied to the SAQ, see Regnier (2015) (Regnier is an experienced attorney).

[25] Shapiro (2011).

we stretch "contemporary" to include ambiguous posthumous evidence like the *First Folio* of 1623.[26]

Since there are no legal "court records" linking the Stratford actor with a literary career, Shapiro must have been referring to the 1595 record of payment to him (along with William Kempe and Richard Burbage), by the royal court, for the performance of unspecified plays.[27] We have no way of knowing whether the plays involved had anything whatsoever to do with the Shakespeare canon. Even if we knew their titles that would not prove that any of the payees *wrote* them. They may have been paid simply as actors, producers, or theatrical company shareholders.

The 1595 record is perfectly consistent with the possibility that Shakspere of Stratford was merely some kind of frontman for a hidden author. Orthodox scholars concede that pseudonyms were common during that era, as they remain today and have been throughout literary history. *Indeed, they concede the name "Shakespeare" was itself used at least sometimes as a pseudonym.* The 1595 record does not in any way "confirm" the Stratfordian theory, nor does any "testimony of contemporary writers" do so before 1623, seven years after Shakspere died. Shapiro, typical of many orthodox scholars on this issue, was blowing hot air.[28]

---

[26] See note 36.

[27] See, *e.g.*, Price, pp. 15, 31-32.

[28] See Part III.A, and Part III.B & note 33 (discussing pseudonyms and frontman theories). Stratfordian scholars like Shapiro, who (missing Wells's memo) insist on repeating the ample early evidence claim, typically obfuscate the crucial question (discussed by Price with crystal clarity): whether anyone during Shakspere's lifetime *personally and specifically identified him as the author*—as opposed to generic impersonal references to the works themselves and to "Shakespeare" simply as their credited author when published. The latter type of evidence obviously cannot pinpoint any Stratfordian (or other) identification nor pierce the veil of a pseudonym.

For example, Professor James Marino (see also note 36; Part III.B & notes 33, 50-54; Part V.C & notes 28-31) has referred misleadingly to "dozens of ... pieces of evidence, early documents in which a wide range of witnesses identify Shakespeare as the poet," Marino (*Penn Press Log*, Nov. 1, 2011), and to "a large stack of historical documents that explicitly name ... Shakespeare, the actor ... as

(footnote continued on next page)

Shapiro's book on the SAQ is well-written, like all his books, with a wealth of fascinating information. But it is also pervasively tendentious and misleading. For the most part it merely analyzes the SAQ as a cultural phenomenon, making little effort to engage its merits.[29] Shapiro's earlier book *Shakespeare and the Jews* (1996), by contrast, was daringly innovative and involved some courageous bucking of conventional wisdom.[30] If only Shapiro would fulfill his early promise as a Shakespeare scholar and revisit more skeptically the Stratfordian myth. Sadly, this seems unlikely.[31] It is not hyperbole, by the way, to use the word "myth." Consider, for example, the outright fraud and fakery in which the Shakespeare Birthplace Trust has been caught red-handed with regard to various buildings in and around Stratford, supposedly associated with Shakspere and his family, as Alexander Waugh has exposed with ferocious wit.[32]

---

(footnote continued from previous page)
the author" and "lots of witnesses who identify Shakespeare, by name, as the writer," Marino (*Dagblog*, Nov. 3, 2011). He is blunter than most in dismissing as "bullshit" and "a lie" the point that "[n]o one ever mentioned Shakespeare as a writer during his lifetime," Marino (*Dagblog*, Dec. 31, 2014). Marino referred mainly, it seems, to impersonal comments on the published name "Shakespeare," though he did claim evidence "nam[ing] ... the actor" and "during his lifetime."

While sorely tempted, I will not respond to Marino's sweeping claims with his own term ("bullshit"), but would instead politely challenge him to identify *any* of this alleged mass of evidence that *clearly and personally* links Shakspere of Stratford to *a career as a writer during his lifetime*. If the answer is one or more of the isolated and ambiguous items cited in note 22, then by all means let's discuss those and other indications of early authorship doubts (the existence of which Marino categorically denies, as discussed in Part V.C, note 29).

[29] See Shapiro (2010). For criticisms, see, *e.g.*, Niederkorn (2010); Cutting (2010); Hope (2010); Hunter (2010); Whalen (2010); Stritmatter (2011, 2013); Ray (2011); Shahan, "Beyond Reasonable Doubt, Part 3"; Wildenthal, "Rollett and Shapiro," pp. 3-7; see also Part II & notes 39-51; Part III.A & notes 10-13.

[30] Shapiro has stated: "My graduate school experience taught me to be skeptical of unexamined historical claims, even ones that other Shakespeareans took on faith. ... That experience, and the [1996] book that grew out of it, taught me the value of revisiting truths universally acknowledged." Shapiro (2010), p. 5.

[31] See Part V.D & notes 54-60 (discussing Shapiro's 2016 radio interview).

[32] See Waugh, "Shakespeare, Birthplace, and Trust" (2014) (and his 2018 video "Shakespeare Birthplace Trust EXPOSED!").

I do not wish to spend too much time on the ample early evidence claim, which is not the main focus of this book. A long line of skeptical scholars, going back more than a century, has gone far to refute that claim. They have shown that the argument for the Stratfordian author is stunningly weak. A large and growing tidal wave of studies indicates that his background and limited education and travels simply cannot be squared with the author's knowledge, perspectives, and life experiences, as revealed over and over again in the works themselves.[33]

As noted above, orthodox scholars sometimes back off from the ample early evidence claim when pressed. They typically cling, however, to the equally false fallback claim discussed above—that other writers of the era allegedly suffer from the same paucity of contemporaneous evidence.

---

[33] See generally, *e.g.*, Greenwood (1908); Greenwood (1916); Looney, ch. 1 ("The Stratfordian View"), pp. 11-67; Ogburn, chs. 1-19, pp. 3-403; Whalen (1994), chs. 1-5, pp. 3-60; Price; Chiljan; Shahan & Waugh; Jiménez (2013 and 2018). On Greenwood's pioneering role, see, *e.g.*, Part IV.2.d & notes 52-59.

A devastating impediment to the Stratfordian theory is Shakspere's 1616 will, which mentions no books and is virtually impossible to square with him being any kind of writer or intellectual. Shapiro (2010), p. 50, dismissed skeptics as "misunderstanding the conventions of Elizabethan wills and inventories," but it is actually Shapiro and other orthodox writers who are ill-informed on the subject. (Shakspere's will, by the way, is *Jacobean*.) Bonner Miller Cutting, by contrast, has studied thousands of early modern English wills. See Cutting "Shakespeare's Will" (2009) and "Poor Anne" (2011) (revised and reprinted in her 2018 book); see also Sobran, pp. 25-28; Bianchi (2017); Campbell (2017). Shahan & Waugh, p. 58, predicted that the 2013 Edmondson-Wells anthology would completely ignore Shakspere's will. Laughably, they were proven right. The will is neither quoted nor discussed in Edmondson & Wells (2013), even though one would think a will would be among any person's most revealing expressions. Compare Shahan & Waugh, pp. 58-68 (reprinting Cutting's 2009 article); pp. 166-67, 193-94; app. A, pp. 225-27 (reprinting the will).

Among modern studies indicating that Shakspere could not plausibly have written the works of Shakespeare (whereas the known education, travels, and life experiences of Edward de Vere are a perfect fit), see, *e.g.*, on Italian culture and geography: Roe (2011); Magri (2014); Waugh, "Italy" (2013); on Greek language and drama: Werth (2002); Showerman (2015); on medicine: Davis (2000); Showerman (2013); and on law, Alexander (2001); Regnier (2013). The foregoing is only a small selection of some of the more compelling studies. See also note 4.

Orthodox scholars often retreat to the posthumous evidence. There are plenty of problems with that too. The posthumous puzzles begin with the strange absence of known reactions—when Shakspere died and for years afterward—even remotely equating to what would be expected in response to the loss of a major literary figure or what actually occurred in response to the deaths of lesser figures. This enduring mystery may well be called the Great Silence of 1616.[34]

The posthumous mysteries continue with the many suspicious oddities of the Stratford Monument and its patently evasive and cryptic inscription,[35] and with the *First Folio* of 1623, also filled

---

[34] It is surely the most remarkable "dog that didn't bark" in literary history (see Doyle, "Silver Blaze," in *Sherlock Holmes*, p. 347), and is viewed by many as the single most compelling reason to doubt the Stratfordian theory. See, *e.g.*, Looney, pp. 37-38; Ogburn, pp. 38, 112; Whalen (1994), pp. 15-16, 51-52; Price, p. 156; Chiljan, p. 23; Shahan & Waugh, pp. 7-8, 194-95; Pointon, "The Rest Is Silence" (2013); Hayes, "Social Network Theory." Orthodox scholars mostly ignore the problem or gloss over it with some weak rationalization. See, *e.g.*, note 17 (discussing Shapiro's evasive and misleading treatment of the issue). The only extended effort (to my knowledge) to really engage the issue, from a Stratfordian perspective, is Kathman, "Shakespeare's Eulogies."

The inexplicable silence *about* Shakespeare in 1616 resonates with two strange silences *by* Shakespeare (if he was Shakspere): upon the death of Queen Elizabeth in 1603 and in 1612 when Prince Henry, the popular heir to King James, died tragically young. See Shahan, "Beyond Reasonable Doubt, Part 1," p. 1 (point 2). As we saw in note 16, Professor Shapiro hypes James's supposed patronage of Shakspere (as an actor). Yet no memorial verse to honor the son of his grief-stricken royal patron? Edward de Vere, by contrast (see note 4 on the Oxfordian theory), was long dead in 1612. As discussed in Part IV.19, Vere's feelings about the queen were probably deeply conflicted and an aristocratic writer hiding behind a pseudonym would feel less pressure to speak out. See also Part III.B & notes 49-53 (discussing Shakspere's 1604 and 1616 problems, in contrast to Vere's alleged, actually nonexistent, "1604 problem").

[35] It has been materially altered since it was first constructed in any event. For a very intriguing analysis, see Waugh, "Moniment" (rev. 2015) (and his 2018 video "Monkey Business at Stratford-upon-Avon"); see also, *e.g.*, Price, ch. 9, pp. 161-75 (defending the integrity of some aspects of the monument while questioning others); Chiljan, ch. 10, pp. 173-90; Whalen, "Stratford Bust" (2013); Goldstone (2012). An influential Stratfordian defense of the monument was Spielmann (1924), promptly debunked by Greenwood (1925) and later by Whalen, "Stratford Bust" (2013) (see p. 148). Orthodox scholars have mostly ignored

(footnote continued on next page)

with teasingly ambiguous wordplay.[36] Even beyond all that—and quite apart from this book's focus on authorship doubts before 1616—additional indications of posthumous authorship doubts arose during the thirty years after Shakspere's death and over the following two centuries.[37]

Nested within the ample early evidence claim are numerous specific subclaims. Many of these lesser canards are comparable in speciousness to the false fallback claim discussed above: that the contemporaneous evidence documenting the literary careers of other writers of the time is allegedly comparable to, or even scantier than, that for Shakspere.

---

(footnote continued from previous page)
Greenwood's excellent work (see note 33), while continuing to rely on Spielmann. See, *e.g.*, Kathman, "Seventeenth-Century References."

[36] See, *e.g.*, Price, ch. 10, pp. 176-200; Chiljan, chs. 8-9, pp. 137-71; Whalen (2011); Whalen, "Ambiguous Ben Jonson" (2013); Rollett, "Doublet" (rev. 2013); Rollett, "Doublet" Video (2015); Waugh, "Avon" (2014) (and his 2018 video "Sweet Swan of Avon"); see also Stritmatter, *First Folio Minority Report* (2016).

Marino, an insightful scholar (see Part III.B & notes 50-54) and strident Stratfordian (see note 28 above; Part V.C & notes 28-31), perceived the "exquisite" nature of Jonson's "ambivalence" in his dedicatory poem, *First Folio,* pp. 9-10 (*e.g.*, his haunting line, "Thou art a Moniment [sic], without a tomb"). Marino observed—with amusing puzzlement—that Jonson "displaces Shakespeare's body ... [and] *bizarrely,* seem[s] to deny that Shakespeare possesses any burial place at all." Marino, *Owning William Shakespeare,* p. 100 (emphasis added). Yo think? Try reading the scholarship cited above and in note 35.

[37] See, *e.g.*, the 1628 Vicars and 1635 Burbage references discussed above in text and notes 7-8. See also, *e.g.*, Chiljan, pp. 28, 103-04, 191-99, 340-41, and app. H, pp. 406-07 (discussing doubts from 1623 to 1640); Shahan & Waugh, p. xiii (discussing 1635 Burbage reference) and pp. 198-99 (discussion by Frank Davis & Peter Dawkins of 1628 Vicars reference and two other items dating from 1623 to 1645); Cleave, p. 32 (discussing doubts from 1645 to 1852); Friedman & Friedman, pp. 1-3 (discussing doubts from 1728 to 1852). The Friedmans' 1957 book (see also note 42) is one of the most valuable, entertaining, and truly essential in the entire literature on the SAQ. Ben Jonson's 1616 *Works* also raised posthumous doubts. See Part III.B & note 38.

It is useful to define "early posthumous" doubts as those arising from 1616 to 1645. A middle period of posthumous doubts may be identified from the 1660 restoration of the British monarchy up to the 1850s, when the Baconians ushered in what I call the "modern era" of authorship doubts.

One of those little Stratfordian canards became especially prominent and annoying during the 2016 *Folio* tour staged by the Folger Shakespeare Library to honor the 400th anniversary of Shakspere's death—a rather ironic celebration given the deafening silence the year he actually died in 1616, and oddly premature in its focus on the 1623 *Folio*, which only turned 393 in 2016.[38] The canard promoted by the Folger *Folio* tour was the claim that it actually was compiled, edited, and introduced by the author's supposed acting "fellows" John Heminges and Henry Condell.

In fact, even orthodox scholars have recognized for 250 years that Ben Jonson probably wrote some or all of the material attributed to Heminges and Condell.[39] The *Folio* credits Jonson with two introductory poems and he prepared a similarly massive folio of his own works in 1616, soon after Shakspere's death—generating, by the way, substantial additional early Shakespeare authorship doubts.[40] Jonson is far more likely than the two actors (who had no known literary experience) to have played the leading role in supervising and editing the 1623 *Folio*. As many skeptics have noted, if we cannot even trust the *Folio* on such a basic point as the Heminges-Condell attributions, how can we rely on anything else it says (or teasingly implies) about authorship?

Yet orthodox writers, especially in communications aimed at the general public, typically gloss over the substantial doubts they

---

[38] See notes 34 and 36. The Folio Tour involved traveling exhibits to all 50 U.S. states (plus Puerto Rico) of original printings of the *First Folio* from the Folger's collection. See Maycock. I visited the exhibit in the San Diego Public Library in June 2016.

[39] See, *e.g.*, Maycock (2016), pp. 15, 26 n. 36, citing a long line of orthodox scholars, including George Steevens (who first noticed Jonson's apparent role in 1770); Edmund Malone's work in 1821; Greg (1955), pp. 17-21, 26-27 ("Note E"); and Donaldson (2011), pp. 370-74, who stated flatly (p. 371) that "the stamp of Jonson's authority is clearly apparent in the 1623 Folio." For analyses by doubters, see, *e.g.*, Greenwood (1921), pp. 11-28 (reprinted in Stritmatter, *First Folio Minority Report*, pp. 61-68); Price, pp. 176-81.

[40] See *First Folio*, pp. 2, 9-10 (Jonson poems); Jonson, *Works* (1616); see also, *e.g.*, Brady & Herendeen. On the doubts generated by Jonson's 1616 folio, see Part III.B & note 38.

themselves widely share about the role of Heminges and Condell. The 2016 Folger *Folio* tour's exhibit guides, printed on large and colorful wall panels, were a sad example—a pathetic dumbing-down of Shakespearean history. They recited the Heminges-Condell claim as if it were an unquestioned certainty. And in a truly astonishing and Orwellian erasure from history—one might say the unkindest cut of all—the exhibits contained *not a single reference to Ben Jonson!* They also censored out any mention of the *Folio*'s two aristocratic dedicatees—one of them a son-in-law of Edward de Vere![41]

In any event, this book argues that the most important Stratfordian canard is the false meme that authorship doubts and questions were unknown during Shakespeare's own time and did not arise until centuries later. The main reason to give it top ranking is that it seems to be the claim that Stratfordians are most desperate to defend and sustain. They think it is the strongest point in the orthodox wall. In fact, as this book shows, it is their Achilles heel.

To be sure, the SAQ in its modern form, with widespread and open discussion of doubts and alternative candidates, did not

---

[41] On the Orwellian overtones of the orthodox approach to the SAQ, see also Part III.A. For another disturbing example of the Folger's approach to Shake-spearean history, see Part IV.20 & note 496. This is all the more regrettable given the Folger's admirable overall work and importance as a Shakespearean scholarly resource.

On the Oxfordian theory supporting Vere as the true author, see note 4. The "incomparable pair of brethren" to whom the 1623 *First Folio* was dedicated, and who may have been its financiers and organizers, were William Herbert, Earl of Pembroke (and Lord Chamberlain, in charge of supervising the theatres, 1615–25), and his younger brother Philip Herbert, Earl of Montgomery (who succeeded William as Earl of Pembroke and Lord Chamberlain). They may have hired Jonson, a longtime beneficiary of William Herbert's patronage, to do the literary labor. Philip was Vere's son-in-law. William discussed marriage with another of Vere's daughters, though he ended up marrying someone else. On the possible role of Jonson and the Herbert brothers, see, *e.g.*, Chiljan, ch. 9, pp. 155-71. On the relationship between the Herberts and Vere's daughters, see, *e.g.*, Anderson, pp. 314, 371-73; Whalen (1994), pp. 81-82.

begin until 1856, 240 years after Shakspere's death. That year marked the rise of the Baconians, a movement vulnerable to caricature as just another mystical 19th-century fad on a par with seances or phrenology.[42]

Vere was more credibly proposed as the true author 64 years later, in a 1920 book by a dedicated British schoolteacher named John Thomas Looney. Cue sophomoric snickers from those defenders of orthodoxy who apparently never outgrew the schoolyard. Since even some very prestigious scholars have been unable to resist mocking Looney's surname, the issue should be squarely addressed, just as bullies and name-calling should always be confronted. For the record, it is a respected family name of Manx origin that some families pronounce "LOH-nee," but which, J.T.L.'s descendants report, he and they have always cheerfully and with proud defiance rendered as "LOO-nee."[43]

It seems to be supremely important to Stratfordians to deny or overlook—whether consciously or not—the reality of early authorship doubts dating back to the 1590s. I have come to believe this is the very heart and fulcrum of the SAQ. After all, what better way to delegitimize doubts than by denying or mini-

---

[42] Baconians believe the true author of the works of Shakespeare was Sir Francis Bacon (1561–1626). Bacon, knighted in 1603, was late in life made Baron Verulam and then Viscount St. Alban. The modern Baconian theory was launched by the American scholar Delia Bacon (no relation), in an 1856 article and 1857 book, and by the British scholar William Henry Smith, who independently proposed the theory in his own 1856 pamphlet and 1857 book.

While the Baconian theory has few supporters today, a sympathetic summary was provided by John Michell in his thoughtful and engaging 1996 book, ch. 5, pp. 113-60. To the extent the theory was based on supposed ciphers or cryptographic messages thought to be embedded in Shakespearean and other works, it was demolished by Friedman & Friedman in their valuable and entertaining 1957 book. See also Michell, pp. 134-53.

[43] For a typical snicker, sadly emanating from one of the world's leading Shakespeare scholars, see Bate, *Genius*, p. 66. It will be immediately obvious to anyone who actually reads Looney's book what a thoughtful, sober, and intelligent scholar he was. The Oxfordian theory would be far more widely embraced if more people would simply read his book. See note 4.

mizing the number of people who ever harbored them and the span of time during which they have existed?[44]

The Stratfordian strategy has so far worked well in this regard. The early doubts seem to be mostly forgotten, despite the Baconian and Oxfordian movements (and those on behalf of other candidates) and all the publicity and interest they have generated. Even many authorship doubters today are not, I think, fully aware of the extent of early doubts. That is a key reason I decided to write this book. I first became interested in the SAQ in 2000, but not until 2015, after many years of reading, did the full scope of the early doubts begin to dawn on me.

The dominant tendency of modern academics has been to dismiss the entire SAQ as a curious anachronism, a byproduct of our modern times and attitudes.[45] "Modern" is defined here, as

---

[44] For about 70 years starting in 1932, even many orthodox Stratfordians accepted the idea that authorship doubts began to circulate in the late 1700s. A claim was published that year that a "Rev. James Wilmot" residing near Stratford began investigating the authorship issue in 1785 and ended up doubting the Stratfordian theory. But this turned out to be based on a manuscript apparently forged by a misguided Baconian. This "Wilmot fraud" was exposed in 2003, *thanks mainly to Oxfordian scholars.* Dr. John Rollett and Professor Daniel Wright, both Oxfordians at the time, deserve primary credit. (Rollett later embraced the theory that the author was William Stanley, Earl of Derby. See Part IV.30 & note 798.) Rollett was the first to explore the Wilmot fraud, though several others were also involved, including the Stratfordian Professor Alan Nelson, who would probably never have gotten involved without Rollett's initial research. See Baca (2003); Shahan & Waugh, pp. 203-04.

A useful account of the Wilmot fraud was provided by Shapiro (2010), pp. 11-13, 283-84, but badly marred by his deceptive insinuations that *he* deserved credit for exposing it—and that fraud and forgery are allegedly typical of writings by authorship skeptics. In fact, as Shapiro is well aware, by far the most important fraudsters in the history of Shakespeare studies have been Stratfordians. See Shapiro (2010), pp. 21-27, 62-66 (discussing two of them); Wildenthal, "Rollett and Shapiro," pp. 3-6.

[45] See, *e.g.*, Shapiro (2010), p. 10 (asserting—with evenhanded criticism, to Shapiro's credit, of his fellow Stratfordians—that "[a]nachronistic thinking" is "as characteristic of supporters of Shakespeare's authorship [*i.e.*, Stratfordians] as it is of skeptics"). More illustrations of this dismissive tendency, including a more extensive quotation of this page in Shapiro's book, are in Part II.

historians often do, to encompass the last 200 years or so,[46] in contrast to the "early modern" Elizabethan-Jacobean period when England was evolving from medieval feudalism into renaissance enlightenment. Perhaps, it is often suggested, the SAQ is just an outgrowth of romantic modern notions of autobiographical authorship.[47] Perhaps it derives from our modern tendency to question authority and "establishment" beliefs.[48]

But what if Shakespeare authorship doubts first arose *during the Elizabethan era*? What if they *predated by decades the first suggestion of the Stratfordian theory itself?* It would then become far more awkward and difficult to quarantine the SAQ in *modern* times as merely a contingent product of our *modern* culture. Authorship doubts could no longer be condescendingly marginalized and dismissed on that basis. On the contrary, such doubts would emerge as an authentic, integral, and persistent part of the very time and culture that gave rise to the works of "Shakespeare."

If authorship doubts were present at the creation and have persisted for more than 425 years, arising again and again and again down through the centuries—resonating with generations after generations of people in very different eras and cultures— what then?

---

[46] See, *e.g.*, Johnson, *The Birth of the Modern* (1991).

[47] See, *e.g.*, Shapiro (2013), pp. 238-39 (discussing "biographical" views of authorship and "Romantic assumptions about artistic creativity").

[48] See, *e.g.*, Edmondson, "Shakespeare Establishment," p. 227 (asserting that "anti-Shakespearians [*sic*; referring to anti-Stratfordians], whose cause is parasitic, need always to oppose something, so 'the Shakespeare establishment' is construed as an edifice for them to contradict and challenge").

## II. The Central Stratfordian Claim: Did Doubts Not Arise Until the 1850s?

It is fascinating—and quite amusing—to document exactly how far out orthodox scholars have ventured on the creaky limb of denying the early doubts about the authorship of Shakespeare. They have ventured well past what would have been a safer and narrower claim: that we do not know of anyone during Shakspere's lifetime who *explicitly and specifically denied* that he wrote the works. That might seem, at first blush, to balance out the absence of any clear and contemporaneous *affirmation* that he did so. But people do not tend to specifically question something they have no particular reason to suspect in the first place.[1]

As noted in Part I, even some leading Stratfordian scholars concede there is little if any surviving evidence that *anyone* during Shakspere's lifetime linked him personally to the works of "Shakespeare" in the first place. None of Shakspere's family members or descendants ever did so, as far as we know. As the scholar Ramon Jiménez has shown, several associates of Shakspere, including his own son-in-law Dr. John Hall, left significant writings—all strangely devoid of any hint of a connection between him and those works, or any writing career at all.[2]

---

[1] See Shahan & Waugh, p. iii (introduction by Shahan). Davies of Hereford's *Scourge of Folly* (c. 1610–11) comes mighty close, however, to directly denying that Will Shakspere the player was a bona fide writer. See Part IV.26.

[2] See Jiménez (2013).

It is important to clarify another distinction. This book focuses on whether evidence supports the existence of authorship *doubts or questions* during a crucial early period. That issue is separate from whether, or to what degree, evidence supports or proves any ultimate *conclusions* about authorship. It is useful to clarify the first issue to advance reasoned discussion of the latter.

Take Professor James Shapiro's assertion in a 2013 essay that "no shred of documentary evidence has ever been found that suggests that anyone other than" Shakspere (plus some alleged "collaborators") was the author.[3] That claim is demolished by the evidence surveyed in Part IV—and also by the extensively documented parallels between Edward de Vere's letters and known early poems and the Shakespeare canon.[4] But strictly speaking, this book need not dispute it. That particular statement by Shapiro did not take a stand on when people began to entertain and express *doubts or questions* about authorship, however strong or weak the basis for those doubts or questions may have been.

But orthodox scholars including Shapiro have gone further, making surprisingly sweeping claims that *nobody* during Shakspere's lifetime expressed *anything* indicating *any doubts at all* about the authorship of the works of Shakespeare. They have sometimes ventured still further out on this limb by asserting that no doubts were expressed *at any time before the 1850s*, when the modern Shakespeare Authorship Question (SAQ) was launched by the Baconians.[5] I am indebted to Julia Cleave for collecting some of the statements below by leading scholars along this line.[6]

---

[3] Shapiro (2013), p. 238.

[4] See generally, *e.g.*, Fowler (analyzing parallels to Vere's letters); "Twenty Poems" (2018) (analyzing poetic parallels, also touching on epistolary parallels); Stritmatter, *Poems of Edward de Vere* (2019) (same); see also Part I, note 4; Part III.B, note 45.

[5] See Part I, note 42.

[6] See Cleave, p. 32, quoting, *e.g.*, Shapiro (2010) (flyleaf); Wells, "Allusions," p. 87; Bate, *Genius*, p. 73.

Before surveying those claims, however, it may be noted that *Wikipedia*, that ubiquitous online encyclopedia, is a useful barometer of the prevailing consensus in recognized published sources. I generally admire the overall *Wikipedia* project and make frequent use of it myself, as any sensible person should.

At the same time, like most professional teachers and scholars, I have deep qualms about how many people (including many of our students) seem unsure how to make *proper* use of it. *Wikipedia* should be approached with caution, and used and cited only in appropriate ways. As I often point out to my students, it is not itself an *authority* in any proper sense and should almost never be cited as such.[7] It is perfectly appropriate, on the other hand, to cite *Wikipedia* if the supported point is precisely about *Wikipedia* itself, such as how it treats a given issue.[8]

*Wikipedia* is rather, primarily, a finding tool (a "tertiary" source, to be technical): one convenient way to track down what primary or secondary sources may exist, and what (tentatively) they seem to say, on a given point. At the same time, like any encyclopedia, *Wikipedia* is often a convenient and generally reliable source of information on questions of a highly specific and

---

[7] There are rare exceptions in my view, such as when *Wikipedia* happens to provide an unusually useful compilation of factual information (of a type it has proven to reliably report), which is not compiled or presented in a comparably useful or accessible way in any other readily available source. The very fact that *Wikipedia* is cited should, by now, be sufficient to alert any discerning reader to potential weaknesses in the citation and the need to proceed with caution before relying too heavily on the cited information. For example, this book (see Part IV.2.d, note 59) cites the *Wikipedia* article on Sir George Greenwood as an authority (in a cautious way, not relying heavily on it for any controversial point), because, unfortunately, there is not to my knowledge any other convenient source (such as a scholarly biography or article) summarizing the basic facts of Greenwood's life. And I freely confess to relying on *Wikipedia* (without specific citations) for other basic facts (not of critical importance to any point of dispute, but often of useful interest), such as birth and death dates for various people and other historical details. *Wikipedia* has proven highly reliable in collecting and reporting facts of this kind.

[8] The issue is often not *what* is being cited but rather *the point for which* it is cited.

factbound nature. Indeed, *Wikipedia* may compare well in this regard to even some prestigious traditional encyclopedias and other reference sources. That is because its highly specific and factbound information is constantly subject to rapid online updating and correction by *Wikipedia*'s vast community of users and editors—a process and resource not available for traditionally published reference works.

But if a question, like the SAQ, is complex, controversial, and laden with numerous contested issues of interpretation, then a source like *Wikipedia* may not provide a reliable answer. If the prevailing academic views on such a question happen to be fundamentally off the mark, which has been known to happen,[9] *Wikipedia* will simply reflect the mistaken conventional wisdom found in most published sources—a classic case of "garbage in, garbage out."

Furthermore, that assumes a best-case scenario in which *Wikipedia* articles are honestly and objectively drafted and edited, with no ulterior agenda, to accurately reflect the current state of an important debated question. As Bill Boyle has discussed, that is unfortunately not the case with regard to *Wikipedia*'s treatment of the SAQ, "an endless battleground where every fact and every interpretation of every fact are in contention. In the Internet age the battle has intensified, nowhere more so than on Wikipedia."[10]

Boyle noted that during 2005–06 a respected Oxfordian, Stephen Moorer (Director of the Pacific Repertory Theatre in Carmel, California), began editing *Wikipedia* articles related to the SAQ. As Boyle noted, under *Wikipedia*'s rules, "anyone can

---

[9] See, *e.g.*, Warren (2015), pp. 193-99 (comparing adherence to the Stratfordian theory among most English literature academics to the stubborn initial rejection by most geologists, in the early 20th century, of Alfred Wegener's later-vindicated theory of continental drift to explain the geology of the Earth's crust), citing, *e.g.*, Oreskes (a leading analysis of the early rejection of continental drift theory).

[10] Boyle (2011), p. 8.

plunge in to create or edit articles."[11] *Wikipedia*, however, enforces rules or "community standards" governing the content, tone, and format of its articles. It does so by a complex process of edits, counter-edits, debates on "talk" pages, and "arbitration" of any resulting disputes by experienced and privileged editors termed "administrators." This may result in people being blocked from further editing.[12]

As Boyle related, "Moorer did his best to work from a neutral point of view,"[13] and many viewed the resulting *Wikipedia* articles on the SAQ as greatly enhanced and more informative. During 2010–11, however, other *Wikipedia* editors succeeded in undoing most of Moorer's work and got him banned from further editing—on the alleged ground that he was biased and had violated *Wikipedia*'s rule against its articles adopting a "point of view" (the POV rule or stigma). Other Oxfordians, including the respected independent scholar Nina Green,[14] were then also attacked and banned when they tried to get involved in editing *Wikipedia* Shakespeare articles. But the POV stigma applied to authorship doubters has somehow not attached to Stratfordians, even though most of them are at least as opinionated as most skeptics, often more biased in favor of their own theory, and generally less interested in any serious study of the SAQ.[15]

---

[11] Boyle (2011), p. 8.

[12] Editors, arbitrators, and administrators are often anonymous and usually volunteers. It is a well-intentioned, generally workable, and admirably decentralized system, but susceptible to abuse in some cases. See generally "Wikipedia: Policies and Guidelines" (*Wikipedia*) (and pages linked therein).

[13] Boyle (2011), p. 8.

[14] See Green, *Oxford Authorship Site*. Other notable websites maintained by independent authorship-skeptic scholars include Boyle's *Shakespeare Online Authorship Resources* (SOAR), as well as, *e.g.*, those created by Mark André Alexander (*Shakespeare Authorship Sourcebook*), the late W. Ron Hess (*Dark Side of Shakespeare*), Stephanie Hopkins Hughes (*Politicworm*), Kurt Kreiler (*Anonymous Shake-speare*), Diana Price (*Shakespeare's Unorthodox Biography*), and Hank Whittemore (*Shakespeare Blog*).

[15] See Boyle (2011), pp. 8-11.

It is certainly understandable that *Wikipedia* articles would tend to emphasize the views of traditionally credentialed writers published by respected and established publishers. At the same time (as mentioned in the Preface), much valuable work on the SAQ, from both orthodox and skeptical perspectives, has been done by honest, well-intentioned, and often quite capable amateur scholars. I myself, a professional and credentialed scholar in the field of law, but an amateur in the field of English literature, would not in any way disrespect or disparage the legitimacy and value of amateur scholarship, whether pro- or anti-Stratfordian.

After all, the true and literal definition of an "amateur" is one who pursues any endeavor for the sheer love of it. Given the extraordinary unpaid efforts so many people (pro- and anti-Strat-fordian) have poured into the SAQ, no one could reasonably question the love we all have for these works and their author. (We just can't agree who it was.) Scholarly work should always be judged on its intrinsic merits.

The problems with *Wikipedia*'s treatment of the SAQ are illustrated, however, by the fact that even fully credentialed and professional authorship-doubting scholars have been treated with disrespect and unfairly tainted by the POV stigma. Yet highly opinionated amateur or independent Stratfordian scholars have been accepted as *Wikipedia* editors and as authorities worthy of citation in *Wikipedia* articles on the SAQ.

For example, one of the *Wikipedia* editors who reportedly led the charge against Moorer and pursued orthodox edits of SAQ-related articles was Tom Reedy, an independent Stratfordian scholar with a bachelor's degree in English. Reedy, at last report, worked for a sheriff's office in Texas. David Kathman, a financial analyst with a doctorate in linguistics, has been fully accepted as a citable Shakespearean scholar on *Wikipedia*.[16] Yet Professor

---

[16] See Boyle (2011), pp. 8, 11; see also, *e.g.*, Reedy & Kathman. Let me be clear about my respect for Reedy, Kathman, Terry Ross, and other independent
(footnote continued on next page)

Roger Stritmatter, a tenured scholar with a doctorate in comparative literature, and many publications on early modern English literature (including in peer-reviewed orthodox journals), appears to be marginalized.[17]

Indeed, even today, the main *Wikipedia* article on the SAQ does not contain *any* citation to *any* work by Professor Stritmatter, but cites *five* articles by Dr. Kathman—four of them on an internet website devoted to Stratfordian advocacy and co-edited by Kathman himself.[18] The separate *Wikipedia* article on the "history" of the SAQ does contain a *single* citation to *one* Stritmatter article, which was published in a peer-reviewed orthodox scholarly journal.[19]

With that essential background in mind, it is unsurprising to see that the main *Wikipedia* article on the SAQ almost categorically denies the existence of *any* early authorship doubts, stating at the outset simply that "Shakespeare's authorship was first questioned in the middle of the 19th century."[20]

---

(footnote continued from previous page)
Stratfordian scholars. That is demonstrated by this book's repeated citations of their work (see the Bibliography), though I often do, to be sure, disagree quite strongly with many of their scholarly arguments. But what justifies their privileged treatment on *Wikipedia* (and elsewhere), as compared to the dismissive and disrespectful treatment often meted out to equally impressive independent scholars—much less tenured professors in the field like Roger Stritmatter?

[17] See Boyle (2011), p. 11.

[18] "Shakespeare Authorship Question" (*Wikipedia*), citing, *e.g.*, Kathman, "Seventeenth-Century References," "Shakespeare's Will," "Spelling," and "Why I Am Not an Oxfordian," all on David Kathman's and Terry Ross's *Shakespeare Authorship Page*. In fairness, while *Wikipedia* cites only the current website version of Kathman's latter article, an apparently earlier version did appear in 1997 in the peer-reviewed (authorship-skeptic) journal *Elizabethan Review* (showing the greater respect typically accorded to orthodox writers by skeptics than vice versa). My own respect for Kathman and his work is shown by this book's frequent citations (see note 16), though I often criticize and disagree with his work. I find his "Spelling" article especially useful (see Part III.A); the others, not so much (but still worthy of citation).

[19] "History of the Shakespeare Authorship Question" (*Wikipedia*), citing Stritmatter (2006) (also cited and discussed in Part IV.4 of this book).

[20] "Shakespeare Authorship Question" (*Wikipedia*).

The article later qualifies that only slightly, stating (in a section on "[h]istory of the authorship question"): "Excluding a handful of minor 18th-century satirical and allegorical references, there was *no suggestion in this period* that anyone else might have written the works." By "this period," the article indicates, it means "the century and a half following [Shakspere's] death."

The article then continues: "The authorship question emerged *only* after Shakespeare had come to be regarded as the English national poet and a unique genius." The time at which that happened, the article indicates, was the 19th century.

Even the qualified restatement quoted above denies and censors out of existence *all* of the documented pre-1616 doubts discussed in Part IV of this book, not to mention the very significant posthumous doubts pre-dating 1700.[21]

*Wikipedia*'s separate article, "History of the [SAQ]," is more nuanced, at the cost of seeming to contradict the blatant falsehood of the article quoted above. The history article devotes its first two sections, respectively, to "*Alleged* early doubts" and "*Alleged* 18th-century allusions." Apparently, the use of "alleged" is viewed as sufficient to paper over the contradiction.

The first section states: "The overwhelming majority of mainstream Shakespeare scholars agree that Shakespeare's authorship *was not questioned during his lifetime or for two centuries afterward.*"[22] This is balanced only by the following dismissive concession: "Proponents of alternative authors, however, *claim* to find hidden or oblique expressions of doubt in the writings of Shakespeare's contemporaries and in later publications."[23] This

---

[21] Emphases added to the latter quotations. On the early posthumous doubts, which this book does not explore, see Part I & note 37.

[22] "History of the Shakespeare Authorship Question" (*Wikipedia*) (emphases added), citing Bate, *Genius*, p. 73 (the same incautiously broad claim by Bate quoted in Cleave, p. 32, and quoted and discussed in text below).

[23] "History of the Shakespeare Authorship Question" (*Wikipedia*) (emphasis added). The article provides some discussion of several of the items surveyed in
(footnote continued on next page)

section then proceeds to detail some of these *"claimed"* expressions.

The second section of the *Wikipedia* article on the SAQ's history focuses in some detail on the 18th-century (post-1700) expressions of doubt barely acknowledged by *Wikipedia's* main SAQ article. This section's heading refers tendentiously to *"Alleged* ... allusions," even though the actual text of the article does not deny the reality of their existence and makes plain that most of them explicitly question Shakespeare's authorship. But, it argues, there is *"nothing* in these [references] to suggest genuine doubts about Shakespeare's authorship, since they are all presented as comic fantasies."[24]

That begs the question why writers during this era were fantasizing about Shakespeare authorship doubts. Why did they think audiences and readers would find such expressions titillating? Why did they not suggest doubts about *other* Elizabethan or Jacobean authors? Do these allusions really suggest *"nothing"*?

The expressions during the 1700s, even if humorous, suggest more widespread percolation of genuine doubts about Shakespeare in the society and culture of the time. The *Wikipedia* article quotes a leading Stratfordian scholar mocking authorship skeptics who "discern" genuine doubts in such references, suggesting doubters "have never been remarkable for their sense of humour."[25] Readers may judge who is actually reading the evidence more obtusely. It's all just a joke! Move along, folks, nothing to see here!

---

(footnote continued from previous page)
Part IV—including writings by Edwards, Hall, Jonson, Marston, and Meres, and the anonymous play *Parnassus 2*—but does not mention others.

[24] "History of the Shakespeare Authorship Question" (*Wikipedia*) (emphases added).

[25] "History of the Shakespeare Authorship Question" (*Wikipedia*), quoting Schoenbaum, *Shakespeare's Lives*, p. 395 (internal quotation marks omitted). Compare Part I & note 37; Cleave, pp. 34-35.

A final note on *Wikipedia:* Its main article on "William Shake-speare" himself deals very briefly with the SAQ and its history. It denies any early authorship doubts, stating that "doubts began to be expressed" only "[a]round 230 years after [his] death." But on a brighter note, it concedes that at least "a small minority of aca-demics believe there is reason to question the traditional attri-bution," and that "interest in the subject, particularly the Oxford-ian theory ... continues into the 21st century."[26] Indeed!

One suspects some editors of these *Wikipedia* SAQ articles are also involved in an article on "Shakespeare Authorship" appearing on an entirely separate website—though deceptively similar—called *RationalWiki.* Despite its effort to claim the mantle of "rational" thought, "Opinionated Wiki" might be more accurate. *RationalWiki,* in an eponymous article about itself, claims to be "a community working together to explore and provide information about a range of topics centered around science, skepticism, and critical thinking."[27]

I have not yet had time to explore many *RationalWiki* articles, but I suspect I should strongly sympathize with many of them. Both my parents are natural scientists: my father a nuclear physicist, my mother a biologist. They trained me to respect logic, evidence, rational argument, and critical thinking. I am a long-time supporter of skeptical pro-science organizations such as the Committee for Skeptical Inquiry.[28]

*RationalWiki* notes that it "uses software originally developed for a well-known online encyclopedia [*Wikipedia*]," but disclaims any effort "to be an encyclopedia" itself.[29] Somewhat refreshingly,

---

[26] "William Shakespeare" (*Wikipedia*), citing (for its denial of early doubts) Shapiro, *Contested Will* (2010), quoted and discussed in text below.

[27] "RationalWiki" (*RationalWiki*).

[28] I have as little patience as most skeptics with regard to far-fetched beliefs (typically based on weak logic and less evidence) questioning events like the Apollo moon landings or 9/11 attacks, embracing theories of aliens visiting Earth to account for all kinds of more plausibly explainable phenomena, *etc.*

[29] "RationalWiki" (*RationalWiki*).

*RationalWiki* also disclaims *Wikipedia*'s "neutral" POV policy and instead embraces what it calls a "scientific point of view" (SPOV) which, it says, means its articles are "not afraid to *clearly* state that some idea is bullshit." It also cheerfully embraces a "snarky point of view" (same acronym, SPOV), even to the point of "sarcasm," "irony," and "subversive humour."[30]

What all this means for the SAQ, as doubters may fear based on the *Wikipedia* experience, is about the same level of condescending and ill-informed hostility—with the addition of a candid blast of snarky contempt and attempted mockery. Thus, *RationalWiki*'s article on the SAQ wastes no time calling it "a fringe theory ... whose mostly unreadable products now tally up to several thousand books and articles." It freely doubles down on accusations that doubters suffer from "snobbery," "classism," and "self-promoting mania," among other sins.[31]

This *RationalWiki* article only comments twice, however, on early authorship doubts. It first denies them, asserting simply that the SAQ "[f]irst developed as an idea in the mid-19th century."[32] In an endnote to that comment, however, it grudgingly concedes: "The Anti-Stratfordians *claim* that there is evidence, *never understood as such for several centuries*, that Shakespeare's identity as a playwright was questioned from the very outset, as far back as 1592."[33]

---

[30] "RationalWiki: What Is a RationalWiki Article?" (*RationalWiki*) (emphasis and Britishism in original).

[31] "Shakespeare Authorship" (*RationalWiki*). Ouch, I say, as I add one more book to the pile—hopefully readable. See Part V.C for more discussion of the "snobbery" slander often falsely directed at authorship doubters.

[32] "Shakespeare Authorship" (*RationalWiki*).

[33] "Shakespeare Authorship" (*RationalWiki*), n. 2 (emphases added here), citing Leahy, "Introduction" (2010), p. 3. In what seems a really weird and petty effort to disparage or discredit Leahy's 2010 authorship-doubting anthology, *RationalWiki* misspells the word *"Critical"* in the subtitle as *"Critcal"* and inserts a gratuitous *"(sic)"* as if correcting a mistake by Leahy or his publisher. The word in fact appears properly spelled as *"Critical"* on both the cover and title page of Leahy's book. Or perhaps *RationalWiki* merely intends to use *"(sic)"* to question

(footnote continued on next page)

But exactly how do the self-anointed scientific skeptics of *RationalWiki* know that *no one for centuries* "understood" that Elizabethans themselves were questioning who wrote the works of Shakespeare? It stands to reason that people who express doubts generally understand they are expressing doubts. And the *continued* expression of doubts for decades and centuries seems to suggest that others understood it too. It seems to be modern orthodox deniers of the early doubts who anachronistically fail or refuse to "understand" them.

I must confess to greatly enjoying the anonymous comment (not by me or anyone of my knowledge) on the "Talk" page for the *RationalWiki* SAQ article, with the heading: *"This article sucks."* Aside from zinging the "poorly developed reading skills" of the "20 something staff of [the *RationalWiki*] site" (which strikes me as perhaps a bit of a low blow), the comment rightly criticizes the article's "pretentious" and unclear use of the term "pseudohistory." It notes that "investigation into" the SAQ is most "certainly" a legitimate form of "history" (thank you!), and concludes:

> I'm guessing it helps exercise your authoritarian tendencies that allow you to get off at seeming like an expert on a topic you haven't actually done any serious research into. Make up scientist gets boring? Be a make believe historian. But we already have a term, in this case, that fits, which I just described: revisionist history. You might want to punch up your pseudoWikipedia.[34]

I myself am sadly unsurprised by the hostility to the SAQ on this supposedly rationalist and skeptical website. Though one would think most people strongly identifying with scientific skep-

---

(footnote continued from previous page)
and mock Leahy's use of the word *"Critical"* (of which *RationalWiki* doubtless thinks it has rightful ownership), and just happens coincidentally to misspell it at the same time? Either way, egg is on *RationalWiki's* face.

[34] "Talk: Shakespeare Authorship" (*RationalWiki*) (emphasis in original, though the heading is actually in large boldface, not italics).

ticism might at least be open to authorship doubts, this is often not the case. I learned this when annoyed by a cover story a few years ago in the magazine *Skeptical Inquirer*, "Did Shakespeare Write 'Shakespeare'?"[35] Aside from the silly circularity of the title—glossing over the spelling issues discussed in Part III.A— the article was sneering, *ad hominem*, and worst of all, thinly researched with mostly outdated citations. It missed or misstated key facts and overlooked or ignored the best recent scholarship on the issue—in other words, much like what is regularly seen in Stratfordian arguments about the SAQ.

I found this especially disheartening because the author, Joe Nickell, is an otherwise outstanding researcher and debunker of paranormal claims, with a doctorate in English literature to boot. I am glad to own several of his excellent books refuting ghost stories, lake monsters, and the like. Almost worse was *Skeptical Inquirer* editor Kendrick Frazier's attack on authorship skeptics as "pseudoscholars ... twisting all reason, logic, and evidence to see what they want to see. Sound familiar?"[36]

Yes, it sounds all too familiar. I suspect professional skeptics are so used to dealing with cranks that in a sense that is who *they* "want to see" when confronted by one more challenge to an established view. The irony seems especially rich since the Stratfordian theory, to a large extent, is exactly the kind of faith-based fable that Nickell and other skeptics normally enjoy debunking. They seem to have forgotten Carl Sagan's cautionary reminder of the "exquisite balance" that thoughtful skeptics must maintain "between two conflicting needs: the most skeptical scrutiny of all hypotheses that are served up to us and at the same time a great openness to new ideas."[37]

---

[35] Nickell (2011).

[36] Frazier (2011).

[37] Sagan, "The Burden of Skepticism" (1987 lecture), quoted opposite the table of contents in the classic book by Michael Shermer (another skeptic I
(footnote continued on next page)

I wrote a letter in protest, concluding: "So who are the real skeptics here? I side with the Oxfordians." *Skeptical Inquirer*, to which I have remained a loyal subscriber, had the decency to publish it. Instead of responding to my serious and substantive points, however, Nickell's brief reply was disappointingly flippant. I had already been mildly interested in the SAQ for more than a decade, but his patently inadequate treatment of it was part of what motivated me to get much more engaged as an active authorship skeptic and Oxfordian.[38]

Let us turn now to what leading Shakespeare scholars have said about the early history of authorship doubts. Cleave quoted the flyleaf of Professor Shapiro's 2010 book, which ventured pretty far out on the creaky limb of early-doubt denial with this neatly circular formulation: "For more than two hundred years after William Shakespeare's death, no one doubted that he had written his plays."[39]

Shapiro explained his primary goal on the very first page of his text: "This is a book about *when* and why many people began to question whether William Shakespeare wrote the plays long attributed to him, and, if he didn't write them, who did."[40] On that same opening page, after mentioning the Wilmot fraud,[41] Shapiro

---

(footnote continued from previous page)
greatly admire), *Why People Believe Weird Things* (1997, rev. 2002). Sagan continued: "If you are only skeptical, then no new ideas make it through to you. You never learn anything new." I discuss in Part V.D another Sagan insight with great value for the SAQ. Shermer himself wrote a 2009 column in *Scientific American* dismissing authorship doubts, to which John Shahan (2009) offered an excellent and thorough response.

[38] See Wildenthal (2012); Nickell (2012). It troubled me then, and still does, that otherwise rational and intelligent people sometimes react so vehemently to anyone daring to challenge the prevailing cherished myths about Shakespeare, as if doubters were heretics questioning a religious doctrine. Shouldn't that trouble Nickell, Frazier, and (see note 37) Shermer too?

[39] Shapiro (2010) (flyleaf), quoted in Cleave, p. 32.

[40] Shapiro (2010), p. 3 (emphasis added).

[41] See Part I & note 44.

dated the surfacing of the authorship "controversy ... in any serious or sustained way" to the mid-1800s.[42]

A few pages later, Shapiro framed the entire SAQ as a modern anachronism, consistently with the dominant academic tendency noted in Part I: "While Shakespeare was a product of an early modern world, the controversy over the authorship of his works is the creation of a modern one. As a result, there's a danger of reading the past through contemporary eyes ...."[43]

Shapiro added—in a remarkably revealing comment—that he found it *"hard to imagine* how anyone before the 1840s could argue that [Shakspere] didn't write the plays."[44] That obtuse mindset helps explain Shapiro's inability or refusal, like that of most orthodox scholars, to perceive the early authorship doubts spread all over the historical record. The historical evidence shows that Shakespeare's own contemporaries suggested, hinted, and implied exactly what Shapiro *could not imagine anyone thinking.*

But let us be fair. Tending to contradict his claims just quoted, Shapiro did in fact briefly acknowledge two items indicating authorship doubts dating from 1759 and 1786. Yet he promptly dismissed both as mere "joke[s] about authorship," underplaying (just like the *Wikipedia* article discussed earlier) the extent to which such humorous or fanciful references probably reflected more serious and widespread doubts percolating in the culture of the time.[45]

Shapiro suggested the latter expressions of doubt could be explained merely because, at that time, *"no document in [Shakspere's] hand had as yet been found* that linked him to the plays published under his name or *attributed to him by contemporar-*

---

[42] Shapiro (2010), p. 3.

[43] Shapiro (2010), p. 10.

[44] Shapiro (2010), p. 11 (emphasis added). Two pages before (p. 9; emphases added), he described "the heart of the controversy" as: "Why, *after two centuries,* did so many people *start* questioning whether Shakespeare wrote the plays?"

[45] Shapiro (2010), p. 20. Compare Part I & note 37; Cleave, pp. 34-35.

*ies.*"[46] Shapiro efficiently packed two separate misleading claims into one sentence there. He also misleadingly minimized the evidence of early doubts he had just conceded. The first emphasized passage deceptively implied that some such documentary evidence has since been found. In fact, none ever has been.[47]

The second emphasized passage was a bit less misleading, just vague enough to comport with the point—conceded even by Sir Stanley Wells—that no clear and *contemporaneous* "attribution" of that kind has ever been found.[48] Presumably Shapiro was referring, in a loose and unclear way, to *posthumous* attributions by people who *had been* contemporaries, such as Ben Jonson's statements in the *First Folio*. Shapiro never acknowledged the ambiguous, equivocal, and thoroughly suspicious nature of Jonson's pre-1616 and posthumous statements and of the *Folio* preface and Stratford Monument generally.[49]

---

[46] Shapiro (2010), p. 20 (emphases added).

[47] Shapiro presumably was not referring to the laughably implausible handwriting attribution supposedly linking the "Hand D additions" of the unpublished manuscript play *Sir Thomas More* with the known purported signatures of Shakspere, since that was not a "play published under his name." (This handwriting attribution should not be confused with the separate issue whether the author Shakespeare, whoever that was, may possibly have authored parts of the *Thomas More* manuscript, regardless of who physically transcribed it.)

The Hand D attribution to Shakspere is doubted even by many orthodox scholars. See, *e.g.*, Marino, *Owning William Shakespeare*, p. 13 (terming it "tendentious"). Only the most desperate kind of confirmation bias and wishful thinking can explain the strange persistence of this claim by some Stratfordians that a linkage can be shown between a handful of tortured signatures (that do not even resemble each other and may not all be from the purported signatory's own hand) and the handwriting of any part of the *Thomas More* manuscript. Some Stratfordians seem truly desperate to overcome the total absence of any literary document in Shakspere's own hand. Greenwood (1924) and Tannenbaum (1927), pp. 179-211, went far to debunk this claim. See also Green, "Myths," Sec. V. The *coup de grâce* (if needed) was administered by Price, "Hand D" (2016). On Shakspere's signatures, see also Davis (2013).

[48] See Part I.

[49] Compare Part I, notes 35-37, and Part III.B, note 38, with Shapiro (2010), pp. 241-42 (briefly summarizing at face value the apparent attributions of the *Folio*, and even more briefly mentioning the monument while neatly avoiding any description whatsoever of it).

Much later in his book, Shapiro briefly discussed several items also discussed in Part IV of this book, dating from 1592 to 1605. But Shapiro's account utterly failed to recognize the authorship doubts they indicated.[50] His entire survey of evidence relating to early doubts, from the 1590s to the late 1700s, totaled a mere five pages out of 280[51]—this in a book, as quoted above, that was touted as *precisely and centrally* "about *when* and why many people began to question" the authorship.

Wells himself, in his 2013 essay, joined Shapiro well out on the limb of early-doubt denial: "No one expressed doubt that [Shakspere] wrote the works attributed to him—give or take ... [some] collaboration with other professional writers ... until the middle of the nineteenth century."[52] Yet Wells, in the very same essay, discussed two items actually indicating early doubts.[53] John Jowett discussed one of those—Greene's *Groats-Worth of Wit* (1592)—in another essay in the very same anthology, which was co-edited by Wells.[54] While Wells missed or ignored the early-doubt implications of both items, Jowett conceded the early-doubt implications of *Groats-Worth*. Was Wells asleep at the switch editing his own book?

As Cleave noted, Wells's essay also contradicted R.C. Churchill's classic 1958 book, described in the very same anthology that Wells co-edited.[55] As Hardy Cook's "Reading List" discussed,

---

[50] See Shapiro (2010), pp. 234-37, briefly noting, *e.g.*, Greene's *Groats-Worth of Wit* (1592), *Willobie His Avisa* (1594), Covell's *Polimanteia* (1595), writings by Camden, Harvey, Meres, and Weever between 1595 and 1605, and two anonymous plays, *Parnassus 2* and *Parnassus 3* (*c.* 1599–1601).

[51] See Shapiro (2010), pp. 20, 234-37.

[52] Wells, "Allusions," p. 87, quoted in Cleave, p. 32. See also Part I (Introduction) for more discussion and quotations of Wells's 2013 essay.

[53] See Part I & note 22, noting Wells's discussion of *Groats-Worth* (1592) and *Parnassus 3* (*c.* 1601) (discussed in more depth in Parts IV.2 and 16).

[54] See Jowett (2013) (discussed in Part IV.2.f).

[55] Churchill, cited in Cook, in Edmondson & Wells (2013), p. 243, cited in Cleave, p. 32.

Churchill surveyed authorship doubts starting in the 1600s.[56] The very first sentence of Ivor Brown's foreword to Churchill's book stated: "The disbelief in William Shakespeare's authorship ... *is a very old one*, as Mr. Churchill reminds the reader in his ... study of the many heterodox opinions."[57]

Indeed, though R.C. Churchill was a Stratfordian himself, he sternly rejected the idea that there were no early doubts. Oh for the good old days—when Stratfordians were a bit more candid and a bit more attentive to historical realities! "The common view about the origin of the [SAQ]," Churchill noted, "assigns it to the [19th] century."[58] "*But*," he said, "*this is ... wrong*," though he also stated that "[w]hether the origins go back to the [17th] century or merely to the [18th] is ... a matter of opinion."[59]

A frequently cited essay posted on the internet by two Stratfordian scholars, Tom Reedy and David Kathman, walks right out to the end of the branch. They assert that "*no person of the Elizabethan and Jacobean eras ever doubted* the attribution" of the Shakespearean works to Shakspere of Stratford, that "*[n]o Elizabethan ever suggested* that Shakespeare's plays and poems were written by someone else," that "*[n]o contemporary ... ever suggested* that the name used by ... the author was a pseudonym," and

---

[56] See Churchill, pp. 28-31, cited in Cook, p. 243.

[57] Churchill, p. ix (foreword by Brown) (emphasis added).

[58] Churchill, p. 27; see also p. 28 (noting "an impressive unanimity ... in the crediting of the origins of the question to the [19th] century"). Churchill, were he still alive, might be even more impressed (or frustrated?) by the similar near-unanimous orthodox view today, *sixty years later*. False memes are remarkably persistent. But as Shakespeare himself once said (if he was Edward de Vere), "truth is truth though never so old, and time cannot make that false which was once true." Quoted in Fowler, p. 771 (letter to Robert Cecil, May 7, 1603).

[59] Churchill, p. 28 (emphasis added). Churchill argued that authorship questions were first suggested by the Essex Rebellion of 1601 (discussed in Part IV.17 of this book). See Churchill, pp. 28, 186-88, 220-21. The other specific items he cited as indicating early doubts began in 1624. See pp. 28-34. On Churchill's own Stratfordian views, see p. 18.

that "the historical record—*all of it*—establishes [Shakspere] as the author of the works traditionally attributed to him."[60]

As Cleave noted, however, it is Sir Jonathan Bate—Professor of English Literature at Oxford University and rival of Wells for the honor of most prominent Shakespeare expert in Britain—"who takes the biscuit."[61] Bate declared, in a 1997 book republished by Oxford University Press in 2008: *"No one in Shakespeare's lifetime or the first two hundred years after his death expressed the slightest doubt about his authorship."*[62]

As a humorous aside, it may be noted that Bate, in the same book, made the *really* baffling claim that "no major actor has ever been attracted to Anti-Stratfordianism."[63] To be fair, there may not yet have been much publicity about the *numerous* authorship-doubting theatre and film stars when he originally wrote the book. But he did not bother to correct this laughable whopper when it was revised and republished a decade later. Perhaps Bate should get out of his study more?

Authorship skeptics in the modern world of the arts include some of the most admired Shakespearean actors of the past century. Bate may want to google the following (in alphabetical order, just from his side of the pond): Sir Charlie Chaplin, Sir John Gielgud, Jeremy Irons, Sir Derek Jacobi, Vanessa Redgrave, Sir Mark Rylance, Joely Richardson, and Michael York. From America, I would throw in Orson Welles, Robin Williams, Sam

---

[60] Reedy & Kathman (emphases added), on Kathman & Ross, *Shakespeare Authorship Page.* For a rebuttal of the essay (but not exploring early authorship doubts), see Kositsky & Stritmatter (2004). The Kathman & Ross website has been endorsed and hailed with approval by leading academics. See, *e.g.*, Shapiro (2010), p. 281; Wells, "Allusions," p. 259 n. 2.

[61] Cleave, p. 32 (a charming Britishism; Americans would say "takes the cake"). While I often disagree with Bate, he is a thoughtful scholar whose work I also praise and rely upon. See, *e.g.*, Part IV.2.c & note 43; Part IV.17.

[62] Bate, *Genius*, p. 73 (emphasis in original), quoted in Cleave, p. 32.

[63] Bate, *Genius*, p. 67.

Shepard (also an admired playwright), and singer-writer-actor Steve Earle.

It would be difficult to get more clear than Bate's published denial of early doubts above, but after two more decades to think about it, he elaborated in a 2017 video interview:

> So if we ask, *when did this begin*, the idea that Shakespeare, the actor from Stratford, was not the author of the plays, the answer is roundabout the Victorian period. That's to say, *for over 200 years* after Shakespeare's death, *nobody questioned* that Shakespeare the man from Stratford, Shakespeare the player, was Shakespeare the writer. *For 200 years the question didn't occur to anybody. Nobody had any doubts.*[64]

For good measure, Bate *tripled* down on the issue in an authorship debate with Alexander Waugh later in 2017. Bate's very first substantive point (after two *ad hominem* jabs at Waugh) was to declare: "Now here's the most important fact of tonight. *Nobody—nobody—for 240 years* after Shakespeare's death, *expressed any doubt* that William Shakespeare, the actor from Stratford-upon-Avon, was the author of the plays and poems."[65]

So much for that. Let us now proceed to test these claims against the documented historical record.

---

[64] Bate & Reid (2017) (at minute 10) (emphases added) (at the outset of this 15-minute video, the interviewer stated that it was intended to "put [the SAQ] to bed once and for all"—good luck with that!).

[65] Waugh & Bate (2017) (at minute 18) (emphases added, though in fact Bate is pretty emphatic in the original video). For an excellent critical dissection of Bate's debate performance, see Steinburg (2018). On Waugh's many contributions to authorship and Oxfordian scholarship, see the Preface, Bibliography, and Part I, note 4. See also Part V.C & note 26 (discussing one of Bate's *ad hominem* jabs at Waugh, alleging that he is a snob—Bate also alleged that Waugh is a "contrarian").

## III. Refuting the Central Claim: Doubts Arose by the Early 1590s

### A. *"What's in (the Spelling of) a Name?"*

Perhaps, as Juliet recognizes, not much.[1] The differences in spelling between "Shakespeare," "Shakspere," and their variants do not provide the strongest argument for authorship doubt (there are many stronger ones). The late Oxfordian scholar Peter Moore (one of our best) went too far in calling it a "zero argument." But I agree with Moore—and to some extent with David Kathman, a Stratfordian scholar—that non-Stratfordians sometimes place too much emphasis on spelling issues and on the occasional hyphenation of the author's name or pseudonym.[2]

Yet the spelling issues do raise interesting questions. They add to the evidence suggesting early authorship doubts. It is useful to address these issues here, before getting into the additional survey of background issues in Part III.B and the extensive discussion of early doubts in Part IV.

---

[1] See *Romeo and Juliet*, act 2, sc. 2.

[2] See Moore, "Recent Developments" (1996); Kathman, "Shakespeare Wrote Shakespeare" (2009), p. 15; see also Kathman, "Spelling." For a cogent response to Kathman, see Whalen (2015) (with which I generally agree). For excellent surveys of stronger reasons for doubt, see the sources cited in Part I, note 33, especially Price's book and the Shahan-Waugh anthology. Moore's contributions to scholarship are collected in *The Lame Storyteller, Poor and Despised* (2009), edited by Gary Goldstein.

Everyone agrees spelling, including of proper names, was highly variable in early modern England. But some orthodox scholars suggest on that basis, quite mistakenly, that spelling had no significance at all. Yet we know Ben Jonson, another great poet and playwright of the time, was very particular and consistent about the spelling of *his* name. He "deliberately and publicly dropped the 'h' from his family name to distinguish himself ...."[3] Jonson's two leading biographers (both Stratfordians) have discussed this.[4] Yet neither they nor any other orthodox writers, to my knowledge, have ever conceded the obvious significance this has for how we might interpret the spellings of "Shakspere," "Shakespeare," and their variants.

Jonson's new spelling, adopted midway through his literary career, "was *not* a casual aberration: [He] would employ it in his printed works and private correspondence for the rest of his life. Names meant a great deal to Jonson."[5] Perhaps most tellingly, in speculating *why* Jonson adopted the new spelling, one biographer noted that it "was an *invented* name that implied autonomy."[6]

This all raises obvious questions. Why should we assume, as Stratfordians do, that the variant spellings of Shakespeare are just "casual aberrations"? Why should we assume the spelling of that author's name (or pseudonym) did not also "mean a great deal" to him? Does the highly consistent spelling of the published name, notably different from how the Shakspere name was spelled in important personal records, suggest it too "was an *invented* name"? If so, invented by whom and for what purpose? Unlike Jonson, Shakspere does not appear to have consistently

---

[3] Pointon (2011), p. 19.

[4] Riggs, pp. 114-15; Donaldson, p. 56.

[5] Riggs, p. 114 (emphasis added); see also Price, p. 66 (quoting Riggs more extensively and noting that "[t]hroughout his works, Jonson was usually deliberate in his spelling, his punctuation, and his treatment of names").

[6] Riggs, p. 115 (emphasis added).

conformed his name's spelling in personal matters to that of the published name.

Because the Stratford man's name appears consistently as "Shakspere" in his birth and death records, because that spelling or close variants appear in almost all other vital family records (and so far as can be made out, in his almost illegible purported signatures), all of which seem likely to reflect his and his family's preferences[7]—and because no documentary evidence during his lifetime clearly links him to the literary works published under a name almost uniformly spelled "Shakespeare" (sometimes hyphenated)—it is amply justified for convenience and clarity to render his name consistently as "Shakspere."[8]

Using this well-documented historical spelling is useful—especially in discussing the Shakespeare Authorship Question (SAQ)—to clarify whether one is referring to the businessman and sometime actor from Stratford or the author "Shakespeare" (whoever that was). It does not unfairly prejudge the authorship issue. It is possible, viewed in isolation (while raising obvious questions), that a man from Stratford named "Shakspere" might have written poems and plays that, for some reason, were published under a name consistently spelled "Shakespeare." Whether that is actually or likely what happened depends mainly on *other* available evidence, quite apart from the spelling issues.

Moreover, some orthodox scholars have proven quite unreliable on the issue of spelling. Stratfordians today seem to want to rewrite history by harmonizing the spelling in all cases as "Shakespeare." An especially egregious example of fitting facts to theory—of literally erasing an inconvenient historical fact—was when Kathman revised the first name of Shakspere's grandson to

---

[7] See Pointon (2011), pp. 17, 24. On his signatures, see Davis (2013).

[8] See Pointon (2011), ch. 3, pp. 11-24; see also Part I (discussing weaknesses of the ample early evidence claim, citing, *e.g.*, Wells, "Allusions," and Price); Pointon, "Man Who Was Never Shakespeare" (2013); Davis (2013); Jolly (2016).

"Shakespeare." He even put it in quotation marks! The child was actually baptized "Shaksper" Quiney in honor of his recently deceased grandfather, and upon his death six months later was buried as "Shakspere."[9]

Professor James Shapiro has falsely claimed that "[t]here's no pattern" to the spelling of the author's published name and that it was sometimes published as "Shakspere."[10] These two falsehoods are among many erroneous, misleading, or tendentious state-ments he has made in his 2010 book and elsewhere.[11] With unintended irony, Shapiro added: "Shakespeare himself [he meant Shakspere of Stratford] didn't even spell his own name the same way."[12] *But the author "Shakespeare" very consistently did.*

No less ardent a Stratfordian than Kathman, whose relevant article was prominently available on the internet when Shapiro wrote, may be cited to debunk Shapiro on the spelling of the author's published name. Indeed, Shapiro hailed with approval the website on which Kathman's article appears. Among 138 published "literary" references, as catalogued and counted by Kathman, 131 (95%) spell the name "Shakespeare" (hyphenated

---

[9] Compare Kathman, "Shakespeare and Warwickshire" (2013), p. 125, with Shahan & Waugh, p. 13 (and pp. ii-iii, discussing a similar alteration of the record in Wells, "Allusions," p. 81, again with deceptive quotation marks). A key point of Kathman's 2013 article, claiming that Shakespeare's "works are pep-pered with dialect words from Warwickshire and the West Midlands," p. 129, was demolished by Barber (2016).

[10] Shapiro (2010), p. 227.

[11] See Part I & notes 16-17, 28-31, 44; Part II & notes 3, 39-51; Part V & notes 54-60; see generally Wildenthal, "Rollett and Shapiro." A less important goof for which Shapiro richly deserves the ridicule he has already received from many doubters—given his purported expert status, his pompous dismissal of skeptics, and because it's the kind of blooper for which we suspect he might mark off an undergraduate for not reading the source carefully—was his erroneous claim (deployed to criticize the focus of some doubters on the hyphenation issue) that "Shakespeare" was hyphenated in the dedications of *Venus and Adonis* and *The Rape of Lucrece*. See Shapiro (2010), p. 225; see also Part III.B (discussing the hyphenation issue).

[12] Shapiro (2010), p. 227.

"Shake-speare" in 21 of those 131 references). Published references to "Shakspere" or "Shaksper" according to Kathman: *Zero*.[13]

Not coincidentally, most authorship doubters suspect, this effort to falsify the historical record conveniently reinforces the Stratfordian theory. It does so, in part, by making it difficult even to discuss the SAQ lucidly. This may readily be seen, for example, when orthodox advocates retreat behind mind-numbingly circular mantras like "Shakespeare Wrote Shakespeare."[14] Embarrassingly for present-day Stratfordians, however, orthodox scholars during the 19th and early 20th centuries frequently referred, as this book does, to "Shakspere."[15] Once again, we can only feel nostalgia for the good old days when Stratfordians were a bit more candid and a bit more attentive to historical realities.[16]

It is hypocritical of Stratfordians to criticize non-Stratfordians for sometimes overemphasizing the spelling issues. Orthodox writers themselves place heavy emphasis on the purported

---

[13] Kathman, "Spelling." Among 33 handwritten references (rather broadly and debatably defined as "literary" by Kathman), it was spelled "Shakspere" or "Shaksper" *only once each* (second 1593 and sixth 1609 references in Kathman's list), in notes jotted down by purchasers (respectively) of *Venus and Adonis* (1593) and the *Sonnets* (1609). According to Kathman, by far the most common handwritten "literary" spelling (12 of 33 references, 36%) was "Shakespeare" and 18 of those 33 (55%) were consistent with the latter in using the medial "e" (notably distinct from "Shakspere" and its variants in that regard). See Kathman, "Spelling"; Kathman, "Literary Spelling List." One would expect, of course, more variability in handwritten records. Shapiro (2010), p. 281, praised the Kathman & Ross website where these articles appear as providing "a point-by-point defense of Shakespeare's authorship." He did not notice that they provide a point-by-point refutation of his own comment about the alleged lack of pattern to the published spelling of Shakespeare's name.

[14] *E.g.*, Kathman, "Shakespeare Wrote Shakespeare" (2009); Reedy & Kathman, "How We Know That Shakespeare Wrote Shakespeare"; Wells, "Allusions," p. 87 (claiming that "[t]he evidence that Shakespeare wrote Shakespeare is overwhelming"). For a rebuttal of Reedy & Kathman, see Kositsky & Stritmatter (2004).

[15] See Pointon (2011), pp. 17-18; Pointon, "Man Who Was Never Shakespeare" (2013), pp. 21-22.

[16] See similar comment in Part II (supported by notes 58-59) on the earlier willingness of Stratfordians to concede early authorship doubts.

identity of the Stratfordian and authorial names, while often (as noted) rewriting the historical record by harmonizing the spellings to fit their theory. The supposed identity of the names is often the very first point asserted in orthodox arguments.[17]

One cannot help but recall the goal of "Newspeak" in George Orwell's *1984*—to make it difficult (if not literally impossible) to articulate or even *think* unorthodox thoughts.[18] As Orwell commented, when Newspeak finally triumphed, "[w]hen Oldspeak [standard English] had been once and for all superseded, the last link with the past would have been severed."[19] In a similar way, some Stratfordians seem determined to sever the last links to the historical reality of early authorship doubts.

"History had already been rewritten," Orwell went on—just as the *First Folio* began rewriting the history of the SAQ as early as 1623—"but fragments of the literature of the past survived here and there, imperfectly censored, and so long as one retained one's knowledge of Oldspeak it was possible to read them. In the future, such fragments, even if they chanced to survive, would be unintelligible and untranslatable."[20]

Orwell commented that no older book "could be translated [into Newspeak] as a whole. Pre-revolutionary literature could only be subjected to ideological translation—that is, alteration in sense as well as language."[21] In a comparable way, altering and suppressing the spelling of "Shakspere" of Stratford is far more than a technical adjustment defensible on grounds of simplicity or clarity. It alters the very sense of the SAQ. It rewrites history.

---

[17] See, *e.g.*, Kathman, "Shakespeare Wrote Shakespeare" (2009), pp. 14-15 ("The Name"); Reedy & Kathman (heading 1, "The Name 'William Shakespeare' Appears on the Plays and Poems," followed by headings 2-5 asserting that "William Shakespeare" was an actor and theatre shareholder from Stratford and author of the plays and poems).

[18] See Orwell, p. 5 & n. 1; pp. 312-26 ("The Principles of Newspeak").

[19] Orwell, p. 324.

[20] Orwell, p. 324.

[21] Orwell, pp. 324-25.

As Orwell finally noted: "A good deal of the literature of the past was, indeed, already being transformed .... Various writers, *such as Shakespeare* ... were therefore in process of translation: when the task had been completed, their original writings, with all else that survived of the literature of the past, would be destroyed."[22] Anti-Stratfordians are determined that the true author "Shakespeare" shall not meet that fate of historical oblivion. His name shall *not* remain buried where his body lies.

Another instance of Stratfordian hypocrisy is that orthodox writers seem unfazed by the compelling circumstantial evidence supporting Edward de Vere as the true author.[23] To the very limited extent they pay any attention to that evidence, they apparently view the numerous connections between the Shakespeare canon and Vere's life and known writings as random and meaningless—even though that implies an extraordinary and quite unbelievable array of coincidences.

Yet Stratfordians reject as unthinkable the idea that a man from that town who became involved in the London theatre scene just happened coincidentally to have a name the same as (or similar to) a pseudonym used by the author of published poems and plays. Stratfordians think they must therefore have been the same person. Many authorship doubters also find it implausible that this could be purely coincidental, though for them that points to some consciously planned "frontman" scenario.

If Shakspere of Stratford was a frontman for a hidden author, then the similarity of the names was obviously *not* coincidental. As an apparent investor and sometime actor conveniently placed in the theatre business, he may have regularly brokered and procured plays. He may have been ideally situated to be hired (or simply used) to pass off certain plays as his own. Doubters have

---

[22] Orwell, p. 325 (emphasis added).
[23] See Part I & note 4.

long mulled over various possible scenarios. Obviously these are speculative, but they are also perfectly plausible in light of the limited known evidence.

Perhaps there was no direct or active coordination between Shakspere and a hidden author. Perhaps, at most, he was paid to just keep quiet and go along with the possible confusion of his name with the author's pseudonym. Perhaps he did not even need to be paid to go along. If a hidden author were powerful and well-connected, veiled threats might well have sufficed. And Shakspere may have found ways to profit from the plays on his own, even without being directly paid by an author. Indeed, perhaps it went the other way. Perhaps *he* paid the author for what may have been a lucrative business opportunity.

Perhaps it was indeed merely a coincidence involving similar names. Perhaps the pseudonym was independently chosen before Shakspere got involved—if he ever did, directly. Is that really so hard to believe? Katherine Chiljan has correctly questioned why it should be "beyond ... comprehension that there could have been two separate people with similar names that had theatrical interest, just like there were two men named John Davies who published poetry and were contemporaries."[24]

---

[24] Chiljan, p. 34, referring to John Davies of Hereford (*c.* 1565–1618) (see Parts IV.20 and 26), and Sir John Davies MP (1569–1626) (see Part IV.9). For more discussion of Shakspere as frontman, see Parts IV.2, 11, 14-16, 18, 26, and 28. Yet a third John Davies was one of the 1601 Essex rebels. See, *e.g.*, Bate, *Soul of the Age*, p. 217 (noting the two poets), pp. 233-36, 250 (discussing Sir John Davies the Essex rebel), p. 460 (index entries for all three); compare Anderson, pp. xxxi, 426 (Davies of Hereford), pp. 288, 321, 534, 556-57 (poet Sir John Davies), p. 332 (Essex rebel Davies), p. 354 (mistakenly referring to "poet and pardoned Essex rebel John Davies"), p. 586 (merging all three in a single index entry); see also Part IV.17 (discussing the Essex Rebellion, but not Davies).

Note also the occasional confusion between the scholar Laurence Nowell (*c.* 1515–*c.* 1571), Vere's childhood tutor, and the clergyman Laurence Nowell (?–1576), Dean of Lichfield Cathedral. See Green, "Myths," Sec. I, pp. 6-7 (and relevant *Wikipedia* articles). While "John Davies" seems to have been a more common name than "William Shakespeare" (even with all the latter's variants), it seems possible that "Laurence Nowell" was more rare.

Stratfordian scholars have confirmed that "Shakspere," "Shakespeare," and their variants were actually *not* especially rare English family names at the time.[25] And William or "Will" was a *very* common given name, even more so then than now.[26] That would make the combination very convenient and attractive as a pseudonym, quite aside from the obvious appeal of the vivid action conveyed by the surname.

The leading biographer of Shakspere of Stratford actually observed—in reference to apparently unrelated persons sharing the name Shakespeare or its variants—that *"the coincidence, while curious, need not startle us."*[27] So why are Stratfordians like that biographer so startled by *this* possible coincidence?

Chiljan, in a lecture summarizing her thinking on the matter, discussed the many literary allusions to spear-shaking, in one form or another, leading up to 1593 when *Venus and Adonis* became the first publication to appear under the "Shakespeare" brand. Speaking of *"invented* names," as discussed earlier, Chiljan reminded us that the author's own dedication of that confident masterwork—how absurd to think it was really the "first" thing he wrote—described it as "the first heir of my *invention.*"[28]

---

[25] See, *e.g.*, Schoenbaum, *Documentary Life*, pp. 12-13.

[26] Apparently more than *one fifth of all Englishmen* (22%) during Shakespeare's time went by "William" or its variants. See De Grazia, p. 111 n. 56, citing Ramsey, p. 23.

[27] Schoenbaum, *Documentary Life*, p. 13 (emphasis added).

[28] See Chiljan, "Origins" (emphasis added); see also Chiljan, pp. 27-31; Ogburn, pp. 93-95. Terry Ross, "Oxfordian Myths: First Heir," attacks the idea that this phrase suggests a pseudonym. His two key points are valid in themselves but do not support his conclusion. His first point—that "heir" reflects typical references by Elizabethan writers to their works as children—synergizes perfectly with Chiljan's reading. His second point, that "invention" was often used to mean a writer's "creativity" or "imagination," is perfectly consistent with it *also* being used to suggest a pseudonym, especially one newly *created* or receiving its public debut. Ross cites four examples of Shakespeare using "invention" in the sense he prefers. Here's a fifth: "Why write I still all one, ever the same, And keep invention in a noted weed ... ?" *Sonnet* 76, lines 5-6.

(footnote continued on next page)

This is not the only instance we will see in which early authorship doubts appear to be hiding in plain sight. Perhaps

---

(footnote continued from previous page)
Ross claims "no instances" in the *OED* where "invention" means "pseudonym." But leaving aside Shakespeare's innovative use of language (of which this might be an example), Ross ignores several *OED* definitions that plainly support the reading he opposes. Two definitions (3.b and 4) do reflect his preferred reading (artistic creativity), which may be the intended *surface* meaning here. And the *OED* does not explicitly cite the word "pseudonym." But definition 2 equates "invention" with "[t]he action of ... contriving, or making up; contrivance, fabrication"; definition 6 (under heading II, a "thing invented") is "[s]omething devised; a method of action ... contrived by the mind; a device, contrivance, design, plan, scheme"; definition 8 a "fictitious statement or ... fabrication"; and definition 9 "an instrument ... originated by the ingenuity of some person." The latter four are supported by 16th-century illustrations, *including two by Shakespeare. OED*, v. 8, p. 40; see also *Henry VI, Part 3*, act 4, sc. 1 ("[King Edward:] What if both ... be appeased By such invention as I can devise?"); *All's Well That Ends Well*, act 3, sc. 6 ("[Bertram:] [W]ill [Parolles] make no deed at all of this that so seriously he does address himself unto? [French Lord:] None in the world; but return with an invention, and clap upon you two or three probable lies.").

Supporting the idea of "invention" as the *debut* of a pseudonym (or "contrivance," "fabrication," *etc.*) are two definitions obsolete today but supported by 17th-century illustrations: 10 ("[s]omething formally or authoritatively *introduced* or established") and 12 ("[c]oming in, arrival"). *OED*, v. 8, p. 40 (emphasis added). Keep in mind the context of the overall phrase: "the *first* heir of my invention." Ross *thrice* mentions the importance of "context." What makes his argument really insufferable, given that he himself ignores the historical and contextual definitions above, is his patronizing scolding about the importance of historical context (my emphases): "[T]he language of Elizabethan dedications is very foreign to modern readers, and ... often *dangerous* to interpret ... in [modern] terms .... [W]e must look at the Elizabethan concept ... before we can understand Shakespeare's phrase. ... [L]et me give some background on this word that seems to *puzzle* so many [doubters]." Yes indeed, "we must" consider the "background" to unpack this "puzzle." How unfortunate that Ross does such a poor job of that. The only *"danger"* here is to Stratfordian orthodoxy.

And surely Ross is joking (or has an overly literal mind) when he suggests (my emphasis) that if the "author had circulated *Venus and Adonis* under any name but his own [or anonymously], he would not have referred to it as an 'heir.' ... [Rather], *it would more properly have been labeled a bastard* ...." Really? In a graceful dedication to a nobleman written *as if* by a fawning commoner? See Part I, note 16. Ross asserts: "Far from ... signal[ing] ... a pseudonym, the dedication ... amounts to a virtual warranty that the work bears its author's actual name." But don't writers using pen names typically want them to be convincing or at least plausible? Nevertheless, I cautiously omit the *Venus and Adonis* dedication from the items in Part IV because it does not strike me as clear enough, in and of itself, as an expression of early authorship doubt. But it certainly adds to the general background of doubts.

theatrical and literary insiders knew perfectly well that Shakspere was no poet or playwright (one can imagine them rolling
their eyes) and that "Shakespeare" was a pseudonym for someone
who really was.[29] Just because we obsess over the similarity of the
names does not mean Elizabethans did. They may have shrugged
indifferently at the nominal linkage. Perhaps they joked about it.
Or perhaps they knew it was better not to talk about it, much less
put anything in writing about it.

Perhaps many people did not know the identity hidden behind
the pseudonym. Perhaps most just didn't give a damn. Perhaps
many people outside literary and theatrical circles, not personally
acquainted with Shakspere or the true author, drew their own
mistaken conclusions. Perhaps over time such confusion was
encouraged and eventually suggested a more systematic merger of
identities, which obviously would have become easier after
Shakspere died.[30]

Did Shakspere of Stratford care as much as Ben Jonson about
how his name was spelled? The truth is, we may never know. But

---

[29] A pseudonym that makes intended use of the actual name of another real
person may be described by the obscure term "allonym." *OED*, v. 1, p. 341. Some
authorship doubters get tetchy about this and suggest it is a mistake to use the
term "pseudonym" at all—which is not just wrong but silly. An allonym, by
definition, *is* a pseudonym—a subset or specific example of the latter. A pseudonym does not imply only a fictitious or invented name, but rather encompasses
any "false or fictitious name." *OED*, v. 12, p. 751. The "allonymic" theory is
generally the assumed, most familiar, and dominant paradigm in the SAQ. Thus,
one could frame the issue in text as whether the Shakespeare "pseudonym" is or
is not *also* an "allonym." But I fear deploying rare vocabulary may be more confusing than helpful.

[30] See Part I & notes 35-36 on the many oddities of the Stratford Monument
and 1623 *First Folio*. See also Part V.A-B on why most people during Shakespeare's time may not have cared (or dared) to explore such issues. There are
admittedly a lot of "perhapses" in the text, which simply reflects how much we do
not (and may never) know. Stratfordian "biographies" are filled with much more
speculation—often much less plausible. See, *e.g.*, the largely fictional and speculative "biographies" by Greenblatt (2004) and Ackroyd (2005). For two excellent
analyses of the fictional Shakespeare biography phenomenon, see Ellis (2012)
and Gilvary (2018).

we do have some clues about how the author "Shakespeare" may have felt. He seemed very focused on the significance of names. Juliet's famous question about Romeo's name expresses her desire to transcend such strictures, but also laments the reality that she knows all too well, that names matter very much.

The author *repeatedly* tells us that his true name is hidden and may never be known. I paraphrased earlier one of his lines to that effect, to which Stratfordians should pay more attention: "My name be buried where my body is ...."[31] Yet, he also teased us: "That every word doth almost tell [or 'fell'?] my name."[32]

## B.  *More Background on Early Doubts*

Part IV surveys in detail the evidence of early authorship doubts and provides the basic refutation of the central Stratfordian claim discussed in Part II. This section, building on the spelling issues discussed in Part III.A, provides some additional background on the puzzling timing and patterns of anonymity and attribution in the published works of "Shakespeare." Those patterns, like the spelling issues, constitute documented facts contemporaneous to Shakspere's lifetime that cast at least some general shadow of doubt over his authorship.

But as with the spelling issues, anti-Stratfordians should be cautious about claiming too much based on either the anonymous publication of many Shakespeare plays or the occasional hyphenation of the author's name. As orthodox scholars rightly point out,

---

[31] *Sonnet* 72, line 11; see also text above (p. 47); Part IV.24 (discussing the 1609 *Sonnets*).

[32] *Sonnet* 76, line 7. The almost universally adopted emendation is "tell," but the original quarto uses "fel," see Booth, pp. 66-67, 265, which may well carry an intended and resonant meaning, as in "felling" or cutting down a tree (compare "time's fell hand" in *Sonnet* 64, line 1)—all points for which I am gratefully indebted to Martin Hyatt.

anonymous publication was routine during that era—though as they tellingly concede, so was pseudonymous publication.[33]

Hyphenation, like spelling, was haphazard and used for both real and pseudonymous names.[34] Not only were real names sometimes hyphenated but pseudonyms obviously need not have been and often were not. Anti-Stratfordians, of all people, must recognize that hyphenation was *not* essential to convey a pseudonym. "Shakespeare" itself appeared most often *without* hyphenation, including in the name's first two published appearances.[35]

---

[33] On anonymous publications, see, *e.g.*, Wells, "Allusions," p. 86. For a good recent anthology, see Starner & Traister, *Anonymity in Early Modern England*. Pseudonyms have been common throughout literary history and remain so today, so it is hardly surprising they were common during Shakespeare's time. Furthermore, *even orthodox scholars concede that the name "Shakespeare" was itself sometimes used pseudonymously*. See, *e.g.*, Wells, "Allusions," pp. 86-87 (conceding various publications pseudonymously using the name "Shakespeare"); Kathman, "Shakespeare Wrote Shakespeare" (2009), p. 15 (noting well-known "Martin Marprelate" pseudonymous publications); Erne, "Mythography," pp. 432-33 & n. 7 (noting widespread view that Henry Chettle, or someone else, used Robert Greene's name as a pseudonym in writing some or all of *Groats-Worth*, which was printed in 1592 by Chettle; see Part IV.2).

Professor James Marino (discussed in text below and notes 50-54; see also Part I, notes 28, 36; Part V.C & notes 28-31) purported to mock Oxfordians for believing that "Shakespeare" was used by Edward de Vere as his pseudonym, which may have been understood as such by many, even if they did not discuss it in writing or, perhaps, such records failed to survive. "I'm not making that up," Marino chortled at this "standard Oxfordian claim." Marino (*Dogblog*, Nov. 9, 2011). But the mockery falls flat, given the undisputed fact noted above (further discussed in text below) that "Shakespeare" *was* used as a pseudonym, a standard *orthodox* claim of which Marino must be aware. And it was likely recognized as such on those occasions, even if we seem to have very few surviving records of anyone commenting on this undisputed fact. As discussed in text below, anti-Stratfordian skeptics merely extend, in a perfectly plausible way, the orthodox view that works published as by "Shakespeare" were not necessarily written by anyone of that name.

[34] See, *e.g.*, Kathman, "Shakespeare Wrote Shakespeare" (2009), p. 15; Moore (1996). However, for useful discussions suggesting greater significance for the Shakespearean hyphens, see Ogburn, pp. 96-98, and Price, pp. 57-60.

[35] See the author's own dedications in Shakespeare, *Venus and Adonis* (1593) and *The Rape of Lucrece* (1594); see also Kathman, "Spelling"; Kathman, "Literary Spelling List." The surname of the pseudonymous author "Martin Marprelate"—like "Shakespeare"—sometimes appeared hyphenated and sometimes
(footnote continued on next page)

One plausible explanation for frequent anonymous publication is simply that plays were not yet taken seriously then by most people as literature—though it seems Ben Jonson and the author Shakespeare were ahead of their time. Indeed, those two writers played a crucial role in changing that general attitude. Jonson's 1616 folio of his own *Works*—like the 1623 Shakespeare *First Folio* in which Jonson seems to have played a major role— marked a fundamental shift in that regard.[36]

At the same time—as authorship skeptics rightly note—the specific timing, context, and circumstances may lend implications of doubt to some patterns of spelling and anonymity. And hyphenation might *sometimes* suggest a pseudonym—or at least something odd.[37] A hyphenation puzzle, for example, is part of the early posthumous doubts raised by the 1616 Jonson folio, though posthumous doubts are outside the primary scope of this book.[38]

---

(footnote continued from previous page)
not. See, *e.g.*, Kathman, "Shakespeare Wrote Shakespeare" (2009), p. 15. Ogburn, however, p. 98, plausibly suggested that even though the author himself chose not to hyphenate the name in its first two appearances, *other* writers (and perhaps publishers?) sometimes did so to signal that it was a pseudonym.

[36] See Jonson, *Works* (1616); Shakespeare, *First Folio* (1623); see generally, *e.g.*, Brady & Herendeen; Erne, *Literary Dramatist*; and discussions of Jonson in note 38, Part I & notes 39-41, and Part IV.28.

[37] See notes 34 and 35.

[38] On posthumous doubts, see Part I & note 37. It is curious that Jonson— so particular about the spelling of his own name, as discussed in Part III.A— spelled the name "Shakespeare" once like that and once hyphenated as "Shake-Speare" (double-capitalized), in *the only two references to that person or author* in the entire 1616 folio of Jonson's own *Works*—published just months after the death of Shakspere of Stratford. Jonson seems to have taken great care in editing his folio. Also strange is that each reference merely lists Shakespeare as a cast member in two Jonson plays when performed many years earlier (among the few published references to him as an actor before 1623). Only six other names in Jonson's folio are set forth in hyphenated, double-capitalized form: the comic characters "Brane-Worm," "Shoo-Maker," "La-Foole," and "Love-Wit," and the epigram targets "Court-Parrat" and "Poet-Ape." See Shahan, "Beyond Reasonable Doubt, Part 1," p. 3 (point 11); see also Price, pp. 65-66.

While the Jonson folio was published just months after Shakspere died and included epigrams praising many other people, Jonson made no *explicit* reference whatsoever to Shakespeare (however spelled) apart from the two cast lists—no
(footnote continued on next page)

As John Shahan has noted, the unfolding of Shakespeare's literary career seems "strange."[39] The name first appeared after dedications (not on the title pages) of *Venus and Adonis* (1593) and *The Rape of Lucrece* (1594), which became wildly popular bestsellers. During the next four years, six Shakespeare plays were published—but only anonymously. Then suddenly, in 1598, Francis Meres first identified "Shakespeare" in print as a playwright, listing twelve plays,[40] and they started getting published under that name—but not always. For many years after 1598, several were still published anonymously, even a few of his most popular (such as *Henry V* and *Romeo and Juliet*). Then the *First Folio* was published in 1623, seven years after Shakspere of Stratford died, containing 36 plays, half of which had never before

---

(footnote continued from previous page)
acknowledgment of him, for example, as a fellow playwright or poet. Stranger still, some (even orthodox scholars) have speculated that Jonson's satirical epigram to "Poet-Ape" might *implicitly* comment on Shakespeare (or perhaps only on Shakspere the theatre shareholder and actor, not on the author). If so, it suggested he was a huckster who bought, stole, rewrote, and plagiarized plays. See, *e.g.*, Michell, pp. 70-74; Price, pp. 87-90; Waugh, "Moniment" (rev. 2015). Because Jonson wrote "Poet-Ape" years before it was published in his 1616 folio, it is discussed in Part IV.28 (together with other Jonson writings) as another indication of early doubts predating 1616.

If the Stratfordian theory were valid, why would Jonson coldly ignore Shakspere's death, merely cite his name without comment in two cast lists, and even worse (it appears), mock a recently deceased and widely admired fellow writer? This adds still more to the mystery of the Great Silence of 1616. See Part I & note 34. Jonson may have felt some rivalry with Shakespeare, but under Stratfordian assumptions this reaction to the author's supposed 1616 death makes Jonson look implausibly mean, small, and silly—and seems wildly inconsistent with Jonson's extravagant praise just seven years later for "my beloved, The AUTHOR," "Star of Poets," "Soul of the Age!" *etc.* See Shakespeare, *First Folio*, pp. 9-10 (capitals in original). Suffice it to say the Jonson folio poses quite a mystery, like so much else about Jonson (see again Part IV.28)—a mystery beyond the scope of this book and crying out for more study.

[39] Shahan, "Beyond Reasonable Doubt, Part 1," p. 2 (point 10). The rest of the paragraph in text paraphrases Shahan's discussion in part, while also elaborating on it to some extent. The ensuing paragraphs are also (in substance) not original to me (or very little so) but rather reflect a synthesis of points previously discussed by many doubters. See, *e.g.*, Sobran, pp. 146-48.

[40] Meres, *Palladis Tamia* (1598). See Part IV.12.

appeared in print. Several of those also lack any known evidence
of performance before 1623.

How does this fit logically with the Stratfordian theory that
the author was a commoner seeking fame and fortune under his
own true name? Why did he not cash in on the success of his early
poems and use his name consistently thereafter? It is not a
convincing response to suggest he lacked interest in his plays as
literature or that only a theatre company or publisher, not a
playwright, could profit from a play. There was money to be made
and Shakspere may well have been a theatre shareholder.

Some Shakespearean works, as well as some that scholars
agree he did *not* write, were published in pirated editions touting
his name. That proves what a lucrative draw the name was. Shakspere was an astute businessman who amassed property and
wealth throughout his life. Yet we are asked to believe that
neither he nor his theatre company, nor any publisher with whom
they may have done business, made any known use of that name
in publications between 1594 and 1598, the crucial early part of
his career? And only strangely inconsistent use later? It seems a
lot of money was left on the table.[41]

The best way to preempt and compete with pirated editions
was obviously to publish authorized editions. But it seems the
author Shakespeare was inhibited for some reason from challeng-
ing or competing with the many pirated editions of his works—
perhaps because he had died by the time some appeared. As we
will see in Part IV, there are several indications in the contemporaneous documentary evidence that the author Shakespeare died
many years before 1616.

Authorship doubters find tiresome the constant and mind-
lessly circular orthodox mantra that *of course* "Shakespeare wrote

---

[41] Regarding the points on this page about publication, finances, and piracy,
see generally, *e.g.*, Price, pp. 136-42. With regard to the interest of the author
(whoever that was) in the literary value of the works, acknowledged even by
some Stratfordian scholars, see generally, *e.g.*, Erne, *Literary Dramatist*.

Shakespeare,"[42] as if only a dimwit could question such a self-evident fact. Yet even orthodox scholars assert that some plays and poems published under Shakespeare's name or initials were *not* written by the alleged Stratfordian author. Those include most poems in *The Passionate Pilgrim* published in 1599, and *Locrine, Thomas Lord Cromwell, The London Prodigal,* and *A Yorkshire Tragedy*—plays published in 1595, 1602, 1605, and 1608.

Most anti-Stratfordians agree that some or all of the foregoing were probably not written by whoever did write the canonical Shakespeare works. We merely extend in a perfectly plausible way the orthodox view that works *published* as by "Shakespeare" were not necessarily *written* by anyone of that name.

Brace yourself. It gets better. Quite a few leading orthodox scholars, devout Stratfordians all, have recently contended that up to *one third of the entire Shakespeare canon* was in fact *co-authored* by up to *ten different writers other than Shakspere of Stratford*, who somehow remained hidden, unknown, and un-credited as such until modern times—including Christopher Marlowe, a perennial anti-Stratfordian authorship candidate. This is the argument of Oxford University Press's prestigious—and for Oxfordians, ironically named—*New Oxford Shakespeare*.[43]

---

[42] See Part III.A & note 14.

[43] See Taylor & Egan (2017) and critical reviews by Pollack-Pelzner in *The New Yorker* and Dudley, Goldstein & Maycock in *The Oxfordian*. Pollack-Pelzner nicely surveyed grounds for skepticism (on which Dudley, Goldstein & Maycock elaborated convincingly) about the dubious "stylometric" basis for these co-authorship claims. Very annoyingly, Pollack-Pelzner also felt obliged to engage in the reflexive ritual seen in far too many news articles touching on the SAQ—a typically snide, ill-informed, drive-by dismissal of anti-Stratfordian doubts. Pollack-Pelzner seemed anxious to distinguish the Marlovian co-attribution from any notion that Shakspere "was a front for an aristocrat, as conspiracy theorists since the Victorian era have proposed." Here we go again (sigh). As this book shows, doubts have been circulating since long before the Victorian era. On the bogus "conspiracy theory" charge (and related "snobbery" slander), see Part V.

Strangely, while Pollack-Pelzner disparaged "aristocrat[ic]" non-Stratfordian theories (see Part I & note 4 on the Oxfordian theory), he did not mention the long-touted theory that Marlowe—certainly no "aristocrat," indeed from a more

(footnote continued on next page)

But *whoa*—wait a second! Isn't that *extremely similar* to what they *ridicule* authorship doubters for thinking? That some writer hiding behind the published name "Shakespeare" could somehow have gone undetected until modern times? What vast "conspiracy theory"—as Stratfordians speciously love to claim doubters indulge in—could possibly explain how all those collaborating ghostwriters were somehow kept secret all that time?[44]

For that matter, while scholars have offered various conjectures about the true authors of the *Passionate Pilgrim* poems and the apocryphal plays cited above, all agree we will probably never know for sure who actually wrote most of them. Nor, apparently, are there any surviving documentary records from the time in which anyone clearly and explicitly identified the real writers of those works—exactly the kind of "smoking gun" documentation that orthodox scholars impatiently demand from Oxfordians, in "put-up-or-shut-up" terms.[45]

So how was all that information kept secret for hundreds of years? Who conspired to suppress it? *Why?* Is it not obvious that "Shakespeare wrote Shakespeare"? How dare you question a published attribution to the sacred Bard of Stratford! What kind of snob, idiot, or heretic would challenge his authorship? And why do you hate commoners so much? You don't think people from modest

---

(footnote continued from previous page)
humble background than Shakspere—did not just co-author some "Shakespeare" plays but was the true primary author of the entire canon. This book cannot deeply explore the Marlovian theory or other alternatives to the leading Stratfordian and Oxfordian theories—notwithstanding my admiration for Marlowe and for the fine scholarly work done by many Marlovian and other non-Oxfordian authorship skeptics. See Parts IV.30 & note 799; V.C & note 37.

[44] Co-authors were sometimes openly credited at the time, as in the first publication of *The Two Noble Kinsmen* (1634) by "John Fletcher and William Shakspere" (*sic*). Why not all the other alleged co-authors? See Part V.B for more discussion of the "conspiracy theory" issue.

[45] If they are serious about smoking guns, they should take a careful look at the stunningly extensive parallels between Edward de Vere's known early poems and the works of Shakespeare, as detailed in "Twenty Poems" (2018) and Stritmatter, *Poems of Edward de Vere* (2019). See Part I, note 4; Part II, note 4.

backgrounds in provincial towns could become great writers? The foregoing is scarcely a parody. It reflects the actual substance and tenor of many commonly heard Stratfordian arguments, including by many otherwise serious, pleasant, and rational people.[46]

Adding to their stupefying chutzpah and hypocrisy, the *New Oxford Shakespeare* editors defend their far-fetched new co-authorship theories by embracing *exactly the same argument* Oxfordians have been making for almost a century now—that identifying the true author (or authors) is not only a legitimate (and important) historical and literary inquiry, but also an ethical imperative.[47] We appreciate them finally getting on board with that!

So let's pause and recap: Orthodox academics agree that "Shakespeare" was used as a pseudonym by whoever else wrote (at least several) plays and poems published under that name. Most also now contend that there were hidden authorial hands in at least parts of the "Shakespeare" canon, which we have not uncovered until modern times and may never fully figure out. Some, like the *New Oxford Shakespeare* editors, carry the latter claim to a remarkable extreme.

But then they turn on a dime and dismiss the entire SAQ as an "unscholarly question."[48] They mercilessly mock anti-Stratfordians for arguing that—*drumroll*—"Shakespeare" was used as a pseudonym by whoever else wrote plays and poems published under that name, and there were hidden authorial hands in the "Shakespeare" canon which we have not uncovered until modern times and may never fully figure out.

The problem is not that Stratfordians think anti-Stratfordian arguments are mistaken. We might well be mistaken about many things. To err is human. Nor do I suggest that *merely* because

---

[46] See, *e.g.*, Part V.C.

[47] See, *e.g.*, Taylor & Egan, p. 20, cited and discussed in Dudley, Goldstein & Maycock, p. 199.

[48] Taylor & Egan, p. 41, quoted in Dudley, Goldstein & Maycock, p. 198.

someone pirated the "Shakespeare" name on a few spurious publications, or because uncredited writers possibly left a mark on some plays, therefore we should (for those reasons alone) doubt the primary Stratfordian theory. What is deeply hypocritical (and irrational) is that Stratfordians *ridicule* doubts about the primary author as absurd and beyond the pale of reason.

Stratfordians mock Oxfordians for thinking that Edward de Vere, who died in 1604, wrote numerous plays that were not published (and possibly not performed) until years later. They ridicule this as implausible, even though the posthumous publication of manuscripts—often many years later, sometimes completed or altered by other writers—is common throughout literary history. This "1604 objection" to the Oxfordian theory is a popular orthodox talking point. But it is not only weak on its face, it has in fact been thoroughly refuted. It is also, again, stunningly hypocritical. The Stratfordian theory itself, as outlined above, necessarily rests on a similar scenario of plays appearing for the first time years after the supposed author died.[49]

---

[49] It is beyond the scope of this book to discuss in depth the "1604 question." For two typical invocations, see Bate, *Genius*, p. 67; Shapiro (2010), pp. 258-59. It seems to be a pervasively implicit point of Shapiro's *The Year of Lear: Shakespeare in 1606* (2015) (thoroughly debunked by Anderson, Waugh & McNeil in 2016). Looney was so concerned by the widespread belief that *The Tempest* was written after 1609 that he unfortunately devoted an appendix to his book to a strained argument (never embraced by most Oxfordians) that it was not up to snuff as genuinely Shakespearean and must have been written by someone else. See Looney, app. I, pp. 429-53. But see Stritmatter & Kositsky (2013) (showing that a post-1604 origin for *The Tempest* is not compelled by the evidence nor even likely). On the dating of the plays generally, see, *e.g.*, Gilvary (2010). For more refutations of the 1604 objection, see, *e.g.*, Anderson (2005), app. C, pp. 397-403; Whalen (2007).

*Much more difficult chronological problems afflict the Stratfordian theory.* It is actually Shakspere (not Oxford) who has a far more puzzling and multifaceted set of "1604 problems"—and two "1616 problems" as well.

*First:* Why did his literary production stall after 1604, as he spent the last dozen years of his life apparently doing little except supposedly collaborating with second-rate co-authors? Oxfordians, more plausibly, suspect the "co-authors" were completing or editing drafts left behind by Vere. See, *e.g.*, Waugh, "My Shakespeare" (2018), pp. 80-81. Even some orthodox scholars have argued

(footnote continued on next page)

The only difference is that it is far more difficult to understand why an ambitious professional theatre man working under his own name would allow unpublished (possibly even unperformed) manuscripts to gather dust. It is far easier to imagine how and why that might occur if the author were an aristocrat writing under a pseudonym, subject to a strong social stigma against pursuing any profession, least of all one dealing with public theatres held in great disrepute at the time.

Professor James Marino, in a very insightful book, has suggested several points about the process of writing and publishing early modern plays that tend to accommodate Shakespeare authorship doubts and further defuse the alleged (actually nonexistent) Oxfordian "1604 problem." That surely is unintended on Marino's part, as he is a very strident Stratfordian.[50]

Marino observed that no early modern play was ever "necessarily a single manuscript, written at a single time, nor is it axiomatic that Shakespeare's plays resulted from acts of integral composition." He offered the very intriguing suggestion that

(footnote continued from previous page)
that Shakespeare stopped writing after 1604 and retired to Stratford, as cited in Looney, pp. 359-60, Anderson, pp. 397-98, 572, and Jiménez (2018), pp. 27, 303 n. 10. As Looney summarized, noting the post-1604 stall, contrasts in verse form between the flood of Shakespearean plays published in 1597–1604 and some of those published later, the apparent conclusion of the *Sonnets* series by 1604, and the occasional orthodox suggestions that the author retired in 1604: "*Surely it is not too much to claim that the date of Oxford's death, instead of being a weakness, is one of the strongest links in the chain of [Oxfordian] evidence.*" Looney, Letter (1920), quoted in Warren, "Looney in *Bookman's Journal*: Five Letters" (2018), pp. 135, 149, and Looney, *Collected Articles*, p. 20 (my emphasis); see also Part I, note 17 (inconsistency between Shakspere's retirement to Stratford and *First Folio*'s comment that author was deprived of the opportunity "to have ... overseen his own writings"); Part I, note 34 (author's failure to respond to Prince Henry's death in 1612); see generally Looney, ch. 14, pp. 345-68.

*Second:* What could explain the mysteriously deafening silence following Shakspere's death in 1616? See Part I & note 34.

*Third:* What could explain the multiple references indicating that the author Shakespeare died years before 1616 (as mentioned in the text above and discussed in Part IV.30)?

[50] See note 33; see also Part I, notes 28, 36; Part V.C & notes 28-31.

"many traditional bibliographical puzzles can be resolved or obviated ... when *Shakespeare's originary authorship is not taken as an axiomatic principle.*"[51] Equally eyebrow-raising, he aptly noted that "Heminges's and Condell's *[First Folio]* account should not be taken for literal truth."[52] He suggested that a typical play was "created through ongoing revision in the theater, a process that did not necessarily begin with Shakespeare's original manuscript *or end when he died.*"[53]

Marino commented perceptively on a dilemma faced by scientists and scholars in every field, a comment with application to the Stratfordian theory that he needs to consider much more carefully: "Evidentiary details are hard to use until they are organized into some theory, *but what use is a theory that obscures and distorts the evidence? ...* [T]heories, *especially in Shakespeare studies,* have driven the treatment of ... facts far more thoroughly, and far longer, than anyone is happy to acknowledge."[54]

If the puzzles raised by spelling, hyphenation, anonymity, pseudonyms, and timing of publications generate a diffuse sense of doubt or unease about the traditional story, Ramon Jiménez's new book, *Shakespeare's Apprenticeship,* poses a more severe challenge to orthodox complacency. Jiménez focuses on five anonymous plays that seem pretty clearly to be the author's early drafts of canonical Shakespeare works. They appear to date from times utterly inconsistent with the Stratfordian theory, or with the Baconian, Marlovian, Nevillean, or almost any other non-Oxfordian

---

[51] Marino, *Owning William Shakespeare* (2011), p. 16 (emphasis added).

[52] Marino, p. 133.

[53] This statement appeared on the flyleaf summary of Marino's book (emphasis added). See also note 49, and Marino, p. 74: "*The Taming of the Shrew* was evidently open to revision after its author was dead, and until a few years before it was printed. ... Early modern plays were never finished; they were merely sent to the printers."

[54] Marino, p. 73 (emphases added).

alternative theory, for that matter—but suggestively consistent in multiple ways with the Oxfordian theory.[55]

Before moving on to the specific items surveyed in Part IV, it is useful to note the limited extent to which some leading skeptical writings have previously explored the early doubts.

The single best summary of the SAQ ever written is the 2007 "Declaration of Reasonable Doubt" (DRD), promulgated by the Shakespeare Authorship Coalition founded by John Shahan.[56] The DRD, of which I am proud to be a signatory, is a *tour de force*: very persuasively crafted and, at only four pages, admirably concise. It has to cover a huge amount of ground, making any omission very understandable.

Yet it is still surprising, in hindsight, that the DRD does not even mention the evidence of authorship doubts expressed during Shakspere's lifetime. It focuses more on modern doubters from the 19th century to the present, though it does discuss the paucity of evidence that contemporaries who knew Shakspere thought he was a writer. Shahan's 2016 update, "Beyond Reasonable Doubt," does, however, outline 17 "additional reasons" to doubt the Stratfordian theory, four of which touch on early doubts.[57]

---

[55] See Jiménez (2018). A point for which Jiménez has offered even more compelling evidence is that *Henry V* (generally agreed to have been written by the middle of the author's career) dates to no later than 1584. See Jiménez (2016); Jiménez (2018), pp. 74-90, 146, 300-01; Part IV.17 & note 407. On the Baconian theory, that the true author was Sir Francis Bacon, born in 1561, see Part I, note 42. On the Marlovian theory, that the true author was Christopher Marlowe, born like Shakspere in 1564, see note 43 (in this part) and Part V.C & note 37. Sir Henry Neville was born in 1562. For more discussion of these and other alternative authorship theories, see Part IV.30 & notes 797-810.

[56] See Shahan, "Declaration of Reasonable Doubt" (2007, rev. 2015) and "Beyond Reasonable Doubt" (Parts 1-3) (2016).

[57] See Shahan, "Beyond Reasonable Doubt, Part 1." Point 10 (p. 2) addresses early doubts indirectly, by discussing anonymous publications and "[t]he way the Shakespeare phenomenon developed over time." Point 11 (p. 3) discusses doubts raised by Jonson's *Works* (1616). See also note 38. Points 12 and 16 (pp. 3-5) discuss two important indications of early *post-1616* doubts (the Vicars and

(footnote continued on next page)

The magnificent Shahan-Waugh anthology published in 2013 discusses early doubts in more detail, though still not in any depth and not as a major focus. The anthology presents a remarkably comprehensive survey of the entire case for Shakespeare authorship doubt in a single fairly concise volume. It lists the existence of early doubts as the sixth of seven major reasons to question the Stratfordian theory. It calls out as false the orthodox "no early doubts" claim and cites "seven instances of doubts expressed during the Elizabethan-Jacobean period."[58]

The Shahan-Waugh anthology actually surveys a total of nine items indicating early doubts up to 1645.[59] With regard to doubts dating before 1616, it briefly discusses five of the items explored in greater depth by this book. Those five items already show that doubts began arising no later than the 1590s.[60] Let us now proceed to a more comprehensive look at these early expressions and indications of doubt.

---

(footnote continued from previous page)

Burbage references discussed in Part I & notes 7-8). But pre-1616 doubts remain out of focus, even in the 2016 update of the DRD.

[58] Shahan & Waugh, p. 10.

[59] See Shahan & Waugh, p. xiii, and pp. 197-99 (Lena Cowen Orlin, Answer to Question 40, and Doubter Response by Frank Davis & Peter Dawkins). Four of those items constitute early posthumous indications of doubts dating from 1623–45 (the Vicars and Burbage references and two others). See also notes 38 and 57; Part I & notes 7-8, 34-37.

[60] See Part IV, discussing, *e.g.*, Greene, *Groats-Worth of Wit* (1592), Marston, *Scourge of Villainy* (1598–99), *Parnassus 3* (c. 1601), *Shake-speare's Sonnets* (1609), and Davies of Hereford, *Scourge of Folly* (c. 1610–11)—all briefly discussed in Shahan & Waugh, pp. 198-99; see also pp. 167-68 (Andrew Dickson, Answer to Question 9, and Doubter Response by Frank Davis) (briefly discussing *Groats-Worth*); p. 204 (Daniel L. Wright, Doubter Response to Question 43, noting that "Shakespeare's authorship was first questioned in his own time"); p. 214 (James W. Brooks Jr., Doubter Response to Question 58, similar comment); p. 216 (Thomas Regnier & Alex McNeil, Doubter Response to Question 60, same).

## IV. A SURVEY OF AUTHORSHIP DOUBTS BEFORE 1616

There are more than thirty separate writings dating before the death of Shakspere of Stratford in 1616 that express or indicate early authorship doubts. I have not strained to divide them up to artificially increase their number. On the contrary, I have lumped them together quite a bit. The vast majority reflect *published* indications of doubt.[1]

These early doubts were expressed by at least twenty or so different known writers—possibly as many as 28, depending on how we count anonymous and possibly pseudonymous authors or the publishers of works like the *Sonnets* and *Troilus and Cressida.* On the following two pages is a table of the items surveyed in Part IV.[2]

---

[1] See, e.g., Part IV.3 (lumping together as one item all the Harvey-Nashe pamphlets of 1592–93 and additional writings dating back to 1578); Part IV.20 (discussing two separate writings by Davies of Hereford); Part IV.24 (discussing several separate indications of doubt in the 1609 *Sonnets*); Part IV.28 (discussing Jonson's "Poet-Ape" epigram and other relevant pre-1616 writings by him). Thus, the total number of writings is actually well in excess of thirty.

[2] Here is an alphabetical list of the writers and publishers with the subparts where they and their works are discussed:

Anonymous (15, *Parnassus 2,* c. 1599–1600) (also wrote *Parnassus 3?*)
Anonymous (16, *Parnassus 3,* c. 1601) (also wrote *Parnassus 2?*)
Anonymous (Smith himself?) (22, *Sir Thomas Smith's Voyage,* 1605)
Anonymous ("M.L."; same as "Willobie"?) (29, *Envy's Scourge,* c. 1605–15)
Barksted, William (23, *Myrrha, the Mother of Adonis,* 1607)
Bonian, Richard (co-publisher) (25, *Troilus and Cressida,* 1609)
Brooke, Christopher (30, *Ghost of Richard the Third,* 1614)

(footnote continued on next page)

---

(footnote continued from previous page)
    Camden, William (21, *Remains*, 1605, and *Britannia*, 1607)
    Chettle, Henry (19, *England's Mourning Garment*, 1603; possible
        ghostwriter, 2, *Groats-Worth of Wit*, 1592)
    Covell, William (7, *Polimanteia*, 1595)
    Davies, Sir John, MP (9, *Orchestra*, 1596)
    Davies, John, of Hereford (20, *Microcosmos*, 1603, and *Humour's
        Heaven*, 1609; 26, *Scourge of Folly*, c. 1610–11)
    Edwards, Thomas (4, *L'Envoy* to *Narcissus*, 1593)
    Fitzgeoffrey, Charles (18, *Affaniae*, 1601)
    Greene, Robert (pseudonym for Chettle?) (2, *Groats-Worth of Wit*, 1592)
    Hall, Joseph (10, *Virgidemiarum*, 1597–99)
    Harvey, Gabriel (3, Pamphlets, 1592–93; 13, *Marginalia*, c. 1598–1600)
    Heywood, Thomas (6, *Oenone and Paris*, 1594)
    Jonson, Ben (28, "Poet-Ape" *etc.*, pre-1616)
    Marston, John (11, *Scourge of Villainy*, 1598–99)
    Meres, Francis (12, *Palladis Tamia*, 1598)
    Nashe, Thomas (1, Preface to *Menaphon*, 1589; 3, Pamphlets, 1592–93)
    Peacham, Henry (27, *Minerva Britanna*, 1612)
    Thorpe, Thomas (publisher) (24, *Sonnets*, 1609)
    Trussell, John (8, *First Rape of Fair Helen*, 1595)
    Walley, Henry (co-publisher) (25, *Troilus and Cressida*, 1609)
    Weever, John (14, *Epigrams*, 1599)
    Willobie, Henry (likely pseudonym; same as Anonymous "M.L."?)
        (5, *Avisa*, 1594)

1.   Thomas Nashe, Preface to Greene's *Menaphon* (1589)

As Katherine Chiljan among many others has discussed,
Thomas Nashe (1567–c. 1601) was a "university wit" playwright,
poet, and satirist. He wrote a preface "To the Gentlemen Students
of Both Universities" to Robert Greene's romance *Menaphon*
(1589), in which he seemed to refer to a play called *"Hamlet."* He
suggested this play contained "handfuls of tragical speeches" and
seemed to identify as its author an unnamed playwright described
as "English Seneca."[3] He did not mention Shakespeare. "Seneca"
is most likely a reference to Lucius Annaeus Seneca (Seneca the
Younger), the ancient Roman stoic philosopher and tragic playwright.[4] As Chiljan noted, "English Seneca is clearly ... an English
dramatist who writes as well as, or like, Roman Seneca."[5]

Nashe attributed to "English Seneca" a phrase, "Blood is a
beggar," not found in any English translation of Seneca. Shakespeare was compared to Seneca by Francis Meres in *Palladis
Tamia* (1598) and by Ben Jonson in the *First Folio* (1623). *Hamlet*
refers to Seneca, the only mention of him in the works of Shakespeare, and *Sonnet* 67 contains a phrase, "Beggared of blood,"
notably similar to "Blood is a beggar" in Nashe's preface.[6] Nashe's
key passage mocked "shifting companions" who "busy themselves
with the endeavors of Art" even though they "could scarcely latin-
ize their neck-verse if they should have need; yet," Nashe noted,
"English *Seneca* read by candle light yields many good sentences,

---

[3] Nashe, p. 9, quoted and discussed in Chiljan, pp. 52-53.

[4] Seneca the Younger (*c.* 4 B.C.E.–65 C.E.) is sometimes confused with his
father, Seneca the Elder (54 B.C.E.–*c.* 39 C.E.), another writer and orator.

[5] Chiljan, p. 53. See Part IV.28 & notes 695-97 (Jonson's *First Folio* praise).

[6] Nashe, p. 9, quoted and discussed in Chiljan, pp. 53-55; *Hamlet*, act 2, sc.
2 ("[Polonius:] Seneca cannot be too heavy, nor Plautus too light."); *Sonnet* 67,
line 10; Spevack, p. 1110 (sole reference to Seneca). On the Meres reference, see
Chambers (1930), v. 2, p. 194; Chiljan, p. 54; see also *First Folio*, p. 9 (Jonson's
veiled reference to Seneca as "him of Cordova dead"), cited in Chiljan, p. 54.

as *Blood is a beggar,* and so forth: and if you entreat him fair in a frosty morning, he will afford you whole *Hamlets,* I should say handfuls of tragical speeches."[7]

Orthodox scholars have long been uncomfortable with the idea that Shakspere of Stratford wrote *Hamlet* by 1589, three years before the first (very shaky) evidence said to place him in the London theatre scene, and a full six years before the next piece of evidence to that effect.[8] It seems dubious, to say the least, that young Shakspere, only 25 years old in 1589 and seemingly still in Stratford as recently as 1587,[9] had not only written some version of *Hamlet* by then but had become well enough known in London and university literary circles as "English Seneca" to be referred to allusively that way and not by his actual name.[10]

*Hamlet* has traditionally been dated to around 1600. Orthodox scholars have thus concocted the convoluted and implausible

---

[7] Nashe, p. 9 (italics in original). Also intriguing is that Nashe commented:

*Seneca* let blood line by line and page by page, at length must needs die to our stage: which makes his famished followers to imitate the Kid in *Aesop,* who enamored with the Fox's newfangles, forsook all hopes of life to leap into a new occupation; and these men renouncing all possibilities of credit or estimation, *to intermeddle with Italian translations ....*

Nashe, pp. 9-10 (latter emphasis added; other italics in original) (both passages quoted and discussed in Chiljan, pp. 53-54). The latter passage recalls (I would note) the "page by page" bloodletting in *Hamlet* and specifically the "play within the play," said to be "written in very choice Italian" (act 3, sc. 2). Chiljan also noted, pp. 55, 413 nn. 15-16, that Nashe's phrase "entreat him fair" (quoted in the text), and a Latin phrase he used, "*tempas edax rerum,*" appear in other Shakespeare plays.

[8] See Greene, *Groats-Worth of Wit* (1592) (discussed in Part IV.2); Price, p. 31 (1595 record of payment to Shakespeare and two theatre colleagues for showing several plays to Queen Elizabeth's court); see also Part I & notes 27-28, and Part IV.2.f, note 97 (discussing this 1595 record).

[9] Price, p. 15 (noting that his wife gave birth to twins in Stratford in 1585 and that he met with a litigant in Stratford in 1587).

[10] See Chiljan, p. 52. For more on *Hamlet's* significance for the SAQ, see Part IV.3 & notes 131-34.

theory of an earlier play by some other author, a play they call the "ur-*Hamlet*," allegedly a source or basis for Shakespeare's *Hamlet* and responsible for Nashe's and other "too early" references to *Hamlet*.[11] The simplest and most logical explanation for the early references to *Hamlet* is that the author we know as "Shakespeare"—by whatever name he was known in 1589—had already written an early version of his masterpiece by then. Recall that the authorial name (or pseudonym) "Shakespeare" did not have its public premiere until the publication of *Venus and Adonis* in 1593. If there is any more blatant violation of Occam's Razor than the ur-*Hamlet* theory, at least in the field of literary history, an example does not readily come to mind.[12]

This reading of Nashe's 1589 preface, to be sure, is reasonably debatable and raises many questions. Mark Anderson, an Oxfordian like Chiljan, accepted the view of some orthodox scholars that "English Seneca" was probably Christopher Marlowe, though Anderson agreed with the more important point that Nashe's reference "shows that ... *Hamlet* was already on the minds and pens of the London literati by the end of the 1580s."[13]

Such questions are the whole point, not only with regard to this item but with all the items discussed here. This item suggests questions and doubts *in 1589* as to whether the author Shakespeare might have been someone other than Shakspere of Stratford. It constitutes perhaps the earliest known indication of authorship doubt.

---

[11] See Chiljan, p. 52; see also pp. 50-59 (additional "too early" references); pp. 114-15, 117-18, 244-45, 361 (item 44) (more discussion of Nashe's preface). Even some orthodox scholars have criticized the ur-*Hamlet* theory. See, *e.g.*, Marino, *Owning William Shakespeare*, pp. 75-79, 105. As noted by Richard Malim (2012), p. 4, the "fictitious" ur-*Hamlet* would have "to be by an otherwise un-evidenced playwright, good enough and well-reputed enough by [1589] to evoke [Nashe's] reference, yet otherwise totally unknown."

[12] On Occam's Razor and the philosophical principle of simplicity, see Baker, and "Occam's Razor."

[13] Anderson, p. 236; see also p. 517. Compare, *e.g.*, Duncan-Jones, pp. 48-50 (discussing Nashe's preface from an orthodox perspective).

2. Robert Greene, *Groats-Worth of Wit* (1592)

    a. The *Groats-Worth* Attack and Chettle's Apology:
       A Stratfordian Dilemma

Part IV.2 focuses on a crucial early expression of authorship doubt: the famous passage in *Groats-Worth of Wit, Bought With a Million of Repentance (GW)*,[14] published as by "Robert Greene" in 1592. For Elizabethans, "wit" meant "wisdom" or "prudence," not just clever humor as today. We still sometimes echo the old usage, as in "keep your wits about you."[15] Part IV.2—subdivided into eight parts, IV.2.a to IV.2.h—also discusses the related apology for *GW* issued a few months later by Henry Chettle.[16]

*GW* is not widely recognized as evidence of early authorship doubts. Quite the contrary. Orthodox scholars have long claimed that this Greene-Chettle episode supports the Stratfordian authorship theory. They think it is the best evidence they have that Shakspere established, as early as 1592, some degree of fame in the London theatrical world as an actor and playwright.

This discussion challenges the key orthodox claims about *GW* and Chettle's apology while also embracing a key insight of one of the best modern Stratfordian scholars, Professor Lukas Erne.[17] It seeks to arrive at a synthesis of the best analyses to date—by both orthodox and skeptical scholars—of these crucial and perennially puzzling Elizabethan documents. It shows that the most persuasive reading deprives Stratfordians of crucial and long-cherished evidence supposedly recording the launch of Shakspere's career.

---

[14] *GW*, pp. 45-46. "A groat was a coin worth four pence." Chiljan, p. 107.

[15] See *OED*, v. 20, pp. 432-34. *GW*'s title, in modern English (or American) language and currency, would thus be *A Pound's (or Dollar's) Worth of Wisdom*.

[16] See Chettle, *Kind-Heart's Dream* (1592), pp. iv-v (preface "To the Gentlemen Readers"), quoted in Erne, "Mythography," pp. 431-32.

[17] See Erne, "Mythography"; see also Erne, *Literary Dramatist*.

This discussion also highlights an ironic dilemma for orthodox scholars—almost a Catch-22. The more *GW* is read in accordance with their preferred view, the more it necessarily raises doubts. Specifically, as we will see, the more they insist that *GW* attacks Shakspere (as the writer Shakespeare), the more they bring into sharper focus the doubts about his authorship it expresses. This is a tangled web and requires careful study. As Erne said about these documents: "Their importance can hardly be overstated."[18]

There is a folk saying in India, originating in village life, about those who foolishly seek out unnecessary trouble: *"Aa bail mujhe maar!"*—"Come ox, hit me!"[19] Stratfordians have similarly confounded themselves by misreading Greene and Chettle. Their readings have defied facts, logic, and common sense in various ways. But why have they gone out of their way to confront this particular ox? The traditional misreadings seem to reflect a tendency to force the facts to fit a preferred theory. Those who think the Earl of Oxford (Edward de Vere) was the likely author would suggest a better ox for them to confront.[20]

The remainder of this subsection (Part IV.2.a) presents the basic relevant text and context of *GW* and Chettle's apology. Part IV.2.b provides a roadmap of the questions they raise, the leading orthodox and post-Stratfordian readings, and an overview of my responses. Parts IV.2.c to IV.2.h set forth the detailed substance of my analysis and conclusions.

---

[18] Erne, "Mythography," p. 430; see also Chiljan, p. 107 (noting that Shakspere's supposed "early theatrical career ... hinges entirely upon" Stratfordian interpretations of this source, which is "perhaps [the] most important proof of all [of the Stratfordian theory] because it puts an end to those long, painfully blank, 'lost years' of the Stratford Man, and establishes an approximate starting point for his supposed acting and writing career").

[19] My mother-in-law, Pushpa, was born in a village in Uttar Pradesh, India, but grew up and lived mainly (as did my husband) in Bombay (now known as Mumbai). See "About This Author."

[20] See Part I & note 4.

*GW* purported to be the deathbed confessions of Robert Greene (1558–92), a "university wit" playwright who died shortly before it was published. The relevant passage, part of a letter to three unnamed fellow playwrights—widely thought to be Christopher Marlowe, Thomas Nashe, and George Peele[21]—warns them generally about actors ("players," as they were called in Elizabethan times), and to beware of one in particular. It centers around a single long sentence:

> Yes trust them not: for there is an upstart Crow, beautified with our feathers, that with his *Tiger's heart wrapped in a Player's hide*, supposes he is as well able to bombast out a blank verse as the best of you: and being an absolute *Johannes fac totum*, is in his own conceit the only Shake-scene in a country.[22]

"Tiger" is likely to mislead modern readers, for whom it may connote strength, ferocity, and even admirable bravery, like "lion-hearted." But that is not what it meant to Elizabethans, for whom

---

[21] Soo Erne, "Mythography," p. 431. But see note 49 (discussing the possibility that one of the playwrights was not Peele but rather Edward de Vere, the likely author "Shakespeare").

[22] *GW*, pp. 45-46. "*Johannes fac totum*," for Elizabethans, was a mocking term for a self-styled know-it-all or jack-of-all-trades who is really an airhead. See *OED*, v. 5, p. 656 ("factotum"). The emphasis of the *"Tiger's heart"* line and *"Johannes fac totum,"* and the lack of emphasis in the rest of the quoted text (including the references to the "Crow" and "Shake-scene") reflect precisely the cited 1923 edition (see Bibliography), which in turn accurately reflects the original as available in the "Early English Books Online" (EEBO) database. In the original, emphasis was actually conveyed not by italics but by putting the text in a different typeface. The late W. Ron Hess very kindly alerted me to these points and provided the relevant EEBO image. Hess pointed out to me that some commentators (both orthodox and skeptical) have on occasion mistakenly claimed that "Shake-scene" is emphasized in this passage, sometimes citing that to claim it must have been a pun on a specific person's name (as opposed to a generic description). I am not persuaded by Hess's suggestion that the *lack* of emphasis means it is *not* a pun on a name, though the issue is certainly open to reasonable doubt. See Part IV.2.g, especially note 117.

a "tiger's heart" connoted cruelty and duplicity.[23] "Tiger's heart
wrapped in a player's hide" paraphrased a line in a Shakespeare
play in which it was used precisely to convey the most depraved
cruelty. In *Henry VI, Part 3*, Richard (Duke of York) castigates
Queen Margaret after she gloatingly waves in his face a cloth
dipped in the blood of his murdered young son, Edmund (Earl of
Rutland): "Oh Tiger's Heart wrapped in a Woman's Hide."[24]

An early version of this play, in which this line appears, was
published anonymously in 1595 as *The True Tragedy of Richard,
Duke of York*. That version was again published anonymously in
1600. It was not published under Shakespeare's name until 1619
(hyphenated "Shake-speare"). It appeared in its final version in
the 1623 *First Folio*.[25] *GW*'s paraphrase of its memorable line is
the earliest known evidence of the play's existence and suggests it
was at least performed by 1592. The reference to "Shake-scene"
suggests it may have been associated by 1592 with an author
known in some way as "Shakespeare"—although, as noted, it was
not published under Shakespeare's name *until 27 years later*.

Most notably, the "Crow"—going all the way back to Aesop's
famous fable—had well established connotations of mimicry and
plagiarism, though it also meant proud or overrated.[26] Right
before that key sentence, *GW* described players like the "upstart
Crow" as "Puppets ... that spake from our mouths" and "Anticks
garnished in our colors" ("our" referring to purported author

---

[23] See Erne, *Literary Dramatist*, p. 30 (describing "tiger's heart" line as, in
part, an "accus[ation] ... of duplicity").

[24] Act 1, sc. 4.

[25] *Henry VI, Part 3*, in *First Folio*, p. 505; see also Bains (discussing the
latter's relationship to *The True Tragedy* published in 1595).

[26] See Price, pp. 48-49 (providing definitions of these and other terms as
understood by Elizabethans). As Hughes recounted, "Greene," p. 8 n. 17, Aesop's
"lowly crow, wishing to attract to himself the respect and admiration reserved for
the peacock ... dressed himself in some of the peacock's discarded feathers."
According to the fable, "the foolish crow paraded past the other birds, basking in
their envy and respect, but when they realized that the feathers he was sporting
weren't his own, they attacked him ...."

Greene and his fellow playwrights),[27] thus reinforcing the image of plagiarism and necessarily raising authorship questions.

Right after the key sentence, the author begged his fellow playwrights to stop writing new material for the players. Instead, "let those Apes imitate your past excellence [*i.e.*, use your previous work], and never more acquaint them with your admired inventions."[28] He implied some players might be moneylenders[29] and described them generally as boorish bosses and paymasters on whom playwrights sadly depended: "[S]eek you better Masters; for it is [a] pity men of such rare wits [as the playwrights], should be subject to the pleasure of such rude grooms [as the players]."[30]

The key related item in the apology by Henry Chettle (*c.* 1564–*c.* 1606), who transcribed and printed *GW*—and who many orthodox scholars believe may actually have written it, using the recently deceased Greene as a convenient cover. In a preface to a book published several months after *GW*, Chettle acknowledged (while strenuously denying) the claim circulating even then that he was the true author. Chettle apologized in any event for his role in publishing *GW*—*but only as to certain statements and only to one person.*

Chettle said *GW*'s "letter written to diverse play-makers [playwrights], is offensively by one or two of them taken ...." Among the playwrights, Chettle identified only Nashe by name, but as to one "of them that take offense," Chettle said, "I am as sorry, as if the original fault had been [mine]." Chettle acknowledged that unnamed playwright for the "civil" nature of "his

---

[27] *GW*, p. 45. For more suggestions of plagiarism and frontmen, see Parts IV.11, 14-16, 18, 26, and 28.

[28] *GW*, p. 46.

[29] He said "the best" of his fellow playwrights "will never prove an Usurer," while "the kindest of them all [the players] will never prove a kind nurse." *GW*, p. 46. At the time, moneylenders were viewed pejoratively as "usurers" if they charged any interest at all, even if not what we today would regard as excessive interest. See Price, p. 49.

[30] *GW*, p. 46.

demeanor," and for his "uprightness," "honesty," and "grace in writing, that approves his art."[31]

*GW*'s attack on the Crow—who orthodox scholars believe was Shakespeare—is startlingly harsh, wildly out of tune with Ben Jonson's lyrical praise in the 1623 *First Folio*.[32] But Stratfordians offer what seems at first blush a plausible interpretation. 1623 was in the posthumous afterglow of Shakespeare's glorious career, while 1592 was near its presumed outset. Stratfordians have long argued that *GW* vented the bitter jealousy of a dying, second-rate writer at the ascent of a new literary star. Chettle's apology, *if it was offered to the Crow (and if the Crow was Shakespeare)*, would be extremely helpful to this interpretation, appearing to counterbalance the *GW* attack, rehabilitate Shakespeare, and explicitly identify him as a writer.[33]

### b.    Four Questions and a Roadmap

This Greene-Chettle episode is bedeviled by four questions long hotly debated, the last three of which implicate the Shakespeare Authorship Question (SAQ):

---

[31] Chettle, *Kind-Heart's Dream* (1592), p. iv (preface "To the Gentlemen Readers"), quoted in Erne "Mythography," pp. 431-32; see also Price, pp. 26-29; Chettle, p. v (twice referring to Nashe).

[32] See, *e.g.*, *First Folio*, pp. 9-10 (praising "my beloved, The AUTHOR," "Star of Poets," "Soul of the Age!" *etc.*) (capitals in original).

[33] See Erne, "Mythography," pp. 430, 434-36, 439-40. Erne himself, as we will see, rejected the idea that Chettle apologized to the Crow. Frank Davis's 2009 article, agreeing with Erne on this point, see Davis, pp. 144-46, provided a very useful overview of the Greene-Chettle episode and the competing interpretations of it by the Stratfordian and authorship-doubting camps, see especially pp. 145-48, each camp having disagreed about it as much among themselves as between the two camps. As explained in Part IV.2.g, however, I disagree with Davis's conclusion, p. 152, that *GW* was about Shakspere of Stratford. Anderson did not address Chettle's apology nor the possibility that the Crow might be someone other than Shakspere; like Davis (and Price, as we will see), Anderson seemed persuaded that *GW* was all about Shakspere the player. Similarly to Price (compare Part IV.2.f), Anderson, pp. 256-58, emphasized the doubts that *GW* (so read) raises about Shakspere being the author Shakespeare.

(1) Did Greene really write *GW* or did someone else (most likely Chettle)? (Yes, another authorship question!)

(2) Was Chettle's apology for *GW* directed to the Crow (thus, under the conventional view, to Shakespeare), or to someone else?

(3) Did *GW* identify and attack the Crow mainly as a *writer*, or mainly as a powerful, arrogant, cruel, and duplicitous *actor*?

(4) Was the Crow Shakespeare (either author or actor), or someone else (most likely Edward Alleyn)?

We can get Question 1 (which might be dubbed the "GWAQ") out of the way first, since it appears to have little if any importance to the SAQ. What matters about *GW* for present purposes is not who wrote it but what (if anything) it said or implied about Shakspere the player or Shakespeare the author. Most scholars (especially the orthodox) seem to think it more likely that Chettle rather than Greene wrote some or all of it.[34]

---

[34] See, *e.g.*, Erne "Mythography," p. 432 n. 7, citing, *e.g.*, *GW* (Carroll ed. 1994). For an interesting argument that Nashe may have written it, see Duncan-Jones, pp. 43-48. I myself tend to think it was in fact written by Greene, though I certainly would not rule out the substantial possibility that Chettle had at least a major hand in it. It seems to me a dying Greene, who in 1592 had amassed a longer and more prolific literary career than Chettle's or Nashe's up to that time, had the clearest motivation to pen the screed. On this point, ironically, I am thus inclined (along with quite a few other Shakespeare authorship doubters) to accept a facial authorship attribution even as most Stratfordians are now doubters as to the GWAQ.

An intriguing variation on the GWAQ is the idea propounded by some Oxfordians that "Robert Greene" was (at least sometimes) used as a pseudonym by Edward de Vere himself. See, *e.g.*, Hughes, "Greene" (1997); Prechter, "Greene" (2015). Such arguments have questioned whether there was any real writer named Robert Greene. I do not reject such theories out of hand (they merit more exploration), though they seem difficult to reconcile with Price's finding, pp. 309, 311, of evidence of a contemporary personal "literary paper trail" for Greene in six of ten categories that she identified (putting him squarely in the middle of 24 Elizabethan-Jacobean writers she surveyed). It strikes me as more plausible that Vere was one of the playwrights to whom Chettle apologized for *GW*, see notes 21 and 49, than that he himself wrote *GW*. My argument here proceeds on the assumption that Greene was a real writer. If he was not, or if Vere actually wrote *GW*, then it would seem to constitute even more compelling evidence of early authorship doubts.

As Diana Price has noted, Question 1 does remind us "that confusion over authorship could and did occur," even back in the day, and that scholars are still struggling "400 years later ... to figure it out."[35] Price quoted John Jowett, an esteemed orthodox scholar, who "admitted" that the GWAQ "detracts from the certainties of literary history."[36] Price expressed the hope that such scholars would "simply extend" that insight to the SAQ itself.[37]

Parts IV.2.c and IV.2.d address Question 2: To whom did Chettle apologize for *GW?* That question has been a huge distraction obscuring the proper understanding of *GW* itself. It thus needs to be dealt with next, even though it follows *GW* chronologically. Part IV.2.e then addresses Question 3: Did *GW* attack the Crow as a writer? Parts IV.2.f and IV.2.g address Question 4: Who was the Crow?

Here is a brief roadmap of the longstanding orthodox view on Questions 2, 3, and 4, compared to my own conclusions: In the orthodox view, Chettle apologized to the Crow (Shakespeare, dubbed Shake-scene), who was attacked by *GW* primarily as an upstart playwright. By contrast, I conclude that Chettle's apology had nothing to do with the Crow. Furthermore, the Crow was not mainly attacked as a writer. And in any event, the Crow (Shakescene) was not Shakespeare, but rather Alleyn. So even if Chettle did apologize to the Crow, he was not apologizing to Shakespeare (whether actor or writer or both), and even if the Crow was viewed (to some extent) as a writer, that writer was not Shakespeare.

My conclusions build mainly upon the excellent studies by Lukas Erne, Diana Price, and Katherine Chiljan. I think a synthesis of their best insights pretty much untangles the web. Each of these scholars, however, has also (in my respectful view) been somewhat mistaken in different ways.

---

[35] Price, p. 30.
[36] Jowett (1993), pp. 453, 476, quoted in Price, p. 30.
[37] Price, p. 31.

Erne seems to have been limited, though not as much as most orthodox writers, by the invisible electronic fence of Stratfordian assumptions within which they have worked for so long. Erne deserves great credit for partly breaking with the old orthodoxy in his landmark 1998 article, providing a convincing answer to Question 2—Chettle did not apologize to the Crow. But Erne failed to grasp the related probability that the attack was never aimed at Shakespeare *or any writer* in the first place.[38]

Price and Chiljan, as authorship doubters, have not been hobbled by Stratfordian tethers. But we doubters no doubt have our own blindspots. With regard to Questions 3 and 4, Price embraced and built upon the insights of Erne and others on Chettle's apology and illuminated the authorship doubts generated by the conventional reading of *GW*. But Price did not recognize that the Crow might have been someone other than Shakespeare entirely.[39]

Chiljan, adding to the analysis of Price, Stephanie Hopkins Hughes, and others, constructed a persuasive answer to Question 4: The Crow was Edward Alleyn, a leading actor and theatrical businessman of the time.[40] Chiljan thus agreed with Erne and Price that Chettle, at any rate, did *not* apologize to Shakespeare. But Chiljan also, without citing or engaging Erne or Price on this point, continued to embrace part of the old orthodox answer to Question 2. Chiljan thought Chettle's apology *was* directed to the Crow—though again, Chiljan thought that was Alleyn.[41]

---

[38] See Erne, "Mythography"; see also Erne, *Literary Dramatist*, p. 91.

[39] See generally Price, pp. 25-31, 45-56; see also Leahy, "Introduction" (2010), pp. 3-5 (citing Price and discussing *GW* as an indication of early doubts).

[40] As discussed in Part IV.2.g, note 108, quite a few scholars anticipated Chiljan's identification of the Crow as Alleyn (the idea was proposed as early as the 1950s), including, for example, A.D. Wraight (in books from the 1960s to the 1990s), Jay Hoster (1993), W. Ron Hess (1996), and Stephanie Hopkins Hughes ("Greene," 1997).

[41] See Chiljan, pp. 107-29. Chiljan cited Price in several chapters (see also list of abbreviated citations, p. 409), but not in chapters 6 or 7 where Chiljan

(footnote continued on next page)

c.    Chettle Did Not Apologize to the Crow

Erne's answer to Question 2 is very convincing. Scholars, both orthodox and skeptical, would be well advised to accept his conclusion unless they are prepared to tackle the difficult challenge of confronting and refuting it. It is not just that the literal text of Chettle's apology is quite clear, though it is—he explicitly apologized to one of the playwrights addressed by *GW*, not to the Crow or any other player that *GW* warned the playwrights about. Equally important, the broader context of his apology, like the *GW* attack itself, drew a basic "opposition" between the playwrights on the one hand (viewed as "gentlemen" and "scholars") and the players (including the Crow) on the other.[42]

Chettle piously claimed he had always tried to "hind[er] the bitter inve[ctive] against scholars," but nothing in his apology hinted at any desire to apologize for *GW*'s invective against the players. Chettle's only concern appeared to be the reaction of one

---

(footnote continued from previous page)
dealt with *GW*. Chiljan did not cite Erne at all, nor any of Hughes's work. For additional valuable articles on *GW* (just a small selection of a vast literature), see, *e.g.*, Hess (1996), Hughes, "Greene" (1997, rev. 2009), Davis (2009), Detobel (2013), and Prechter, "Greene" (2015).

[42] See Erne, "Mythography," pp. 432-34. As discussed in Part IV.2.d, Erne's conclusion and much of his supporting analysis were anticipated much earlier by other scholars, including authorship skeptics Greenwood and Ogburn. Chiljan, pp. 125-29, while not citing or responding to Erne, Price, or the earlier scholars on this issue, made several points in support of her conclusion that Chettle *did* apologize to the Crow. (I again note Chiljan's view, with which I agree as discussed in Part IV.2.g, that the Crow was not Shakspere but rather Edward Alleyn.) For example, Chiljan, p. 125, emphasized that Chettle referred to the recipient of his apology as "the other," a term also used by Gabriel Harvey to refer (apparently) to the Crow ("the worst of the four ... *[GW]* upbraidest," quoted in Chiljan, p. 127). It seems clear from Chettle's text and context, however, that he was simply referring to "the other" playwright who took offense at *GW:* "With neither of them that take offence was I acquainted, and with one of them I care not if I never be: the other, whom at that time I did not so much spare, as since I wish I had [in publishing *GW*] ... I am as sorry, as if the original fault had been [mine] ...." Chettle, *Kind-Heart's Dream*, p. iv.

or more of the playwrights. In short, the apology was very selec-tive and the Crow was decidedly left out. Sir Jonathan Bate, to his credit, embraced Erne's reading and bluntly observed that "[t]he upstart crow d[id] not rate a mention."[43]

Erne conceded the first-blush impression many have gained—that in comparison to the Crow (or Marlowe, who was accused of atheism, a dangerous allegation at the time), the other two play-wrights addressed by *GW* did not seem to have as much to be offended about.[44] That has understandably caused some to wonder why they would expect or need an apology. But Erne debunked the obvious mistake, still repeated by some, that nothing in *GW* could have offended the other playwrights. On the contrary, *GW* strongly implied that all three were involved in "drunkenness," "lust," "loose life," "sin," and other "irreligious" behaviors.[45]

One might point to Chettle's acknowledgment of the recip-ient's "honesty," while questioning whether *GW* ever specifically attacked the honesty of the three playwrights, as it certainly did attack the Crow's honesty. But *GW*'s implied castigation of the playwrights' sinful and irreligious behavior was more than broad enough to make sensible an apology affirming the "honesty" of one of them. One of several valuable points clarified by Robert Detobel is that "honesty" was used quite loosely at that time, certainly carrying its primary present meaning but also used interchange-ably with terms like "civil," "upright," and "virtuous."[46] We still

---

[43] Bate, *Soul of the Age*, p. 35. It is admirable that Bate, in this instance, was willing to completely reverse the position he took on this point in his 1997 book, before Erne's article was published. Compare Bate, *Genius*, pp. 17-18. However, when the latter book was republished in 2008 with an extensive new afterword, see pp. 341-57 (the same year *Soul of the Age* was first published), Bate did not bother to correct or update this point, thus problematically perpet-uating an important mistake—and making himself appear a bit of a fool, pub-lishing two diametrically opposed views on this issue the very same year.

[44] See Erne, "Mythography," p. 436.

[45] *GW*, pp. 46-47; see also Erne, "Mythography," p. 437.

[46] See Detobel (2013), pp. 17-18; *OED*, v. 7, pp. 349-50.

sometimes use "honesty" to refer to moral virtue in a general sense, as in the comment (offered jokingly today) that marriage might make someone an "honest woman (or man)."

That at least two of the playwrights were offended we can only infer from *GW* itself and Chettle's apology. But we know for a fact that Nashe was offended, even if Chettle seems unclear on exactly how many of the playwrights expressed offense. Nashe's angry published reaction showed that merely being associated with Greene and Marlowe was likely to cause offense.[47]

Erne could have added, as Price did, that *GW* labeled the playwrights "[b]ase minded men all three of you, if by my misery you be not warned ...."[48] Note the similarity of that hectoring injunction to the famous trick question: "Have you stopped beating your wife?" If the playwrights accepted the advice without protest, they might well be viewed as confessing to various past sins; otherwise, they were sinfully defiant. Who would *not* be offended by this Catch-22 insult?

Erne concluded that Chettle's apology was probably directed to Peele,[49] though that remains less clear—and unimportant for purposes of the SAQ—than the conclusion that it was not, in any event, directed to the Crow.

---

[47] See Erne, "Mythography," pp. 436-37; Davis, p. 145.

[48] *GW*, p. 45; see also Price, p. 26.

[49] See Erne, "Mythography," pp. 437-38. Detobel argued that Chettle apologized neither to Peele, Shakspere, the Crow (who he thought was Alleyn), nor any commoner, but rather to an aristocrat, who may have been the pseudonymous author "Shakespeare." Thus, apparently, in Detobel's view, the third playwright (other than Nashe and Marlowe), and the one to whom Chettle apologized, was not Peele but Edward de Vere (Earl of Oxford)—though puzzlingly, Detobel (an Oxfordian) left this point implicit, not discussing or even mentioning Vere except briefly in endnote 10. See Detobel (2013), pp. 15-18. Ogburn, p. 727, not cited by Detobel, similarly opined (more explicitly) that Chettle was apologizing to "Oxford-Shakespeare." This idea strikes me as intriguingly plausible, but I do not feel competent to express a strong view on it. It is not crucial to *GW*'s status as an indication of early authorship doubt. I hope someone returns to these issues and builds upon and synthesizes (better than I can) the analyses by Greenwood, Ogburn, Erne, Price, Chiljan, Detobel, and others.

d.   Reflections on Chettle's Apology

Erne's analysis of Chettle's apology showed him to be relatively candid, insightful, and even daring among modern Stratfordian scholars. He offered a devastating critique of how virtually all leading conventional biographers up to 1998 treated Chettle's supposed apology to Shakespeare as if it were "established *beyond doubt*."[50] Most orthodox scholars had ignored not only the sheer implausibility of that reading but also five dissenting scholars (apparently all Stratfordians) who pointed out the inconvenient truth in 1874, 1886, 1905, 1912, and 1949.

Erne sounded almost eerily like an exasperated anti-Stratfordian when he asked: "Is it possible that so many [scholars] were not aware of at least one of the [dissenting] articles ... ? Or *is it possible* ... that biographers, aware of the alternative reading, chose to pass over it in silence so as not to compromise their account of Shakespeare's early years in London?"[51]

*Could it be?* Welcome to our world, Professor Erne! This is a world in which orthodox scholars routinely ignore post-Stratfordian scholarship or never bother to educate themselves about it in the first place, even as many of them loftily disparage skeptical scholars. Without intending to associate Erne with such attitudes, it must be noted that his own account of the earlier scholars who anticipated his view of Chettle's apology regrettably overlooked not one but *two* major anti-Stratfordian studies, from 1908 and 1984, that explored the issue in some depth.[52]

---

[50] Erne, "Mythography," p. 434 (emphasis added).

[51] Erne, "Mythography," p. 435 (emphasis added).

[52] See Greenwood (1908), pp. 308-19; Ogburn, pp. 58-61. Both cited one of the same scholars (Fleay, 1886) that Erne did. See Erne, "Mythography," p. 435 & n. 20; Greenwood (1908), p. 315; Ogburn, p. 59.

Erne mistakenly thought the analyses in 1912 and 1949 were "the last attempts ... to go against the orthodox reading of Chettle's apology."[53] No, my dear Professor Erne, they and you are not the only ones who attempted "to go against the orthodox reading" there *or on so many other points of traditional Shakespeare studies.* Let me tell you, anti-Stratfordians have been banging their heads against this wall a lot longer than you.

Sir George Greenwood (1850–1928), a writer largely forgotten and hugely underappreciated today, was to a large extent the founder of serious post-Stratfordian scholarship. Perhaps because he and his name are not easily ridiculed, he is much less widely known than his fellow Englishman, J. Thomas Looney, founder of the Oxfordian theory.[54] Stratfordians almost never mention Greenwood, much less engage with his powerful scholarly work. Disgracefully, but not at all surprisingly to non-Stratfordians, the supposedly definitive Edmondson-Wells anthology (titled "Shakespeare *Beyond Doubt*") completely ignored Greenwood.[55]

Greenwood published two major books on the SAQ in 1908 and 1916, as well as five shorter works from 1916 to 1925.[56] He cited and relied heavily on other scholars, as any good scholar

---

[53] Erne, "Mythography," p. 435.

[54] See Looney (1920); Part I & note 4. Despite Greenwood's insight, Looney, pp. 49-50, passed briefly by the Greene-Chettle episode, accepting the orthodox view of it. Looney, p. 78, praised Greenwood's work as "the first milestone in the process of scientific research" on the SAQ.

[55] See Edmondson & Wells (2013) (emphasis added). Greenwood is not mentioned in Cook's "Selected Reading List" of "anti-Shakespearean studies," see pp. 246-48, nor in the anthology's main index, see pp. 279-84. The anthology also ignored Chiljan and other important authorship-doubting scholars—even though it purported to be a systematic response to the SAQ. It cited Price only once, p. 247 (mistakenly, as an Oxfordian). Price's book is actually, like those of Greenwood, agnostic on the likely author. The substance of Price's extremely important scholarly work—which could not have been more centrally relevant to the Edmondson-Wells anthology—was essentially ignored.

[56] See Greenwood (1908); Greenwood, *Shakespeare Problem?* (1916); see also (his shorter works) Greenwood, *Law and Latin* (1916); Greenwood, *Law* (1920); Greenwood, *Jonson* (1921); Greenwood, *Shakspere Signatures* (1924); Greenwood, *Stratford Bust* (1925).

should. But reflecting the sharp barrister's mind (and tongue and pen) that brought him success as a lawyer and Member of Parliament, Greenwood also repeatedly applied his own reason and common sense in analyzing the primary sources and the overall weight of the evidence.

Among countless cogently argued points, Greenwood's 1908 book discussed and refuted the traditional misreading of Chettle's apology.[57] For example, Greenwood anticipated Erne's refutation of the oft-repeated claim that Chettle's reference to "the quality ... professe[d]" by the recipient of his apology pinpointed that person as an actor. In fact, "quality" could refer to any occupation, including that of professional writer. Greenwood and Erne both relied on the very same example in *The Two Gentlemen of Verona*, also cited by the *Oxford English Dictionary*, where Shakespeare himself used "quality" to refer to *outlaws*.[58]

Greenwood was a fascinating and admirable character. He excelled at Eton and Cambridge (studying the classics), and at cricket, was called to the bar by the Middle Temple, and pursued politics for thirty years as a candidate of the old British Liberal Party, eventually winning election to Parliament (1906–15). His

---

[57] Greenwood (1908), pp. 308-19.

[58] Act 4, sc. 1; *OED*, v. 12, p. 974 (definition I.5); see also Greenwood (1908), p. 317 n. 2; Erne, "Mythography," p. 438. The *OED* says the word, when used in this "obsolete" sense relating to professions, referred "especially"—*but not exclusively*—to "actors." *OED*'s full definition: "a. Profession, occupation, business, *esp.* that of an actor. b. Fraternity; those of the same profession; *esp.* actors as a body. *Obs.*" While one must hesitate to argue with the *OED*, the usages it cites (including that by Shakespeare) do not in fact support any special focus on actors. The *OED* cites plays by John Fletcher (1625) and Philip Massinger (1626) referring to *fortune-tellers* and *traitors*. The only cited usage that appears to relate to actors, Davies of Hereford's *Microcosmos* (1603) (discussed in Part IV.20 & note 464) ("*Players*, I love ye, and your *Quality*"), does not suggest any special linkage to actors. It merely indicates the writer happens to admire actors, and thus the profession they happen to pursue. Detobel (2013), p. 18, unfortunately repeated the mistaken claim that the word only relates to acting. See also Chiljan, p. 126 (stating it was "a word often used to describe the acting profession," in support of her argument, mistaken in my view, that Chettle therefore apologized to actor Alleyn—whom she and Detobel identified, correctly in my view, as the Crow).

causes included preventing cruelty to animals and—strikingly unusual and ahead of his time for an English politician during that era—support for India's independence. Also unusual, for an anti-Stratfordian of that time, he resisted the Baconian movement, instead remaining agnostic about who the author Shakespeare may have been.[59]

Erne commented that some of his fellow Stratfordian scholars had in the past "been extremely unwilling to abandon" their misreading of Chettle's apology.[60] This turned out to be a prescient prediction of the future as well. Granted, some have accepted Erne's conclusion, including Sir Jonathan Bate and Sir Brian Vickers.[61] Others, not so much. Some prominent orthodox scholars since 1998 have continued to cling stubbornly to the old misreading. Some have at least cited Erne, though without offering much meaningful response.[62]

For example, the late Professor D. Allen Carroll—perhaps the leading modern expert on *GW*—cited Erne and Vickers but made no real effort to engage Erne's reasoning, while stubbornly resisting his conclusion.[63] In a puzzling error, Carroll suggested both Erne and Vickers were "anti-Stratfordians." We wish! He dismissed them as merely "seiz[ing]" upon a literal reading of the apology.[64] Carroll repeated the long-debunked mistakes that the Crow and Marlowe were the only people touched by *GW* who had

---

[59] While joining forces with J. Thomas Looney in authorship activities after 1920, Greenwood apparently never publicly endorsed the Oxfordian theory. See "George Greenwood" (*Wikipedia*) (and sources cited therein).

[60] Erne, "Mythography," p. 435.

[61] See, *e.g.*, Bate, *Soul of the Age*, pp. 34-35, 429 (see also note 43); Vickers, pp. 140-41.

[62] See, *e.g.*, McCrea (2005), pp. 37-38, 228-29 n. 19 (rejecting Erne's view but at least citing and engaging it, albeit very briefly and only in an endnote).

[63] Carroll (2004), pp. 277, 291-94. Carroll edited the standard modern (1994) scholarly edition of *GW*.

[64] Carroll (2004), p. 292 & n. 104 (also mistakenly claiming that Erne, in support of his conclusion, cited only "two" rather than five "traditional Shakespeare scholars").

reason to expect an apology,[65] and that the word "quality" necessarily referred *only* to the acting profession.[66]

Carroll's implausible *pièce de resistance* was to argue that the word "spare" as used by Chettle—as when he confessed that in printing *GW*, "I did not so much spare [one], as since I wish I had"[67]—was, like "Shake-scene," a deliberate play on "Shakespeare."[68] Get it? "Shake-*spare*"?[69]

Others have just ignored Erne, doubling down on the misreading.[70] The treatment of the issue by Sir Stanley Wells in his 2013 essay was disingenuous at best. Wells avoided explicitly asserting that Chettle apologized to the Crow, ignoring Erne, Bate, and Vickers on this point. Wells instead cited another article for the point that Chettle might have written *GW*, an issue with no relevance to the SAQ.[71] Recall that Wells's essay, and his entire co-edited anthology in which it appeared, purported to be a systematic response to the SAQ.

Wells gave prominent treatment to Chettle's apology, implying that it was among "strong reasons to identify the object of *[GW's]* attack with Shakespeare."[72] He quoted the apology at

---

[65] But see Part IV.2.c

[66] But see discussion in text above and note 58. Compare Carroll (2004), pp. 292-93.

[67] Chettle, *Kind-Heart's Dream*, p. iv.

[68] Carroll (2004), p. 293.

[69] This seems like exactly the kind of strained and far-fetched cherry-picking of supposed verbal linkages and clues that Stratfordians often claim anti-Stratfordians indulge in too freely—and concededly, some doubters have at times. "Spare" was and is an utterly commonplace word. Its use here was probably mere coincidence.

[70] See, *e.g.*, Greenblatt (2004), pp. 214-15; Ackroyd (2005), pp. 189-90; Kathman, "Why I Am Not an Oxfordian." Greenblatt's endnotes did briefly and generally cite Erne's important 2003 book for an unrelated point. See Greenblatt, p. 403, citing Erne, *Literary Dramatist*. Ackroyd, perhaps blacklisting Erne altogether for giving aid and comfort to heretics, did not cite anything at all by him among hundreds of sources in Ackroyd's extensive bibliography. See Ackroyd, pp. 537-48.

[71] See Wells, "Allusions," pp. 73-74, 259 n. 3, citing Jowett (1993).

[72] Wells, "Allusions," p. 73.

length, including (of course) its reference to "grace in writing."[73] Wells concluded: "The cryptic nature of the *[GW]* attack ... means that we cannot say *definitively* that it refers to Shakespeare."[74] That neatly avoided the point that *we can say*, quite confidently, that Chettle's apology was *not* directed to Shakespeare, at least not to Shakspere nor any player.

Wells recommended the Kathman & Ross website, *The Shakespeare Authorship Page*, as "[t]he best recent account of the [early Shakespeare] allusions."[75] The only noteworthy discussion of *GW* among the articles posted on that website appears to be in an article by Kathman, which asserts that the person to whom Chettle apologized "is generally taken to be Shakespeare,"[76] ignoring Erne and relying instead on scholarship long predating Erne's 1998 article. Given the contrary views of such leading Stratfordian scholars as Erne, Bate, and Vickers—all ignored by Kathman on this point—this fails even to pass muster as an accurate summary of orthodox views.

Kathman insists there is ambiguity in Chettle's clear text, speculates implausibly that Chettle did "not writ[e] with Greene's exact words in front of him, but rather was recalling the episode in general terms" (ignoring the substantial possibility that Chettle himself may have *written* "Greene's words"), recycles the debunked canard that the Crow and Marlowe were "the only two people likely to have taken offense," and generally ignores the broader context carefully explained by Erne.[77]

---

73 Wells, "Allusions," p. 74; see also pp. 73-74.

74 Wells, "Allusions," p. 74 (emphasis added).

75 Wells, "Allusions," p. 259 n. 2.

76 Kathman, "Why I Am Not an Oxfordian."

77 Kathman, "Why I Am Not an Oxfordian." It seems a bit rich in this light that Kathman, while legitimately questioning several (apparently minor) mistakes in Ogburn's book, devotes much of this very same article to lambasting Ogburn for "arrogantly" committing various alleged sins, including failing to consider "context." See also Kathman, "Shakespeare Wrote Shakespeare" (2009), pp. 13, 22-23 (similarly disparaging anti-Stratfordian scholars in general, and Diana Price and Professor Roger Stritmatter in particular, in remarkably harsh,

(footnote continued on next page)

Many people understandably question whether there could be any real substance to the SAQ, given that most established academics dismiss it so scornfully and adhere so firmly to the Stratfordian theory. Well, here we have an answer. As so often in the field of Shakespeare studies—and in other academic fields that come to mind, such as law (in which I have worked for decades)—established scholars (even very prestigious ones) often do not acquit themselves well.

To be very clear, I do not endorse the lazy and all-too-fashionable popular trend to reflexively and cynically distrust all established scholars and conventional authorities. But all authorities should be subject to reasonable questions. Scholarly work must always be subject to critical examination and should only be followed to the extent justified by its intrinsic merits.

e.    Was the Crow Attacked as a Writer?

Erne's 1998 article focused mainly on Question 2: To whom did Chettle apologize? He accepted the orthodox answers to Question 3: Did *GW* attack the Crow mainly as a writer or as an actor?—and to Question 4: Was the Crow Shakespeare (either author or actor)? The orthodox answers, as noted earlier, are that the Crow was attacked mainly as a writer, and that the Crow was indeed Shakespeare, both author and actor.

It is useful now to focus on Question 3, because the writer-actor issue arises regardless of whether the Crow was Shakespeare, Alleyn, or someone else. We can then wind up, in Parts IV.2.f and IV.2.g, by discussing the identity of the Crow (Question

---

(footnote continued from previous page)
snide, and offensive terms). Kathman, a scholar whom I respect and whose work I sometimes find helpful (see, *e.g.*, Parts II & notes 16, 18; III.A & notes 2, 13; IV.21 & note 535; IV.24, note 601; IV.26 & notes 676-77), should recall the saying about glass houses. Compare, *e.g.*, Parts II & note 60; III.A & note 9; IV.16 & notes 380-84; IV.23; IV.26 & notes 676-81.

4). Only if the Crow was Shakespeare would *GW* appear to express major Shakespeare authorship doubts.

The *GW* attack was primarily and pervasively aimed at actors as such—and in particular at the Crow, who seems to have been an especially arrogant and powerful player. The Crow especially, and to some extent the players generally, were depicted not only as actors but as theatrical bosses, managers, or paymasters. Review the key sentence in *GW* (see Part IV.2.a), including what came before and after it. It seems a fair inference that some of the targeted actors may have been theatre shareholders.

In about a full page's worth of invective against the players, only 17 words in *GW*, part of that one sentence, suggested the Crow was also a writer, or had pretensions as such. By far the stronger evidence that the Crow was a writer has always (supposedly) been Chettle's apology with its explicit reference to the recipient's "grace in writing." But as we have seen, it is almost certain that Chettle did not apologize to the Crow.

The 17 words in *GW* stated much more vaguely that the Crow "supposes he is as well able to bombast out a blank verse as the best of you," the last word referring to the three playwrights addressed. Indeed, remove seven of those 17 words ("as well ... as the best of you") and it might seem to suggest only that the Crow bombastically belted out lines on stage.

But it clearly suggested more than that, as orthodox scholars rightly emphasize. The Crow was *to some extent* depicted as a writer. The comparison to the playwrights was explicit. The Crow was perceived as not just reciting "verse" but to some extent writing or at least producing it—albeit pretentiously and fraudulently, as the attack also suggested. "Bombast" meant literally stuffing or filling, as of a pillow, and thus here, metaphorically, filling out or embellishing dramatic lines.[78]

---

[78] See, *e.g.*, Carroll (2004), p. 286; Detobel (2013), p. 15.

Chiljan suggested this phrase indicated the Crow "was a bombastic actor."[79] Chiljan also argued that the Crow "wrote plays."[80] Perhaps he did, and I agree with Chiljan in any event that the Crow was probably Alleyn (see Part IV.2.g). Chiljan appeared to base her statement that he was a playwright on evidence extraneous to *GW*—some of it specifically pertaining to Alleyn[81]—but also, in part, based on her view (mistaken, I think) that the Crow was the graceful writer to whom Chettle apologized.[82]

At the same time, Stratfordian scholars have stretched *GW* well past what it can bear by claiming the Crow was recognized *primarily*, or in any serious way, as a rival writer. As Price summarized, the Crow was

> resented, not as a promising dramatist who threatens the *status quo*, but as a paymaster, callous usurer, and actor who *thinks* himself capable of extemporizing blank verse. He is arrogant enough to presume that his ad-libbing can compete with or improve upon the lines written by professional dramatists, the very same writers whom he hires. Moreover, he thinks he can pass off their words as his own.

In sum, the "warning was about a particular actor who exploits the playwrights, not a rival dramatist who could write better than they." The playwrights were advised "to write for a 'better' master rather than the one with a 'tiger's heart'."[83]

Price supported her reading of the *GW* attack with a careful contextual analysis of the often-overlooked preceding and following sections of *GW*. The first section described the adventures of

---

[79] Chiljan, p. 113; see also p. 110. As Chiljan discussed, pp. 113-15, the style and typical roles of Alleyn were notably "bombastic."

[80] Chiljan, p. 112. On whether Alleyn was a writer, see Part IV.2.g (especially note 112).

[81] See Chiljan, p. 112.

[82] See Chiljan, pp. 125-26.

[83] Price, p. 50 (italics in original); see also Chiljan, pp. 108-17.

"Roberto," a writer clearly representing Robert Greene, and a player who resembles the Crow. The later section related a fable about, as Price describes, a "profligate Grasshopper" (again Greene) and a "greedy," "miserly," "tiger-hearted Ant" (again the Crow). The Ant cruelly refuses the Grasshopper's pleas for help and allows him to die.[84]

Price also noted the similarity of the "bombast out a blank verse" line with one published three years earlier in Nashe's preface to Greene's *Menaphon* (1589). Nashe described "idiot art-masters ... mounted on the stage of arrogance," who "think to outbrave better pens with the swelling bombast of a bragging blank verse."[85]

Most striking of all, Price pointed out that a 1603 attack on the theatre business, *Virtue's Commonwealth*, discussed "noble," "gift[ed]," and "ingenious" playwrights "basely employed" by pretentious, plagiarizing, and profiteering players, in terms remarkably reminiscent of *GW*.[86] Indeed, the 1603 attack echoed verbatim the "bombast" line from *GW*, mocking players like the Crow: "He that can but bombast out a blank verse, and make both the ends jump together in a rhyme, is forthwith a poet laureate" and will "hang out the badge of his folly."[87]

---

[84] *GW*, pp. 7-43, discussed in Price, pp. 46-47 (Roberto and player); *GW*, pp. 47-50, discussed in Price, pp. 50-52 (Grasshopper and Ant); see also Chiljan, pp. 109-10, 115-16 (discussing the same parts of *GW*); Davis (2009), pp. 139-41, 143-44 (same).

[85] Nashe (1589), pp. 5-6, quoted and discussed in Price, p. 50; see also Chiljan, pp. 114-15 (also discussing this passage); Baron (2019), p. 17 (same); Duncan-Jones, pp. 48-49 (discussing it from an orthodox perspective). A different part of Nashe's preface is discussed in Part IV.1.

[86] Crosse, p. 122, quoted and discussed in Price, pp. 53-55. *Virtue's Commonwealth* was purportedly written by "Henry Crosse," but as Price noted, no other record of such a person has been found and the name sounds suspiciously like a thinly veiled pseudonym for Henry Chettle. Price, p. 53 n. †. That seems especially so, given that "Crosse" appeared to plagiarize (or repeat his own language in?) much of *Groats-Worth*. See Price, pp. 54-55.

[87] Crosse, p. 109, quoted in Price, p. 54.

That is powerful and relatively contemporaneous support for Price's reading. Whichever Elizabethan wrote *Virtue's Commonwealth*, that writer's view of *GW* and players like the Crow seems utterly "at odds with [modern Stratfordian] interpretations." Yet this striking piece of evidence "has been ignored by [Stratfordian] biographers."[88] It strongly suggests that the Crow in 1592, just like the bombasters of blank verse mocked in 1603, "commanded no respect whatsoever, was hardly the subject of any professional envy, and ... was an incompetent hack and broker who took credit for someone else's literary effort ...." The author of *Virtue's Commonwealth* "did not detect resentment toward a budding playwright" but rather "a braggart who passed off somebody else's writing as his own" and was involved in "usury, brokering, and profiteering."[89]

f.   The Implications of a Shakespearean Crow

Price agreed with the orthodox answer to Question 4—that the Crow (Shake-scene) was Shakespeare—at least that he was Shakspere the player. If so, then *GW* necessarily expressed doubts that he was any kind of serious writer, far less the greatest poet of the age. It would "confirm Shakspere's presence in London's theatrical world, but not in the role usually assigned to him. Instead of the emerging playwright of legend, we find a rather obnoxious actor and usurer who pays playwrights to write for him."[90]

Orthodox scholars have long insisted the Crow was Shakespeare the author as well as Shakspere the actor. There was and is no reason in principle why an actor could not also be or become

---

[88] Price, p. 53.

[89] Price, p. 55; see also Davis (2009), p. 149; Ogburn, pp. 57-58.

[90] Price, p. 56; see also Shahan & Waugh, pp. 168, 198 (brief discussions of the authorship doubts raised by *GW* by Frank Davis and Peter Dawkins).

a writer. As they fairly point out, some leading writers of the era, including Ben Jonson, were actors at one time. So was Molière, the great 17th-century French playwright. There are modern examples too, like playwright Sam Shepard, who by the way was himself a Shakespeare authorship doubter.[91] But was this *particular* player recognized as a rising literary star in 1592?

The dilemma faced by Stratfordian scholars is that they cannot seem to resist claiming that *GW* attacked the Crow (Shakescene) primarily as a writer. They tend to exaggerate the extent to which it did.[92] In fact (see Part IV.2.e), it was overwhelmingly about abuse and exploitation by the players. It singled out the Crow *not* mainly as a purported writer but as an especially powerful, arrogant, cruel, and duplicitous *player*. The complaint was that he—like all the other players *but more so*—exploited writers.

Why do most orthodox scholars read the evidence differently? It seems they assume as a premise that the Crow was the great writer Shakespeare. But that amounts to circular reasoning. They have put the cart before the horse.

In any event, the more orthodox scholars insist that *GW* attacked Shakespeare the author, the more they bring into sharper focus the doubts about the Crow's writing and authorship expressed by *GW*. If Stratfordians really want to claim ownership of *GW* (all of it, in full context) as an attack on Shakespeare, they are "faced with the embarrassing problem of ... explain[ing] why

---

[91] See Cott (*Rolling Stone* interview, 1986).

[92] See, *e.g.*, Jowett (2013), pp. 89-90. Bate characterized *GW* as indicating that "the players have added insult to injury. It is not *merely* that they have taken advantage of the university playwrights; now, one of the actors has trespassed on their territory by setting himself up as a writer." Bate, *Genius*, p. 15 (emphasis added). But is that really the best reading, to suggest *GW* objects to the players (including the Crow) "tak[ing] advantage of the ... playwrights," *merely* as some sort of incidental springboard to launching a *primary complaint* about the Crow becoming a rival writer? It seems quite the reverse.

an emerging literary genius would hire 'scholars' to write plays for him, just as he is supposedly struggling to make his own debut."[93]

If the Crow (Shake-scene) was a writer, the accusations published in 1592 were that he *wrote* as a Crow (a symbol of mimicry and plagiarism); that he wrote "from [other writers'] mouths"; that he was "garnished in [other writers'] colors"; that he was "beautified with [other writers'] feathers"; and that he merely *"suppose[d],"* that is, feigned or pretended, as the verb "suppose" also meant at that time[94]—or perhaps *deluded himself* as a "conceit-[ed]" and foolish *"Johannes fac totum"*—that he could "bombast out a blank verse" like the *real* writers.

This all resonates very well with one or more plausible anti-Stratfordian theories: that perhaps Shakspere—an investor and sometime actor conveniently placed in the theatre business—may have regularly brokered and procured plays and may have been an ideal frontman for some hidden author, passing off certain plays as his own.[95]

To be sure, as Stratfordians might object, *GW* was an *attack* and must be taken with a helping of salt. Whoever wrote it may have been biased, jealous, or driven by other malign motives. My suggestion is not, and I do not take Price's to be, that we should accept at face value everything GW said. The point is that it raised contemporaneous questions. And what contemporaneous evidence counterbalances its derogatory doubts?

Stratfordians concede that *GW* is "the first surviving reference to" Shakspere in any theatrical or literary connection[96]—if in fact it refers to him at all (see Part IV.2.g). The next reference in any theatrical connection was not until three years later in 1595,

---

[93] Price, p. 56.

[94] Price, p. 48; Anderson, pp. 257, 525; *OED*, v. 17, p. 263 (defs. 12 and 13).

[95] See Part III.A & notes 23-30. For more suggestions of plagiarism and frontmen, see Parts IV.11, 14-16, 18, 26, and 28.

[96] Bate, *Genius*, p. 16.

but that minimal record said nothing—not even derogatory like *GW*—about any role as a writer.[97] During the entire 31-year span between *GW* and the posthumous 1623 *First Folio*, only two other documents (to my knowledge) even arguably connect Shakspere the player with any suggested role as a writer or literary figure.[98]

If there were any evidence around the time of *GW*—or any time before 1623—clearly affirming Shakspere the player as any kind of admired or serious writer, then it would be easier to view *GW* as *another* acknowledgment that he was a writer, however hostile or biased (again assuming it referred to him at all). That, again, is why Chettle's apology has always been so important to Stratfordians and why so many have clung to it so fiercely. If Chettle apologized to Shakspere and praised his "grace in writing," that would corroborate the very limited extent to which *GW* suggested he was any kind of writer at all, while defusing and counterbalancing all the derogatory authorship doubts so explicitly and emphatically expressed by *GW*.

But again, alas for Stratfordians, Chettle's apology has been pried loose from their hands—by a Stratfordian! It has nothing to do with Shakspere (see Parts IV.2.c and IV.2.d). *GW* stands alone. However biased it may be, they have essentially nothing to counterbalance it. Assuming for the moment that *GW* does attack Shakspere, the doubts and ridicule it rains upon him as any kind of writer stand essentially unrebutted in the contemporaneous documentary record. On the contrary, the authorship doubts it

---

[97] See Price, p. 31 (discussing the well-known 1595 record of payment to "Shakespeare," as spelled in this particular record, and two theatre colleagues, for presenting several unspecified plays at Queen Elizabeth's court, which could very easily reflect merely a role as actor or theatre shareholder on his part—we have no idea what plays were involved; they might have had nothing to do with anything *written* by "Shakespeare"); see also Part I & notes 27-28 (discussing this 1595 record).

[98] See *Parnassus 3* (c. 1601) (last of the three anonymous *Parnassus* plays) and Davies of Hereford's *Microcosmos* (1603). Their limited value as Stratfordian evidence is undermined by the fact that they also, like *GW* and *Parnassus 2*, express significant authorship doubts. See Parts IV.15, 16, and 20.

expresses are corroborated by all the other items during this era expressing early authorship doubts.

Some Stratfordians in recent years have begun to recognize that *GW* is for them a double-edged sword—that it is in fact a very early indication of authorship doubts. But they have seemed hesitant and conflicted in doing so.

Sir Stanley Wells, in his 2013 essay, categorically denied that any authorship doubts were ever expressed before the mid-19th century.[99] Yet Wells discussed *GW* in the same essay. He seemed oblivious to the authorship doubts it expressed, generally depicting it as supporting the Stratfordian theory.[100] He conceded it was "cryptic" and that "we cannot say definitively that it refers to Shakespeare."[101] But he seemed equally oblivious to the fact that John Jowett's essay—immediately following in the same anthology that Wells himself co-edited—conceded that *GW* raises authorship doubts.

Jowett, while generally clinging to the traditional reading, conceded that *GW* accused Shakespeare of being "guilty ... perhaps of plagiarism." He promptly tried to fog the issue, stating: "If plagiarism is one possible implication ... yet it is not quite the right term ...." Jowett concluded with a comment better suited to his own treatment than to the source he was discussing: "The exact implication of the charge against Shakespeare's writing techniques may well be left deliberately obscure."[102]

---

[99] See Wells, "Allusions," p. 87.

[100] See Wells, "Allusions," pp. 73-74.

[101] Wells, "Allusions," p. 74; see also Part IV.2.d (discussing Wells's disingenuous treatment of Chettle's apology).

[102] Jowett (2013), p. 90. Andrew Dickson, theatre editor of the *Guardian*, is another Stratfordian who has conceded that *GW* raised authorship doubts, see Shahan & Waugh, p. 167 (Answer to Question 9) (*GW* "accuse[d] Shakespeare of plagiarism"), though as with the others, Dickson did not seem to grasp the implications, as briefly outlined in Frank Davis's cogent response, p. 168.

Sir Jonathan Bate also conceded that *GW* suggested plagiarism.[103] But he took a rather curious approach to this obvious indication of early authorship doubts. He seemed to try to discount it by linking it to *modern* authorship doubts, which he viewed as inherently foolish and ill-founded and hoped his readers would as well. "It is one of the ironies of the Shakespeare story that the first surviving reference to him *[GW]* concerns the very lack of a university degree which three hundred years later led people to start supposing that the plays must have been written by someone more educated."[104]

There are several things wrong with Bate's foregoing statement. As this book shows, people began questioning the authorship during Shakespeare's own time, not 300 years later. The modern SAQ has never been based primarily on Shakspere's lack of university education, though that is one factor to consider. And it was quite a stretch for Bate to suggest that *GW* attacked the Crow and other players *primarily* because they were uneducated, though it is true that status-based disdain permeated the attack.

Bate claimed that *GW*'s "principal emphasis [was] the new boy's 'rudeness', his lack of an advanced education."[105] But *GW* never once referred to the Crow's lack of education. It called him and the other players "rude grooms," but that rather general insult was merely collateral to its *principal* attack on the Crow as arrogant, cruel, exploitative, and duplicitous.

Bate was quite correct to perceive *an* irony here. But (ironically) it is not *the* irony he thought he perceived. As we have seen (Part IV.2.e), the primary focus of the *GW* attack had nothing to do with writing. To the extent it did relate to writing, the focus

---

[103] See Bate, *Genius*, pp. 15-16. So has Marino, *Owning William Shakespeare*, p. 35 (noting that it makes "at least an equivocal accusation of plagiarism"). For more suggestions of plagiarism that orthodox scholars would do well to consider, see Parts IV.11, 14-16, 18, 26, and 28.

[104] Bate, *Genius*, p. 16.

[105] Bate, *Genius*, p. 16.

was not on education or lack thereof, but rather on the repeated implications that the Crow was a *plagiarist*. That issue—the false attribution of authorship—is what the SAQ is all about. The true irony here is that it was, in fact, anticipated by *GW* more than four centuries ago and yet Bate can't see it.

A newspaper article by Robert McCrum, a respected journalist and author, seemed to combine (even more strangely) a concession that *GW* raised early authorship doubts with an attempt to discredit it:

> Even in his own time, Shakespeare drove people mad with his modest Stratford origins. In 1592, rival dramatist Robert Greene made a deathbed attack on the "conceit" of the "upstart crow" from the provinces .... For Greene, and every subsequent Shakespeare conspiracy theorist, there was something enraging about the poet's genius. The explanation must be that Shakespeare was not original but an impostor "beautified with our feathers."[106]

First of all, McCrum again misread *GW*. He distorted the text beyond recognition by suggesting that *GW's* author was primarily "enraged" by the Crow's "genius." Beyond that, McCrum's entire approach was patently illogical. *GW* should be taken as the historical starting point. McCrum seemed to dismiss it, anachronistically, because of his own *modern* scorn for authorship doubts.

*GW* is direct and powerful contemporaneous evidence of what an Elizabethan thought. It should be respected as such. Under the

---

[106] McCrum (2010). The suggestion that modern authorship doubters are somehow "enraged" by "the poet's genius" can only be described as bizarre. The obvious mystery of Shakespeare's genius, knowledge, and evident life experiences, in comparison to the known facts of Shakspere's life, does not "enrage" us—it merely mystifies us. The most comical of McCrum's various mistakes (the article does not inspire confidence in the *Guardian's* fact-checkers) is his assertion that Looney—as solid a Briton as they come—was actually *(quelle horreur!)* "another American."

prevailing traditional reading that the Crow was Shakespeare, *GW* thus provides a powerful indication of *Elizabethan* authorship doubts. So read, it corroborates and supports *modern* authorship doubts. Our view of *GW* should not be clouded by arbitrary assumptions (like McCrum's) that the entire concept of authorship doubt is foolish nonsense to be pushed away. That would simply blind us to what the historical evidence is trying to tell us.

Yet the final irony, when all the hurly-burly's done, is that *GW* may not actually add much to early doubts after all. That is because *it probably never attacked Shakspere the player or Shakespeare the author in the first place.* As we will shortly see, the Crow was probably Edward Alleyn. *Most of us, doubters and Stratfordians alike, have focused on the wrong player all along.*

Perhaps *GW* should thus be stricken from the roster of evidence of early doubts—and from the much scantier roster of pre-1623 evidence (touted by Stratfordians) for Shakspere's supposed literary career. Shall we make a deal to strike it from both? It seems unlikely most orthodox writers would agree. They are too deeply invested in Greene, Chettle, and the "mythography"[107] they have constructed on these 1592 writings.

But as we have seen, that mythography boomerangs against Stratfordians. They are hoisted by their own petard. This earliest and crucial foundation stone of the Stratfordian theory—*if that is even what it is*—comes at the very outset with a poison pill of profound authorship doubt. What a dilemma!

g.    The Crow Was Probably Edward Alleyn

Katherine Chiljan is far from the first scholar to identify the Crow as Edward Alleyn (1566–1626). The idea was suggested as early as the 1950s. Jay Hoster and Stephanie Hopkins Hughes, among others, published detailed arguments in the 1990s. But

---

[107] See Erne, "Mythography."

Chiljan has constructed the most persuasive overall argument to date, backed up by a recent essay by Robert Detobel.[108] Stratfordians should carefully consider this argument, especially given the ironic damage their traditional reading of *GW* does to their own authorship theory. (And once they crack Chiljan's book, maybe they will keep reading. Hope springs eternal.)

Alleyn was actually two years younger than Shakspere. But it is generally agreed, supported by much more evidence than we have for Shakspere's career as a player, that Alleyn became a major actor by around 1587, when he was only 21. Shakspere was probably still in Stratford then.[109] "By 1592 ... Alleyn was wealthy, famous, a box-office draw, and in a position of power."[110] By contrast, even orthodox scholars agree that 1592 was closer to the starting point of Shakspere's London career.

Greene, or whoever wrote using his name, seemed to recount grievances accumulated over years, and described a powerful and

---

[108] See generally Chiljan, pp. 111-24; Detobel (2013), p. 15; see also Part IV.2.b, note 40; Chiljan, pp. 112, 115-16, 417 n. 3, 418 n. 12 (crediting the 1993 book by Hoster, a Stratfordian scholar; and also A.D. Wraight, a Marlovian scholar whose arguments for Alleyn date to the 1960s). Stritmatter (2017) (at minute 26), in addition to citing Hoster, Wraight, and Chiljan, noted that Oxfordian scholars Hughes ("Greene," 1997, pp. 5-8) and Detobel (in 2010), and Marlovian scholars Pinksen (2008, 2009) and Farey (2009), also identified Alleyn as the Crow (as Stritmatter himself did as well). Stritmatter apparently referred to Detobel's privately published (difficult-to-obtain) book, *Shakespeare: The Concealed Poet* (2010) (which Detobel himself, however, did not cite in his own 2013 essay). See Cutting (2011) (reviewing Detobel's 2010 book). Anderson, p. 525 (note to p. 257), dated Detobel's endorsement of Alleyn as the Crow to an unpublished 2004 manuscript. Hess (1996), pp. 47-48 (citing Wraight), also supported Alleyn as a strong candidate to be the Crow, as did Sobran (1997), p. 34 (citing Hoster).

Interestingly, the Stratfordian scholar Erne, while accepting the traditional Shakespearean identification of the Crow, observed "a curious echo of the *[GW]* attack" in some lines in *Parnassus 3* (*c.* 1601). Erne stated that the anonymous author of *Parnassus 3*, in launching a similar attack on players, was "probably thinking of Shakespeare or Alleyn, or of both." Erne, "Mythography," p. 433.

[109] See Price, p. 15 (noting that his wife gave birth to twins in Stratford in 1585 and that he met with a litigant in Stratford in 1587).

[110] Chiljan, p. 111.

well-established theatrical player and manager. That fits much better with Alleyn in 1592. "Upstart" would fit either Shakspere or Alleyn, but resonates well with Alleyn's unusual combination of youth (he was still only 26 in 1592) and precocious success.

*GW* itself is the only evidence we have—murky and highly debatable as it is—for any success of Shakspere by 1592. Alleyn's career is independently well-documented. The argument for Shakspere as the Crow, by comparison, has to pull itself up by its own bootstraps. Even more striking, Alleyn's acting company had performed two of Greene's plays multiple times earlier in 1592. We have specific evidence that Alleyn played the title role in Greene's *Orlando Furioso* in early 1592, just months before *GW* was published.[111]

Perhaps the clincher, documented by Detobel and resonating strongly with *GW*'s reference to the Crow thinking he could "bombast out a blank verse," is that we have specific evidence that Alleyn in fact embellished his role in that very play by adding lines to it.[112]

---

[111] Chiljan, pp. 111, 115; Detobel (2013), p. 15; Hughes, "Greene," p. 7 (citing Edmund K. Chambers's multi-volume work, *The Elizabethan Stage*, for the point that Alleyn, as manager of the Rose theatre, opened the 1592 season with Greene's *Friar Bacon and Friar Bungay*; Hughes noted that this "places Alleyn and Greene at the same place and the same time in the very situation we see reflected in Greene's *[GW]* diatribe"); see also Hughes, "Greene," p. 5 n. 9 (supporting the "bootstrap" point in text about the lack of other evidence before 1595 for Shakspere's supposed career).

[112] "Among Alleyn's papers at Dulwich College is a manuscript of the part of Orlando in Robert Greene's *Orlando Furioso*, probably played by Edward Alleyn," containing "corrections and insertions, some of which certainly, and probably all, are by Alleyn ...." Detobel (2013), pp. 15, 18 n. 4 (citing and quoting Henslowe papers edited by Walter W. Greg; internal quotation marks omitted here). Alleyn "had the temerity to add some 530 lines of his own," Detobel (2013), p. 15; see also Chiljan, p. 115 (briefly noting this evidence but not linking it to the "bombast" reference); p. 112 (discussing additional evidence suggesting Alleyn may have written or embellished plays); Marino, *Owning William Shakespeare*, pp. 88-90. Davis's 2009 suggestion, p. 148, citing a 1998 conference presentation by Dick Lester, that "there is no evidence [Alleyn] ever wrote or pretended to be a writer," thus appears to be mistaken.

But of course, I have not yet addressed the two elephants in the room. What about *GW*'s two key references—*first*, describing the Crow by paraphrasing the tiger's heart line from a Shakespeare play, and *second*, referring to the Crow thinking of himself as Shake-scene?

Stratfordian scholars have been supremely confident that the combination of those references provides absolutely killer evidence that the Crow was Shakespeare. Bate put it concisely: "There can be no doubt that this refers to Shakespeare. A pun on his name is combined with a parody of one of his lines."[113]

Such confidence is badly misplaced, for reasons I will now explain. Chiljan unlocked the puzzle in what I think is one of her best insights, in a study filled with meticulous research, solid analysis, and some provocative speculations. Stratfordians would benefit from "look[ing] ... on ... h[er] book."[114] The following elaborates on her insight.

First, however, it must be conceded that most anti-Stratfordian efforts to challenge readings like Bate's have tended to dance around the edges, quibbling here and there with one or the other reference without effectively tackling both. For example, one might reasonably argue that the play now known as *Henry VI, Part 3*, from which the "tiger's heart" reference was drawn, was published only anonymously before 1619 (not at all until 1595). Thus, that play or that line, *viewed in isolation*, may not have been associated with "Shakespeare" in 1592.[115] Whether that

---

[113] Bate, *Genius*, p. 15.

[114] See *First Folio*, p. 2.

[115] See Part IV.2.a (discussing *Henry VI, Part 3*, and the tiger's heart line). Detobel (2013), p. 15, for example, questioned the connection between the tiger's heart line and Shakespeare, as did Hughes, "Greene," p. 7. Hess (1996), pp. 41-46, discussed various reasons to doubt that the tiger's heart reference originated with Shakespeare or in any version of *Henry VI*. Hess showed, pp. 45-46, that the concept of a hidden tiger's heart was a meme common to numerous sources long predating the early 1590s. It is thus at least *possible*, as Hess suggested, p. 48, that the line "was a common, traditional ... metapho[r] upon which both Shake-
(footnote continued on next page)

name appeared on playbills or similar performance ephemera is unknown. A related issue is whether the primary author of the Shakespeare canon (whoever that was) wrote all of that play, including the tiger's heart line.[116]

But those arguments are never going to convince most people. *GW*'s reference to "Shake-scene" is corroborating evidence that someone known in some way as "Shakespeare" was already spoken of as the author of the paraphrased play (or as somehow associated with it). Even if someone going by that name did not actually write it—and even if the line did not originate in that play—the entire play (including that line) may still have been commonly credited to or associated with "Shakespeare" by 1592.

Likewise, one might argue that Shake-scene, *viewed in isolation*, might be a mocking or humorously admiring nickname for *any* bombastic actor who stomps about the stage. It might be a mere generic description of a "scene-shaker," not necessarily an intentional pun on Shakespeare or anyone's name in particular.[117] Indeed, if we can only get past the *combination* of the

---

(footnote continued from previous page)

speare and *[GW]* drew, but which neither ... originated in themselves or copied from the other." Still, as discussed in text below, the mutually corroborating references to the tiger's heart and to "Shake-scene" lead me to hew more cautiously to the traditional reading that they do—*at least in some way*—connect to Shakespeare. At any rate, as I think I show, even if we stipulate some such connection, the broader orthodox view of *GW* falls apart.

[116] Some orthodox scholars, *e.g.*, Taylor & Egan *et al.*, now credit Christopher Marlowe as co-author of all three *Henry VI* plays. See Part III.B & note 43; Part V.C & note 37.

[117] See Hess (1996), pp. 46-48 (discussing theories suggested by Winifred Frazer, Nina Green, and A.D. Wraight); see also note 22. The lack of emphasis of "Shake-scene" in *GW*'s original text might arguably suggest it is *not* a pun on a name, though that seems a weak inference to me. Its capitalization might arguably suggest it *is* a pun, though that also seems weak evidence. *GW* appears to consistently capitalize and emphasize all proper names. But nouns referring to specific persons in a generic way appear not to be emphasized, though they are still capitalized, *e.g.*, "Bridegroom" and "Father," *GW*, p. 27. "Shake-scene," viewed as a pun on someone's name, fits well within the latter category, as does "Crow" (likewise capitalized but not emphasized). However, even non-personal nouns were often capitalized in early modern English (and in modern English at

(footnote continued on next page)

Shake-scene and tiger's heart references, the image of a scene-shaking actor resonates strongly with Alleyn's well-documented career, which included star turns in larger-than-life roles like the title characters in Marlowe's *Tamburlaine, Doctor Faustus*, and *The Jew of Malta*.[118]

But can we get past the combination of those references? Surely Shake-scene (and thus the Crow) must be Shakespeare (or at least Shakspere the player). The references seem mutually reinforcing. While Shake-scene seems to describe an actor (not a writer), we also have that paraphrase of the tiger's heart line later credited to Shakespeare. As noted earlier, one could be both an actor and a writer. Alleyn himself may have been both.

A play on a line in a play *could* refer merely to an actor known for performing a role in that play, perhaps even known for delivering that very line. Chiljan, by the way, cited records showing that Alleyn's acting company performed a play called *"Harry the VI"* no fewer than 14 times in early 1592. That suggests Alleyn himself might actually have delivered the tiger's heart line on stage while possibly playing the Duke of York. As Hughes noted, "it was in all probability Alleyn himself who made the line famous."[119] But Shakspere could also have performed the

---

(footnote continued from previous page)
least through the 18th century, and are still generally capitalized, for example, in modern German), including references to generic places, things, and concepts, *e.g.*, "Park," *GW*, p. 26, and "Death," "Atheism," and "Comedy," p. 44. Many nouns in the U.S. Constitution (a late 18th-century text heavily influenced by English law) are capitalized, inconsistently and with no apparent significance.

[118] See Chiljan, p. 113; see also p. 123 (suggesting that "Shake-scene" alluded to "Alleyn's loud, stalking and stamping acting style"); Hughes, "Greene," pp. 6-7 (earlier making the same point).

[119] Hughes, "Greene," p. 7; see also Chiljan, pp. 112, 417 n. 2 (citing Henslowe papers edited by R.A. Foakes); Anderson, p. 258. While it is true we have no *explicit or conclusive* evidence that Alleyn performed this role, it thus seems an overstatement that Davis (2009), p. 148 (emphasis added), asserted "there is *no* evidence" to that effect. While admittedly only indirect, the cited evidence seems highly suggestive. But Davis, p. 148, conceded only that identifying Alleyn as the
(footnote continued on next page)

role. Most records have been lost. If Shakspere both wrote and performed it, that might make the *GW* attack, which also puns on his name, more convincing as a zinger against him than Alleyn.

We could go in circles like this indefinitely, but it is better to go back and dissect Bate's reading more carefully. It has two parts. Let us concede at least *arguendo* that his second sentence looks very solid: "A pun on his name is combined with a parody of one of his lines."[120] It is indisputable that *GW* paraphrases a line from *Henry VI*, whether intentionally linked to that play or not.[121] And it seems very likely that Shake-scene is an intentional pun on Shakespeare. It could in theory be a coincidence, but how many people will ever believe that? I don't think it's coincidental and neither does Chiljan.[122]

It is Bate's first sentence that overreaches: "There can be no doubt that this refers to Shakespeare." Wait a second, you may object, didn't Chiljan and I just admit that it *does* refer to him? Well, what Bate obviously *meant* was that there was (in his view) no doubt that *GW attacked* Shakespeare. That is the precise point in dispute and it is on that point that I dissent from Bate.

My point, building on Chiljan's, is that *referring to* someone and *attacking* someone are not the same thing. It is certainly possible (perhaps typical, depending on the context) to attack and refer to the same person simultaneously. But it is also quite possible to *refer to* Person A in the course of *attacking* Person B, and I think that is exactly what happened here. The insight is Chiljan's:

---

(footnote continued from previous page)

Crow "is not entirely implausible." His conclusion in 2009, p. 152, was that it was more likely Shakspere.

[120] Bate, *Genius*, p. 15.

[121] See note 115, and Part IV.2.a.

[122] See Chiljan, p. 110 (asserting that *GW* "was definitely punning upon the name 'Shakespeare' with 'Shake-scene' because of the usage of Shakespeare's 'tiger's heart' line"). Compare discussion in text above and notes 115, 117, and 119.

The word "only" in "the only Shake-scene in a country" implies that there was another "Shake-scene," the original one—otherwise the Upstart Crow would not fancifully single himself out as one ("in his own conceit"). It is implied that there was another Shake-scene, one whose reputation was well established .... [The] Crow conceitedly thought of himself as *another* Shakespeare .... [The] Crow was not Shakespeare, he just fancied himself another great writer or scene-shaker ....[123]

I would add that he fancied himself another great "bombast[er]" of "blank verse."

In other words, just because you make a pun on someone's name, or paraphrase a line credited to that person, or refer to some other characteristic associated with that person (or do all those things), does not mean you are necessarily attacking that very same person. You might well be attacking *someone else* (Person B) by playing upon some similarity or association with Person A's name or characteristic.

Take heed that *GW*'s author did not directly or immediately label his target as Shake-scene. He identified him first as "an upstart Crow," then as a cruel, deceitful *"Tiger"* in actor's clothing. Only several lines later, more than 40 words after "Crow," did he ridicule the Crow's *"own conceit[ed]" view of himself* as "the only

---

[123] Chiljan, pp. 110-11 (emphasis in original). I do not agree with all of Chiljan's arguments in support of this conclusion. For example, she argued that the "insulting picture of the Upstart Crow-Player-Ant and warning about his devious character makes it unlikely that [the author] would make an obvious pun upon this person's real name." Chiljan, p. 110. But the personalities involved could hardly have been a secret to people at the time (especially in theatre circles), as Chiljan's own powerful circumstantial argument for Alleyn demonstrates. While Greene used the figleaf of not explicitly naming names—and Chettle may have used the deceased Greene as a pseudonym for additional protection—the author clearly wanted those addressed to know whom he was warning them about. Otherwise, what was the point of scolding them as "[b]ase minded ... if ... you be not warned," *GW*, p. 45?

Shake-scene in a country."[124] In fact, as this parsing of the text should remind us, the author *never did* directly label the Crow as Shake-scene! Instead, he characterized the Crow as *thinking of himself* as Shake-scene. There is a difference.

One might draw an analogy to current politics. Suppose one wished to mock an obscenely boorish blowhard of a politician, as bearing some resemblance to—President Donald Trump? One might easily mock some *other* public figure who *resembles* him— some governor or senator perhaps, or a small-town mayor like Shakspere's father?—by labeling him or her a "Trumpster." Or, dare I suggest, "Trump-scene"? Anyone can understand what that means, whether you love Trump or hate him. "That conceited Mayor Shakspere, he thinks he's the biggest Trumpster in the county!" Some have suggested Doug Ford, the premier of Ontario, might be the biggest Trumpster in Canada.[125]

But would it make sense for anyone to mock *Trump himself* by saying, for example: "Trump is such a conceited oaf, he's the biggest Trumpster in America!" No—that would fall totally flat. It would be too obvious and strangely circular—even more odd to mock Trump for *thinking "in his own conceit"* that he's the biggest Trumpster around. That would not be a "conceit" but an obvious reality. Of course *Trump* resembles Trump!

Chiljan's insight, similarly, is that it would not logically seem to be a "conceit" for Shakespeare *himself* to think he was "the only Shake-scene." Whoever's name was being punned upon as Shake-scene was likely the original Shakespeare (Person A)—just as Trump is the original Trump (for better or worse). But that original Shakespeare would most logically be someone *other than* the target being mocked (Person B, the conceited Crow) for having Shakespearean *pretensions*. For this argument to succeed, it is not necessary to show anything more than a reasonable *possibility*

---

[124] *GW*, pp. 45-46 (emphasis of *"Tiger"* in original; second emphasis added).
[125] Ford has disowned this debatable comparison.

that "Shake-scene" (even if referring to Shakespeare) could have been used to mock someone else. The point is to refute the claim that the Shake-scene and tiger's heart references *necessarily* prove the Crow was Shakespeare.

So do the references *compel* the conclusion that *GW* attacked Shakespeare *himself* as the Crow? No. Given the compelling evidence pointing to Alleyn as the Crow (and thus Shake-scene), it is not even *likely* that Shake-scene was Shakespeare. Admittedly, it cannot be ruled out as a *possible* reading. But on balance, it seems unlikely that *GW* was mocking a conceited Shakespeare. The whole point of using a fairly mild pun on the name was probably not to mock Shakespeare *himself* but rather someone else (like Alleyn) who evoked some association with the name—someone with Shakespearean *pretensions*.[126]

Shakespeare's plays, by 1592, are generally thought to have included not just early versions of all three *Henry VI* plays but also *Titus Andronicus*, that over-the-top revenge-fest. All lend themselves to scene-shaking actors like Alleyn. As noted above, we have evidence suggesting Alleyn may have acted in a play called *"Harry the VI"* in early 1592, perhaps delivering the very line paraphrased in *GW*. As Chiljan noted, Alleyn liked to perform outsize *title roles*.[127] Recall that the title of *Henry VI, Part 3*, when it was published anonymously in 1595 and 1600, was actually

---

[126] Again, it is certainly *possible* (even common) to attack and refer to the same person simultaneously. One might well attack someone by punning on his name. But usually such a pun would be patently derogatory. For example, a late-night comedian sought to ridicule Trump by altering his name to "Drumpf"—supposedly the name's original German form, with (it seems) an intended echo of Hitler's *Mein Kampf*. A derogatory variation on "Trumpster" might be "Dumpster." But "Trumpster," while a workable insult to mock someone with Trumpian *pretensions*, is not patently or inherently derogatory and is thus too lame, obvious, and circular to effectively attack Trump himself. "Shake-scene," likewise, works well as mockery of someone with Shakespearean *pretensions*, but is also not inherently very derogatory and thus seems a weak jab at the very author of scene-shaking lines.

[127] See Chiljan, pp. 111-14.

*Richard, Duke of York*, the character who utters that very line. It all starts to fit together.

In sum, the best reading of *GW*'s mocking reference to Shake-scene is that it suggested the Crow arrogantly thought of himself as the greatest Shakespearean actor of his day. And perhaps he was. Perhaps one known as a bombastic player who stomped about literally shaking the stage. Perhaps one who performed leading roles in plays written by *others*, like Marlowe's *Tambur-laine* or "Shakespeare's" *Henry VI*, perhaps including the role of the Duke of York lamenting a tiger's heart wrapped in someone's hide. Perhaps one who pompously thought he could embellish and improve upon the scripts he was given. Perhaps one who was a wealthy moneylender. Definitely one who was a powerful and well-established figure in the London theatre scene, a cruel and deceitful "Master." As Chiljan argued, that all fits far better with Alleyn—in terms of internal textual logic, known facts, and exter-nal context, especially in 1592—than with Shakspere the player or Shakespeare the author.

### h.   Conclusion

All that remains to consider is where this revisionist reading of *GW* leaves us with regard to the SAQ. Let us first recap: Strat-fordians have long argued that (1) the Crow (Shake-scene) was both Shakspere the player and Shakespeare the author. Despite Erne, many still argue that (2) Chettle's apology (to a graceful writer) was directed to the Crow. But as we have seen:

(1) Chettle did not apologize to the Crow.

(2) Even if he did, the Crow was probably Edward Alleyn.

(3) Even if the Crow were Shakspere, *GW* depicted him as a plagiarist, not any kind of serious writer.

(4) Under Stratfordian assumptions *GW*, far from supporting their theory, is instead a wellspring of early authorship doubts.

Yet the reading adopted here—by replacing Shakspere with Alleyn—may, ironically, deprive anti-Stratfordians of a significant early indication of authorship doubts. (But never fear, we have plenty more. See the rest of Part IV.) More importantly, however, this reading deprives Stratfordians of evidence supposedly recording the launch of Shakspere's career as an author.

It should be kept in mind that retargeting *GW* to Alleyn does not eliminate it as evidence about Shakespeare the author (whoever that was). It just alters its significance. Even if Alleyn was the Crow, it is still probably true (and very interesting) that *GW* referred for the first time in print (albeit punningly) to Shakespeare—the year before that author's name (or pseudonym) first appeared *in haec verba* under the dedication to Henry Wriothesley (Earl of Southampton) in *Venus and Adonis* (1593).

But under this revisionist view, *GW* no longer suggests that Shakespeare the author was a player. Indeed, we no longer have any reference at all to Shakspere as a player in 1592, or any time before 1595. We seem to have lost any documented connection during the 1590s—other than the similarity of the names, recalling (see Part III.A) that they were not rare names—between Shakspere the player and any writing career he may have had. We have lost the only 16th-century connection we thought we had between Shakspere the player and whoever wrote the tiger's heart line—an author now more mysterious than ever.

This revisionist reading, to be sure, does not by itself rule out the possibility that Shakspere was both a player and author of the tiger's heart line. The implications are simply that (1) there was *some* playwright in 1592 with a name or pseudonym easily punned upon as Shake-scene, (2) this pun was used to mock *someone else* (the player Alleyn), and (3) perhaps actors playing this writer's characters were (like Alleyn) notorious for "shaking" the stage, or Shake-scene was a play on the name of Shakespeare the author, or both. As Chiljan noted, a fourth implication is that

Shakespeare the author already had a well-established reputation by 1592—not an "upstart" like Alleyn the Crow.[128] That still does not completely rule out Shakspere of Stratford as the author. Marlowe, at the same age in 1592, was well-established as a playwright. But the more we sift the evidence, the less likely it seems that Shakspere was the Crow, much less a real writer.

So perhaps this revisionist view of *GW* does not entirely dissolve its significance as an early expression of doubt. It belongs on the list until Stratfordians themselves arrive at a consensus to remove it by abandoning the traditional misreading. The ball is in your court, dear orthodox colleagues. Keep us posted on when and how you resolve your dilemma. And look out for that ox!

3.   Thomas Nashe and Gabriel Harvey, Pamphlets (1592–93)
     (with glances back to 1578)

Thomas Nashe (1567–*c.* 1601), whom we met in Part IV.1, was a playwright, poet, and satirist. Gabriel Harvey (*c.* 1553–1631), whom we will meet again in Part IV.13, was also a writer, who apparently dabbled in poetry but was known more as a scholar and pamphleteer. They were both educated at Cambridge University, Harvey in the late 1560s and Nashe during the 1580s. Harvey also, by the 1580s, earned a law degree at Oxford University and began practicing law in London.

They engaged in a famous "pamphlet war" from 1592 to 1596, of which the most notable entries for present purposes were Nashe's *Pierce Penniless* (1592) (postdating Greene's *Groats-Worth of Wit*, discussed in Part IV.2), followed by Harvey's *Four Letters* (1592), Nashe's *Strange News* (1593), and Harvey's *Pierce's Supererogation* (1593) and *New Letter of Notable Contents* (1593).

It is undisputed that in 1599 the Archbishop of Canterbury ordered all of Nashe's and Harvey's writings to be destroyed—an

---

[128] Chiljan, pp. 110, 124.

order thankfully not fully executed! The reasons for that order remain unclear. But given the many indications that Edward de Vere (Earl of Oxford) figured significantly in the Nashe-Harvey pamphlets, Oxfordians reasonably infer that it may have been in part because the rival pamphleteers, in the heat of their sparring, wrote too freely about Vere and his hidden literary activities.[129]

Even some orthodox scholars have opined that the pamphlet war arose from the well-known rivalry, both literary and personal, between Vere and Sir Philip Sidney, who died in 1586. Harvey was generally on the side of Sidney and his many admirers, with Nashe more or less allied with Vere.[130] The high (or low) point of the Vere-Sidney feud was their famous "tennis court quarrel" in 1579.[131] Some orthodox scholars have opined that Polonius's comment in *Hamlet* about "falling out at tennis" may be a topical reference to the incident,[132] which raises very troublesome questions about the traditional authorship theory. Shakspere was a 15-year-old boy in Stratford when it happened and only 22 (probably still in Stratford or at most very recently departed) when Sidney died at age 31 from battle wounds—causing him to be "revered as an English national hero. Would a commoner, writing after that" (especially for the public stage?), "dredge up an unsavory incident from many years before?"[133]

Stratfordian scholars think *Hamlet* was written around 1600. But see Part IV.1, discussing Nashe's 1589 reference to *Hamlet* as if it were then already a well-known play. It is very difficult to

---

[129] In support of the foregoing three paragraphs and much of Part IV.3, see, *e.g.*, Anderson, pp. 138-41, 246, 255-56, 258-64, 267-71, 321; Anderson, "Apis Lapis" (1999); Anderson & Stritmatter, "Harvey"; Barrell; Chiljan, pp. 247-53; Ogburn, pp. 629-31, 723-27; Van Dreunen, pp. 215-35, cited in Anderson, p. 529, and Anderson & Stritmatter, "Harvey," online reprint, *SOF*, n. 7. See also Barber (2009); Waugh, "My Shakespeare" (2018), pp. 58-62.

[130] See Ogburn, p. 629 (citing McKerrow edition of Nashe's works).

[131] See, *e.g.*, Anderson, pp. 149-56; Ogburn, pp. 619-25.

[132] *Hamlet*, act 2, sc. 1; see also, *e.g.*, Chambers (1895), p. 142.

[133] Stritmatter, *Poems of Edward de Vere* (2019), v. 1, pp. 95-96.

explain that reference, except by supposing that some early version was performed in royal court, aristocratic, inns of court, or university settings—long before Shakspere could possibly have written it but fitting perfectly with the Oxfordian theory. Vere's life story contains many more parallels with *Hamlet*, most of them more compelling than the tennis court quarrel, some quite stunning. Even orthodox critics have long sensed that *Hamlet* is a deeply personal expression of the playwright.[134]

While orthodox scholars reject the Oxfordian theory of Shakespeare authorship, they cannot reasonably dispute the well-documented and long-discussed fact that Vere was publicly praised on multiple occasions as a poet and playwright by his contemporaries during the Elizabethan-Jacobean period. Nor do we have anything close to a sufficient corpus of surviving works, openly acknowledged as Vere's, to account for how he earned such praise.[135]

As a recent survey of Vere's known youthful poems noted, his stature as a leading Elizabethan literary light was praised even by Stratfordian scholars into the early 20th century. It was conceded by Professor Steven May, the leading orthodox expert on Vere's poetry, in scholarly analyses published from the 1970s to the 1990s. "The modern decline in Oxford's reputation among most other orthodox scholars appears to be an anachronistic reac-

---

[134] See, *e.g.*, Anderson, pp. 109-21, 189-92, 206, 219-20.

[135] The best effort by a Stratfordian to quibble over these points appears to be Ross, "Oxford's Literary Reputation." But see note 180 below and related text (debunking one of his arguments). Ross cites May, "Poems" (1980) in his bibliography, but does not further cite, quote, or discuss that or any other work by May, who has praised Vere's distinction as an Elizabethan poet. See May (1975); May, "Poems" (1980); May (1991). Ross ignores altogether the praise for Vere's importance as a literary figure by late-19th and early-20th century orthodox scholars (before he was proposed as "Shakespeare" in 1920). It is absurd to dismiss the praise (as Ross and most other Stratfordians do) as merely flattery of a powerful nobleman. Some puffery may have been involved, but there were more powerful and highly regarded aristocrats in England than Vere (who suffered from various scandals throughout his career), and few of them were praised as poets (much less playwrights) to the extent Vere was.

tion to his emergence, since 1920, as the leading non-Stratfordian [Shakespeare] authorship candidate."[136]

Perhaps the most telling contemporary praise for Vere is in the anonymous 1589 book, *The Art of English Poesy:*

> I know very many notable gentlemen in the [royal] court that have written commendably and suppressed it again [meaning "afterward"], or else suffered it to be published without their own names to it, as if it were a discredit for a gentleman to seem learned and to show himself amorous of any good art.[137]

A later but clearly related passage stated that

> in her Majesty's time ... are sprung up another crew of courtly makers, noblemen and gentlemen of her Majesty's own servants, who have written excellently well, as it would appear if their doings could be found out and made public with the rest. *Of which number is first that noble gentleman Edward Earl of Oxford ....*[138]

Some Stratfordians, well aware of the importance of this evidence, have gone to astonishing lengths to try to rationalize it away. Terry Ross, for example, argues that the author of *Poesy* did not intend to include Oxford among the "noblemen and gentlemen ... who have written excellently well ... if their doings could be found out," but rather to lump him in "with the rest" whose works were already publicly known.[139] That bizarre misreading, while hypertechnically permissible in a grammatical sense, is plainly refuted by the context and focus of the quoted paragraph—and by

---

[136] "Twenty Poems" (2018), p. 10; see also May (1975); May, "Poems" (1980); May (1991); Stritmatter & Wildenthal, "Methodological," pp. 175-84.

[137] *Art of English Poesy*, p. 112 & n. 56 (book 1, ch. 8). The book is widely attributed to George Puttenham.

[138] *Poesy*, p. 149 (book 1, ch. 31) (emphasis added).

[139] See Ross, "What Did Puttenham Really Say?"

its explicit content, since it describes Vere as a *"noble gentleman"* in terms echoing verbatim the description of the group *("noblemen and gentlemen")* from which Ross would *exclude* him.

Vere was well-known as a courtier poet, as attested by ample independent evidence. Only some of his early work was ever published under his name or initials. Most of it, like that of other "courtly makers," evidently circulated privately in manuscript—except to whatever extent it was later published anonymously or under the "Shakespeare" pseudonym. Incredibly, Ross *equates* a work privately "circulating in manuscript" with it being "made public"—the very *contrast* the author of *Poesy* was obviously seeking to *highlight*.[140] On the next page of *Poesy*—as Ross quotes without noticing it destroys his own argument—Oxford is again cited, as one of only two writers "deserv[ing] the highest price [meaning 'praise'] ... for comedy and interlude."[141] No "comedy" or "interlude" (nor any dramatic work) was ever published under his name or initials.

Ross also quotes (again obtusely) the *third* reference to Oxford in *Poesy*, which yet again refers to him as "a most noble and learned gentleman," praises "his excellence and wit," and quotes some lines from one of his few surviving acknowledged poems.[142] Ross misses the relevant point that this Oxford poem was never published in full during the Elizabethan era. It is known in full, aside from its partial quotation in *Poesy*, only from manuscript

---

[140] Ross, "What Did Puttenham Really Say?" (referring to writing having "been 'made public' either by being printed or by circulating in manuscript"). That ignores *Poesy*'s own explicit equation, in the quoted and obviously linked passages, between writing *"to be published"* and to be *"made public."* How could a nobleman's writing (at least of poetry) become known at all, to *Poesy*'s author or anyone, if it was not at least circulated privately in manuscript? Here as in many cases, common sense is perhaps the key missing element in Ross's analysis.

[141] *Poesy*, p. 150 (book 1, ch. 31); see also *OED*, v. 12, p. 451 ("price").

[142] *Poesy*, p. 291 (book 3, ch. 19) (quoting "When Wert Thou Born, Desire?"); see also Stritmatter, *Poems of Edward de Vere* (2019), v. 1, pp. 85-88. "Wit" means intelligence or wisdom, not just humor. See *Poesy*, p. 448; *OED*, v. 20, pp. 432-34; Part IV.2.a & note 15.

sources in which it apparently circulated privately.[143] Ross dismisses the poem as "charming." He might want to consider its parallels to the Shakespeare canon, including one noted by a leading Stratfordian scholar in 1910—before Vere became a threat to Stratfordians to be disparaged at all costs.[144]

Ross oddly suggests that these discussions and quotations of Vere in *Poesy* somehow contradict Vere's own obvious preference not to publish writing under his own name. "Remember," Ross hectors, "the reason [*Poesy*] gives" for aristocrats' reluctance to publish work under their own names

> was that they thought it "unseemly" for a gentleman to "seem learned," and yet in this passage [*Poesy's* author] not only quotes Oxford's poem, he names Oxford and calls him "a most noble and learned gentleman." Clearly, [he] does not regard Oxford [as] one of those who thought it unseemly .... Oxford wrote poems and a comedy or interlude under his own name. [He] does not suggest that Oxford ever published anything under a pseudonym ....[145]

Ross's analysis is hopelessly confused. *Poesy's* point is to gently express regret for this aristocratic coyness, by praising writings that the "noble and learned gentlemen" were unwilling to toot *their own* horns about. But one suspects, given human nature, they might have been glad for *Poesy* to do it for them. Ross's statement that *Poesy* "does not regard Oxford [as] one of [them]" is inexplicable. *Poesy* says *exactly the opposite.*

Vere himself did not publish anything "under his own name," aside from a handful of suitably aristocratic introductions (includ-

---

[143] See Looney (Miller ed. 1975), v. 1, app. III, pp. 568-69 (from Looney's 1921 edition of Vere's poetry); May, "Poems" (1980), pp. 73-74.

[144] Ross, "What Did Puttenham Really Say?"; see also Stritmatter, *Poems of Edward de Vere* (2019), v. 1, pp. 85-88 (providing the quoted poem's text and parallels). The parallels to this poem are outshone by those to many other early poems by Vere, who was proposed as "Shakespeare" in 1920. See Part I & note 4.

[145] Ross, "What Did Puttenham Really Say?"

ing one poem) contributed to a few courtly treatises. *Others* published, perhaps with his plausibly deniable "suffer[ance]," only a few more of his early poems.[146] It is unclear what Ross means by vaguely asserting that "Oxford wrote ... under his own name,"[147] except to obfuscate the relevant distinction between writing *privately* (to a restricted social circle) as opposed to *publicly*. Contra Ross, *Poesy* surely at least "suggests" that Oxford might have "published [some]thing under a pseudonym," since it *explicitly states* that "many notable gentlemen ... suffered [their writing] to be published *without their own names* to it." Granted, this might refer to anonymous as well as pseudonymous publications. To the extent *Poesy* failed, in 1589, to clairvoyantly predict that Vere might later publish pseudonymous writings (or perhaps "suffer" some "to be published"), Ross apparently forgot, in the tendentious heat of his argument, that the "Shakespeare" name was not used in print until 1593, four years later.

---

[146] See, *e.g.*, Cardano, *Comfort* (Bedingfield trans. 1573) (Vere's prefatory letter and poem); Stritmatter, *Poems of Edward de Vere* (2019), v. 1, pp. 27-32 (reprinting his 1573 poem and discussing parallels to it and to his 1573 prefatory letter); Stritmatter & Wildenthal, "Methodological," pp. 175-84 (general discussion); Anderson, pp. 31, 121-23 (discussing several youthful poems by Vere published with his initials in the 1576 courtier poetry collection, *The Paradise of Dainty Devices*), pp. 52-53 (discussing Vere's prefatory letter in the 1572 Latin translation of Castiglione's classic, *The Courtier*), pp. 62-65 (discussing his 1573 prefatory letter and poem in Cardano's *Comfort*).

[147] Ross, "What Did Puttenham Really Say?" Even many unpublished manuscript poems thought to be by Vere (or possibly so) contain only his initials or no clear attribution at all. Not even a manuscript has ever been found of any dramatic work with any Oxfordian attribution (no manuscript of any canonical "Shakespeare" play has ever been found either), rendering Ross's assertion that "Oxford wrote ... a comedy or interlude under his own name" a classic instance of "making stuff up" (to use the polite formulation). That Oxford was obviously, as *Poesy* testifies, *known* in his time for writing some highly praised dramatic works—now lost to us, unless they are those of "Shakespeare"—does not mean he ever *promoted or published them* "under his own name." *Poesy*'s precise point—going completely over Ross's head—is that he demurely did *not* do so, or at least had not by 1589 when *Poesy* was published. Plays might not even have been circulated in manuscript; unlike poetry, they might have been known only through live performances and the author's identity only through word-of-mouth.

Mind you, this is the same Terry Ross—an amateur Shakespeare scholar himself—who dismisses anti-Stratfordian scholars in remarkably arrogant and condescending terms.[148] The same Ross (with David Kathman), relying entirely on a single article by Professor Steven May, dismisses as a "myth" the Elizabethan aristocratic "stigma of print" to which *Poesy* prominently testifies. Diana Price replied convincingly on the stigma of print.[149] Profes-

---

[148] See, *e.g.*, "Ross's Supererogation," 1:3, p. 29, in Anderson & Stritmatter, "Harvey" (quoting Ross: "[o]ne of the difficulties in helping someone like Ken Kaplan with ... texts written in the 1590s is that Ken does not know a great deal of Elizabethan literature," whereas, Ross noted, "I've read a fair amount"); Price, "Mythical" (2002) (quoting David Kathman's comments that "Terry Ross and I have both been far too busy with more important matters to write up a comprehensive response to Price," and that "doing exciting *real scholarship* is somehow much more fulfilling than refuting *pseudo-scholarship*") (my emphases); see also Part III.A, note 28 (debunking Ross's condescending dismissal of a reading of the *Venus and Adonis* dedication); Part IV.2.d, note 77 (noting Kathman's snide and offensive attacks on anti-Stratfordian scholars).

Despite my frequent frustrations with Ross's *analysis*, I myself (even more of an amateur in this field) do not dismiss or disparage Ross himself, who holds master's degrees in English literature and creative writing and is a program manager at the University of Baltimore's Center for Excellence in Learning, Teaching, and Technology. I have the utmost respect for Stratfordian scholars, perhaps especially dedicated amateurs like Ross, Kathman, and Reedy who are willing to engage the merits of the SAQ. I have made clear my respect and admiration for them and amateur scholars in general. "Amateur" is not a pejorative term in my view. I wear it proudly in this field (though I am a professional legal scholar). Though sorely tempted, I do not stoop to their swooping and regrettable name-calling, however much I criticize on the merits some particular *arguments* they make. See Part II & notes 16, 18. Anti-Stratfordians ignore at their peril the often helpful scholarly work of Ross, Kathman, and Reedy. See, *e.g.*, note 173; Ross, "Oxfordian Myths: Burghley" (appearing to refute what may be a relatively minor mistake repeated by some Oxfordians). But Ross's misreading of *Poesy* is not a minor mistake. It is a remarkably contorted mischaracterization of a key passage in perhaps the most important work of literary criticism of the Elizabethan era.

[149] See Kathman & Ross, *Shakespeare Authorship Page*, citing and reprinting May, "Tudor" (1980); Price, "Mythical" (2002). The tendentious bias of Ross's analysis of *Poesy* is tellingly revealed by his bizarre suggestion that an aristocrat like Vere who observed this prevailing social custom of discretion would thereby be a "*cowardly* poet," a mischaracterization that he falsely claims "the Oxfordian position requires." Ross, "What Did Puttenham Really Say?" (emphasis added). Ross also misses the point that, however strong or weak the stigma of print may

(footnote continued on next page)

sor Roger Stritmatter and Andrew Hannas further demolished Ross's absurd misreading of *Poesy*.[150]

Returning to the Nashe-Harvey pamphlets of 1592–93, as explored by Gerald Phillips in 1936, Charles Wisner Barrell in 1944, and decades later by Charlton Ogburn Jr., Mark Anderson, Roger Stritmatter, Elizabeth Appleton van Dreunen, and Katherine Chiljan: They seem to suggest, as we will see, that Vere was the author of *Venus and Adonis* (1593), the first work published under the "Shakespeare" name, and was known and addressed in terms strongly resonating with that very name.

Nashe's *Strange News*, in early 1593, suggested Vere was known by the nicknames "Gentle M. [Master] William," "Will. [*sic*] Monox," and "Master *Apis lapis*." The resonance of the first two with "William Shakespeare" hardly needs pointing out. The latter two allude to "ox," thus suggesting "Oxford"—"Monox" being a sort of pidgin Franglais for "my ox" and *Apis* being a classical term for an ox worshipped by ancient Egyptians.[151] *Lapis* is a Latin word meaning "stone," thus here implying a stony, stubborn, or inactive ox.[152] Master William *Apis* is addressed as a "copious Carmin-

---

(footnote continued from previous page)
have been, and however much it may have eroded over time, that may have very little to do with whatever specific reasons (pertaining to Vere's own life and family) may also have motivated the creation and perpetuation (even long after his death) of Vere's particular pseudonym.

[150] See Stritmatter, "Matter" (1996); Hannas, "Rest Is Not Silence" (1996).

[151] See, *e.g.*, Barrell, pp. 52-66; Ogburn, pp. 725-27 (but missing reference to "Gentle M[aster] William"); Anderson, pp. 255-56, 258-60; Anderson & Stritmatter, "Harvey," 1:3, p. 28, and online reprint, *SOF*, n. 2; Chiljan, pp. 247-50; see generally sources cited in note 129. Barrell, pp. 53, 56, and Ogburn, pp. 725, 861, 871, credited Phillips (1936) with identifying *"Apis lapis"* with Oxford.

[152] See *Cassell's Latin Dictionary*, p. 336; see also Anderson, p. 259 (suggesting *"Apis lapis"* meant, in this particular context, "insensate," "lacking empathy," and a "stubborn old ox"); Anderson, "Apis Lapis" (1999), p. 24 (suggesting it meant "a *do-nothing* sacred ox"). Anderson, while generally praising and relying on Barrell's excellent pioneering work, noted that Barrell's interpretation of *"Apis lapis"* to mean simply a castrated bull (*i.e.*, an ox), Barrell, pp. 55-56 (see also Ogburn, p. 725, noting this reading), was too simplistic. Anderson noted that Elizabethans understood "Apis" alone to be a classical reference to a sacred ox. See Anderson, "Apis Lapis" (1999), pp. 19, 24.

ist"—a prolific poet, at least one who had been until a recent lull.[153]

With regard to "Will Monox," Nashe comments in *Strange News*, "Hast thou never heard of him and his great dagger?" The letter opening the pamphlet, dedicating it to "Master *Apis lapis*" and "Gentle M[aster] William," refers to "your dudgeon dagger" and "your round cap." The "dagger" may refer to Vere's ceremonial sword of state as Lord Great Chamberlain. It may also allude to the name or pseudonym "Shakespeare," perhaps already bandied about before its first explicit appearance in print in 1593, under the dedication of *Venus and Adonis*. None of Nashe's pamphlets, however, ever referred to Shakespeare, by any spelling. This omission has been viewed, even by some orthodox scholars, as "curious."[154]

A round cap was customarily worn by Elizabethan men of high social rank and power. That Nashe's dedicatee was of high social rank was also suggested by Nashe addressing him as "your Worship." Vere, it should be noted, is referenced more explicitly in other parts of this and other Nashe-Harvey pamphlets. One can imagine various reasons why the references discussed here were more veiled and irreverent.[155] By the way, in the sole Shakespearean passage referring to "lapis," the word is likewise juxta-

---

[153] See, *e.g.*, Barrell, p. 55; Ogburn, pp. 725-26; Chiljan, p. 248. The preceding time period fits well as one during which Vere probably felt beaten down and depressed, and was perhaps artistically quiescent. See also discussion in text below (related to note 176) regarding Spenser's reference to "Willy" being "dead of late." Vere's first wife had died young in 1588 and he was saddled by the worst financial difficulties of his life, though things began to look up in 1592 after his marriage to his second wife. See, *e.g.*, Anderson, pp. 244-51.

[154] See, *e.g.*, Barrell, p. 62; Ogburn, pp. 725-26; Anderson, p. 256; Chiljan, p. 248-49. On Nashe's "curious" failure ever to mention Shakespeare, see Price, p. 147 (quoting Charles Nicholl). That "Shakespeare" may already have been associated with Vere by 1592–93 is suggested by the discussion below in text; that it may already have been bandied about, at least in a general way, is suggested by the 1592 "Shake-scene" reference in *Groats-Worth* (see Part IV.2).

[155] See, *e.g.*, Barrell, p. 62; Ogburn, pp. 725-26; Anderson, p. 256; Chiljan, p. 248-49.

posed to "William," as a schoolmaster in *The Merry Wives of Windsor* tests a boy on his Latin: "What is 'lapis,' William?"[156]

Nashe was daringly impudent, it seems, to use such familiar nicknames and a form of address like "Master"—while also, as noted, dropping many hints that he was addressing a nobleman. Perhaps Vere, slumming around with literary friends, tolerated such ribbing familiarity as long as the references were not explicitly linked to him. But the 1599 order to destroy the Nashe-Harvey pamphlets—and the fact that the *Strange News* dedication, in later editions, was reprinted in reduced type or omitted altogether—suggest that Nashe overstepped.[157]

At this point it is useful to go back fifteen years, to 1578, and recall that Harvey, then a fellow at Cambridge University, wrote a Latin address to Vere, part of a set of tributes to Queen Elizabeth and several of her courtiers. Harvey's 1578 address is

---

[156] Act 4, sc. 1; Spevack, p. 685 (only three references to "lapis" in Shakespeare canon, all occurring in this scene); see also, *e.g.*, Barrell, p. 56; Chiljan, p. 248. There are many additional linkages in *Strange News* both to Vere and to the works of Shakespeare, too many to elaborate here in text or footnotes. For example, it referenced the Vere heraldic colors (tawny and blue) and the boar in the Vere coat-of-arms. See, *e.g.*, Barrell, pp. 56, 64-65; Ogburn, p. 725. For more details, see, *e.g.*, Barrell, pp. 55-66; Ogburn, pp. 725-27; Anderson, pp. 259-64; Chiljan, pp. 248-49.

[157] See, *e.g.*, Barrell, p. 52; Ogburn, pp. 726-27; Chiljan, pp. 249-50, 252-53. Anderson, p. 526 (note to p. 259, "Stubborn old ox"), noting that "Nashe was playing games with caste," suggested that he "had a middle-class 'William' in mind" and that Nashe (though mainly addressing Vere, as Anderson concurred) may also have been playfully alluding to William Shakspere the player from Stratford. This strikes me as dubious. As Chiljan noted, p. 247, Shakspere at that time was not even a "gentleman" yet. His father's coat-of-arms had apparently not yet been granted then. While "Master" was an improper form of address to an aristocrat, "Gentle" was at least a gesture in the right direction. On the evolving meaning of "gentle" at the time, see Part IV.20 & note 482.

Anderson's 2005 book adhered to the traditional view that *Groats-Worth* in 1592 referred to Shakspere as the Crow and "Shake-scene." See Part IV.2.a, note 33, citing Anderson, pp. 256-58. But if, as Part IV.2 suggests, *Groats-Worth* did *not* attack or refer to Shakspere at all (even if punning upon some author known as "Shakespeare"), there seems little reason to think Nashe's *Strange News*, a few months later, alluded to him either. The first clear evidence linking Shakspere to any London theatrical role dates to 1595. See Part IV.2.f & note 97; see also discussions of *Parnassus 3* (c. 1601) in Parts IV.2.f & note 98, and IV.16.

interesting in part for how it corroborates other contemporary comments (noted above) praising Vere's literary prowess—"how greatly thou dost excel in letters." Harvey indicated that Vere had written "many" Latin verses and even "more" English poetry, and had "drunk deeply" of the Muses of France and Italy and was learned in the manners, arts, and laws of many countries.[158]

Harvey's main point, however, was that Vere should give up "bloodless" and impractical "books" and "writings" and instead gear up as a warrior to fight for his country.[159] Anderson's conclusion that Harvey's address left Vere "unimpressed" seems sound,[160] but more doubtful was his suggestion that Harvey was auditioning to be Vere's personal secretary.[161]

---

[158] Harvey's address is often described as if given orally to the queen and her guests, but Nina Green points out it was apparently delivered in manuscript form and published not long after. Green, "Harvey's *Gratulationes*," pp. 1-2. On the Muses, see note 180. Harvey's Latin text was translated with questionable accuracy in Bernard Ward's 1928 biography of Vere, pp. 157-58, although, as we will see, Ward may have hit close to the best translation of its three most disputed words. Ogburn, pp. 596-97, followed Ward's translation in full; Anderson's 2005 biography did so for the most part, while omitting some parts of Ward's translation. Anderson noted that Professor Alan Nelson's 2003 biography, p. 181, relied for his translation (as does Green) on a 1938 dissertation by Thomas Hugh Jameson. Jameson's translation is also debatable. See Anderson, pp. 139, 481; A. Nelson (2003), p. 464 (ch. 32, n. 12), p. 499 (bibliography).

All four cited books, by Ward, Ogburn, Nelson, and Anderson, are carefully researched and merit scholarly respect (whatever mistakes each may contain). As mentioned in Part I, note 4, however, Nelson's biography is deeply biased against Vere and the Oxfordian theory, while Ward's biography in turn has been criticized (perhaps justly) as overly hagiographical (dismissed as such by Nelson himself, p. 250). Ward, like Ogburn and Anderson, was an Oxfordian. Anderson's account achieves to my mind the most judicious balance (see Hughes's thoughtful 2005 review), unflinchingly criticizing Vere where due while avoiding Nelson's tendentious hostility. Ogburn was also under no illusion that Vere was any kind of angel (rather, a deeply flawed cad on many occasions), while perceiving (contrary to Nelson's obtuseness, shared by many anti-Oxfordians) that this hardly rules him out as an artistic giant.

[159] See Anderson, p. 139; A. Nelson (2003), p. 181.

[160] Anderson, p. 140.

[161] See Anderson, p. 139. Anderson, pp. 140-41, suggested that a poetic lampoon of Vere by Harvey in 1580 was motivated by bitterness over not getting hired by Vere following his 1578 address. The more economical interpretation is

(footnote continued on next page)

Nina Green suggests more plausibly that Harvey, then working for Vere's archenemy Robert Dudley (Earl of Leicester), "sought to curry favour with Leicester by mocking and insulting Oxford (under cover of extravagant praise)."[162] Harvey was in effect publicly urging the young aristocrat—presumptuously, to say the least—to give up effete and pointless literary obsessions and "be a man" (my words, not Green's or Harvey's).

A great deal of argumentative ink has been spilled over the three most intriguing words in Harvey's address—that, as he put it in Latin, Vere's *"vultus tela vibrat."* The first Oxfordian translation, by Bernard Ward in 1928, was *"thy countenance shakes a spear"*—a startlingly early connection, it seems, between Vere and his likely literary pseudonym.[163] The word translated as "spear" (*tela*) is the plural form of *telum*, so Ogburn and Anderson corrected this to read *"shakes spears."*[164]

By contrast, the Stratfordian (and decidedly anti-Oxfordian) scholar Alan Nelson—relying on a 1938 translator (Jameson) who apparently had no dog in the authorship fight—read the same phrase as "your glance shoots arrows."[165] Anderson, finally, citing Andrew Hannas, contended that *vultus* was best understood as neither "countenance" nor "glance" but rather "will"—thus (insert drumroll), "thy *will shakes spears.*"[166]

---

(footnote continued from previous page)
that the 1580 attack, like the mocking 1578 address in the first place, reflects Harvey's general aligment with Leicester and Sidney in opposition to Vere.

[162] Green, "Harvey's *Gratulationes*," p. 2; see also pp. 1-2. This reading, and my paraphrase in text, are actually not far from Anderson's reading, which recognized that "Harvey's exhortation was brash and unsolicited," in effect saying: "You, milord, are wasting your time in pursuing a career based on poetry and the courtly stage." Anderson, p. 139.

[163] Ward, p. 158 (my emphasis); see also note 158.

[164] Ogburn, p. 597; Anderson, pp. 139, 481 (emphasis added); see also note 158; *Cassell's Latin Dictionary*, p. 596 (*telum*; referring, *e.g.*, to *tela militaria*).

[165] A. Nelson (2003), p. 181; see also note 158.

[166] Anderson, pp. 139, 481 (Anderson's emphasis), citing Hannas, "Harvey" (1993); see also Chiljan, pp. 251, 426 n. 10 (also citing Hannas to embrace this reading); Waugh, "My Shakespeare," p. 65 & n. 37 (also embracing it).

How should we sort all this out? In context, Harvey's declaration climaxes a sentence beginning, in the Jameson-Nelson translation (Ward's differs stylistically but not in substance *except for the last three words*): "[Y]our blood boils in your breast, virtue dwells in your brow, Mars keeps your mouth, Minerva is in your right hand, Bellona reigns in your body, and Martial ardor, your eyes flash, your *glance shoots arrows*."[167] The standard modern translation of *vultus* is "expression of the face," "countenance," "look," or "aspect"—for example, a "threatening frown."[168] So both the Ward-Ogburn and Jameson-Nelson versions seem equally fine to that extent. But Hannas and Anderson noted that dictionaries in the 1500s also provide "will" as an alternative meaning for *vultus*.[169] Fair enough, though one may doubt Harvey would likely have intended, or would have been understood, to embrace this more "obscure" meaning.[170]

The context of Harvey's own sentence is strong and specific evidence against the Hannas-Anderson reading and in favor of the standard translation of *vultus* in facial terms. Harvey refers to "your brow," "your mouth," and "your eyes flash[ing]," so by parallel logic he was building up to a point about how—one might colloquially suggest—Vere's *looks could kill*, or at least that his face offered the threatening appearance of shaking or hurling a deadly weapon of some kind.

The standard modern dictionary translation of *vibrat* is to "brandish," "shake," or "hurl."[171] *Telum* (plural *tela*) does translate as "spear," but also as other projectile weapons like "missile,"

---

[167] A. Nelson (2003), p. 181 (emphasis added here to highlight the disputed words); compare Anderson, p. 139 (following Ward and Ogburn except as to the last three words).

[168] *Cassell's Latin Dictionary*, p. 650 (*vultus* or *voltus*).

[169] Hannas, "Harvey" (1993), p. 3; Anderson, p. 481; see also Chiljan, "Origins" (2015); Waugh, "My Shakespeare," p. 65 n. 37.

[170] Hannas, "Harvey" (1993), p. 3 (conceding it was "obscure"). "Will" more clearly translates to *volo* in Latin. See Part IV.28, note 728.

[171] *Cassell's Latin Dictionary*, p. 640 (transitive sense of *vibro* or *vibrare*).

"dart," "javelin," or "arrow."[172] Nelson's preferred translation ("shoots arrows") is thus plausible. But it seems awkward. *Vibrat*, in the sense of brandish or shake, fits better with "spear," since one does not typically shake or brandish an arrow, whereas one certainly may brandish, shake, or hurl a spear.[173]

Thus, Ogburn's amended Ward translation—that Vere's "countenance" (or "glance" or "expression" or "look" if you prefer) "shakes spears"—seems reasonable, and better than the Jameson-Nelson version. The Hannas-Anderson variation ("thy will shakes spears") seems possible but unlikely. No definitive translation is feasible in any event, given the various available meanings. Furthermore, the fact that Harvey wrote in Latin obscures any arguable linkage to the name "Shakespeare." Still, Harvey's 1578 address to Vere is intriguing. At the very least, it suggests how easy and natural it may have been for Vere to hit upon such an evocative *nom de plume*.[174]

---

[172] *Cassell's Latin Dictionary*, p. 596 (*telum*); see also pp. 272, 836 (*hasta* as more specific Latin word for "spear").

[173] It seems significant, as Anderson noted, p. 481, that two standard translations of Ovid's *Metamorphoses*, including the Elizabethan translation by Arthur Golding (Vere's uncle, as it happens), translate *tela* as "spears" or "boar-speare." Hannas, "Harvey" (1993), pp. 3-4, 8, actually favored the more vague and encompassing term "missile." He suggested, p. 3, that "spear" is "a bit of an Oxfordian liberty." But Hannas also, p. 3, cited standard Latin-English dictionaries of the 1500s translating *vibro* (thus *vibrat*; see note 171) as to "shake" or "brandish" something.

Errors are inevitable even in the best scholarship, and Oxfordians have made their fair share. We should be grateful to Stratfordian scholars like Terry Ross, David Kathman, and Tom Reedy for caring as much as we do about the SAQ and keeping us on our toes. Ross, "Oxfordian Myths: Burghley," notes for example that Hannas and others have erred in asserting that William Cecil (Lord Burghley, Vere's father-in-law, widely viewed even by many Stratfordian scholars as a possible model for *Hamlet*'s Polonius), was referenced by Harvey in his 1578 addresses by the nickname "Polus." See also Green, "Myths," Sec. III, pp. 7-11. However, neither Ross nor any scholar, to my knowledge, has refuted Hannas's primary analysis in his cited article (his comment about "Polus" being a passing sidenote of little importance).

[174] See Part III.A & notes 23-32; Chiljan, pp. 27-31; Chiljan, "Origins."

Another intriguing set of references—one explicitly to Vere and some debatably implicit—may be found in the poems of Edmund Spenser. For example, resonating with Harvey's 1578 address—and more compellingly with Nashe's 1593 references to "Will" and "William"—Oxfordians have noted that in *The Shepherd's Calendar* (1579), Spenser referred to a poet named "Willy" or "Willie" (originally spelled "Willye").[175]

Oxfordians also cite Spenser's "Tears of the Muses" (part of his *Complaints*), apparently written by 1590 and published in 1591. This poem refers to a writer who had once been active and prolific, apparently known to Spenser prior to the latter's long sojourn in Ireland (1580–89), but who was recently withdrawn (figuratively "dead") from the literary scene: "Our pleasant *Willy*, ah is dead of late."[176] Spenser "laments the degradation of the comic stage" by a new breed of vulgar writers.[177] Seemingly again referring to "pleasant Willy," Spenser writes: "[T]hat same gentle Spirit, from whose pen Large streams of honey and sweet nectar flow, Scorning the boldness of such base-born men ... Doth rather choose to sit in idle Cell, than so himself to mockery to sell."[178]

A connection between these two poets named "Willy," in 1579 and 1591, seems more than plausible. Recall that in 1579 Shakspere was a 15-year-old boy in Stratford. He is generally thought to have just begun his London career by around 1500. Spenser's poet "Willy" seems to be a very well-established figure by 1590. Many Oxfordians think these references may relate to Vere, with

---

[175] *The Shepherd's Calendar* (March and August Eclogues), in Spenser, *Shorter Poems*, pp. 52-59, 107-15.

[176] "The Tears of the Muses" (line 208), in Spenser, *Shorter Poems*, p. 197 (italics in original). See note 153 on why Vere may have been withdrawn during this period. On the Muses, see note 180.

[177] Chiljan, p. 245.

[178] "The Tears of the Muses" (lines 217-19, 221-22), in Spenser, *Shorter Poems*, p. 197; compare Chambers (1930), v. 2, pp. 186-87.

the poets "Willy" and "Perigot" in *Shepherd's Calendar* representing Vere and his rival Sir Philip Sidney.[179]

The explicit reference to Vere is the sonnet by Spenser honoring him, one of several addressed to leading courtiers of Queen Elizabeth in the 1590 preface to Spenser's masterwork, *The Faerie Queen*. Spenser refers to Vere's "love, which thou doest bear To th'*Heliconian* imps, and they to thee, They unto thee, and thou to them most dear ...."[180] The sonnet, while doubtless intended partly

---

[179] See, *e.g.*, Looney, pp. 284-91; Barrell, pp. 49-50; Ogburn, pp. 401, 718-20; Chiljan, pp. 245-47.

[180] Spenser, *Faerie Queen*, p. 26 (italics in original). The Muses in Greek mythology are associated with Mount Helicon and its legendary springs. The Muses have long been commonly said to live on Helicon, and the Muses and the springs have long been viewed as sources of poetic inspiration. The ancient Greek poet Hesiod's *Theogony* refers to "the Heliconian Muses." "Heliconian imps" could (perhaps often did) refer to *poets* as figurative children of the Muses. See Spenser, p. 1073 (editorial note); *OED*, v. 7, pp. 693-94 ("imp" as child or offspring, sometimes with devilish or mischievous overtones). Looney, p. 123, and Ogburn, p. 718 (among others), have proposed that Spenser's words instead (or also) refer to *the Muses themselves* (thus praising Vere as a poet).

Most modern Stratfordians insist that Spenser meant *only* poets. See, *e.g.*, Ross, "Oxford's Literary Reputation" (asserting that "Oxford is called not a poet himself but a lover of poets" and that the sonnet indicates Spenser thought "Oxford's reputation as a poet was not worth mentioning"). But the Looney-Ogburn reading seems preferable, indeed compelling. Ross's reading, yet again, is strikingly unpersuasive. (For other examples of Ross's misreadings, see notes 135-50 and related text, and Part III.A, note 28.) We know from other evidence that Vere *was* a poet, highly regarded in his own time. It would be very odd if Spenser's flattering sonnet failed to salute him as such. Some of Vere's poetry was published starting in the 1570s and he was praised in *The Art of English Poesy* (1589), just a year before *The Faerie Queen*. See notes 135-50 and related text. This reading is also corroborated by Angel Day's similar (more explicit) praise that Vere was "ever sacred to the Muses," in Day's dedication of *The English Secretary* (1586). See Ogburn, p. 688.

The Muses, as daughters of Zeus (Jove) and Mnemosyne, might easily be called *their* "imps." They were so described in an earlier 16th-century poem. See *Tottel's Miscellany* (1557), p. 100 (Nicholas Grimald, first line of "The Muses": "Imps of King Jove, and queen Remembrance"). Grimald's poem, with which Spenser may well have been familiar, strongly supports the Looney-Ogburn reading of Spenser's 1590 sonnet. I am indebted to a reference by Oxfordian scholar Christopher Paul for alerting me to Grimald's poem and its relevance.

"Heliconian imps" thus very easily describes the Muses: as literal children of the gods, and entities who live on Helicon, thus also figurative children of the mountain, or at least associated with it. The phrase also, to be sure, describes

(footnote continued on next page)

as flattery, resonates with other contemporary praise for Vere. It may also imply that Vere himself, under the pseudonym "Ignoto" (Italian for "unknown"), wrote one of the tributary poems addressed to Spenser which also preface *The Faerie Queen*.[181]

The final Spenserian reference associated with Vere and Shakespeare is in *Colin Clout's Come Home Again*, probably written by 1591 though published in 1595. Praising several poets, Spenser says "last not least is *Aelion*, A gentler shepherd may no

---

(footnote continued from previous page)
poets, who are also figuratively children of (or at least associated with) the Muses, the mountain, and its springs. There seems no reason to think either meaning would have been any more or less unavailable or incomprehensible to Elizabethans. See the definition of "Heliconian" in *OED*, v. 7, p. 113: "Pertaining to Helicon, or to the Muses." The *OED*'s two 16th-century examples are another Grimald poem in *Tottel's*, p. 107 ("To m. D.A.," line 11: "th[']Heliconian Nymphs"), and another part of Spenser's *Faerie Queen*, book II, canto 12, stanza 31, line 2, p. 368 ("th'*Heliconian* maids") (italics in original), both of which clearly refer to the Muses.

The flattering context of Spenser's sonnet to Vere, while perhaps a reason to discount its praise, counsels strongly in favor of this reading. (Stratfordians like Ross and Kathman harp on the importance of "context." See, *e.g.*, Part III.A, note 28; Part IV.2.d & note 77; Part IV.16 & note 382.) It is far more likely that Vere would be praised in terms of mutual love with the Muses (imps of the gods) than merely with poets (imps of the Muses, and mostly of lower social rank than Vere). Describing *only* mutual love between him and poets would have risked insulting him. But Spenser may well have meant to praise him in both senses. Poetic license very typically allows double meanings.

Spenser refers to these "imps" as "they" and "them." But "we" and "us" seem more appropriate if he meant *only* to describe poets *like himself* who appreciated Vere's patronage. His contraction of "the" before "Heliconian" shows he sought to avoid using an extra syllable. "Imps" would thus have been more attractive than "Muses" (or even "nymphs") in terms of poetic rhythm. With typical poetic allusiveness, he may not have wanted to refer explicitly to the Muses anyway. He may well have been striving for the suggested double meaning. Describing them as "Heliconian" thus appears an artful choice. But Heliconian ... *whats?* "Imps" seems very apt. No equally sonorous one-syllable alternative comes to mind.

Why should it take a lawyer like me to remind literary experts that this is a *poem* we are expounding? A famous quotation in my own line of work, from one of Chief Justice John Marshall's greatest U.S. Supreme Court opinions, is that "we must never forget that it is *a constitution* we are expounding." *McCulloch v. Maryland*, 17 U.S. 316, 407 (1819) (emphasis in original).

[181] See "To Look Upon a Work of Rare Devise," in "Commendatory Verses," in Spenser, *Faerie Queen*, pp. 22-23; see also, *e.g.*, Ogburn, pp. 718-19.

where be found: Whose *Muse* full of high thoughts invention, Doth like himself Heroically sound."[182]

As Chiljan noted, even some orthodox scholars have thought "Aetion" must refer to "Shakespeare," a surname with an obvious "heroic" and martial "sound." Yet that is difficult to square with the Stratfordian theory. Spenser's statement that no "gentler" poet may be found is a clear indication that "Aetion" held high (probably aristocratic) social rank.[183] It also echoes Spenser's reference to the "gentle spirit" Willy in "Tears of the Muses," who by chronological context, as noted above, cannot possibly have been Shakspere of Stratford.[184] Once again, signs point to Vere as the more likely poet.

Returning again to the Nashe-Harvey pamphlets: Anderson and Stritmatter have discussed how Harvey in April 1593, just two weeks after *Venus and Adonis* by "Shakespeare" was registered for publication, registered his pamphlet *Pierce's Supererogation*. The timing and content of the pamphlet suggest that Harvey had some insider connections affording him a preview of the famous erotic poem, which became a very hot seller.[185]

Harvey's pamphlet made several obvious references to *Venus and Adonis*, while never mentioning the purported author "Shakespeare." Harvey suggested the poem was by a writer he identified with the nickname "Pierce Penniless," whose art, he suggested, built upon that of Sidney and Spenser and "blossom[ed] ... in the

---

[182] *Colin Clout's Come Home Again* (lines 444-47), in Spenser, *Shorter Poems*, p. 357 (italics in original); compare Chambers (1930), v. 2, p. 187.

[183] "Gentleness" referred at the time to social rank more than to kindly personality. See Part IV.20, note 482, for a more detailed discussion. Chiljan, p. 247, noted that Shakspere of Stratford, a commoner who was never part of the aristocracy, did not even become an ordinary "gentleman" until 1596 at the earliest; that "[m]ost of the poets Spenser ... admired in this short work have been identified as courtier poets"; and that Vere as "Earl of Oxford held the highest title among courtier poets."

[184] See Chiljan, pp. 246-47.

[185] See Anderson & Stritmatter, "Harvey," 1:2, p. 28; Anderson, p. 270.

rich garden of poor Adonis."[186] Harvey also parodied the reference to "idle hours" in the dedication, which states that if the Earl of Southampton (Henry Wriothesley) is "pleased" with it, "I ... vow to take advantage of all idle hours, till I have honoured you with some graver labour." (The "graver labour" is generally taken to be *The Rape of Lucrece*, published in 1594.) Harvey stated: "I write only at idle hours that I dedicate only to *Idle Hours*."[187]

So who was "Pierce Penniless," imputed by Harvey to be the author of *Venus and Adonis*? Anderson noted good reasons to link him with Edward de Vere. Harvey sometimes used "Pierce Penniless" to refer to Nashe, given Nashe's 1592 pamphlet of that very title. But Nashe, in his pamphlet *Pierce Penniless*, was obviously not referring to *himself* by that name. Rather, Nashe referred to "Pierce Penniless" as "an older and more experienced writer [who was] also Nashe's patron."[188] Harvey's 1592 pamphlet *Four Letters* similarly referred to "Pierce Penniless" as Nashe's patron—who, it appears, was Vere.[189]

Thus, Anderson suggested, Harvey in *Pierce's Supererogation*, the very same month that *Venus and Adonis* was registered, publicly implied that the poem's author was none other than Vere himself.[190] Anderson and Stritmatter, citing Appleton van Dreunen, also noted that Harvey described "Pierce Penniless" with

---

[186] Anderson, p. 270.

[187] Anderson, p. 270 (italics in Harvey's original). The "garden of Adonis," Anderson noted, was an idiom suggesting a "worthless toy" or "perishable goods," implying that *Venus and Adonis* was (as Anderson put it) "a mere novelty, a trendy poetic trinket aimed at pleasing the younger crowd." A well-known comment by Harvey written in the margin of a copy of the works of Chaucer, *c.* 1598, stated: "The younger sort take much delight in Shakespeare's Venus and Adonis; but his Lucrece, and his tragedy of Hamlet, Prince of Denmark, have it in them to please the wiser sort." Anderson, p. 529 (second-to-last note to p. 270); see also Part IV.13 (discussing Harvey's 1598–1601 marginalia).

[188] Anderson & Stritmatter, "Harvey," 1:3, p. 29; see also Anderson, p. 270.

[189] See Anderson & Stritmatter, "Harvey," 1:2, p. 27; Waugh, "My Shakespeare," pp. 58-59 & n. 22.

[190] Anderson, p. 270; see also Baron (2019), pp. 16-18.

some of the same terms he had used more than a decade earlier, in 1580, to mock Vere as a nobleman with Italian pretensions. (Vere spent almost a year in Italy in 1575–76.) They further noted that a "recurrent theme in Harvey's commentary on Pierce Penni-less is that [he] is an author with a huge store of unpublished materials," including some "miraculous" works "being held 'in abeyance' by unnamed institutional forces ...."[191]

Chiljan has discussed another reference to *Venus and Adonis* in Harvey's *Supererogation*. Harvey's pamphlet was not actually published until July 1593, three months after it was registered.[192] Harvey explained that he delayed its publication so it would not be overshadowed by "that fair body of the sweetest Venus in Print, as it is redoubtably armed with the complete harness of the bravest Minerva."[193] Harvey feared there would be "small hope of any possible account, or regard of mine own discourses,"[194] while, as Chiljan noted, "the literary world was caught in the sensation" of the bestselling erotic poem.[195]

As Chiljan suggested, Harvey in this passage almost "openly stated that Shakespeare is a pen name."[196] "[B]ravest Minerva" refers to the Greek goddess Athena by her Roman name, who according to well-known legend leaped fully formed from the head of Zeus brandishing a spear, which she is often depicted holding. The implication is that *Venus and Adonis* was somehow clothed, armored, or shielded by the authorial name attached to it.[197] This seems a very odd way to refer to an author's *real* name, especially

---

[191] Anderson & Stritmatter, "Harvey," 1:3, p. 29. On Vere's sojourn in Italy, see, *e.g.*, Anderson, pp. 80-107.

[192] Chiljan, p. 251.

[193] Quoted in Chiljan, p. 252; see also Part IV.27 (discussing Minerva).

[194] Quoted in Chiljan, pp. 251-52.

[195] Chiljan, p. 252. *Venus and Adonis*, registered for publication in April 1593, was in general circulation by June. Chiljan, p. 250.

[196] Chiljan, p. 252; see also Baron (2019), pp. 18-19.

[197] See Chiljan, p. 252; see also Waugh, "My Shakespeare," pp. 64-65.

a supposed newcomer publishing his first work. It is precisely a *pseudonym* that typically provides some kind of cover or shield.

Harvey oddly skirted any explicit reference at all to "Shakespeare," the name printed under the dedication of *Venus and Adonis* but oddly absent from the title page. Another oddity is that *Venus and Adonis* was initially registered as an anonymous work. Yet another is the dedication's reference to the poem as "the first heir of my *invention*."[198]

Furthermore, as Chiljan noted, Harvey's very next sentence, following his reference to "bravest Minerva," also suggested the author was hiding behind some cover: "When *his necessary defense* hath sufficiently acleared him, whom it principally concerneth to acquit himself ...."[199] Chiljan suggested the author may not have wanted (or dared?) to publicly and explicitly associate himself with a poem that "principally concerneth" a powerful, petulant, and seductive woman (Venus) who could well be interpreted as representing Queen Elizabeth—and was so interpreted by some, starting right away in 1593.[200]

Harvey said of this Venus, often referred to in the poem as a "queen": "She shall no sooner appear ... but every eye ... will see a conspicuous difference between her, and other mirrors of Eloquence"—that is, compared to other depictions of her.[201] As Chiljan noted, there seems little "difference" in one more depiction of the notorious love goddess as a seductress—here ardently pursuing, almost sexually assaulting, a blushing teenage boy who dodges her libidinous advances. But the poem poses a *very* "conspicuous difference" compared to depictions of Elizabeth as the "Virgin Queen," the spotlessly virtuous mother of her country.[202]

---

[198] Quoted (my emphasis) and discussed in Part III.A & note 28.
[199] Quoted in Chiljan, p. 252 (Chiljan's emphasis).
[200] See Chiljan, p. 252; Anderson, pp. 267-70.
[201] Quoted in Chiljan, p. 252 (my ellipses).
[202] See Chiljan, p. 252.

Would a commoner writing under his own name dare to publish an erotic poem implicitly depicting the revered queen in such a scandalously mocking way? It is far easier to imagine a "bad boy" nobleman doing so, at least under the polite fiction of a pseudonym (even if most people in court circles may have known who wrote it). It is especially easy to imagine the author being an aristocrat like Vere, about whom we know Elizabeth was surprisingly tolerant and forgiving—sometimes only after fits of angry pique—with regard to various other instances of misbehavior.[203]

As Chiljan also discussed, Harvey's *New Letter of Notable Contents*, dated September 1593 (registered in October), may be read as raising still more questions about the authorship of *Venus and Adonis*. The *New Letter* concluded with two poems mentioning various "wonders" and "miracles" of 1593, including several international events, the death of Christopher Marlowe, and—in a veiled way—the publication of *Venus and Adonis*.[204] Harvey's key lines were as follows:

A Stanza declarative: to the Lovers of admirable Works.

Pleased it hath a Gentlewoman rare,
With Phoenix quill in diamond hand of Art,
To muzzle the redoubtable Bull-bare,
And play the galliard [valiant] Championesse's part.
Though miracles surcease, yet Wonder see
The mightiest miracle of Ninety Three.

Vis consilii expers, mole ruit sua.[205]

The last line is a Latin epigram of Horace: "Power without good sense comes crashing down under its own weight."[206]

---

[203] See, *e.g.*, Anderson, pp. 70-72, 161-65, 172-73, 192-93, 209-12.

[204] See Chiljan, pp. 250-51.

[205] Quoted in Chiljan, p. 250 (omitting italics and underlining in original and added by Chiljan).

[206] Chiljan, p. 426 n. 9.

Chiljan offered good reasons to view the "Gentlewoman rare" as Queen Elizabeth and the "muzzle" as the pseudonym imposed on the author of *Venus and Adonis*. (For her full argument, please purchase her excellent book.) Harvey's *Four Letters* (1592) had used the same odd term "bull-beare" (echoed by "Bull-bare" in the 1593 lines above), in a passage explicitly referring to the Earl of Oxford (though not, in 1592, specifically labeling *him* as the "bull-beare"). "Redoubtable" indicated high social status. "Bull," interchangeable with "ox," may have been a pun on Oxford's name.[207] On Chiljan's reading, it "pleased" the queen to require or expect Vere ("the redoubtable Bull-bare") to "muzzle" his true identity with a pseudonym when writing *Venus and Adonis*—and, by implication, all other works of "Shakespeare."

The Anderson-Stritmatter reading of the Nashe-Harvey pamphlets has been disputed in various ways, for example by Stratfordian scholar Terry Ross and even by Oxfordian scholar Nina Green.[208] Anderson and Stritmatter may possibly be mistaken (as may Chiljan), though they seem to me to have the better of the argument. But that's really beside the point, which is that these pamphlets, at the very least, may reasonably be read as raising public and precisely contemporaneous questions about the authorship of the very first work credited to "William Shakespeare." They obviously merit further careful study as part of the broader array of early authorship doubts.

---

[207] See Chiljan, pp. 250-51; *OED*, v. 2, p. 640 ("bull-bear": obsolete, possible corruption of "bugbear"; an imaginary bogeyman or scarecrow); v. 11, pp. 7-8 ("ox": a bull or cow, or any bovine, most commonly a castrated or domesticated bull); v. 13, p. 424 ("redoubtable": to be "feared or dreaded; formidable," or "revered, commmanding respect"; "redoubted": "reverenced, respected; noted, distinguished"; both used, *e.g.*, "redoubtable" in 1550, in connection with "sovereigns"; "redoubted" in 15th-17th centuries "[v]ery common[ly]" so used).

[208] See Anderson & Stritmatter, "Harvey," 2:2, pp. 26-28.

## 4.   Thomas Edwards, *L'Envoy* to *Narcissus* (1593)

More doubts about the identity of the author Shakespeare, again relating to *Venus and Adonis*, were expressed in a poem by Thomas Edwards, registered for publication in October 1593 and thus presumably written by then. Very little is known about Edwards, not even the years of his birth or death. The poem is *L'Envoy*, an epilogue to his longer work *Narcissus*, published in book form in 1595 together with *Cephalus and Procris*.[209]

The poem offers veiled homages to several English poets, mostly identified by their works (or characters therein), including Edmund Spenser, Samuel Daniel, and Christopher Marlowe. It is generally agreed that the eighth stanza honors Shakespeare, identified as "Adon" from *Venus and Adonis*:

> *Adon* deafly [obscurely] masking through,
> Stately troupes rich conceited [fancifully devised
>     or costumed],
> Showed he well deserved to,
> Love's [Venus's] delight on him to gaze,
> And had not love [Venus] herself intreated,
> Other nymphs had sent him bays.[210]

As Katherine Chiljan noted, this seems to depict "Venus ['Love'] and Adonis as characters in a masque," with the suggestion that if Venus were not chasing this beautiful boy, others would be.[211]

---

[209] See Edwards (Buckley ed. 1882), pp. 61-64; Chiljan, p. 253.

[210] Edwards, p. 62 (italics in original); see also Price, p. 231; Stritmatter (2006), p. 37; Chiljan, p. 253. On "deafly," see *OED*, v. 4, p. 294 (adj. "deaf," def. 5, "hardly or indistinctly heard; muffled"; "deafly" def. b, indistinctly or obscurely to the ear); on "conceited," v. 3, p. 649 (defs. I.4.b, "fancifully dressed or attired"; II.6, ingeniously devised or conceived; II.7, fancifully made in general; could carry its primary current meaning of "vain," but not then its primary meaning).

[211] Chiljan, p. 253.

Controversy centers around the poem's ensuing ninth and tenth stanzas, which even some orthodox scholars used to view as continuing to relate to Adon (Shakespeare).[212] Stratfordians these days generally insist those stanzas must be about some *other* mystery poet—nothing to see here, move along now—but concede they have no idea *whom*. But as Diana Price noted, these stanzas (unlike the eighth or others) do *not* clearly seem "to introduce a new poet."[213] Here are the lines in question:

> Eke [also] in purple robes distained,
> Amidst the Center of this clime,
> I have heard say doth remain,
> One whose power floweth far,
> That should have been of our rhyme,
> The only object and the star.
> Well could his bewitching pen,
> Done the Muses objects to us,
> Although he differs much from men,
> Tilting under Frieries,
> Yet his golden art might woo us,
> To have honored him with bays.[214]

Many have noted that the references to "purple robes" and "power flow[ing] far" seem to indicate a person of high social rank, probably an aristocrat, while "distained" suggests some kind of dishonor, disgrace, or defilement.[215] That fits very suggestively with Edward de Vere, Earl of Oxford, a known courtier poet who

---

[212] See, *e.g.*, Price, p. 232 (citing 19th-century scholars); Stritmatter (2006), p. 37 (same). Anti-Stratfordian scholars—such as Price, pp. 231-32; Anderson, p. 181; Stritmatter (2006); and Chiljan, pp. 253-54—have generally suggested that all three stanzas are about the same poet. I agree, as discussed in the text.

[213] Price, p. 232.

[214] Edwards, p. 63; see also Chiljan, p. 253. On "eke," which then carried the meaning (now obsolete) of "too" or "also," see *OED*, v. 5, p. 105.

[215] See, *e.g.*, Price, p. 232; Anderson, p. 181; Stritmatter (2006), p. 37; Chiljan, pp. 253-54; see also Parts IV.10 & note 287, IV.18 & notes 438-43, IV.20 & notes 474-79, 515-17, IV.23 & notes 578-81, and IV.24 & note 605.

suffered several disgraces. It certainly clashes very puzzlingly with the Stratfordian theory that an up-and-coming commoner (not known ever to have been disgraced) wrote *Venus and Adonis*.

There are several specific textual reasons, in addition to Price's point noted above, to link the eighth stanza (pretty clearly about the poet of *Venus and Adonis*) with the ninth and tenth stanzas about a mysterious disgraced nobleman "whose power floweth far." Chiljan pointed out that in the latter part of 1593, "the star" of English poetry ("of our rhyme") was most certainly the author of the hugely successful *Venus and Adonis*.[216] But if "Shakespeare" were a pseudonym, as discussed in Parts III and IV.3, that would resonate strongly with Edwards's suggestions of a poet hidden "in purple robes distained," apparently at the "center" of the literary world, yet who somehow was not (though he "should have been") the "object" and "star" of literary fame.

The statement that this poet "differs much from men" may also obscurely imply some social distinction or divide.[217] The implication of the tenth stanza, like the ninth, is that his contemporaries *should* or *would* "have honored him with bays" (that is, a poet's laurels) but for some reason could not—at least not openly.

All these hints of hidden or mysterious identity in the ninth and tenth stanzas link back to the eighth stanza's opening reference to a "mask." Indeed, the introduction of the poet as "*Adon* [obscurely] masking through" quite vividly, almost explicitly, suggests an author passing by in some unheralded way.

Perhaps the clincher, explored in a landmark 2006 article by Professor Roger Stritmatter, is the tenth stanza's reference to "Tilting under Frieries." Stritmatter showed that this very likely referred to violent altercations, notably in the Blackfriars district

---

[216] Chiljan, p. 254; also noting, p. 253, that—like Adonis (Adon), the object of Venus's ardent "attention"—this mysterious, unnamed, aristocratic poet is depicted as "someone else who deserves attention."

[217] See Stritmatter (2006), p. 38; Chiljan, p. 254.

of London, between Vere and his retainers, on one side, against several of his enemies including the Knyvet-Vavasour family.[218]

## 5.   Henry Willobie, *Avisa* (1594)

This book-length poem, fully titled as *"Willobie His Avisa,"* amounts to a satirical novel in verse. It appeared in 1594, several months after *The Rape of Lucrece*, to which it makes reference.[219] *Lucrece* was the second published work by "William Shakespeare," following *Venus and Adonis* in 1593. *Avisa* depicts—perhaps with mocking irony—an admirably (or supposedly) virtuous and faithful wife of that name, not unlike the steadfast and more earnestly depicted Lucrece of Shakespeare's poem. Her virtue is tested by a series of suitors. Scholars have long believed these characters satirize real people, in the nature of a *roman à clef*, but there is no consensus on exactly who they are.[220]

*Avisa* purported to be published by an Oxford University student, Hadrian Dorrell, without the consent of the supposed

---

[218] See Stritmatter (2006); see also Anderson, pp. 181, 495 (crediting, in 2005, Stritmatter's then-unpublished manuscript); Chiljan, p. 254 (surprisingly, Chiljan's 2011 book nowhere cited Stritmatter's important article). Vere fathered an out-of-wedlock son with Anne Vavasour in 1581, one of the queen's maids of honor, bringing disgrace and scandal upon her as well as him. This led to years of feuding with her family during the first half of the 1580s. See Anderson, pp. 161-66, 172-73, 178-81; Stritmatter (2006), pp. 39-40 n. 20. "Blackfriars had been a theatrical enclave for many decades" and Vere in the early 1580s was a patron of Blackfriars Theatre, Stritmatter (2006), p. 37 (Blackfriars "catered to the upper class," Chiljan, p. 254), though it was closed between 1584 and 1600, thus "impl[ying] that [the author] Shakespeare was active there in 1583 or before," Chiljan, p. 254, an obvious impossibility for Shakspere (then still a teenager in Stratford). See also Waugh, "Vulgar Scandal" (2015) (at minute 43) (drawing more connections between *L'Envoy*, Vere, and Lady Penelope Rich).

[219] *Avisa*, p. 15 (prefatory poem by "Contraria Contrarijs," "In praise of *Willobie His Avisa*, Hexameton to the Author," commenting in the second stanza, line 12, that "Shake-speare paints poor Lucrece['s] rape").

[220] See, *e.g.*, Ogburn, pp. 736-37; Price, pp. 228-29; Anderson, pp. 251-53; Chiljan, ch. 14, pp. 233-41; Prechter (2011); Hamill (2012); Waugh, "Vulgar Scandal" (2015); Hamill (2017).

author, Henry Willobie, claimed by Dorrell to be a fellow student conveniently out of the country at the time. That all smells very much like a pseudonymous conceit concocted to cover up a hidden author—not surprisingly, given that the book was viewed as scandalous and banned in 1599. It seems very doubtful there was any such person as "Dorrell." And if there was a real "Willobie," his name was probably borrowed to cover up for the real author, whoever that was.[221]

*Avisa* has been the subject of at least one book-length study, published almost fifty years ago by an orthodox scholar,[222] and it cries out for another that might synthesize and update the many intriguing analyses since then. I fear I can add little meaningful value here, except to briefly summarize what some other scholars have noted about the early authorship doubts that *Avisa* raised.

First of all, who was Avisa herself supposed to represent? Quite a few scholars have suggested Queen Elizabeth.[223] But in relation to Avisa's suitor "Henrico Willobego"—a curiously Italianized or Hispanicized version of the purported author's name,[224] thereafter abbreviated as "H.W."—other possibilities have been suggested. Edward de Vere's biographer Mark Anderson argued in 2005 that Avisa (at least in relation to H.W.) was Elizabeth Trentham, Vere's second wife, whom he married in late 1591.[225]

---

[221] See Price, pp. 228-29; Chiljan, pp. 234-35; Prechter (2011), pp. 135-36.

[222] De Luna (1970).

[223] See, *e.g.*, Ogburn, p. 737, and Prechter (2011), pp. 137-38, both citing, *e.g.*, Akrigg (1968) and De Luna (1970).

[224] *Avisa*, p. 90 (introduction to canto 44), describes him as "Italo-Hispalensis." The odd way in which the supposed author seems to describe himself as one of Avisa's suitors, in the third person (*e.g.*, introduction to canto 44, pp. 90-91), supports the conclusion that "Willobie" (or "Willobego") is a transparent pseudonym—a point further suggested by the way it appears crafted, as noted below in text, to evoke the name of a real person no one seriously suspects as the author, one who in fact appears to be one of the targets of the satire: Henry Wriothesley, Earl of Southampton.

[225] See Anderson, pp. 251-53, 282-85; see also Hamill, "Dark Lady" (2005); Hamill (2012). Anderson and Hamill, however, have since embraced the theory that she was Lady Penelope Rich. See Waugh, "Vulgar Scandal"; Hamill (2017).

(footnote continued on next page)

Katherine Chiljan, on the other hand, has argued that she was Anne Vavasour, an earlier lover of Vere.[226]

A newer and well-argued theory is that Lady Penelope Rich, an Elizabethan aristocrat with a scandalous reputation, was the model for Avisa. Two independent Stratfordian scholars first promoted that view, which has been developed more recently by Oxfordian scholars Alexander Waugh and John Hamill.[227] It might also be noted that in different parts of the poem, read at different levels, Avisa could perhaps be understood to represent more than one real person.

Many scholars have seen connections between Avisa's suitor H.W. and Henry Wriothesley (Earl of Southampton), to whom both *Venus and Adonis* and *Lucrece* were dedicated and who is widely viewed as the "fair youth," the beautiful young man at the heart of *Shake-speare's Sonnets*. They share the same initials and the same first name.[228] *Avisa* depicts H.W. as a "headlong youth," "want[ing]" in "years."[229] And can it be mere coincidence that the book describes H.W.'s "familiar" and "faithful friend" as an "old player" with the initials "W.S."?[230]

If *Avisa's* "W.S." is Shakespeare and "H.W." is Southampton, that generates obvious authorship questions. If "Shakespeare" were really a commoner from Stratford and a "player," a young man of low social status who just turned 30, why would he be des-

---

(footnote continued from previous page)
The identification of Avisa as Trentham originated in a 1937 article ("Light on the Dark Lady") by Pauline Angell.

[226] Chiljan, pp. 237-39.

[227] See Wilson (1992); Mooten (2010); Waugh, "Vulgar Scandal"; Hamill (2017). Hamill (like Anderson) had favored Trentham but both have been persuaded by Waugh's argument. See note 225; see also Part V.B & note 13.

[228] See, *e.g.*, Ogburn, p. 737; Chiljan, pp. 235-37; Hamill (2012), pp. 138-40.

[229] *Avisa*, p. 108 (canto 55); see also, *e.g.*, Chiljan, pp. 235-36.

[230] *Avisa*, p. 90 (introduction to canto 44) ("his familiar friend W.S."), p. 91 (introduction to canto 44) (describing W.S. as "the old player"), p. 93 (canto 44) (H.W. on W.S.: "yonder comes my faithful friend"), p. 94 (canto 45) (W.S.: "Well met, friend Harry"). See generally Part IV.24 (discussing the *Sonnets*).

cribed as "old" and on implausibly intimate terms with an aristocrat he addresses as "friend Harry"?[231] W.S. fits much better as a
sly reference to Vere, the likely author hiding behind the "Shakespeare" pseudonym. Vere, a well-traveled 44 when *Avisa* was published, may have "slummed" on occasion as an actor.[232] *Avisa*
indicates "the old player" W.S. had previously courted (perhaps
won?) Avisa and now mocks H.W.'s "like passion"—taking
"pleasure for a time to see him bleed"—while also advising the
younger man how to win over Avisa for himself.[233]

This triad of Avisa, H.W., and W.S. brings to mind (as many
have noted) the central love triangle of *Shake-speare's Sonnets*
between the poet, the "fair youth," and the "dark lady." As a
result, many have suggested the Dark Lady and Avisa must represent the same woman.[234]

Where all this ultimately leads is far from clear. *Avisa* is a
notorious rabbit-hole of mystery and contested interpretation. But
Chiljan aptly described it as "[o]ne of the most revealing" sources
of early Shakespeare authorship questions. "The book dropped
major clues about" the author's identity, describing him as an "old
player" and implying he was an aristocrat—specifically, perhaps,
Edward de Vere, 17th Earl of Oxford. But "[i]nstead of following

---

[231] See note 230; Sobran, pp. 159-60; see generally Hamill (2012).

[232] See, *e.g.*, Malim, "Oxford the Actor" (2004); Waugh, "My Shakespeare"
(2018), pp. 52-53; see also Parts IV.20 & notes 468, 485-87, and IV.26 & notes
676-77.

[233] *Avisa*, p. 91 (introduction to canto 44); see generally pp. 92-98 (cantos 44-
48). W.S. may be identified with Avisa's "French" suitor "D.B.," see *Avisa*, pp. 57-
73 (cantos 23-33), both possibly representing Edward de Vere. See Waugh,
"Vulgar Scandal," and "My Shakespeare," pp. 67-68. Chiljan, pp. 239-41, and
Hamill (2012), pp. 139-40, outlined additional grounds to link W.S. with Vere.

[234] See, *e.g.*, Ogburn, pp. 739-40; Anderson, pp. 282-85; Chiljan, ch. 14, pp.
233-41; Waugh, "Vulgar Scandal." How this may fit with various theories about
Emilia Bassano Lanier, see, *e.g.*, Hughes, "New Light on the Dark Lady" (2000),
is unclear. Much remains to be explored. See Parts IV.24 (discussing the *Sonnets*); IV.30 & note 805 (Bassano as Shakespeare authorship candidate).

these ... leads," orthodox scholars "ignore them because they do not fit with their conception of the great author."[235]

## 6.    Thomas Heywood, *Oenone and Paris* (1594)

Ogburn and Chiljan have discussed another poem, registered for publication in May 1594, that openly expressed doubts about the authorship of *Venus and Adonis. Oenone and Paris* by "T.H."—thought to be Thomas Heywood (*c.* 1570–1641)—is an obvious parody of *Venus and Adonis*.[236] Heywood's dedication of *Oenone* to "Courteous Readers," mockingly imitating the phrasing of the 1593 *Venus* dedication, clearly indicated that he viewed "William Shakespeare," the purported author of *Venus*, as a pseudonym.

Heywood's dedication self-abasingly conceded "how rude and unpolished" his own poem "may seem in your eagle-sighted eyes ... and therefore, fearing the worst, I have sought in some way to prevent it."[237] He sought to cover his behind—or rather, to mock Shakespeare for covering *his* posterior—by, as Ogburn put it, "offering the poem under concealed authorship in imitation of the Greek painter Apelles so that he might see how the dedicatees like it,"[238] before venturing to submit another work for their consideration. In just the same way, Ogburn noted, Shakespeare hesitantly offered *Venus* to Southampton, promising that "if your

---

[235] Chiljan, p. 233. Wells, "Allusions," p. 75, typifies the orthodox attitude. Even as he conceded that "Shakespeare is probably the person referred to" as W.S., Wells declared, in a brisk washing-of-hands *non sequitur:* "We may pass quickly over [that] reference"—and everything else about *Avisa*'s main text— "since ... only initials are given."

[236] See Ogburn, pp. 95-96; Chiljan, pp. 256-57.

[237] Quoted in Ogburn, p. 96.

[238] Ogburn, p. 96; see also Part IV.14 (discussing Weever's Epigram No. 11 and its reference to Apelles).

Honour seem but pleased," he would next submit "some graver labour" (which he did, with *The Rape of Lucrece* in 1594).[239]

Heywood explicitly declared that, "imitat[ing] the painter [Apelles]"—and by clear implication, *imitating Shakespeare*—he would present his *work* "openly to the view of all," while "*hiding himself* closely in a corner of the work-house, to the end, that if some curious and carping fellow came to find any fault, he might amend it against the next market."[240]

Heywood, publishing *Oenone* coyly under the initials "T.H.," stated that he was—just as he implied Shakespeare was with *Venus and Adonis*—"lurking in the meanwhile obscurely."[241] The echo of Edwards in *L'Envoy* to *Narcissus*, similarly depicting the author of *Venus and Adonis* as "deafly [silently] masking through," is hard to miss.[242]

None of this makes sense if *Venus and Adonis* and *Lucrece* were in fact—as the Stratfordian theory insists—the debut publications of an ambitious young writer publishing openly, for the first time, under his own true name.

## 7.   William Covell, *Polimanteia* (1595)

One of the most striking early expressions of authorship doubt—or actual knowledge that "Shakespeare" was a pseudonym for a hidden author—appears in the text and adjoining marginal note of a letter appended to *Polimanteia*, a book published anonymously in 1595 by Cambridge University. The dedication on a surviving copy of the book indicates it was written by William Covell (?–1613), a Fellow of Queens' College at Cambridge, as

---

[239] See Ogburn, p. 96.

[240] Quoted in Chiljan, p. 256 (also quoted in Ogburn, p. 96, though Ogburn quoted the poem as referring to "gaping fellow" rather than "carping fellow") (emphasis added here); see also Part IV.14 (Weever's 1599 reference to Apelles).

[241] Quoted in Ogburn, p. 96, and Chiljan, p. 256.

[242] See Part IV.4.

explored in several fascinating articles by Alexander Waugh and Patrick O'Brien.[243]

The Covell letter appears on the surface to be a rhetorical message "from England to her three daughters"—her leading universities: Cambridge, Oxford, and the Inns of Court—urging them to cooperate in celebrating their respective histories and graduates.[244] The key passage comments, in part, "*Oxford* thou maist extoll thy courte-deare-verse happy *Daniel*," thus inviting Oxford University to celebrate its former student, the poet-playwright Samuel Daniel, referencing three of his writings.[245]

Much more widely known than this obscure passage is the marginal note printed right next to it, referring to "*Sweet Shakspeare*."[246] As Waugh noted, orthodox scholars, even the meticulous Sir Edmund Chambers, have long cited this brief and rare early published reference to Shakespeare while apparently ignoring or overlooking the adjacent passage.[247]

---

[243] See Waugh, "Covell" (2013), pp. 2-3; O'Brien (2014) (further exploring connections between Covell, Cambridge, and Edward de Vere, who was educated at Queens' College for a time as a boy); see also Waugh, "Shakespeare Nom de Plume" (2013) (and follow-up discussion in January 2014 *De Vere Society Newsletter*); Waugh, "My Shakespeare" (2018), p. 68; and Waugh's videos "Vulgar Scandal" (2015) (starting at the one hour 9 minute point), "William Covell Knew" (2017), and "Fair Youth Dark Lady" (2018). Waugh and O'Brien also discussed the connections between Cambridge and William Cecil, Lord Burghley—Vere's father-in-law and, when Vere was a boy, his guardian—who in 1595 (among several important roles, including top advisor to Queen Elizabeth, in effect her prime minister), was chancellor of the university.

[244] Waugh, "Covell," p. 2.

[245] Quoted in Waugh, "Covell," p. 3 (italics in original). I have modernized spellings here (as the Preface notes I customarily do in quoting archaic sources), but I have not altered the spelling of the crucial and puzzling phrase or compound adjective "courte-deare-verse."

[246] Quoted in Waugh, "Covell," p. 4 (italics in original). The marginal note omits the first "e" in "Shakespeare" and also hyphenates the name, both perhaps for reasons of space, since "Sweet Shak-" barely fits in the margin, followed below by "speare."

[247] See Waugh, "Covell," p. 3, citing Chambers (1930), v. 2, p. 193, and discussing Chambers's failure to discuss or even provide the adjoining text.

Waugh's discovery was to observe four striking points that appear in combination:

(1) The reference to Shakespeare is aligned precisely to the line of text in which "courte-deare-verse" appears.

(2) The reference to "Oxford" appears directly above that very odd, distinctive, and noticeable phrase.[248]

(3) This phrase contains the words "our," "de," and "verse" in that order, which (omitting the "s" in "verse") reads "our de vere."

(4) This phrase ("courte-deare-verse") is a perfect anagram[249] of "our de vere a secret."[250] It would be implausible to dismiss this as mere coincidence. Covell seems to have chosen, for whatever reasons, to hint at some connection between "Shakespeare" and Edward de Vere (Earl of Oxford).[251] "Our" could mean "England's" and perhaps also, more specifically, "Cambridge's."[252]

---

[248] The phrase is not nonsensical, though as Waugh suggested it seems "convoluted" at best. Waugh, "Covell," p. 3. It may be thought to convey that Daniel's "verse" was "dear" to the (royal) "court." The very fact that this distinctive and discrete three-word combination is so odd and awkward is a dead giveaway that it must have been crafted intentionally to facilitate the creation of the anagram it contains. See note 249.

[249] An anagram is formed by rearranging the letters in a string of text. A "perfect" anagram is one in which no letter is left unused nor used more than once. See Friedman & Friedman, p. 92. Another impressive feature of this anagram is that the string of text from which it derives need not be subjectively chosen but rather appears in the original source as a discrete and distinctive three-word phrase calling obvious attention to itself (a single compound adjective modifying "happy Daniel"). For reasons stated in text and note 248, it seems very likely that this anagram was intentionally crafted to convey some message about Vere.

[250] See Waugh, "Covell," pp. 4-5. Price, pp. 84, 232, discussed Covell's marginal reference to Shakespeare and adjacent textual reference to Daniel, suggesting they conveyed authorship doubts, but did not notice the anagram discovered by Waugh. Waugh elaborates on broader possible meanings of this Covell passage in his very intriguing 2018 "Fair Youth Dark Lady" video, which builds on his 2015 "Vulgar Scandal" video. See also Part IV.27 (discussing the title page of Peacham's *Minerva Britanna*, which appears to contain another Oxfordian anagram, more debatable and less significant for the SAQ).

[251] See notes 248 and 249.

[252] See note 243; O'Brien (2014), p. 11; see also Part IV.14 (discussing the authorship doubts expressed by John Weever, who was tutored by Covell).

It must be noted that many Shakespeare authorship doubters today, no less than orthodox Stratfordians, have developed a well-earned skepticism—even aversion—toward cryptographic theories and other claims about coded messages or word puzzles. The Baconians famously drove themselves into a ditch with byzantine theories of this kind.[253] I myself share and sympathize with that skepticism as a general matter.

The Baconian "cipher" theories were thoroughly debunked in a deftly scholarly and entertaining book by William and Elizebeth Friedman, a married team of cryptologists who served American and allied governments with great distinction in both world wars of the 20th century.[254] The Friedmans also set forth useful criteria by which to assess the potential validity of purported cryptographic systems and messages.[255]

A full assessment of the weight which should be given to this Covell anagram and other possible cryptograms (coded messages) relating to the SAQ is beyond my expertise and the scope of this book.[256] But for present purposes, it may be noted that a message using an anagram is a type of "unkeyed transposition cipher."[257] It is thus, as the Friedmans suggested, less useful to convey an unambiguous (and securely encrypted) message than a cipher or cryptographic system employing a rigorous "key." As they noted, "[e]ven when [an] anagram has only a few letters there may be more than one 'solution'; and when it has many letters there can

---

[253] See, *e.g.*, Hess (an Oxfordian), "Shakespeare Cipher Systems." On the Baconian theory of Shakespeare authorship, see Part I & note 42.

[254] See Friedman & Friedman (1957); see also Part I, notes 37, 42. There is no typo in "Elizebeth"; she spelled her given name with three e's. For a recent study of her fascinating life and career, see Fagone (2017).

[255] See Friedman & Friedman, ch. 2, pp. 15-26.

[256] See also Part IV.24, note 617 (noting Rollett's, Prechter's, and Waugh's cryptographic theories about the dedication and other aspects of *Shake-speare's Sonnets*). For more possible anagrams, see Parts IV.25, note 650; IV.27.

[257] Friedman & Friedman, p. 18; see generally chs. 2, 7-8, pp. 15-26, 92-113.

be many 'solutions'—all equally valid."²⁵⁸ The Friedmans suggested a secure cryptogram using a keyed cipher system requires a
minimum length of at least 25 letters, in order to ensure only one
reliable and unambiguous solution.²⁵⁹ But a shorter anagram may
be very significant (that is, *not* a product of random chance)—
though obviously not as useful to send a message requiring great
secrecy—precisely because it is much less likely to have multiple
solutions (if any) spelling out any meaningful message.

The Friedmans' main criticism of the alleged Baconian anagrams was precisely that "any *lengthy* sequence of letters with the
normal proportions of ... vowels and consonants may be anagrammed *in a large number of ways*," such that no solution "will
carry any objective conviction."²⁶⁰ By contrast, the short and well-
defined nature of the Covell "plain text,"²⁶¹ together with the reinforcing clues provided by the associated references to Shakespeare
and Oxford, seems to lend much greater rigor and reliability to its
apparent anagrammatical message.

The Covell anagram seems risky if ensuring utmost secrecy
were the top priority. True, it was missed by all of the many
hundreds (even thousands) of modern professional and amateur
Shakespeare scholars until Waugh noticed it in 2013, after the
modern debate over Shakespeare authorship had been underway
for more than 150 years.²⁶² But it was probably far more readily
recognizable to Covell's contemporaries.

Presumably, Covell did not create this anagram in order to
*preserve* "a secret" that would be passed down for centuries only to

---

²⁵⁸ Friedman & Friedman, p. 19; see generally pp. 18-19.

²⁵⁹ See Friedman & Friedman, pp. 22-23.

²⁶⁰ Friedman & Friedman, p. 113 (emphases added).

²⁶¹ "Plain text" refers to the original text which, when subjected to a "keyed"
cipher, or transposed (reshuffled) in an "unkeyed" way as with an anagram,
produces the encoded or intended text or message. See Friedman & Friedman, p.
18. The 16-letter "plain text" by Covell is "courte-deare-verse." The asserted
message, seemingly encoded therein by anagram, is "our de vere a secret."

²⁶² See Part I & note 42 on the rise of the Baconians in the 1850s.

be discovered much later, such as in our own time. On the contrary, he probably intended to call attention—albeit in a slyly coy and artful way—to what may have been an open or at least widely known "secret" in his own time.[263]

## 8.   John Trussell, *The First Rape of Fair Helen* (1595)

This poem by John Trussell (c. 1575–1648) seems inspired by Shakespeare's *The Rape of Lucrece* and is prefaced by a sonnet in which Trussell equivocates about whether and how to praise an unnamed poet. As Chiljan discussed, that poet seems to have been the author Shakespeare. So why would Trussell be reluctant to praise him openly by name? "My praise cannot disparage thee a whit," Trussell stated, which seemed oddly to imply the possibility that praise *might* disparage the author of *Lucrece*.[264]

The logical implication, Chiljan noted, was that the unnamed poet "had high social rank," as also suggested by Trussell's reference to being "commanded" by the poet's friendship.[265] It is inexplicable why Trussell would have treated the poet's identity so coyly and obscurely if the author were the up-and-coming Shakspere of Stratford publishing *Lucrece* under his own name.

## 9.   Sir John Davies MP, *Orchestra* (1596)

Sir John Davies (1569–1626) was a lawyer and Member of Parliament as well as a poet. His *Orchestra, or a Poem of Dan-*

---

[263] In this sense, the Friedmans' comment, p. 26, that it is generally *not* "reasonable to expect that, if cryptic messages actually were inserted in the text, they would be clearly signalled in some way," would not seem to apply to Covell's anagram, and perhaps not to other authorship-related cryptograms. To be sure, as a general matter "[o]ne does not put something in a secret hiding-place and then put up a sign saying 'Notice: Secret hiding-place.'" Friedman & Friedman, p. 26. But that may well be exactly what Covell intended in this instance.

[264] Chiljan, pp. 257-58.

[265] Chiljan, p. 258.

*cing*, was registered in 1594 and published in 1596.[266] The last four stanzas praise several poets. As Katherine Chiljan noted, given the "recent acclaim" and popularity of *Venus and Adonis* and *The Rape of Lucrece*, it would be odd if Shakespeare were not among those poets.[267] But he was not identified as such, even though other poets were clearly identified. Instead, the last three stanzas of *Orchestra* dwelt on extravagant praise for a mysterious *unnamed* poet whom Davies addressed as "sweet Companion" and "the Swallow," who was said to "under a shadow, sing."[268]

Chiljan noted several lines by Davies about the "Swallow" that appear to echo Shakespearean passages, thus implying that the unnamed poet was indeed the author Shakespeare. For example, Davies rhapsodizes that some lines by the Swallow "so enchant mine ear, And in my mind such sacred fury move, As I should knock at heav'n's great gate above"[269]—reminiscent of *Sonnet* 29's "the Lark at break of day arising" that "sings hymns at Heaven's gate."[270]

So why all the mystery? Davies appeared very anxious to maintain public discretion so as not to offend the unnamed poet ("that singing Swallow"), "[t]o whom I owe my service and my love."[271] As Chiljan noted, this servile attitude suggested the poet held high rank within the rigidly stratified society of that time. It is difficult to imagine why Davies, a knight and prominent public official himself, would defer in such a way to a poet or playwright who was a commoner with lower social standing—like Michael

---

[266] He should not be confused with John Davies of Hereford, nor Sir John Davies the Essex Rebellion supporter. See Parts III.A & note 24; IV.20 and 26.

[267] Chiljan, p. 255; see generally pp. 254-56.

[268] Quoted and discussed in Chiljan, pp. 254-55, and very briefly in Ogburn, pp. 105, 814.

[269] Quoted in Chiljan, p. 255.

[270] *Sonnet* 29, lines 11-12; see also *Cymbeline*, act 2, sc. 3 ("hark, the lark at heaven's gate sings"); both discussed by Chiljan with other parallels, pp. 255-56.

[271] Quoted in Chiljan, p. 255.

Drayton (one suggested candidate for the unnamed poet) or Shak-spere of Stratford.[272]

## 10. Joseph Hall, *Virgidemiarum* (1597–99)

The Baconian theory of Shakespeare authorship, it turns out, may have originated not in the 1850s[273] but in the 1590s. As John Michell and Diana Price have noted, even some Stratfordians have acknowledged that satires by Joseph Hall (1574–1656) and John Marston (1576–1634) (see Part IV.11) may be read to suggest that Sir Francis Bacon was the author of *Venus and Adonis* and *The Rape of Lucrece*.[274] Hall was a writer and clergy-man who eventually became a bishop in the Church of England. His satires appeared in *Virgidemiarum*, which was published and revised in several installments during 1597–99.[275]

Even if Hall and Marston did believe "Shakespeare" was Bacon, that does not prove they were right.[276] The Baconian theory seems to have far fewer adherents today than the Oxford-ian theory. The relevant point is that Hall's and Marston's writ-ings provide still more evidence that *doubts and questions* about the authorship of the works of "Shakespeare" were in fact circulat-ing quite publicly during the 1590s.

Hall satirized a writer whom he disguised with the sobriquet "Labeo." In one of Hall's more famous and oft-quoted passages, he seems to criticize Labeo for hiding his true identity:

---

[272] See Chiljan, p. 256. Chiljan also noted that when Davies republished the poem in 1622, he oddly deleted the last four stanzas with a note falsely stating that they had "describ[ed] Queen Elizabeth." Chiljan, p. 256.

[273] See Parts I & note 42; IV.30 & note 797.

[274] See Michell, pp. 126–29, and Price, p. 232 (both citing, *e.g.*, the Stratford-ian scholar H.N. Gibson).

[275] Hall's satires were initially published anonymously, but were identified as his by 1599. See Morris (2013), p. 5; Morris (2016), p. 33.

[276] See, *e.g.*, Michell, p. 129 (quoting H.N. Gibson).

Long as the crafty Cuttle [cuttlefish] lieth sure
In the black Cloud of his thick vomiture,
Who list [desires to] complain of wronged faith or fame[277]
When he may shift it to another's name?[278]

Michell argued that "Hall seems to hint at Labeo's connection with Shakespeare's early poems," but conceded that Hall himself never clearly identified him.[279]

More recent articles by Carolyn Morris and Alexander Waugh have opened a new front in studying Hall's *Virgidemiarum*, suggesting that it contains veiled commentary on Edward de Vere that supports the Oxfordian theory of Shakespeare authorship.[280] We have already seen ample evidence in the preceding sections of Part IV, and they provide still more, that the Oxfordian theory—while not promulgated in modern times until 1920[281]—was also publicly foreshadowed as far back as the 1590s.

Reconciling these interpretations of Hall's obscure and complex writings is beyond the scope of this book. But a few points of interest are worth noting. Morris agreed that Labeo represents the author Shakespeare, but she argued that Hall implicitly identifies him with Oxford, not Bacon.[282] Morris also argued that two other characters satirized by Hall, "Lolio" and his son (the

---

[277] "List," as used here, means "desires" or "wishes to." See *OED*, v. 8, pp. 1020-21.

[278] Quoted and discussed, *e.g.*, in Michell, pp. 127-28.

[279] Michell, p. 128. As discussed in Part IV.11, Michell, pp. 128-29, argued that Marston did. Mark Anderson has discussed authorship doubts raised by another clergyman, Thomas Bastard (yes, that's his name) (c. 1565–1618), in a 1598 collection of epigrams, *Chrestoleros*. Anderson, p. 320, compared Bastard to Hall as also scolding an unnamed author who "writes sinful works, is widely admired, and hides behind another man's identity."

[280] See, *e.g.*, Morris (2013); Morris (2016); Waugh, "From the Pulpit" (2015), pp. 2-3 & n. 3.

[281] See Part I & note 4.

[282] Morris (2013), pp. 13-14; see also Morris (2016), pp. 38-39, 60-61, 73-75. She also argued that several other characters in Hall's satires add up to a collective description of Vere and further link him to the author Shakespeare. Morris (2013), pp. 13-18; see generally Morris (2016).

latter curiously unnamed), represent John Shakspere of Stratford and his son William.[283]

Waugh agrees that Labeo is both "Shakespeare" and Oxford. He argues that Hall more openly satirized Vere with the mocking title of "Great Osmond."[284] As Waugh has noted, Hall's Osmond

> wonders how he shall be remembered once he is "dead & gone." His name is not attached to any of his works and he is reviled for his living deeds. Hall insists that no fancy tomb will ever save his "rotten name," and suggests that once [he] is dead he should be "inditched in great secrecie where no passenger might curse [his] dust."[285]

Hall's vicious attack eerily foreshadowed the mystery that in fact surrounds Vere's ultimate resting place.[286] It is also poignantly corroborated by *Shake-speare's Sonnets*, replete with mournful lamentations by a poet who perceives all too well that his name has "receive[d] a brand," that he is "despised," an "outcast," with "vulgar scandal stamped upon [his] brow," "vile esteemed," "in disgrace with Fortune and men's eyes," that his "name [will] be buried where [his] body is ... no more to shame nor me nor you," and that he, "once gone, to all the world must die."[287]

---

[283] Morris (2013), pp. 7-13; see also Morris (2016), pp. 53-59, 62-64.

[284] Waugh, "From the Pulpit," pp. 2-3 & n. 3; Waugh, "Moniment" (rev. 2015) (point 3, "Shakspere: With Whom Quick Nature Died").

[285] Waugh, "From the Pulpit," p. 2.

[286] For Waugh's solution of that mystery, see, *e.g.*, his article "Moniment" (rev. 2015) and his videos "Where Shakespeare Is REALLY Buried" (Parts 1-4).

[287] See, respectively, *Sonnets* 111 (line 5), 37 (line 9), 29 (line 2), 112 (line 2), 121 (line 1), again 29 (line 1), 72 (lines 11-12), and 81 (line 6), quoted in Waugh, "From the Pulpit," p. 3; see also Sobran, p. 199. This clashes very puzzlingly with the Stratfordian theory that an up-and-coming commoner was the author—a popular and admired poet-playwright writing openly under his own name, not known to have been touched by public scandal or disgrace. See Parts IV.4 & note 215; IV.18 & notes 438-43; IV.20 & notes 474-79, 515-17; IV.23 & notes 578-81. See generally, on the *Sonnets*, Part IV.24 (especially notes 603-05).

### 11. John Marston, *The Scourge of Villainy* (1598–99)

According to Michell, John Marston—a poet-playwright and "literary enemy" of Joseph Hall—confirmed Hall's identification of Labeo with the author Shakespeare and Bacon.[288] Morris and Waugh, as discussed in Part IV.10, have instead connected Labeo with Edward de Vere, Earl of Oxford.[289] What is clear, in any event, is that both Hall and Marston wrote about the author of *Venus and Adonis* and *The Rape of Lucrece* in a way that simply makes no sense if they believed the Stratfordian theory of Shakespeare authorship.

Price also suggested that Marston's satires in *The Scourge of Villainy*—published in 1598 and revised in 1599—include a curious echo of a character, "Gullio," in the second anonymous *Parnassus* play.[290] Gullio and Marston's character both woo a lady named "Lesbia" and both may be read as satirizing Shakspere of Stratford—as a buffoon who plagiarizes lines from plays written by others, including *Romeo and Juliet*.[291]

### 12. Francis Meres, *Palladis Tamia* (1598)

Francis Meres (*c.* 1565–1647), another clergyman and writer, is most famous for his commentary on Shakespeare in *Palladis Tamia*, a "commonplace book"—a type of compilation or published

---

[288] Michell, pp. 128-29; see also Price, p. 232. Michell, p. 128, cited both Marston's satires and a 1598 poem ("Pigmalion's Image").

[289] See, *e.g.*, Morris (2016), pp. 60-61.

[290] *Parnassus 2* was apparently first performed *c.* 1599–1600 and may have been written around the same time as Marston's *Scourge of Villainy*. See Part IV.15. We may never know which writing echoed the other.

[291] See Price, pp. 85-86. For more discussions of suggested plagiarism, see Parts IV.2, 14-16, 18, 26, and 28. Mark Anderson, pp. 317, 545, has discussed authorship doubts raised by the anonymous play *Histriomastix, or, The Player Whipped* (*c.* 1599, published 1610), generally thought to be written by Marston.

scrapbook popular in the Elizabethan era, vaguely analogous to a modern almanac or similar popular reference work. It is largely a collection of quotations or paraphrases of other commentators (mostly uncredited) along with various lists of writers.[292] *Palladis* was published the same year (1598) that plays started appearing in print with the "Shakespeare" name on them, five years after that name first appeared below the dedication of the hugely popular book-length poem *Venus and Adonis*.

Scholars have differed over how seriously to view Meres as a "literary critic."[293] The few paragraphs and lists in *Palladis* mentioning the published author Shakespeare never even provide his first name, are brief and impersonal in nature, shed no light on who that author actually was, and in particular fail to provide any support for the Stratfordian authorship theory.

Yet *Palladis* still offers by far the most clear, direct, and extended commentary on this author and his works before the 1616 death of Shakspere of Stratford and indeed before the 1623 publication of the *First Folio*. And Meres's commentary provides good reasons to think he had an "inside track" on what was going on in Elizabethan literary circles.[294] Thus, it has understandably attracted great attention.

Meres offers (or passes along) high praise for this author, whoever he was. He calls him "mellifluous" and "honey tongued," possessing "the sweet witty soul of *Ovid*." While mostly just listing him among other writers, he singles him out to declare that "the

---

[292] See Chambers (1930), v. 2, pp. 193-95 (quoting Meres's comments); see also, *e.g.*, Detobel & Ligon (2009), pp. 97-100; Price, pp. 143-44.

[293] Detobel & Ligon opined that it "seems very wide of the mark indeed" to dignify Meres with the term "literary critic" or to call *Palladis* (as one scholar has) an "extremely valuable survey of English literature." They also noted that from a modern perspective we might be tempted to dismiss him as a mere plagiarist, though they suggested this would be unfair and anachronistic. Detobel & Ligon, p. 100. They argued that "the driving force behind" *Palladis*, p. 100 (see also p. 99), was one of the men involved in publishing it, Nicholas Ling.

[294] See Stritmatter (2017) (at minute 34); Detobel & Ligon, p. 100.

Muses would speak with *Shakespeare's* fine filed phrase, if they would speak English." Among English writers of dramatic comedies and tragedies, Meres also singles out Shakespeare as "the most excellent in both kinds for the stage."[295]

Somewhat oddly, however, when Meres lists "the best among our [England's] poets," "our best for tragedy," and "[t]he best for comedy amongst us," Shakespeare's name is buried in the middle or even toward the end in each case (the lists are not alphabetical)—fourth among five English poets, tenth of 14 writers of dramatic tragedies, and ninth of 17 comedy writers.[296]

The lists appear to prioritize social rank, with "Shakespeare" grouped among writers who appear to be commoners, not listed first or even toward the top among them.[297] "Lord Buckhurst" (Sir Thomas Sackville, later made Earl of Dorset by King James[298]) is listed first among "our best for tragedy," and "Edward [de Vere] Earl of Oxford" appears first on the list of those "best for comedy amongst us."[299]

---

[295] Quoted in Chambers (1930), v. 2, p. 194 (italics in original). On the Muses, see Part IV.3, note 180.

[296] Quoted in Chambers (1930), v. 2, pp. 194-95.

[297] Stratfordians, naturally, are fond of pointing that out, but please note that "Shakespeare," regardless of whether that was a real author's name or a pseudonym, *had to be viewed as a commoner*, since there would have been no way to invent a fake addition to the well-known ranks of the nobility in the small world of the Elizabethan elite. The whole *point* of such a pseudonym would have been to hide the aristocratic status of the author and *pretend* he was a commoner. See Part I & note 16.

[298] Sabrina Feldman has argued that Sackville (1536–1608) was the primary author behind the "Shakespeare" name. Her argument is not nearly as strong as the case for Vere (see Parts I, note 4, and IV.30), but both of her books are thoughtful and informative and merit careful reading. See Feldman, *Apocryphal* (2011) and *Sackville* (2015); see also Hess, "Literary Mentor" (2011); Feldman, "Response" (2011). Feldman holds a doctorate in physics and is a real-life "rocket scientist" who manages the Planetary Science Instruments Office at NASA's Jet Propulsion Laboratory. Like many authorship skeptics, she hardly fits the stereotype of the flaky kook or "conspiracy theorist" so often falsely portrayed by orthodox Stratfordians. See Part V.B-D.

[299] Quoted in Chambers (1930), v. 2, pp. 194-95 (omitting italicization of "Buckhurst" and "Edward" in Meres's original).

Oxfordians sometimes mistakenly assert that Vere was singled out as "best for comedy," but Meres's description clearly applies to the entire list, on which Vere simply happens to appear first—with that position most likely due only to his aristocratic status. On the other hand, Stratfordians sometimes foolishly suggest that Vere's appearance on the list *at all* might be due only to his rank, seeking to obfuscate the undeniable fact that Meres recognized him—among very few aristocrats and many more commoners—as among the "best" English writers of his day. Meres thus corroborated what other commentators of that era said.[300]

Stratfordians often gleefully invoke the fact that Vere and Shakespeare *both* appear on Meres's "best for comedy" list. Professor James Shapiro gloated almost giddily: "*Crushingly*, for those who want to believe that the Earl of Oxford and Shakespeare were one and the same writer, Meres names both ... while omitting Oxford from the list of leading tragedians."[301] This is one of those arguments that makes me wonder if some Stratfordian scholars really are as obtuse as they often seem to be—or if (more likely) they just think the rest of us are stupid enough to fall for such patently weak arguments.[302] To be sure, at first blush, the simplest way to interpret the listing of both Vere and Shakespeare is that it is *consistent* with them being different authors. Occam's Razor always has some force.[303] But does it *disprove* the theory

---

[300] See Part IV.3 & notes 135-50, 180; Stritmatter & Wildenthal, "Methodological," pp. 175-84.

[301] Shapiro (2010), p. 236 (emphasis added).

[302] Two other examples are the arguments that: (1) the obsequious tone of "Shakespeare's" dedications of *Venus and Adonis* and *The Rape of Lucrece* to a young nobleman somehow proves the writer could not have been an older and higher ranking aristocrat (but see Part I & note 16); and (2) the wordplay over the name "Will" in some of *Shake-speare's Sonnets* (*e.g.*, 135-36) somehow proves the author's real (not just published) first name must indeed be William (but see Part IV.24 & notes 607-16).

[303] See Part IV.1 & note 12, Baker, and "Occam's Razor." Occam's Razor, however, is not an ironclad law of nature, merely a cautionary guide to analysis. Sometimes a more complex explanation is true.

that "Shakespeare" was Vere's pseudonym? Not at all—certainly not "crushingly."

*If, by hypothesis,* Shakespeare was a pseudonym for a high-ranking aristocrat—the very point in question—then Meres's discussion is perfectly consistent with what we might reasonably expect to see in a published commentary, given likely sensitivities over "outing" such a person. On the other hand, *if* the Stratfordian theory is correct, then yes, it would obviously follow that the two names listed by Meres represent different people. That all merely *begs the question* of how likely the pseudonym hypothesis itself may be, a separate issue dependent mainly on other evidence. In fact, as we will shortly see, *Palladis* itself, including this very list, tends to corroborate the numerous doubts about the Stratfordian theory raised by all the other writings discussed in this book.

Meres might have been unaware that Shakespeare was a pseudonym. Or if he did know, he may not have known the name of the true author hidden behind it. As noted above, nothing in his commentary suggests any personal knowledge of the author, nor anything specifically supporting the Stratfordian theory. I tend to think, for reasons elaborated below, that Meres must have known or suspected the truth. But even if so, by listing both names he might easily have been playing along with the pseudonym or helping to preserve or promote it.[304]

It is very unlikely that Meres would have dared to embarrass an aristocratic author in print by explicitly blowing his cover as the true Shakespeare—even though he did comment publicly in this passage on Vere's facility for comedy, which may already have been common knowledge anyway (like his well-known affinity for poetry). We would expect a writer like Meres to coyly maintain at least plausible deniability, to pay lip service (at least) to a polite fiction about a powerful and well-connected nobleman.

---

[304] See, *e.g.*, note 305.

That Meres was in fact seeking to convey some coy message about Vere is suggested, first of all, by how he listed him among the best comedy writers but not among the best poets. Shapiro, curiously, overlooked the latter point, even while emphasizing Vere's omission from the list of tragedy writers. We have independent evidence that Vere was well-known and highly regarded as a poet. Some of his poems had been published long before 1598 in connection with his name or initials. But no extant plays were ever published in connection with his name, as Meres must have known. If Meres was nominally going along with the cover name, he may also have been slyly yanking at the veil.[305]

Alexander Waugh, building on studies by Professor Roger Stritmatter and a 2009 article by Robert Detobel and K.C. Ligon, has demonstrated that far more is going on in *Palladis* than Shapiro or other Stratfordian devotees have cared to explore. Meres, albeit in veiled fashion, did in fact express doubts about—even implicitly contradicted—the idea that "Shakespeare" wrote literary works under his own name.[306] As Waugh put it, "[c]areful consideration of Meres' method and purpose ... reveals the very opposite [of Shapiro's claim] to be the case ...."[307]

---

[305] See, *e.g.*, Part IV.3 & notes 135-150 & 180, Stritmatter & Wildenthal, "Methodological," pp. 175-84. It seems surprising Meres went as far as he did to suggest Vere's association, not just with poetry (more respectable for courtiers), but also stage drama. But Meres balanced his daring jab, in listing Vere among those "best for comedy," by listing Vere's pseudonym separately, thus bolstering his cover at least as to the publicly known comedies of "Shakespeare." Meres also, as noted, avoided listing Vere as a tragic dramatist.

[306] See Waugh, "My Shakespeare" (2018), pp. 69-72 (and his 2018 video "Francis Meres Knew"); Detobel & Ligon, pp. 101-07; Stritmatter (2017) (at minutes 31-54). Stritmatter's 2017 lecture built in part on his earlier lecture and unpublished paper, "By the Numbers: *Palladis Tamia* and the Shakespearean Question" (SOF Annual Conference, Madison, Wis., Sept. 12, 2014). See Waugh, "My Shakespeare," p. 71 (citing Stritmatter's 2014 study). Stritmatter (2017) (at minutes 44-45) has credited Detobel & Ligon's pioneering work. Waugh, while also citing and building on Detobel & Ligon's study, corrected a minor mistake in their analysis. See Waugh, "My Shakespeare," p. 70 n. 40.

[307] Waugh, "My Shakespeare," p. 70.

Meres was enamored of numerology. He went out of his way to set forth symmetrical lists of English writers in various categories, set against equal numbers of classical or other non-English writers. He was also very fond of sets of three, reflecting the Christian religious significance of the trinity. In the opening dedication of *Palladis*, Meres declared in Latin: "Tria sunt omnia" (literally, "Three is all," or "All things come in threes").[308]

It may be tempting for present-day Stratfordians to ridicule interpretations of *Palladis* in such numerological terms, just as they may ridicule and dismiss the anagrams in Covell's *Polimanteia* or Peacham's *Minerva Britanna*. But that would merely defy in a silly and anachronistic way the fact that writers of that time were very much into numerology and believed in its significance, just as they were fascinated by anagrams and similar puzzles.[309] We may not put much stock in them today, *but they did then* and we are trying to understand *their* historical and literary context.

Meres was very "persistent" in his numerological approach. In "only four of his 58 paragraphs" in his "comparative discourse" on English and classical or foreign writers does he even "appear to abandon triadic or symmetrical structures and on close examination even these anomalies are shown to be illusory." In three of those four paragraphs, "Meres uses a single name to represent two different persons," thus preserving the desired symmetry.[310]

In the fourth seemingly anomalous paragraph, Meres—in a neat reversal—uses two names to represent a single person. This is the paragraph setting forth the comparative lists of the best writers of comedy for the stage. As noted above, Meres includes 17

---

[308] See Detobel & Ligon, p. 102, and generally pp. 101-03; Waugh, "My Shakespeare," pp. 69-70.

[309] See, *e.g.*, Stritmatter (2017) (at minutes 39-44). On the Covell and Peacham anagrams, see Parts IV.7 and 27.

[310] Waugh, "My Shakespeare," p. 70. Wells, "Allusions," p. 76, perceived dimly that "there is something mechanical about" all this list-making, but he spurned further inquiry, brushing off Meres's approach as "mindless."

English playwrights in the second list in this category, with the Earl of Oxford (Vere) listed first and "Shakespeare" ninth. Yet only 16 classical playwrights appear in the first list, seeming to violate his preferred symmetry. The balance would be restored if any two of the English names may be viewed as duplicative.[311]

Given the ample independent evidence pointing to Vere as the author hidden behind the Shakespeare name,[312] those two names are the obvious candidates to represent a single person. Much of that evidence has been explored in modern times. But as we have seen, hints to that effect were already circulating publicly in the 1590s. People in literary and court circles probably knew much more. The *publicly expressed* doubts during that era must surely be the proverbial tip of the iceberg of *privately circulating* doubts (or outright knowledge). As noted above, Meres seems to have been well informed.

That all seems very suggestive, but how can we *know*, or at least deduce a higher probability, that Meres actually intended to convey such an artfully cloaked message? Was he indeed slyly hinting at the pseudonymous nature of "Shakespeare" and his linkage to Vere? Or are we reading too much into this?

Waugh and Stritmatter pointed to several features of this passage that seem too contrived to be coincidental. It is the 34th paragraph in Meres's "comparative discourse" and 34 equals two times 17. The asymmetry, as noted, suggests an excess of one name on the English side. Could this suggest—and would it have suggested to an Elizabethan reader—that someone on the English list, in some way represented by the number 17, is "somehow doubled in paragraph 34?"[313]

Vere is not only the first of the 17 English names listed but also the 17th of the 33 names listed overall, following the 16

---

[311] See Waugh, "My Shakespeare," pp. 70-71.
[312] See Part I & note 4.
[313] Waugh, "My Shakespeare," p. 71.

classical comedy writers. And he was the 17th Earl of Oxford. Waugh noted that this places Vere at the center of the two lists combined, both preceded and followed by 16 names. "Shakespeare," meanwhile, is at the center of the English list, both preceded and followed by eight names on that list—another way in which they are implicitly paired.[314]

Stritmatter's insight was to carefully compare the two lists of names preceding and following Vere's. What he discovered seems far too artful to be coincidental. Following the order in which Meres listed them, each of the 16 classical playwrights (with one odd *apparent* exception) matches up to one of the 16 English playwrights sharing significant similarities.[315]

By contrast, if we follow the obtuse insistence of Shapiro and other Stratfordians and simply take the English list at face value, as reflecting 17 different playwrights, and then compare the writers in order starting with Vere on the English side, Meres's carefully crafted parallel linkages do not work. The Stratfordian reading actually *destroys* the artful symmetry that Meres evidently labored to create.

---

[314] Waugh, "My Shakespeare," p. 71. Waugh suggested that Meres's fascination with the trinity is reflected in the threefold identification of Oxford here with the number 17: as the 17th earl of that name, as the 17th name listed from the top, and as the 17th name counting up from the end as well. See Waugh, "Francis Meres Knew" (2018).

[315] For example, "Menander (first on the classical side) pairs with Gager (first on the English side) because Menander was the imitator of Euripides and Gager the adapter of Euripides ...." Waugh, "My Shakespeare," p. 71 (citing Stritmatter). The points noted in text already imply that Vere is the odd one out. Waugh further noted that for Elizabethan numerologists: "One properly is no number." See also Shakespeare's *Sonnet* 136, line 8: "Among a number one is reckoned none." Waugh, "My Shakespeare," p. 71. Thus Vere, being at first glance number "one" on the English list, could properly be renumbered as zero and treated as "none," inviting and justifying his removal for purposes of the ensuing comparison of the 32 remaining names, as pursued by Stritmatter. The propriety of that maneuver is further justified and reinforced, in hindsight, given that retaining Vere would preclude and destroy the symmetry of Meres's evidently intended comparison of the classical and English writers on each list.

There is one final twist that further clinches this reading of *Palladis* as a potent source and expression of early authorship doubts. Which classical playwright did Meres implicitly compare to "Shakespeare," the eighth English comic playwright he lists (omitting Vere)? The eighth classical comedian listed is Aristonymus, an ancient Greek writer about whom little is known.

What little we do know about Aristonymus does *not* match up well to Shakespeare as conventionally understood: the commoner on the make from Stratford. Ah, but does he match up to *Vere?* Does anything about him suggest that the author Shakespeare was not Shakspere of Stratford but rather a cloaked aristocrat? Well, by marvelous coincidence—if you're a really determined believer in coincidences—what we do know is that "Aristonymus" *literally means an aristocratic (or noble) name* and that he was famous for ridiculing Aristophanes, his far better known contemporary and master of stage comedy. And why did he ridicule Aristophanes? Because Aristophanes sometimes used a front man to produce his own plays.[316] Enough said?

## 13.  Gabriel Harvey, Marginalia (*c.* 1598–1600)

Gabriel Harvey (*c.* 1553–1631), the pamphleteer we met in Part IV.3, wrote some marginal comments in a book he purchased. The book was published in 1598 and for various reasons it seems likely the comments date to some time within the following two years. Harvey's comments are famous mainly because they are among the few recorded remarks on the works of Shakespeare dating before the 1623 *First Folio.*[317]

---

[316] See Stritmatter (2017) (at minutes 50-53); see also Waugh, "My Shakespeare," p. 72 (discussing the meaning of Aristonymus's name but not his connection to Aristophanes).

[317] See, *e.g.*, Chambers (1930), v. 2, pp. 196-98; Price, pp. 232-33.

Harvey commented on something of a generation gap among admirers of the works of the author Shakespeare. He noted that "[t]he younger sort takes much delight in Shakespeare's Venus & Adonis." He then observed: "[B]ut his Lucrece, & his tragedy of Hamlet, Prince of Denmark, have it in them, to please the wiser sort." Harvey then quoted Latin lines by Ovid from the title page of *Venus and Adonis*, followed by the somewhat obscure comment: "quoth Sir Edward Dyer, between jest, & earnest."[318]

Dyer (1543–1607) has sometimes been suggested as a Shakespeare authorship candidate.[319] He was a poet and courtier who was knighted by Queen Elizabeth in 1596.

As Diana Price has noted, this marginalia may be read to suggest that Harvey suspected Dyer was the author of *Venus and Adonis*.[320] While that specific proposition is very dubious, and Harvey's comment is obscure and debatable, this constitutes one more item suggesting that doubts and questions were circulating in the 1590s about who the author Shakespeare really was.

## 14. John Weever, *Epigrams* (1599)

Alexander Waugh has observed that the poet and antiquarian John Weever (1576–1632), somewhat similarly to Meres (see Part IV.12), referred in a curiously linked way both to "Shakespeare" and to another writer who appears to be the same person.[321]

Weever's *Epigrams*, published in 1599, address various other poets of his time. Epigram No. 22, his most famous, is addressed explicitly to "Shakespeare" and seems to praise the author highly, though in a saucy tone. The first four lines read:

---

[318] Quoted in Chambers (1930), v. 2, p. 197.

[319] See Price, p. 8; see also Brooks (1943); Part IV.30 & note 801.

[320] See Price, pp. 232-33.

[321] See Waugh, "Weever" (2014); Waugh, "My Shakespeare" (2018), p. 72 (and his 2018–19 videos "John Weever Knew," Parts 1 and 2).

> Honey-tongued *Shakespeare* when I saw thine issue
> I swore *Apollo* got them and none other,
> Their rosy-tainted features clothed in tissue,
> Some heaven born goddess said to be their mother ....

The poem goes on to mention the characters Adonis, Venus, Lucrece, and Tarquin from Shakespeare's book-length poems of 1593–94, *Venus and Adonis* and *The Rape of Lucrece*.[322]

As Waugh suggests, No. 22—even taken by itself—is pregnant (my pun) with authorship doubts generally ignored by orthodox scholars. It openly suggests that this author's "issue" (literary works) are fathered by someone else (Apollo)—in other words, that they are plagiarized. Waugh construes "Apollo" as a veiled reference to Edward de Vere, which seems likely based on all the other evidence pointing to Vere as "Shakespeare," but must count as speculative if based strictly on Epigram No. 22.[323]

As Waugh first discussed in a fascinating 2014 article, however, more compelling evidence of authorship doubt is furnished by comparing No. 22 with Weever's Epigram No. 11, which is mysteriously prefaced (in Latin): *"In Spurium quendam scriptorem"* ("To Spurius, a certain writer"). The adjective "spurious," applied to a writing, means: "Not really proceeding from its reputed origin, source, or author."[324]

Epigram No. 11, only four lines long, states:

> *Apelles* did so paint *Venus* Queen,
> That most supposed he had fair *Venus* seen,
> But thy bald rhymes of *Venus* savour so,

---

[322] Quoted in Chambers (1930), v. 2, p. 199 (italics in original).

[323] See Waugh, "My Shakespeare," p. 72.

[324] Waugh, "Weever," p. 12; Waugh, "My Shakespeare," p. 72; *OED*, v. 16, p. 376. For more suggestions of plagiarism and frontmen, see Parts IV.2, 11, 15-16, 18, 26, and 28.

That I dare swear thou dost all *Venus* know.[325]

This epigram, like No. 22, seems clearly to refer to *Venus and Adonis*. "Spurius" must therefore be the purported author of that poem: "William Shakespeare." The two epigrams contain similarly leering innuendo. No. 22, as noted, implies illicit paternity. No. 11, more ribaldly, suggests the author *it* addresses has not only "seen" Venus in "all" her (naked?) beauty, but has actually "known" her ("all" of her)—in the biblical sense, readers are clearly meant to think.[326]

One implied message of No. 11, taken by itself, seems equally obvious: The author of *Venus and Adonis* writes under a pseudonym. The combination of Nos. 11 and 22—addressing the same author first as "Spurius" and then as "Shakespeare," while openly questioning his literary paternity in the second epigram—reinforces that message very strikingly indeed.[327]

Extending Waugh's analysis a bit further,[328] it may be recalled that Apelles—an ancient Greek painter known for lifelike depictions of Venus[329]—was also known for hiding his own creative role in presenting his artistic work. Weever's reference to

---

[325] Quoted in Waugh, "Weever," p. 12, and Waugh, "My Shakespeare," p. 72 n. 42 (italics in original). Nos. 11 and 22 both appear in the same chapter ("The Fourth Week") of Weever's book. See Waugh, "Weever," pp. 13-14.

[326] See Waugh, "Weever," pp. 12-14; Waugh, "My Shakespeare," p. 72.

[327] See Waugh, "Weever," p. 14; Waugh, "My Shakespeare," p. 72.

[328] Waugh himself extended his analysis, in a concededly more speculative vein, by noting that Weever went oddly out of his way—a case of "protesting too much"?—to *deny* any significance in the numbering of his epigrams. See Waugh, "Weever," p. 13. Given that two epigrams imply "Shakespeare" is a "double" for an unnamed author, Waugh suggested Weever may have amplified that hint (and suggested the linkage of the two epigrams) by numbering them so that the second (No. 22) is double the first (No. 11), with each of those numbers, in turn, being composed of doubled numerals. See Waugh, "Weever," pp. 13-14. Whether this is too much numerology for you is, I suppose, a matter of taste. Compare Part IV.12. The cursory treatment of Weever in Wells, "Allusions," p. 76, declined to quote No. 22's lines indicating authorship doubt and simply ignored No. 11 altogether.

[329] See Waugh, "Weever," pp. 12, 15 n. 3.

Apelles in No. 11 recalls the commentary on this painter by Thomas Heywood in his 1594 poem *Oenone and Paris*, discussed in Part IV.6—which was itself yet another commentary, more veiled than Weever's, on the author of *Venus and Adonis*.

Patrick O'Brien and Waugh have discussed the fascinating links between Weever, Cambridge University, Vere, and William Covell, whose 1595 anagram linking Vere with Shakespeare is discussed in Part IV.7. Covell was Weever's tutor at Cambridge, where Vere studied as a young boy.[330]

### 15. The *Parnassus* Plays: *Parnassus 2* (c. 1599–1600)

The three anonymous *Parnassus* plays, like Weever and Covell, provide more connections between Cambridge University and the SAQ. These plays were satirical comedies performed by and for the students of St. John's College at Cambridge. It is possible they were all written by the same author but we don't really know.[331]

*The Pilgrimage to Parnassus* ("*Parnassus 1*") is thought to have been written and performed by 1598 or 1599. The first part of *The Return From Parnassus* ("*Parnassus 2*") is thought to date from 1599 or 1600. The third play in the series, the second part of *The Return From Parnassus (The Scourge of Simony)* ("*Parnassus 3*"), dates to around 1601. *Parnassus 3* was published in 1606, but the first two plays are known only from surviving manuscripts. All three were mostly forgotten until published in a scholarly edition in the late 19th century.[332]

The *Parnassus* plays allegorically describe the progress of students through a traditional course of university education, as if

---

[330] See, *e.g.*, O'Brien (2014); Waugh, "My Shakespeare," p. 72.

[331] See Macray, pp. v-xi; see also, *e.g.*, Price, pp. 78-86; Ogburn, pp. 106-08; Chiljan, pp. 211-15.

[332] Macray (1886); see also Greenwood (1908), pp. 320-21.

undertaking a long journey in which they ultimately must climb Mount Parnassus.[333] The characters often bemoan the impoverished, disrespected, and discontented plight of scholars dependent on wealthy patrons and employers. The plays seem to satirize various targets, though many of their allusions "are by no means clear."[334] Yet they remain funny and quotable. One of many *bon mots* might work well as a t-shirt slogan to be worn by denizens of some academic departments even today: "I'll be a scholar, though I live but poor."[335]

The second and third plays are of interest here. As Diana Price among many scholars has noted, they "contain explicit allusions to Shakespeare, as well as some indirect hits."[336] As discussed in Part IV.2, *Groats-Worth of Wit* (1592) attacked the "upstart Crow" ("Shake-scene") as an arrogant and pretentious fraud and plagiarist who "beautified" himself with the words of others. Orthodox scholars insist the Crow was Shakespeare—a conclusion questioned in Part IV.2 but which, if true, highlights significant early authorship doubts.

Either way, even some orthodox scholars have noted that "Gullio," a character in *Parnassus 2*, seems reminiscent of the Crow and may also be seen as a satire of Shakspere the player. Indeed, an interlocking web of satirical references seems to connect the Crow, Gullio, Shakspere, and at least two characters in works by Ben Jonson: "Sogliardo" in his play *Every Man Out of His Humour* (1599) and the subject of his epigram "Poet-Ape."[337]

---

[333] Mount Parnassus is located in Greece above Delphi. According to Greek mythology it is sacred to Dionysus and Apollo. In some traditions it is viewed as the home of the Muses (mythical beings who inspire poetry, music, art, and learning); other traditions accord that honor to Mount Helicon, which is part of the same range. See Part IV.3, note 180.

[334] Macray, p. viii.

[335] *Parnassus 1*, act 1, line 64 (Consiliodorus), in Macray, p. 3.

[336] Price, p. 78.

[337] See Part IV.28 (discussing Jonson's pre-1616 writings); see also, *e.g.*, Part IV.16 & notes 365-69 (discussing *Parnassus 3*'s suggestions of plagiarism),

(footnote continued on next page)

Gullio is a vain, foppish, gullible braggart—literally a "gull."[338] He is not an aristocrat nor even a knight, but has pretensions of social standing, comparing himself to Sir Philip Sidney and boasting that he wears at least two outfits every day at court.[339] "Ingenioso," another character in *Parnassus 2*, is a one-time scholar who now works for a printing house.[340] Ingenioso mocks Gullio's social pretensions in a way that seems to go over Gullio's head: "I wonder such a gallant as you are scapes the marriage of some Countess."[341]

As Price observed, *Parnassus 2* ridicules Gullio as a plagiarist who borrows from the author Shakespeare and who "never spoke [a] witty thing but out of a play."[342] When Gullio lifts a garbled line from *Romeo and Juliet*, Ingenioso remarks in an

---

(footnote continued from previous page)
notes 386-96 (discussing "Sir Adam Prickshaft" in Dekker's *Satiromastix*); Price, pp. 66-75, 78-82, 87-90; Chiljan, ch. 12, pp. 203-16; Michell, pp. 67-74.

[338] *Parnassus 2*, act 3, sc. 1, lines 854-55, in Macray, p. 52, quoted in Chiljan, p. 211 (Ingenioso addressing the audience as Gullio enters): "Now, gentlemen, you may laugh if you will, for here comes a gull." "Gullio" and "gull" may also be seen as puns on "Gulielmum," the Latin version of William Shakspere's first name. See Price, p. 79; Chiljan, pp. 203, 211.

[339] Act 3, sc. 1, lines 922-27, 957-62, in Macray, pp. 54-55. Among other comparisons, Gullio muses daftly that Sidney "died in the Low Countries, and so I think shall I." Act 3, sc. 1, lines 961-62, in Macray, p. 55. He claims friendship with "[a] Countess and two lords," *id.*, lines 1060-62, in Macray, p. 58. He later claims: "The Countess and my lord entertained me very honorably [at dinner]." In a line that seems reminiscent of Edward de Vere (Earl of Oxford) and efforts to marry off his three daughters, Gullio asserts: "Indeed they used my advice in some state matters, and I perceived the Earl would fain have thrust one of his daughters upon me; but I will have no knave priest to meddle with my ring." Act 4, sc. 1, lines 1123-27, in Macray, p. 60. Ingenioso, in an aside to the audience, ridicules Gullio's claims. *Id.*, lines 1130-33, in Macray, pp. 60-61; see also Anderson, pp. 279-80 (also connecting this scene with Vere, while suggesting that Gullio is satirizing Henry Wriothesley, Earl of Southampton).

[340] See act 1, sc. 1, lines 137-64, in Macray, p. 30.

[341] Act 3, sc. 1, lines 935-36 (see also lines 937-46), in Macray, p. 54.

[342] Act 5, sc. 1, line 1467, in Macray, p. 71, quoted in Price, pp. 78, 86; see generally act 3, sc. 1, act 4, sc. 1, and act 5, sc. 1, in Macray, pp. 52-58, 60-64, 68-72; Price, pp. 78-79, 81-82; Chiljan, pp. 211-14.

aside to the audience: "O monstrous theft!"[343] Gullio vainly re-
works lines from *Venus and Adonis* as his own, changing "thus
she began" to "thus I began."[344] Gullio is quite unabashed about
his fondness for regurgitating Shakespeare, perhaps suggesting
that authorship questions were an open secret at the time.

Gullio hires Ingenioso to write verses to woo the female
objects of his affection in the style of several poets, including
Shakespeare. Gullio exclaims: "O sweet Mr. Shakspeare! I'll have
his picture in my study at the court."[345] Later he comments: "I'll
worship sweet Mr. Shakspeare, and to honour him will lay his
*Venus and Adonis* under my pillow ...."[346] But Gullio is spurned as
a plagiarist even by one of the ladies he pursues.[347]

---

[343] Act 3, sc. 1, line 1015, in Macray, p. 57, quoted and discussed in Price, p.
82, and Chiljan, p. 212.

[344] Act 3, sc. 1, lines 1018-23, in Macray, p. 57, quoted and discussed in
Price, p. 81, and in Chiljan (who noted that "Alden Brooks [in 1943] first noticed
that Gullio was here attributing these Shakespeare lines to himself"), pp. 213,
424 & n. 14, citing Brooks.

[345] Act 3, sc. 1, lines 1054-55, in Macray, p. 58; see also lines 1037-52, in
Macray, pp. 57-58. When Ingenioso recites his verses in Shakespeare's "vein"
(they parody *Venus and Adonis*), Gullio exclaims with approval: "I am one that
can judge according to the proverb, *bovem ex unguibus.*" Act 4, sc. 1, lines 1212,
1220-21, in Macray, p. 63 (italics in original).

Alexander Waugh noted that Gullio's Latin phrase oddly revises the well-
known proverb, to "know the lion by its claw," to an unfamiliar version, to "know
the ox by its hoof," thus hinting intriguingly that Edward de Vere (Earl of Oxford) was the author hidden behind the name "Shakespeare." Waugh noted evidence that Vere was known to some associates by the nickname "Ox." Waugh, "My
Shakespeare" (2018), pp. 63-64 & n. 31; see also *Cassell's Latin Dictionary*, p. 79
(*bovillus* or *bovum* as "relating to oxen"), p. 624 (*ungula* or *unguis* as "hoof, claw,
talon").

[346] Act 4, sc. 1, lines 1223-25, in Macray, p. 63. The manuscript source of
*Parnassus 2* (which was apparently never printed in its own time) spells the
author's name consistently as "Shakspeare." See Part III.A (discussing the variability of spelling in early modern England and especially, in note 13, that one
would expect more variability in handwritten manuscripts).

[347] Act 5, sc. 1, line 1441, in Macray, p. 70 (quoting Lesbia with regard to a
letter Ingenioso delivers to her from Gullio: "I am sure not a word of it proceeds
from his pen ...."); see also *id.*, lines 1377-84, in Macray, p. 68. These references
resonate with similar suggestions of plagiarism and frontmen discussed in Parts
IV.2, 11, 14, 16, 18, 26, and 28.

The meaning of all this satire remains obscure, as noted earlier. *Parnassus 2* is far from the strongest early expression of authorship doubt explored in this book.[348] Katherine Chiljan noted: "There is a clear separation between Gullio and Shakespeare: ... he cannot actually be Shakespeare."[349]

But as Price and Chiljan suggested, Gullio may be viewed as a send-up of Shakspere of Stratford, thus differentiating both from the *author* Shakespeare. As Price noted, "when it comes to identifying 'Shakespeare,' [the *Parnassus* plays] convey two distinctly separate images." Depictions of Gullio—and of Shakspere the player in *Parnassus 3*, as we will see in Part IV.16—"are distinct from" those of "Shakespeare, the admired poet."[350]

Chiljan noted that since Gullio seems to be "imitating and impersonating" the author Shakespeare, we may look to Gullio's boasts and lies about himself for clues about how the author was perceived and understood.[351] In that light, *Parnassus 2* suggests, very intriguingly, that the author was among other things a champion jouster who lived in a grand home, who socialized with aristocrats, traveled to Italy, was a patron of scholars and poets, was celebrated by students when visiting Oxford University, and was often compared to the courtier poet Sir Philip Sidney.[352]

---

[348] Price, pp. 81-82, suggested that *Parnassus 2* implicitly attributes *Romeo and Juliet* to Samuel Daniel. See act 3, sc. 1, lines 1015-17, in Macray, p. 57 (after Gullio's garbled quotation of the play, Ingenioso exclaiming: "Mark, *Romeo and Juliet!* O monstrous theft! I think he will run through a whole book of Samuel Daniel's!"). I disagree with that reading. As Price herself noted, *Romeo and Juliet* was publicly credited to "Shakespeare" in 1598 by Francis Meres's *Palladis Tamia* (see Part IV.12). *Parnassus 2* dates to *c.* 1599–1600. I think the more likely reading is that Ingenioso is simply commenting on Gullio's theft from Shakespeare and then suggesting something like: "Next thing you know, he'll steal even more from another writer, Samuel Daniel."

[349] Chiljan, p. 214.

[350] Price, p. 84.

[351] Chiljan, p. 214.

[352] See Chiljan, pp. 214-15; see also note 339 above and related text.

Those attributes fit far better, overall, with Edward de Vere (Earl of Oxford) than with William Shakspere of Stratford.[353]

## 16. The *Parnassus* Plays: *Parnassus 3* (c. 1601)

The third *Parnassus* play is the longest of the three and generally the least enjoyable and most difficult to follow. The leading characters of the trilogy, struggling scholars Philomusus and Studioso, have sought their fortunes in Rome but now return in abject failure to England. Studioso comments that "it's as good to starve mongst English swine, As in a foreign land to beg and pine."[354]

Giving up the honest ideals of scholarly life, Philomusus and Studioso explore various other professions and resort to being conmen and grifters.[355] One gambit they pursue is acting for the stage, a calling generally held in low regard at the time. They are auditioned by characters representing real-life theatrical personalities Richard Burbage (1567–1619) and Will Kempe (?–1603).[356]

Burbage, the tragic actor and successful theatrical businessman, was a colleague of William Shakspere of Stratford and is thought to have been his friend. Burbage seems to have achieved (for an actor) a rare degree of popular respect and even adulation. His death, said to have almost eclipsed that of King James's consort Queen Anne just ten days earlier, occasioned an enormous outpouring of grief and numerous elegies—in curious and striking contrast to the deafening relative silence that greeted Shakspere's

---

[353] See note 339, and Part I, note 4.

[354] *Parnassus 3*, act 1, sc. 4, lines 402-03, in Macray, p. 90; see also *id.*, lines 384-91, in Macray, p. 90.

[355] See, *e.g.*, act 1, sc. 4, lines 422-46, in Macray, pp. 91-92.

[356] See act 4, sc. 3, in Macray, pp. 138-43. Leading up to this, Philomusus and Studioso reach a truly desperate state by act 3, scene 5, bemoaning their lot in almost suicidal terms, *e.g.*, lines 1443-44, in Macray, p. 126 (Studioso: "Not long this loathed life can run, Soon cometh death, and then our woe is done.").

death three years before.[357] Kempe, a comedian, was a theatrical colleague of Burbage and Shakspere, though he parted ways in unclear circumstances and died in obscurity.

The main interest of *Parnassus 3* for the SAQ is a brief bit of dialogue between "Kempe" and "Burbage" as they await the arrival of the forlorn scholars. Kempe expresses doubt that university students can act well, ridiculing a play he saw at Cambridge— seemingly a self-referential jab at the *Parnassus* plays themselves that surely got a good laugh from the student audience. Burbage replies: "A little teaching will mend these faults, and it may be besides they will be able to pen a part."[358] Kempe retorts:

> Few of the university [men] pen plays well, they smell too much of that writer *Ovid*, and that writer *Metamorphosis* [*sic*], and talk too much of *Proserpina* and *Jupiter*. Why here's our fellow *Shakespeare* puts them all down, [aye] and *Ben Jonson* too. Oh that *Ben Jonson* is a pestilent fellow ... but our fellow *Shakespeare* hath given him a purge ....[359]

Burbage, apparently referring to Shakespeare, agrees that he's "a shrewd fellow indeed."[360]

---

[357] See Part I & note 34. *Parnassus 3* testifies to the fame of Burbage and Kempe. The character "Kempe" boasts to Philomusus and Studioso (in humorously self-serving lines which yet have the ring of truth):

> [B]e merry my lads, you have happened upon the most excellent vocation in the world for money: they come North and South to bring it to our playhouse, and for honours, who of more report, than *Dick Burbage and Will Kempe*, he is not counted a Gentleman, that knows not *Dick Burbage and Will Kempe*, there's not a country wench ... but can talk of *Dick Burbage and Will Kempe*.

Act 4, sc. 3, lines 1828-35, in Macray, p. 139 (italics in original).

[358] Act 4, sc. 3, lines 1804-05 (see also lines 1801-03), in Macray, p. 138.

[359] Act 4, sc. 3, lines 1806-12, in Macray, p. 138 (italics in original; bracketed "men" added by Macray; bracketed "aye" added here, replacing original "I").

[360] Act 4, sc. 3, line 1814, in Macray, p. 139.

This certainly seems at first blush to be intriguing evidence supporting the Stratfordian authorship theory—perhaps the best piece of contemporaneous evidence the Stratfordians have. Counting the debatable 1592 reference to "Shake-scene" in *Groats-Worth of Wit*, discussed in Part IV.2, this is (to my knowledge) one of only three references predating the *First Folio* of 1623 that connect the author Shakespeare to an actor who more typically spelled his name Shakspere. Stratfordians like David Kathman have often touted *Parnassus 3*, very understandably.[361]

The problem for Stratfordians is that this same passage, viewed in context, mocks and questions that very connection. Their best (and lonely) piece of evidence—a brief satirical reference in an anonymous play—is simultaneously (like the other two references mentioned above) an early expression of authorship doubt. Sir George Greenwood was (to my knowledge) the first scholar to discuss this in print, in 1908. He noted it was "surely needless to point out"—but apparently doubters *do need to keep pointing it out*—"that a University dramatist, writing for a University audience, did not intend to be taken seriously when he made player Kempe say, 'few of the University men pen plays well'!"[362]

Indeed, the entire scene ridicules uncultured *nouveau-riche* players like Kempe and Burbage—and their "fellow Shakespeare" to the extent that refers to Shakspere the actor. But how, one may ask, can this be reconciled with the respectful admiration in both the second and third *Parnassus* plays for the works of the *author* Shakespeare? The answer, as suggested in Part IV.15, is that they

---

[361] See, *e.g.*, Kathman, "Shakespeare Wrote Shakespeare" (2009), p. 17; Reedy & Kathman (item 5a); see also Greenwood (1908), pp. 319-20 (noting that even then, this passage was "constantly cited" by Stratfordians). The third reference, which they don't seem to tout as much, is in Davies of Hereford's *Microcosmos* (1603). See Part IV.20.

[362] Greenwood (1908), p. 322 (omitting brackets and modernizing spelling in Greenwood's quotation of the play, but leaving his capitalization of "University").

seem to draw a curious distinction between the two.[363] As soon as Kempe and Burbage are out of earshot,[364] the scholars vent their contempt for the players. Philomusus fumes: "[M]ust the basest trade [acting] yield us relief? Must we be practiced to those leaden spouts [actors], That nought [do] vent but what they do receive?"[365] In other words, players do nothing but recite lines they are given by the true authors of the plays they perform. As Charlton Ogburn Jr. noted, this could not possibly be true of Shakespeare if he actually was both a player and a writer, and thus the *Parnassus 3* author could not have seriously believed or meant to imply that he was.[366]

In the next scene, the scholars having joined a band of itinerant fiddlers, Studioso continues to seethe with scorn for players, mixed with bitter envy and resentment at the actors' recently improved social standing:

---

[363] See Price, pp. 80, 84. An earlier passage in *Parnassus 3* refers briefly but respectfully to *"William Shakespeare"* as an author (emphasis in original), with no hint there of any connection to a player from Stratford. The character "Judicio," a publisher who seems well-educated and well-informed, comments: "Who loves [not *Adons* love, or *Lucrece* rape?] His sweeter verse contains heart [throbbing line], Could but a graver subject him content, Without love's foolish lazy languishment." Act 1, sc. 2, lines 304-08, in Macray, p. 87 (italics in original; brackets by Macray); see also Chiljan, p. 215. The gentle chiding that Shakespeare should direct his talents more to "graver subjects" seems odd, since *The Rape of Lucrece* itself is a very grave work of art, and *Parnassus 3* later quotes the memorable opening lines of the eminently serious play *Richard III*. See *Parnassus 3*, act 4, sc. 3, lines 1876-79, in Macray, p. 141 (Philomusus, at Burbage's instruction, reciting: "Now is the winter of our discontent, Made glorious summer by the son of York."). Compare Price, pp. 80-81.

[364] There is no explicit "exit" stage direction at line 1885, but Burbage and Kempe indicate they are leaving at that point to confer with their "fellows" and they invite Philomusus and Studioso to follow them. See act 4, sc. 3, lines 1881-85, in Macray, p. 141. The players have no further lines and do not respond to the ensuing insults by Philomusus. Dialogue between the scholars rounds out the scene as they continue to lament their lot. See *id.*, lines 1886-1952, in Macray, pp. 141-43.

[365] Act 4, sc. 3, lines 1886-88, in Macray, p. 141 (first two sets of brackets added here; bracketed "doe" added by Macray, with spelling modernized here as usual; see my Preface), quoted and discussed in Greenwood (1908), p. 330.

[366] See Ogburn, p. 108.

Better it is mongst fiddlers to be chief,
Than at [a] player's trencher [plate] beg relief.
But ist not strange [these] mimic apes should prize
Unhappy Scholars at a hireling rate.
Vile world, that lifts them [players] up to high degree,
And treads us [scholars] down in groveling misery.
*England* affords those glorious vagabonds,
That carried erst their fardels[367] on their backs,
Coursers [fine horses] to ride on through the gazing
    streets,
Sooping[368] it in their glaring Satin suits,
And Pages to attend their masterships:
With *mouthing words that better wits have framed,*
They purchase lands, and now Esquires are [named].[369]

Greenwood provided further essential context in which to consider Kempe's reference to "our fellow Shakespeare" as a playwright who "puts ... down" all the university-educated writers. His reference to a writer named "Metamorphosis" (*Metamorphoses* being a work by Ovid), was obviously intended as a thigh-slapper highlighting his ignorance as a player.[370] And if any writer "smell[s] too much of ... Ovid ... and talk[s] too much of Proserpina

---

367 *I.e.*, that used to carry their bundled belongings on their backs. "Erst" is an archaic term for "formerly" and "fardel" for "bundle." *OED*, v. 5, pp. 379, 729.

368 "Soop" is a Scottish and northern English dialectal verb (mostly archaic) meaning to sweep or clear away. *OED*, v. 15, p. 1013.

369 Act 5, sc. 1, lines 1956-68, in Macray, pp. 143-44 (first italics in original, second added here; bracketed "a," "these," and "named" added by Macray; other brackets added here), quoted and discussed in Greenwood (1908), pp. 329-30.

As many have noted, there is a striking resonance between these passages in *Parnassus 3* and the diatribe against players (including the Crow) in *Groats-Worth of Wit*. Studioso goes on to lament that "fortune" has converted "ragged grooms" like the players into "gallants," act 5, sc. 1, lines 1971-72, in Macray, p. 144, just as the *Groats-Worth* author, in 1592, lambasted players as "rude grooms." See, *e.g.*, Part IV.2.a (quoting and discussing similar passage in *Groats-Worth of Wit*); Price, pp. 84-85; Erne, "Mythography," p. 433 (discussed in Part IV.2.g, note 108); see also Part IV.15 & note 337 (discussing linkages between *Parnassus 2*, *Groats-Worth*, and Ben Jonson characters). For more discussions of suggested plagiarism and frontmen, see Parts IV.2, 11, 14-15, 18, 26, and 28.

370 See Greenwood (1908), p. 322; Ogburn, p. 106; Price, pp. 82-83; Chiljan, p. 215.

and Jupiter," that would be Shakespeare himself.[371] His deep debt to Ovid, in addition to being well-documented by modern orthodox scholars, was well-known when *Parnassus 3* was written and performed, having been prominently noted just a few years before.[372] Shakespeare refers copiously to deities in classical mythology, including Jupiter and Proserpina.[373]

In sum, Greenwood argued, Kempe's praise-by-contrast for Shakespeare is so absurdly and humorously mistaken as to make it "obvious ... that the passage, so far from being intended to be taken in its literal sense, conveyed to the audience the very opposite meaning."[374] As Ogburn similarly argued, it tells us that

> only an ignoramus would be able to believe that Shakespeare was a fellow of such as Kempe the clown. If the passage is not mocking the attribution of Shakespeare's works to an ill-educated fellow of two actors, then I should like to have the Stratfordians explain why Kempe is made to speak as he does.[375]

As Chiljan summarized, both the second and third *Parnassus* plays seem to have "mock[ed]" and "ridiculed the confusion between the Stratford Man and the great author's pen name."[376]

More cautiously than Greenwood, Ogburn, or Chiljan (though I find their analysis rather persuasive), I would align myself here only with Greenwood's more measured suggestion (quoted in part by Price) that the Kempe-Burbage passage in *Parnassus 3*, at the

---

[371] See Greenwood (1908), p. 323; Ogburn, pp. 106-07; Price, p. 83; Chiljan, p. 215.

[372] See Meres, *Palladis Tamia* (1598), quoted and discussed in Part IV.12 & note 295, and in Ogburn, p. 107; see also Bate, *Shakespeare and Ovid* (1993).

[373] See Greenwood (1908), p. 323; Ogburn, p. 107; see also, *e.g.*, Spevack, pp. 654, 1019 (35 references in 11 works to Jupiter; three references in three works to Proserpina, including a memorable one by Perdita in *The Winter's Tale*, act 4, sc. 4, cited by Greenwood and Ogburn).

[374] Greenwood (1908), p. 323.

[375] Ogburn, p. 107; see also Price, pp. 82-85; Anderson, p. xxxi.

[376] Chiljan, p. 215.

very least, "is quite consistent with the theory that Shakespeare was a mask name" and that "[t]he whole scene is evidently a burlesque in which the poor players are held up to ridicule for their ignorance generally, and for their distorted notions as to 'Shakespeare' and Jonson in particular."[377] In other words, the scene raises intriguing questions and implies strong doubts (at least) about the Stratfordian authorship attribution playfully suggested on its literal surface.

It must be kept in mind, however, as Ogburn conceded, that this passage shows the player Shakspere of Stratford was "being spoken of as the poet-dramatist [Shakespeare]"[378] by around the turn of the 17th century—if only in a satirically mocking way. Perhaps many people had come to view him by then as a playwright, either mistakenly or as part of a widely accepted polite fiction. This passage may be read as hinting that he was widely known or suspected as a frontman for a hidden author. Perhaps he was mocked as someone known to be fond of passing himself off as a writer. This all suggests, among other things, that even if the similarity of the names began as merely coincidental, some connection had been created or drawn by around 1600.[379]

Kathman was given an excellent opportunity in 2009 to offer the best possible Stratfordian response to Ogburn's above-quoted challenge on *Parnassus 3*. He was invited to publish an article summarizing the Stratfordian theory in *The Oxfordian*, a scholarly journal devoted primarily to exploring evidence for Edward de Vere's authorship of the Shakespeare canon. This illustrates the eagerness of authorship doubters to engage in serious and constructive debate, even as Oxfordian and other skeptical studies remain almost completely excluded from orthodox journals and

---

[377] Greenwood (1908), pp. 328-29 (emphasis added); see also Price, p. 83 (quoting the latter comment).

[378] Ogburn, p. 108.

[379] See Part III.A & notes 23-24.

conferences and skeptical scholars continue to be treated by Stratfordians (for the most part) with contempt and derision.[380]

Kathman gave prominent treatment to *Parnassus 3*, understandably citing it as "evidence" that "tie[s] actor Shakespeare explicitly to author Shakespeare." His relevant analysis is quoted in full here:

> The 1601 Cambridge play *[Parnassus 3]* includes Will Kempe and Richard Burbage of the Chamberlain's Men as characters, and at one point Kempe refers to "our fellow Shakespeare" as a rival of the university playwrights and Ben Jonson.
>
> Charlton Ogburn [Jr.] asserts that Kempe's mention of "that writer Ovid, and that writer Metamorphosis" shows that he is too ignorant to be taken seriously, and that the whole passage is mocking the idea that the writer Shakespeare could have been an actor. The passage makes perfect sense if the phrase in question is emended to "that writer's Metamorphosis," but even if we treat it as a comic blunder by Kemp[e], Ogburn's attempt to make it mean the opposite of what it says is typical of his aggressively deceptive rhetorical style. Kemp[e] and Burbage are clearly comic characters being used by the Cambridge playwright to make fun of professional actors, but that doesn't mean that everything they say is false. In fact, the *Parnassus* scene merely reinforces all the other evidence ... for identifying actor Shakespeare with author Shakespeare.[381]

---

[380] Ironically, this very article became an example of that rude contempt. It disparaged anti-Stratfordian scholars in general, and Diana Price and Professor Roger Stritmatter in particular, in remarkably snide and offensive terms. See Kathman, "Shakespeare Wrote Shakespeare" (2009), pp. 13, 22-23; see also Part IV.2.d & note 77. Kathman, I note again, is nonetheless a scholar whom I respect, whose work I often find valuable. See, *e.g.*, Parts II & notes 16, 18, III.A & notes 2, 13, IV.21 & note 535, IV.24, note 601, and IV.26 & notes 676-77.

[381] Kathman, "Shakespeare Wrote Shakespeare" (2009), p. 17 (footnote citing Ogburn, pp. 106-08, omitted here). The "other evidence" to which Kathman referred, dating from Shakspere of Stratford's lifetime, fails to connect him in

(footnote continued on next page)

But if this is the best a leading Stratfordian can do, with their strongest single item of contemporaneous evidence, their theory has serious problems. Kathman's argument illustrates the inadequate treatment of context—and sheer obtuseness and lack of common sense—too often seen in Stratfordian polemics. Yet he and other Stratfordians are fond of railing against authorship doubters for allegedly paying inadequate attention to "context."[382]

That Kathman suggested rewriting a key line as "that writer's Metamorphosis" is almost as funny as the play he proposed to mangle. Hello! *Parnassus 3* is a comedy! You want to eliminate part of the humor? Greenwood, by the way, noted more than a century before Kathman's article that two orthodox scholars had mistakenly rendered that line exactly as Kathman proposed to consciously alter it. Greenwood noted they did "not seem to have perceived that the players are being held up to ridicule."[383]

What's Kathman's excuse? As quoted above, he grudgingly acknowledged the passage's satirical intent. "Emend" the phrase, my foot. The alteration obviously would *not* cause the line, as Kathman absurdly claimed, to "make perfect sense." It would *destroy* its contextual (comedic) sense and intent. It would render the line more literally accurate, but the play is not a school lesson. What the alteration would mainly do is clear away a small impediment to the Stratfordian theory. So inconvenient, sometimes, that documentary record!

The alteration would not even accomplish much for Kathman. The passage would remain sarcastic and satirical. It would still (on the surface) criticize the university writers for features actually more associated with the (purported) object of Kempe's praise,

---

(footnote continued from previous page)
any direct, specific, or personal way with the literary works of Shakespeare. That is typical of most Stratfordian "ample early evidence" claims. See Part I.

[382] See, *e.g.*, Kathman, "Why I Am Not an Oxfordian" (discussed in Part IV.2.d & note 77); Ross, "Oxfordian Myths: First Heir" (discussed in Part III.A, note 28); see also Part IV.3, note 180.

[383] Greenwood (1908), p. 322 n. 1.

"our fellow Shakespeare." The *context* would continue to support Ogburn's reading and undermine Kathman's. Grant Kathman's point that the context does not mean "everything [the players] say is false." That's a red herring. Ogburn did not claim (and need not have) any such thing. He argued that we cannot rely on Kempe's comment at face value and even, as Kathman complained, that it may "mean the opposite of what it says." But doesn't comedy often consist of saying something that unwittingly means the opposite of what the speaker appears or intends to say?

On a more serious note, we must pause at Kathman's charge that Ogburn—a deeply thoughtful writer and scholar with many fine books to his credit, on the SAQ and a diverse range of other subjects—was "aggressively deceptive." The charge is puzzling at best—and gratuitously offensive—since Ogburn accurately quoted the text at issue and transparently set forth his reasons for reading it as he did. He might in theory be wrong, even wildly wrong, but not "deceptive."

Kathman, likewise, was not being deceptive in openly proposing—however laughably and wrongheadedly—to rewrite part of the documentary record by altering a key line. But it does call to mind another article by Kathman. Was Kathman deceptive in silently altering the documented spelling of the name of Shakspere's grandson?[384] Stratfordians seem not to be very comfortable with the historical record confronting all of us.

Sir Jonathan Bate has briefly discussed this same passage in *Parnassus 3*. Unlike Kathman, he did not fight the fact that "Kempe reveals his ignorance by thinking that *Metamorphosis* [*sic*] is the name of a writer rather than a work by Ovid."[385] Bate, blithely wedded to the Stratfordian theory, seemed otherwise obli-

---

[384] See Kathman, "Shakespeare and Warwickshire" (2013), p. 125, discussed in Part III.A & note 9; see also Part IV.26 & notes 678-81 (discussing a clearly deceptive argument by Kathman and Tom Reedy).

[385] Bate, *Soul of the Age*, p. 354.

vious to the authorship doubts implied by this passage and its context, even as his own discussion unwittingly proceeded to amplify those doubts.

Bate connected Kempe's reference to Shakespeare giving Ben Jonson a "purge" to Thomas Dekker's play *Satiromastix* performed in the fall of 1601, apparently not long before *Parnassus 3*.[386] That linkage seems sound enough, part of the "poets' war" (*poetomachia*) in which Jonson (in his play *Poetaster*) and Dekker (in *Satiromastix*) made playfully figurative use of "emetic pills" and "purges."[387] Bate explained why Kempe did not refer to *Dekker* giving Jonson the purge by noting that *Satiromastix* was performed by the Lord Chamberlain's Men.

Bate suggested that Shakespeare acted in the play. While he conceded uncertainty as to which role he may have played, Shakespeare may have been sufficiently associated with the purge to make the *Parnassus 3* reference understandable and funny. Bate noted that one character in *Satiromastix*, "Sir Adam Prickshaft," may have been named precisely to poke fun at the phallic overtones of Shakespeare's own name.[388]

This is all very logical and amusing as far as it goes. What is downright funny is that Bate—even while insisting that Shakspere the player was also "Shakespeare ... the ... company

---

[386] *Satiromastix*, which Bate noted meant "the whipping of the satirist," was published under that title (used consistently here for clarity, as Bate did) in 1602, but was performed the autumn before as *The Untrussing of the Humourous Poet.* See Bate, *Soul of the Age*, p. 355. One might argue that Dekker (*c.* 1572–1632) and *Satiromastix* merit separate treatment as an early source of authorship doubt. But I elect to be cautious and combine them here with *Parnassus 3*— with a note of appreciation to Bate for drawing the connection.

[387] See Bate, *Soul of the Age*, pp. 354-55; Donaldson, pp. 168-74.

[388] See Bate, *Soul of the Age*, pp. 355-59. Just to be clear, credit (or blame) for the use of "poke" here rests with me, not Bate. We agree that, as Bate put it: "The combination of *shake* and phallic *speare*, especially in conjunction with the first name Will, has robust bawdy possibilities." Bate, p. 356 (emphases in original). So, yeah ... doesn't that (among *many other reasons*) cause Bate to suspect, just a tiny bit, that it might be a pseudonym?

dramatist"[389]—conceded that the author of *Parnassus 3* "may [in this passage] be [making] an allusion to Shakespeare the actor as well as, *or instead of*, Shakespeare the writer."[390] Exactly so!

Even more startling—right after linking Shakespeare with "Sogliardo" from Jonson's *Every Man Out of His Humour*[391]—Bate began discussing parallels between Prickshaft and Shakespeare. Prickshaft, Bate observed, *"is a bad amateur writer, a foolish aspirational gentleman poet."*[392] Sounds an awful lot like Gullio in *Parnassus 2*, and how all the players (including Shakespeare) are satirically mocked in *Parnassus 3*.[393] Bate proceeded to describe other ways in which Prickshaft seems to be a satire of Shakespeare—*"the actor,"* Bate suggested in conclusion.[394] So wait a second—did Bate just agree with Greenwood, Ogburn, Price, and Chiljan that some sly distinction was being drawn here between the Shakespearean *doppelgängers*—player and writer? Not quite. The Stratfordian blinders still obscured his vision. "It would have been very witty," averred Bate, for this fake would-be writer to be "played by the supreme professional, Master William Shakespeare."[395]

Possibly. But *that* would only make fun of *Prickshaft*. Is it not *more* funny (in a meta sort of way) to imagine Prickshaft being played by the very actor (and similarly fake would-be writer) that his character appears to satirize? More credit to Shakespeare the

---

[389] Bate, *Soul of the Age*, p. 356.

[390] Bate, *Soul of the Age*, p. 357 (emphasis added).

[391] See Part IV.15 & note 337 (further discussed in Part IV.28).

[392] Bate, *Soul of the Age*, p. 356 (emphasis added).

[393] For similar suggestions of plagiarism and frontmen, see Parts IV.2, 11, 14-15, 18, 26, and 28.

[394] Bate, *Soul of the Age*, pp. 356-57 (noting a parallel in Prickshaft's opening lines to those of Justice Shallow in *Henry IV, Part 2*, and that *Satiromastix* repeatedly mocks Prickshaft for being partly bald, just like purported images of Shakespeare; emphasis added to *"the actor,"* p. 357). Bate refrained from observing that the gags about Prickshaft's baldness and "remnant or parcel of hair" (*Satiromastix*, quoted in Bate, p. 357), may well add to the phallic humor.

[395] Bate, *Soul of the Age*, p. 356.

player if he had a big enough sense of humor to go along with that! After all, Bate himself, in this very same discussion, documented (as noted above) how Dekker seems to use Prickshaft precisely to make *Shakspere* the ultimate butt of the joke.[396]

These competing readings of the *Parnassus* plays do cause me to wonder: If the author Shakespeare was in fact an actor from Stratford, how would a satire, *circa* 1600, most likely target him and his works? Not, I daresay, by posing a contrast with features criticized in and attributed to other writers, that are actually found more clearly in Shakespeare's own works, that do not in fact merit criticism, and that would not likely *be* criticized by an educated audience.

Perhaps a satirist might offer laughably excessive praise for the works? *Parnassus 2* (via Gullio), as discussed in Part IV.15, offers some gestures in that direction. But as we have seen, the *Parnassus* plays generally do *not* target Shakespeare's literary works with any strong criticism. Rather, they express considerable respect and admiration for his works.[397]

One would think a satire aimed at a writer seriously understood as a common player might be harsher and might target (and explicitly link him to) features of his plays that seem designed to curry popular favor. *Parnassus 1*, as it happens, ridicules the popularity of clown characters in plays, in a scene that makes a passing swipe at Kempe.[398] Clowns and fools, as we all know, pop

---

[396] See note 394 and related text.

[397] On this point, I disagree with Greenwood, who stated, p. 327, that "[t]o be eulogised by this fool [Gullio], is, of course, the reverse of recommendation." See generally Greenwood (1908), pp. 326-28. I would suggest, in agreement with Price, pp. 78-84, and Chiljan, pp. 211-15, that *Parnassus 2* ridicules Gullio (and perhaps the Stratford actor whom he may represent), not the author Shakespeare.

[398] Toward the end of act 5 (which consists of a single long scene), a character named Dromo comes on stage "drawing a clown in with a rope." The clown understandably objects and Dromo replies: "Why, what an ass art thou! Dost thou not know a play cannot be without a clown? Clowns have been thrust into plays by head and shoulders ever since Kempe could make a scurvy face ...."

(footnote continued on next page)

up in quite a few Shakespeare plays. But *Parnassus 1* does not allude to Shakespeare (actor or author), there or elsewhere.

*Parnassus 2*, when it does allude to Shakespeare, quotes and refers mainly to his beloved romantic works *Romeo and Juliet* (no classic clown or fool character) and *Venus and Adonis* (his epic erotic poem).[399] *Parnassus 3* refers again to *Venus and Adonis*, and to its more sober and high-minded follow-up poem *Lucrece*, and later quotes the serious and admired play *Richard III* (again no clown character).[400]

And, as we have seen, *Parnassus 3* refers to a "fellow [player] Shakespeare"—with no linkage to any literary work by him except the quotation of *Richard III* several pages later—in a scene designed to ridicule all such players and, it seems, to mock the very idea that such a player might actually be a writer.[401]

---

(footnote continued from previous page)
Lines 671-77, in Macray, p. 22, quoted and discussed in Greenwood (1908), pp. 323-24. The poor clown asks: "But what must I do now?"

> *Dromo[:]* Why, if thou canst but draw thy mouth awry, lay thy leg over thy staff, saw a piece of cheese asunder with thy dagger, lap up drinking on the earth, I warrant thee they'll laugh mightily. Well, I'll turn thee loose to them; either say somewhat for thy self, or hang and be *non plus* [*i.e.*, no more].

Lines 679-85, in Macray, p. 22 (italics in original; bracketed phrase added here). The clown, while continuing to kvetch (*e.g.*, lines 686-88, in Macray, p. 22: "[W]hen they have nobody to leave on the stage, they bring me up, and, which is worse, tell me not what I should say!"), improvises awkwardly. See lines 688-710, in Macray, pp. 22-23.

[399] See, *e.g.*, act 3, sc. 1, lines 1009-24, in Macray, pp. 56-57; act 4, sc. 1, lines 1211-25, in Macray, p. 63.

[400] See, *e.g.*, act 1, sc. 2, lines 304-08, in Macray, p. 87; act 4, sc. 3, lines 1876-79, in Macray, p. 141.

[401] Act 4, sc. 3, in Macray, pp. 138-43. Price, p. 84, suggested that in the *Parnassus* plays, "the admired poet [Shakespeare] is safely distanced from the profession of playwriting." See Part IV.15 & note 350.

## 17. The Essex Rebellion and Treason Trials (1601)

This section, in contrast to the other items in Part IV, does not deal with any specific document or publication. But since a leading orthodox scholar, R.C. Churchill, has treated this episode as an early instance of authorship doubt—and because it does raise such questions—it merits discussion. Churchill's 1958 book on the SAQ conceded that authorship questions were raised on several occasions at least back to the early 17th century.[402]

Churchill devoted several pages to discussing the rebellion by Robert Devereux (Second Earl of Essex) and his allies—who included Henry Wriothesley (Third Earl of Southampton), widely believed to be the beloved youth of *Shake-speare's Sonnets* and to whom "Shakespeare" floridly dedicated *Venus and Adonis* and *The Rape of Lucrece* in 1593–94. The Essex plotters claimed self-servingly not to target Queen Elizabeth personally. Their main grievances were against her advisors led by her powerful Secretary of State, Sir Robert Cecil. But after the failure of the rather farcical revolt on Sunday, February 8, 1601, Essex, Southampton, and several others were convicted of treason.[403]

The Essex rebellion would seem, by all logic, to have put Shakspere of Stratford in a very delicate and dangerous position. On the afternoon of Saturday, February 7, 1601, Shakspere's theatre company, the Lord Chamberlain's Men, put on a performance at the Globe of *Richard II*, depicting the deposition, imprisonment, and murder of that English monarch. The production was

---

[402] See Part II & notes 55-59; Churchill, pp. 28-34, 186-88, 220-21.

[403] Essex was beheaded at the Tower of London on February 25, 1601. A few others were also executed, but Southampton's life was spared. He remained imprisoned in the Tower until the 1603 accession of King James, who pardoned him and restored his titles. See, *e.g.*, Bate, *Soul of the Age*, pp. 233-43; Anderson, pp. 330-36; Cutting (2018), ch. 4, pp. 84-85, 96-98; see also Churchill, pp. 186-88, 220-21; For an intriguing further discussion relating to Southampton, see Chiljan, pp. 296-302.

arranged on short notice by some of Essex's supporters.[404] Later in 1601 Elizabeth reportedly—apocryphally, it seems—exclaimed to one of her officials, in supposed reference to the rebellion: "I am Richard II, know ye not that?"[405] The play was first published anonymously in 1597, but two quarto editions appeared in 1598 under the purported authorship of "William Shake-speare."[406]

Still worse for Shakspere, it would seem, were the dedications noted above by "Shakespeare," just a few years earlier, to Southampton—one of Essex's top henchmen and now fellow convicted traitor! How strange—if the Stratfordian theory were true—that there is no hint in any known historical record that Shakspere

---

[404] See, *e.g.*, Bate, *Soul of the Age*, pp. 233-43, 248-49. The oft-suggested rationale is that they sought to rouse the London populace in support of Essex, who already enjoyed considerable fame and popularity. Perhaps so, though Bate, p. 239, pointed out that Essex's actions on February 8 were to a large extent improvised in response to events occurring *after* the play's performance.

[405] Bate, *Soul of the Age*, pp. 263-67, offered convincing reasons to doubt the historical basis for that anecdote.

[406] Hyphenation in original. It seems to be widely assumed, though apparently we don't really know, that the February 1601 performance included the passage commonly known as the "deposition scene." That scene was not published in the 1597–98 editions of the play. It appeared later in a 1608 quarto and the 1623 *First Folio*. But as Bate astutely pointed out, see *Soul of the Age*, pp. 240-41, there is no direct evidence of any censorship and it is far from clear that the scene should be viewed as making the play any more "subversive" than it already was without it. Indeed, Bate suggested, p. 241, "Shakespeare may have written it as an addition after the real-life drama of February 1601, in order to give the impression of a formal, stately handing over of power, as opposed to the disorder in the original version now tarred by association with the trial of Essex and his accomplices." I would suggest Oxfordians should be open to this interpretation, though of course we differ with Bate over the likely identity of the author.

Pointon (2011), p. 275, listed Bate, *Soul of the Age*, in his bibliography, but did not seem much influenced by Bate's discussion of the Essex rebellion. Pointon himself asserted without cited support that *Richard II* "was performed in London at least forty times as a prelude to the rebellion, complete with the scene showing the forced abdication ... (which was normally omitted)." Pointon, p. 136. Pointon's book—which I find insightful and often valuable, see, *e.g.*, Part III.A & notes 3, 7-8—generally lacks specific citations, an unfortunate shortcoming. The idea that the play was performed "forty times" in early 1601 originated in the same dubious anecdote discussed in the text and note 405. See also the discussion of Pointon's treatment of the Essex rebellion in note 415.

was ever arrested or even questioned or suffered any adverse consequences at all! Did the authorities at the time know something that modern Stratfordians refuse to consider?

The only Lord Chamberlain's player whose name appears to be recorded in connection with the Essex affair was Augustine Phillips. He testified that the players were hired to perform the play—paid "more than their ordinary" to do so. He said they were reluctant at first (yielding only under pressure), on the ground that the play was "so old and so long out of use" that few would show up.[407] The queen evidently had no doubts about their loyalty. She invited the company to perform before her at court a few weeks later, "[o]n the very eve of Essex's execution."[408]

Shakspere's invisibility in this whole episode, and his apparent teflon coating, appear all the more strange when we consider that historian John Hayward got in a very sticky mess over *his* authorship of a 1599 book about Richard II, which included a dedication to Essex himself.[409] During 1600, even before the uprising, Elizabeth's officials were trying "to put together a treason case against Essex" based in part on Hayward's book.[410]

---

[407] Quoted in Bate, *Soul of the Age*, p. 240. Bate, p. 240, repeated the orthodox view that *Richard II* was written and first performed around 1595. But there is compelling evidence that Shakespeare's second history tetralogy—*Richard II*, *Henry IV* (Parts 1 and 2), and *Henry V*—dates to no later than the early 1580s. See Jiménez (2016); Jiménez (2018), pp. 74-90, 146, 300-01; Part III.B & note 55. That is intriguingly consistent with Phillips's quoted testimony and would by itself go far to devastate the Stratfordian theory, given that Shakspere turned twenty in 1584 and the second tetralogy is thought to date to about the midpoint of the author's career. See also Part IV.30.

[408] Bate, *Soul of the Age*, p. 263.

[409] The title of Hayward's book was *The First Part of the Life and Reign of King Henry IV*, but it was mainly about Richard II and was apparently often confused with the play of that title—and appears in fact to have drawn heavily from the play, as discussed in note 411. See Bate, *Soul of the Age*, pp. 244-62. The dedication stated that Essex was "great ... in hope, greater in the expectation of future time." Quoted in Bate, p. 246. Hayward was born around 1564, the same year as Shakspere, was knighted by King James in 1619, and died in 1627. Lee, "Hayward," pp. 311-12.

[410] Bate, *Soul of the Age*, p. 247, and see generally pp. 244-48, 258-62.

Hayward may have been no more guilty of any actual seditious intent than whoever wrote the play *Richard II*.[411] But it is documented that he was brought before the Star Chamber, interrogated, and imprisoned in the Tower.[412] Showing what a small world Elizabethan England was, none other than Francis Bacon, who became a leading Shakespeare authorship candidate in the 19th century,[413] spared Hayward much worse treatment. The queen urged Bacon, then a crown prosecutor, to have Hayward tortured on the rack.[414]

Bacon dissuaded Elizabeth from that cruel recourse, but her reasons provide fascinating testimony that hidden authors using frontmen were a well-known phenomenon at the time. The queen suspected that Hayward had not written the book to which his name was attached but was "shield[ing] 'some more mischievous' person" who was the true author, perhaps Essex himself.[415]

---

[411] Compare, *e.g.*, Lee, "Hayward," p. 311 (stating that "suspicion [of his intent] was hardly justified"), and Bate, *Soul of the Age*, p. 245 (arguing that his "intention was in no way seditious"), with Anderson, pp. 330-31 (describing Hayward as "a supporter of Essex and Southampton" and arguing that his book "none too subtly drew parallels" between Elizabeth and Richard II and "implied that a similar fate should befall the queen"). Bate, pp. 257-61, argued that Hayward's book was in fact deeply indebted to Shakespeare's play, closely echoing some of its incidents and language.

[412] See Lee, "Hayward," pp. 311-12 (indicating he was released some time after Essex's execution); Bate, *Soul of the Age*, p. 258 (indicating he was imprisoned in July 1600 and not released until after Elizabeth's death in 1603).

[413] See Part I & note 42.

[414] See Bate, *Soul of the Age*, p. 245; Cutting (2018), ch. 4, pp. 84-85, 96-98.

[415] Lee, "Hayward," p. 311; see also Churchill, p. 187 (noting that Hayward was imprisoned "because it was wrongly suspected that his [1599 book] had been written by a noble author with a treasonable purpose"). I am puzzled by the uncited claim in Pointon (2011), p. 136, that "[a]fter Essex was captured, Elizabeth ordered that the author of *Richard II* be found and brought for examination, but without success." If this had documented support (I am not aware of any), it would be a smoking-gun refutation of the Stratfordian theory. Equally dubious and devoid of cited support is Pointon's claim, p. 136, that the queen "was sure [Hayward] must know who had written the play, if he had not written it himself." Pointon surely confused the play with Hayward's book. See also the discussion of Pointon's treatment of the Essex rebellion in note 406.

(footnote continued on next page)

My discussion here relies heavily on an account of the Essex revolt—and its connections to Shakespeare and Hayward—by Sir Jonathan Bate. His analysis is thoughtful and often perceptive, except for the distortions introduced by his stubborn adherence to the Stratfordian theory.[416] Bate never concedes the elephant in the room: that this entire episode seems deeply peculiar under that theory and obviously raises serious questions about it.

Bate weakly suggested that Elizabeth's notoriously efficient and pitiless security agents did not pursue Shakspere "[b]ecause the rebellion proved so farcically ineffective"[417] or because the testimony of player Phillips did not directly link Essex to the play's performance, only his "outer circle."[418] That seems naive at best. As Bate himself conceded:

A few years before ... the theaters had been closed down and ... Ben Jonson imprisoned on the far lesser provocation of some few seditious lines in a play called *The Isle of Dogs*. Surely in this case, Cecil would have argued, the Globe must be closed, the acting company disbanded, and Master Shakespeare, tarred with the Southampton brush, thrown in the Tower.[419]

---

(footnote continued from previous page)
    If Elizabeth herself did not already know perfectly well who wrote *Richard II* (I suspect she did and that she knew it was not Shakspere), she certainly would have insisted that Shakspere be put to the rack—the kind of action that Pointon, p. 137, noted she and her officers did *not* take. Pointon, see pp. 136-37, made the same essential point suggested here (in common with many previous authorship doubters): that it seems very difficult to reconcile Shakspere's supposed authorship of *Richard II* with his "surviv[al] [of] the Essex rebellion unscathed," and that the orthodox attempts to explain this have been "weak" and "speak of desperation rather than conviction." Pointon, p. 137; see also Anderson, p. 331 (noting by contrast that the entire scenario is perfectly consistent with Edward de Vere, Earl of Oxford, being the author).
    [416] See Part II & notes 61-65.
    [417] Bate, *Soul of the Age*, p. 238.
    [418] Bate, *Soul of the Age*, p. 262.
    [419] Bate, *Soul of the Age*, p. 238; see also Pointon (2011), p. 137: "In [Elizabeth's] reign, writers such as Jonson, Marston, Dekker, Chapman, Kyd and
(footnote continued on next page)

Yes—"*surely*"! So why didn't he and why wasn't he?

R.C. Churchill, while conceding that the 1601 episode raised an early authorship question, insisted the queen's agents must have conclusively resolved that question in favor of Shakspere's authorship. But his reasoning is faulty and his conclusion plainly does not follow.

Churchill did ask the right question: "Why did nothing happen to Shakespeare himself?" And he promptly conceded the typical doubter response: that the queen or her agents may have known "that Shakespeare was just a cover for a noble author."[420] He stated, in a passage that makes perfect sense if one merely substitutes "Shakspere" for "the author": "They must have found"— or, I would add, *might already have known of—*

> evidence of Shakespeare's authorship so utterly convincing that there was no need even to take *the author [substitute: Shakspere]* to the Tower and torture him. The evidence which they found convincing must also have convinced the Queen, one of the shrewdest politicians in English history and at that moment the most suspicious person in England.[421]

Where Churchill went astray was his assumption that if Shakspere were *not* the playwright, "he would have been forced to confess the identity of the real author."[422] It did not occur to Chur-

---

(footnote continued from previous page)
Nashe were sentenced to imprisonment in circumstances much less serious than those surrounding *Richard II*, and Kyd did not survive."

[420] Churchill, p. 187. As Churchill noted at the end of the quoted paragraph, p. 187, "there is no evidence that [Shakspere] was ever taken to prison at all, let alone 'put to the question'."

[421] Churchill, p. 188 (emphasis and brackets added).

[422] Churchill, p. 187; see also p. 188 (arguing that "if [Shakspere] *had* been a figurehead, the secret police, suspecting just that thing, would have got the name of his noble author out of him" in very quick time) (emphasis in original); p. 220 (arguing that "[i]f there had been any doubt about [the authorship], Shakespeare would have been imprisoned until he revealed the identity of the

(footnote continued on next page)

chill that Elizabeth and her officers perhaps already knew exactly who the author was without any need for Shakspere's help. And they may have had full confidence in the author's loyalty. This would make perfect sense, for example, if the author were Edward de Vere (Earl of Oxford), a high-ranking nobleman well-known to the queen. Despite the dedications to Southampton, it may also have been known by 1601 that Vere was an adversary of Essex— perhaps because he was jealous of his relationship with Southampton. Essex has been cited as a candidate to be the "rival poet" of the *Sonnets*.[423]

This hypothesis, that the true author of *Richard II* was already known (at least to the queen and her agents) as a loyal person of high rank, has great explanatory power with regard to the known facts. It would instantly clear Shakspere and his fellows of any taint with regard to the Southampton dedications or the play's content. It would explain why Phillips's testimony was so readily accepted and why the queen herself hired the same company a few weeks later to perform before her, as they probably did on many occasions.

To argue that the Essex rebellion and treason trials indicate serious authorship doubts, however, is not to claim they conclusively refute the Stratfordian theory—or even that such doubts are among the strongest of those discussed in this book. While we have no evidence of any interaction between Shakspere and the queen's agents, many records of the time are lost. It is *possible* that he was discreetly questioned, and satisfied Elizabeth and her goons (as R.C. Churchill argued) that his "innocence was that of a

---

(footnote continued from previous page)
nobleman they assumed to be behind him"). Churchill, p. 220, claimed without citation—baselessly to my knowledge—that officials "were searching for a noble author at the express command of the Queen." As with Pointon (discussed in note 415), Churchill seems to have confused the authorship of the play *Richard II* with Hayward's authorship of his book about Richard II. See Churchill, pp. 187, 220 (discussing Hayward).

[423] See Moore, "Rival" (1989), in Moore (2009), p. 2; Anderson, pp. 299-301.

professional dramatist who had written the play as one of a series of historical subjects, with no thought of a contemporary application."[424] *Possible*—but not very likely. It seems especially unlikely that this happened *and* that we have no record of it.

As we have seen, Phillips apparently persuaded the powers that were that his and Shakspere's theatrical troupe were merely innocent hirelings paid extra to mount a command performance. More puzzling is how, under Stratfordian assumptions, they could have explained away so easily the Shakespearean dedications to Southampton—*exactly* the kind of thing that got Hayward into such hot water. And why is that angle not mentioned in the same extant records that document Phillips's testimony, Hayward's own predicament, and numerous other aspects of the rebellion?

## 18. Charles Fitzgeoffrey, *Affaniae* (1601)

In 1601 Charles Fitzgeoffrey (1576–1638), a witty young poet (and future clergyman), published *Affaniae,* a collection of Latin epigrams. As Mark Anderson has discussed, Fitzgeoffrey praises many of the leading names in English literature, including Ben Jonson, Edmund Spenser, George Chapman, Samuel Daniel, Michael Drayton, John Marston, and Thomas Nashe. But Shakespeare, at least on the surface, is "[g]laring[ly] ... absen[t]."[425]

Anderson observed that Fitzgeoffrey "include[s] a series of couplets addressed to a writer he cryptically calls 'the Bard.' One ... suggests that [he] consider complete literary self-censorship."[426]

---

[424] Churchill, p. 188.

[425] Anderson, p. 336; see generally pp. 336-37; Sutton, "Introduction"; Fitzgeoffrey, *Affaniae* (Sutton ed.). His surname is sometimes spelled "Fitzgeffrey" (as in Anderson). *Affaniae,* according to Sutton's Introduction, is "a non-classical [Latin] word which means 'trivial, trashy talk' "—thus "gossip," it would seem to me. The full title is *Affaniae: Sive Epigrammatum Libri Tres,* which thus seems to translate as "Gossip: or Epigrams in Three Books."

[426] Anderson, p. 336; see also p. 337 (quoting this epigram).

Another comments on the Bard's plans to publish some of his poems posthumously, and seems to agree that is at least preferable to publishing while he is still alive, which Fitzgeoffrey suggests would badly harm the Bard himself or his reputation.[427]

Anderson noted that if this "Bard" refers to Shakespeare, it would appear to be the first reference to him by that now-common nickname.[428] The English word "bard" and the Latin *bardus*[429] both derive from Gaelic or Celtic words for a poet or wandering minstrel. They may also denote a prophet or seer.[430] The word appears twice in the Shakespeare canon, clearly referring to a prophet on one occasion.[431]

The first epigram quoted by Anderson, "To the Bard" (Book II, No. 64), is translated there as follows: "Are you healthy, he who writes for the last generation? *[posterity?]* Let 'the letter' *[the Sonnets?]* never be handed over, O Bard. Be silent."[432] Professor Dana Sutton translates it as: "Is he sane, who writes for far posterity? The letter will never be delivered, [Bard], hold your

---

[427] See Anderson, pp. 336-37 (second of two epigrams quoted on p. 337).

[428] Anderson, p. 551 (third note to p. 336).

[429] Sutton's English translation retains the Latin *Bardus* in the epigrams referencing him. See Fitzgeoffrey, *Affaniae* (Sutton ed.) (English version), Book I, Nos. 21, 35; Book II, No. 64. The original Latin epigrams use the object form (*In* or *Ad Bardum*, i.e., "On" or "To" the Bard) and the second-person-address form (*Barde*). See Fitzgeoffrey, *Affaniae* (Sutton ed.) (Latin version).

[430] *OED*, v. 1, p. 950. According to *Cassell's Latin Dictionary*, p. 631, the more common Latin term for bard or poet is *vates*. *Cassell's*, p. 73, does not list the noun *bardus* (only an adjective *bardus* meaning stupid, slow, or dull).

[431] *OED*, v. 1, p. 950; Spevack, pp. 89-90 ("bard" and "bards"); *Richard III*, act 4, sc. 2 ("[King Richard:] [A] bard of Ireland told me once I should not live long after I saw Richmond."); *Anthony and Cleopatra*, act 3, sc. 2 ("[Enobarbus:] But [Lepidus] loves Caesar best; yet he loves Anthony: Ho! hearts, tongues, figures, scribes, bards, poets, cannot Think, speak, cast, write, sing, number, ho! His love to Anthony. But as for Caesar, Kneel down, kneel down, and wonder. [Agrippa:] Both he loves.").

[432] Anderson, p. 337 (italics and brackets added by Anderson). Anderson, p. 551 (first note to p. 337), credits Roy Wright-Tekastiaks and Roger Stritmatter for "assistance" in his translations.

silence."[433] "Sane" appears, in context, a better translation than "healthy."[434]

The second epigram quoted by Anderson (Book I, No. 35), "On the Bard,"[435] is translated there as: "You have been cautious, saying, 'I will publish verses after my death.' I would not so hurriedly crucify yourself, O Bard."[436] Sutton's translation: "You have been cautious, [Bard], saying 'I shall publish my verse posthumously,' lest I wish you a speedy hanging."[437]

As Anderson suggested, these two epigrams seem possibly to be discussing *Shake-speare's Sonnets*.[438] The concern that the Bard himself (or at least his reputation) might be endangered by the publication of certain poems, resonates very strongly with the scandalous content of the *Sonnets*. It is universally agreed they are sexually provocative, both in their sometimes racy imagery and in their suggestions of a bisexual love triangle and a possible homosexual affair, at a time when the latter was a death-penalty

---

[433] Sutton provides the citations to book and number. Fitzgeoffrey, *Affaniae* (Sutton ed.) (English version), Book II, No. 64 (brackets added here; as mentioned in note 429, Sutton for some reason does not translate *Bardus* into English). For those who know Latin (sadly, I don't), the original reads: "*Ad Bardum: Sanus est, ad seram qui scribis posteritatem? Tradetur nunquam litera, Barde, sile.*" Fitzgeoffrey, *Affaniae* (Sutton ed.) (Latin version); see also Anderson, p. 551 (first note to p. 337).

[434] See note 433. *Sanus* primarily means "healthy" or "sound," but an alternative figurative meaning—surely intended here—is "*of sound mind, rational, sane.*" *Cassell's Latin Dictionary*, pp. 533-34 (italics in original).

[435] Anderson gives the title as "To the Bard," but the original reads *In Bardum* ("On the Bard"). See note 437.

[436] Anderson, p. 337.

[437] Fitzgeoffrey, *Affaniae* (Sutton ed.) (English version), Book I, No. 35 (brackets added here; see note 429). The original reads: "*In Bardum: Cavisti dicens, 'Edam post funera versus,' Optarem properam ne tibi, Barde, crucem.*" Fitzgeoffrey, *Affaniae* (Sutton ed.) (Latin version); see also Anderson, p. 551 (first note to p. 337). The meaning may be slightly stronger than either translation suggests, more like "wary" than "cautious." See *Cassell's Latin Dictionary*, p. 96 (translating *caveo* as "*to guard against, beware,*" and *cautus* as "*cautious, wary*") (italics in original).

[438] Anderson, p. 337. See generally Part IV.24 (discussing the *Sonnets*).

offense in England. Some scholars have also suggested they have politically explosive content.[439]

This reinforces, first of all, the tentative identification of Fitz-geoffrey's Bard as the author of the *Sonnets*. If so, then his epi-grams point further to an author more like Edward de Vere (Earl of Oxford) than Shakspere of Stratford. If Shakspere wrote the *Sonnets* and other works under his own name, why would Fitz-geoffrey omit the name and refer to him only cryptically as the Bard? That in itself is yet another hint, among many discussed in this book, that "Shakespeare" was widely viewed as a pseudonym.

The Bard's apparent plan to have certain poems published only after his death *could* fit with Shakspere (who died in 1616), if the 1609 publication of the *Sonnets* were unauthorized (a perenni-ally debated issue). But it fits better with Vere, who turned 51 in 1601 (Shakspere was 37), and died in 1604, and was thus more likely to be contemplating such matters. If the author was Vere, then the *Sonnets* obviously *were* published posthumously, precise-ly in line with the Bard's stated plan.

Fears about the Bard "crucify[ing]" himself do not resonate well with Shakspere, who under the Stratfordian theory was a successful, popular, up-and-coming writer not known ever to have been touched by any public scandal or disgrace.[440] To be sure, it is possible Shakspere feared some scandal we do not know about, perhaps one revealed by the *Sonnets* themselves. But we have no other evidence of that. Vere, by contrast, is well-documented to have endured multiple scandals, including accusations of homo-sexual encounters.[441] His reputation took a nose-dive around

---

[439] See Anderson, pp. 283-85, 299-301, 308-09, 333-36; Sobran, pp. 197-201.

[440] See, *e.g.*, Parts IV.4 & note 215, and IV.20 & notes 474-79, 515-17.

[441] See, *e.g.*, Anderson, pp. 167-69; Sobran, pp. 124-26; Part IV.4 & note 218 (discussing Vere's affair and out-of-wedlock child with Anne Vavasour).

1590, for unclear reasons.[442] The *Sonnets* are fairly riddled with laments about "scandal," "disgrace," and "shame."[443]

Anderson also mentioned in an endnote a third epigram "On the Bard" (Book I, No. 21), translated there as: "You say that you always write your poems hurriedly. It is true; from others all things, O Bard, you snatch."[444] Sutton's translation: "You say that you always write your poetry in snatches. Quite right: you snatch everything from others."[445]

As Anderson noted, this echoes the theme of plagiarism discussed earlier—aimed on several occasions at Shakspere of Stratford or characters seeming to reflect him.[446] Is it possible Fitzgeoffrey's Bard—like the references to Shakespeare in the *Parnassus* plays—carries a double meaning?[447] Might he represent *both* a possible frontman like Shakspere *and* a discreet or hidden author? Did Fitzgeoffrey possibly communicate only with the frontman, or perhaps only know about him?

It is interesting, as noted above, that Fitzgeoffrey—unlike, say, Weever, whoever wrote the *Parnassus* plays, or (possibly) the author of *Groats-Worth* with his debatable "Shake-scene" reference[448]—is too reticent to use or even suggest any variant of the published authorial name Shakespeare. He alludes merely and mysteriously to the unnamed Bard.

I tend to disagree with Anderson's suggestion (though it cannot be ruled out) that Fitzgeoffrey "may not himself have known

---

[442] See Moore, "Order of the Garter" (1996), in Moore (2009), p. 263.

[443] See Parts IV.10 & note 287, IV.23 & notes 578-81, and IV.24 & notes 603-05; see also, *e.g.*, *Sonnets* 25, 29, 37, 72, 81, 90, 111, 112, and 121.

[444] Anderson, p. 551 (first note to p. 337).

[445] Fitzgeoffrey, *Affaniae* (Sutton ed.) (English version), Book I, No. 21. The original reads: "*In Bardum: Scribere te raptim semper tua carmina dicis: Verum est; ex aliis omnia, Barde, rapis.*" Fitzgeoffrey, *Affaniae* (Sutton ed.) (Latin version); see also Anderson, p. 551 (first note to p. 337).

[446] See Parts IV.2, 11, and 14; IV.15 & notes 337-50; IV.16 & notes 365-69, 386-96; IV.26; IV.28.

[447] See Parts IV.15-16.

[448] See Part IV.2.

the identity of the [*Sonnets'* author]."[449] Just three years earlier, Francis Meres (*Palladis Tamia*, 1598) referred in print to Shakespeare circulating "his sugared Sonnets among his private friends."[450] The circulation was not *very* "private," being discussed in a published book. *The Passionate Pilgrim* was published in 1599—purportedly by "Shakespeare"—containing two of the 1609 *Sonnets* among other poems (some of doubtful authorship).[451]

Meres and Fitzgeoffrey were probably among many literary insiders who read at least some of the *Sonnets* a decade or more before they were all published in 1609. They may have been in communication with each other. Meres praised Fitzgeoffrey as a poet in *Palladis Tamia*, and Fitzgeoffrey responded by thanking Meres in *Affaniae*.[452] Just as Meres probably knew the author's true identity, as discussed in Part IV.12, it seems likely Fitzgeoffrey did as well.

---

[449] Anderson, p. 337. Anderson qualified this suggestion, p. 551 (second note to p. 337), by noting yet another curious feature of Fitzgeoffrey's *Affaniae*—that it contains multiple references to a "Hilary Vere." Anderson did not explore this angle, but this person appears to be no relation to Edward de Vere. According to Sutton's Introduction to *Affaniae*, this "Vere" was a young man actually named Digory Whear, a beloved friend of Fitzgeoffrey who studied with him at—*first facetious drumroll*—*Oxford* University. See, *e.g.*, Book III, No. 131 ("To His Oxford Friends," referring to "Vere, the choir-leader of my dear friends"). Sutton explained that Whear, "perhaps with an eye to the Earl of Oxford's surname, and because his Cornish Christian name sounded foreign to Home County ears[,] signed himself in Latin as 'Hilarius Verus.' " Hilarious indeed!

And seriously, it must be coincidental that the first introductory dedication in Book I is from young "Vere" to a man described by Sutton as an older friend of Fitzgeoffrey, named—*second facetious drumroll*—*Edward* Michelborne. "Vere" tells Edward that "your Charles and mine ... has sent these three books of epigrams." The second dedication is from Edward "To His [presumably Fitzgeoffrey's] Hilary Vere." The third and final dedication is from "C.F.G." (presumably Fitzgeoffrey) to another apparent friend, William Raleigh—presumably no relation to Sir Walter Raleigh. For other references to "Vere," see Book I, Nos. 23, 80; Book II, Nos. 5, 100, 126; Book III, Nos. 38, 43, 44, 52, 101, 102, 131.

[450] Quoted in Chambers (1930), v. 2, p. 194.

[451] See, *e.g.*, Anderson, pp. 320-21.

[452] See Sutton, "Introduction"; Fitzgeoffrey, *Affaniae* (Sutton ed.) (English version), Book II, No. 24.

## 19.  Henry Chettle, *England's Mourning Garment* (1603)

Henry Chettle (*c.* 1564–*c.* 1606), the printer, transcriber, and possible ghostwriter of *Groats-Worth of Wit* (1592), whom we met in Part IV.2, was also an Elizabethan author in his own right. He wrote a booklet, *England's Mourning Garment*—an elegy to Queen Elizabeth and a retrospective on her reign—that was published not long after her death in 1603.

As Robert Detobel and Katherine Chiljan have discussed (among many scholars), Chettle made a clear reference to Shakespeare—though like Fitzgeoffrey (see Part IV.18), never using the published authorial name. In a poetic passage urging other writers to join him in eulogizing the late queen, and lamenting that they had not yet done so, Chettle commented:

Nor doth the silver tongued *Melicert*,
Drop from his honeyed muse one sable tear
To mourn her death that graced his desert
  [*i.e.*, she had rewarded his merit],
And to his lays[453] opened her Royal ear.
Shepherd, remember our *Elizabeth*,
And sing her Rape, done by that *Tarquin*, Death.[454]

The last line is an obvious reference to *The Rape of Lucrece*, thus pinpointing "Melicert" as Shakespeare, as orthodox scholars have long agreed.[455]

This brief passage is a rich source of authorship doubts. First of all, it reminds us that Shakespeare *never did* eulogize Eliza-

---

[453] "Lays" refers to poetry or verse, especially if intended to be sung as lyrics. In Elizabethan times it was also a general poetic synonym for "songs." See *OED*, v. 8, p. 723.

[454] Chettle, *England's Mourning Garment* (Detobel ed.) (italics in original); see also Detobel, "Melicertus" (2004); Chiljan, pp. 258-59; Anderson, p. 346.

[455] See, *e.g.*, Chambers (1930), v. 2, p. 189 (quoting this passage).

beth. While he was not alone in that failure, as Chettle's lament shows, it seems strange that Shakespeare of all writers would not publicly mourn her passing. It seems especially difficult to understand why Shakspere of Stratford, the upwardly mobile actor and supposed playwright, would not have published a laudatory elegy of some kind.[456]

Note that Chettle clearly indicated the queen had rewarded this author. We have no evidence of any royal patronage directed to Shakspere of Stratford *as a writer*, though his company of players is generally thought to have been invited and paid on many occasions to perform before her.[457] But if he actually was a writer, even the latter would seem likely to have prompted some written expression of appreciation upon her passing.

It is well-documented, on the other hand, that the queen in 1586 began giving Edward de Vere (Earl of Oxford) an annuity of 1,000 pounds a year—for reasons that remain unclear—which was renewed through the end of her life and then by King James up to Vere's death in 1604. This was an enormous sum over almost two decades, worth many millions in present-day dollars.[458] It could well be this to which Chettle referred in saying the queen had "graced his desert."

Truth be told, the author's failure to eulogize the queen seems strange at first blush even under the Oxfordian theory, especially given that stipend. But Vere's biography provides ample reasons to think his feelings about the queen were deeply conflicted. An aristocratic writer hiding behind a pseudonym would also feel far

---

[456] See Part I, note 34. The conclusion of *Henry VIII* (act 5, sc. 4) celebrates the birth of Princess Elizabeth, the future Queen, with an extended prophecy of the glories of her reign, including that she would live, rule, and die a virgin. But *Henry VIII* is generally believed (including by orthodox scholars) to have been co-authored (or revised) by John Fletcher, who is commonly credited with writing half or more of it, including that scene.

[457] They became the King's Men under James I. See Part I & notes 15-16.

[458] See, *e.g.*, Anderson, pp. 210-12; Cutting, "Sufficient Warrant" (2017), pp. 80-89.

less pressure to speak out on such an occasion. In 1603 Vere, unlike Shakspere, was near the end of his life and probably embittered. Despite the annuity, the queen had frustrated his desires and denied or ignored his petitions on other occasions.[459]

Vere also may well have recalled how Elizabeth, either herself or by allowing some of her favorites and top officials to do so, had essentially robbed him as a result of the royal "wardship" to which he was subjected after his father's death, when he was not yet of legal age. Vere, fairly or unfairly, has been called an extravagant spendthrift. But the abusive wardship system that the queen carried over from her own father, Henry VIII, helps to explain how he lost most of his inherited wealth.[460]

Chettle also mentioned "Melicert" (the author Shakespeare) earlier in his pamphlet, in a passage defending Elizabeth against the charge that she was to blame for breaking the truce with Spain, which led to the Spanish Armada's attempted invasion of England in 1588. One of Chettle's characters asks another to recall songs or stories by three poets, including "smooth tongued *Melicert*," about this period in the mid-1580s—impossibly early for Shakspere of Stratford's career timeline.[461]

---

[459] See, e.g., Anderson, pp. 337-49, 353; see also Part I, note 34. Vere repeatedly, without success, petitioned the queen for various lucrative monopolies of the kind she handed out to other favorites. As Anderson noted, p. 210, "Elizabeth seldom gave direct gifts of money to the nobility, preferring to give monopolies in goods and commodities like sweet wine or wool or tin. The new monopolist could then earn out a comfortable living, all without withdrawing a penny from the state's coffers." See also Anderson, pp. 340-41, 343; Cutting, "Sufficient Warrant" (2017), p. 83. While the queen stipulated that Vere did not have to account to anyone else for how he spent the annuity (disbursed quarterly), she herself could have cut it off at any time. The effect was to keep him on a short leash, thus explaining why he continued to press her for a more desirable monopoly or lucrative office. See Cutting, "Sufficient Warrant" (2017), pp. 82-83.

[460] See, e.g., Anderson, pp. 16-18, 21; Green, "Earl in Bondage" (2004); Green, "Fall" (2009); Cutting, "Evermore in Subjection" (2016).

[461] Chettle, *England's Mourning Garment* (Detobel ed.) (italics in original), quoted and discussed, Chiljan, pp. 258-59; see also Detobel, "Melicertus" (2004), pp. 224-29; Part IV.1 & note 9 (Shakspere, 23, still in Stratford in 1587).

Furthermore, a poet and "shepherd" with a very similar name, "Melicertus," appeared in Robert Greene's 1589 romance, *Menaphon*. Part IV.2 discusses the close connections between Chettle and Greene. As Chiljan noted, it is eventually revealed in *Menaphon* that Melicertus is "actually [a] nobleman, Lord Maximus."[462] All these references, at the very least, raise serious questions about the Stratfordian attribution. They seem much more consistent with Vere as the true author.

### 20. John Davies of Hereford, *Microcosmos* (1603) and *Humour's Heaven on Earth* (1609)

This John Davies (*c.* 1565–1618), known by the town of his birth, is not to be confused with his slightly younger contemporary, Sir John Davies MP.[463] Davies of Hereford mostly wrote what may be described as poetic miscellanies. *Microcosmos* (1603), as orthodox scholars agree, refers to the "players" (actors) William Shakspere and Richard Burbage, identified as "W.S." and "R.B." Davies states that he "loves" players and their "quality" (profession of acting). He further states that he loves "some" players (citing W.S. and R.B.) for pursuing the "pass time" of either "paint-

---

[462] Chiljan, p. 259; see also Detobel, "Melicertus" (2004), pp. 229-33; Part IV.1 (discussing Nashe's preface to *Menaphon*); Greene, *Menaphon* (Arber ed.), pp. 40-41, 50-52, 73-76, 81-85, 90-92. Chiljan, p. 259, noted that an unattributed poem ("Sonetto") in *Menaphon* (Arber ed.), pp. 88-89, was credited to Vere (using his initials "E.O.") in the 1600 anthology *England's Parnassus*. See also Greene, *Menaphon* (Detobel ed.), in which Detobel (n. 10) observed that this "Sonetto" turns out to be a loose translation of an older French poem, albeit one having considerable resonance with Vere's early known poetry and with several lines ("Love is a smoke," *etc.*) in *Romeo and Juliet*, act 1, sc. 1.

[463] See Part IV.9. Nor should either poet John Davies be confused with Sir John Davies the Essex Rebellion supporter. See Part III.A & note 24. None of the three were related as far as I know. See also Part IV.26 (discussing Davies of Hereford's *Scourge of Folly*, *c.* 1610–11). Miller, "Family Affair," pp. 29-30, outlined the connections that Davies of Hereford may have had, by way of dedications and possible patronage, with family members and associates of Edward de Vere (Earl of Oxford).

ing" or "poesy."[464] As Katherine Chiljan has noted, this description makes sense for Burbage, who was best known for his primary profession of acting. While one might debate Chiljan's comment that Burbage "was not renowned for his painting," it may have been viewed as more of a pastime for him.[465]

But as Chiljan suggested, it seems strange—if Davies thought Shakspere the player from Stratford and Shakespeare the author were the same person—that he would describe *his writing* as a pastime. Davies, like others we have seen, may have been making a sly double reference to *another* "W.S." well-known at the time: the authorial name (or pseudonym) William Shakespeare. He may have been hinting at the true identity behind *that* W.S.—that he "was a nobleman who acted and wrote poetry as a pastime, not for his livelihood."[466] That would be consistent with the "stigma of print" and general disapproval of money-making professional acti-

---

[464] Davies, *Microcosmos* (1603), p. 215, excerpted and discussed in A. Nelson, "Davies, *Microcosmos*" (2017). We met Burbage in Part IV.16, in connection with his parody character in *Parnassus 3*. While "quality" clearly refers *here* to the profession of acting, *it was not limited to that meaning*. It could refer to *any* occupation or profession. See Part IV.2.d & note 58, citing Greenwood (1908), Erne, "Mythography," and *OED*, v. 12, p. 974 (def. I.5).

*Microcosmos* is one of only three references before 1623 (to my knowledge) that arguably connect Shakspere the player to any possible role as a writer. The other two are *Groats-Worth of Wit* (1592) (very doubtfully, see Part IV.2) and *Parnassus 3* (c. 1601) (see Part IV.16). Unfortunately for Stratfordians, all three also indicate early authorship doubts. See Part 1 & note 22; Part IV.2.f & note 98; Part IV.16 & note 361. Some might also claim Davies of Hereford's *Scourge of Folly* (c. 1610–11), at least the title of Epigram No. 159, as a possible literary linkage for Shakspere the player. But as discussed in Part IV.26, nothing in the text of Epigram No. 159 (or elsewhere in *Scourge*) suggests any such linkage. On the contrary, the titles of Epigrams No. 159 and No. 160 form an unusually powerful expression of authorship doubt.

[465] Chiljan, p. 259. Diana Price gave up too quickly on trying to analyze *Microcosmos* and *Humour's Heaven*. Without citing either title, she merely commented that "Davies wrote ... two [epigrams] in which the initials 'W.S.R.B.' appear in the margin. ... Both ... are riddles that have defied attempts at deciphering." Price, p. 64 n. *. I disagree, though undeniably parts of both are quite obscure. See note 507; see also Ogburn, pp. 105, 814 (citing and quoting two lines of *Microcosmos* and one of *Humour's Heaven*, but with no discussion).

[466] Chiljan, p. 260.

vities which applied to aristocrats during that era—a stigma that may have evolved and eroded over time.[467] It would also be consistent with the theory that the author behind the Shakespeare name was Edward de Vere (Earl of Oxford).

To be sure, the reference to W.S. *as a player* clearly relates at least in part, and probably as the primary and nominal surface meaning, to Shakspere of Stratford. But this reference could also hint at the possibility that Vere himself acted on occasion—which would have been viewed as a pastime at best, disreputable slumming at worst—and a substantial danger to his reputation if it were publicly known. While this is a debatable conjecture, it has some support and fits with much of what we know about Vere's life. We know he had lifelong exposure to and interest in theatre, starting with the acting troupe his father sponsored when he was a boy and continuing with his own sponsorship of players.[468]

It is possible that Shakespeare the author (whoever that was) may have been viewed, especially by 1603, as primarily a playwright. Perhaps "poesy" was viewed as more of a sideline for him. But if the author was writing and publishing under his own name, then he was likely gaining financial success from his poetry as well as his plays. And his plays contain much poetry. *Venus and*

---

[467] See Part IV.3 & note 149; Price, "Mythical" (2002).

[468] See Part IV.5 & note 232 (discussing "Willobie's" *Avisa*, which in 1594 referred to "W.S." in somewhat similar ways); see also Part IV.26 & notes 676-77; Malim, "Oxford the Actor" (2004); Waugh, "My Shakespeare" (2018), pp. 52-53; Anderson, pp. 3-4, 187-88.

In *Sonnet* 110, lines 1-2, the author famously laments, in what seems a likely reference to acting on the stage: "Alas 'tis true, I have gone here and there, And made myself a motley to the view ...." Stratfordians may be tempted to argue that points to the author being Shakspere the player. But as many skeptics have suggested, why the mournful breast-beating? If Shakspere is the author, the appropriate reaction is puzzlement and something along the following lines: "*Duh!* What else is new? Tell us something we don't know! And why the angst? You're a well-known player and big success in the theatre business. Not bad for an ordinary boy from Stratford. Stop whining and get over it already." The lines fit far better with an author (and sometime actor) who had high social rank and thus more social standing to lose.

*Adonis* and *The Rape of Lucrece*, first published in 1593–94, remained bestsellers for years. If Shakspere of Stratford were the author, it is difficult to see how his poetry could be described as a pastime.[469]

Here is the full relevant passage in *Microcosmos* (numbering the lines for convenient reference):

(1) *Players*, I love ye, and your *Quality* [your
     profession of acting[470]],
(2) As ye are Men, *that* pass time not abused:
     [*i.e.*, not only do I love your professional work,
     I also love that you don't abuse your free time;
     your pastimes are also praiseworthy]
(3) And ᶜ some I love for ᵈ *painting, poesy*,
(4) And say fell *Fortune*[471] cannot be excused,
(5) That hath for better *uses* you refused:
(6) *Wit, Courage, good shape, good parts*, and all *good*,
(7) As long as all these *goods* are no *worse* used,
(8) And though the *stage* doth stain pure gentle *blood*,
(9) Yet ᵉ generous ye are in *mind* and *mood*.

[marginal notes in original, linked to superscripted "c," "d," and "e" in original text above:]

---

[469] Defenders of the Stratfordian theory sometimes argue that authors, especially playwrights, did not benefit much financially from their writings during that era—that perhaps only theatre companies or publishers profited after a given work was initially sold or performed. But that would ignore the fact that Shakspere was apparently also a theatrical shareholder and businessman. The author Shakespeare was obviously prolific (whoever he was), constantly generating new material. If he was also Shakspere the shrewd businessman, it defies credulity to suggest that he or his theatre company were somehow unable to enter into mutually lucrative business arrangements with publishers, so as to leverage ongoing income for Shakspere from his (presumed) ongoing stream of new writings. See Part III.B & note 41. It is well-documented and beyond dispute that Shakspere retired and died quite wealthy.

[470] See note 464, and Part IV.2.d & note 58, on the meaning of "quality."

[471] *I.e.*, cruel Fortune, the latter word meaning chance or luck, often viewed as a goddess or lady. *OED*, v. 5, p. 814 ("fell" as an adjective); v. 6, p. 104 ("fortune"). The Romans called her Fortuna—or in modern parlance, Lady Luck.

c W. S. R. B.

d Simonides saith, that painting is a dumb Poesy, & Poesy a speaking painting.

e Roscius was said for his excellency in his quality [his acting[472]], to be only worthy to come on the stage, and for his honesty to be more worthy than to come thereon.[473]

The assertion by Davies in lines 4-5, that "fell Fortune cannot be excused, That hath for better uses you refused," is very intriguing, as Chiljan noted. Davies was saying, in effect, that he found it inexcusably cruel that the goddess of luck[474] had "refused" W.S. and R.B. But refused them *what?* Davies, as Chiljan conceded, did not provide "further explanation." Chiljan drew the inference that he meant they were denied recognition for the pastime talents he praised (painting and poetry).[475]

Chiljan observed that this could, like the pastime description itself, make sense for Burbage, who was better known as an actor than a painter. But for Shakespeare, if he was writing under his own name, it made no sense at all. The name "Shakespeare *was much renowned* for ... poetry."[476] This "can only mean," Chiljan argued, "that Davies believed 'Shakespeare' was a pen name" and that the true "author was not getting recognition for his poetry"—at least not public credit under his actual name.[477]

Chiljan also noted the resonance between the ill-treatment of W.S. by Fortune and the suggestions by the author of the *Sonnets*

---

472 See note 464, and Part IV.2.d & note 58, on the meaning of "quality."

473 Davies, *Microcosmos* (1603), p. 215 (italics in original; bracketed explanations added here), excerpted and discussed in A. Nelson, "Davies, *Microcosmos*" (2017); see also Chambers (1930), v. 2, p. 213 (quoting this passage).

474 See note 471.

475 Chiljan, p. 259.

476 Chiljan, p. 259 (emphasis in original).

477 Chiljan, p. 259.

that he was spited and disgraced by Fortune.[478] As we have seen, this clashes with the Stratfordian image of Shakespeare as a popular and successful actor and writer, not known to have been touched by any disgrace.[479]

Chiljan's argument is debatable, though I find it attractive. Acting was a profession held in very low esteem at the time, though actors like Burbage himself, and Edward Alleyn, helped start the process of changing that.[480] Davies could be read to suggest merely that it was unfortunate Shakspere and Burbage had to make their primary living as actors or theatrical businessmen, whatever more elevated sidelines or pastimes they pursued.

As Chiljan's argument suggests, however, that reading sits uneasily beside the undeniable fact that Shakspere, if he was the author Shakespeare, also had a brilliant and successful career as a poet and playwright. As discussed above, it is hard to see how writing could have been viewed as merely his sideline or pastime. There was far more plentiful and laudatory contemporary praise for Shakespeare (however spelled) as a writer than as an actor. *Microcosmos* itself is one of very few published references to him as an actor before 1616, and it appears to be the only such reference that clearly *praises* him as such.[481]

---

[478] See Chiljan, p. 259, citing *Sonnets* 25, 29, 37, 90, and 111. Perhaps the best-known example is *Sonnet* 29, line 2: "When in disgrace with Fortune and men's eyes, I all alone beweep my outcast state ...."

[479] See notes 515-17 and related text; see also Parts IV.4 & note 215; IV.10 & note 287; IV.18 & notes 438-43; IV.23 & notes 578-81; IV.24 & note 605.

[480] See Parts IV.2.g (discussing Alleyn) and IV.16 (discussing Burbage).

[481] Four other references (or possible references) to him as an actor appear in Greene's *Groats-Worth of Wit* (1592) (very debatably, see Part IV.2), in the anonymous play *Parnassus 3* (c. 1601) (see Part IV.16), and in two later works by Davies of Hereford: *Humour's Heaven* (1609), discussed in this part, and *Scourge of Folly* (c. 1610–11), discussed in Part IV.26. The only other published mentions of Shakespeare as an actor before the 1623 *First Folio* (to my knowledge) are the posthumous (and very curious) cast-list references in Ben Jonson's 1616 *Works*, discussed in Part III.B, note 38.

More compelling is the inference Chiljan drew from the comment in lines 8-9 that "the stage doth stain pure gentle blood, yet generous ye are in mind and mood." Neither Shakspere of Stratford nor Burbage had "gentle blood" in the sense of being members of the nobility.[482] But as Chiljan noted and this book has discussed, "many overlooked remarks about [the author] Shakespeare say or imply that he was an aristocrat."[483] We should also keep in mind the many strong indications to that effect woven through the works themselves.[484] Yet again, this all happens to reinforce the Oxfordian theory that Vere was the author. It also reinforces the other indications that Vere himself may have dabbled at times with acting.[485]

Chiljan thus argued that lines 8-9 were "meant for [the author] Shakespeare only," who was depicted as "generous" for being willing to risk his social standing by appearing on stage,

---

[482] The primary meaning of "gentle" during Shakespeare's time related not to kindness or mild disposition but rather high social rank. "Gentle," as an adjective relating to persons, was "originally used synonymously with *noble*." *OED*, v. 6, p. 450 (def. 1.a) (italics in original). As the *OED* discusses, it later expanded, a transition still occurring during Shakespeare's time, to include people of lower (but still elevated) social rank, such as knights, and also "gentlemen" who (like Shakspere of Stratford and his father by the late 1590s) acquired a coat-of-arms. See also *OED*, v. 6, p. 450 (def. 2.a, "gentle" as an adjective relating to "birth, *blood*, family"; def. 3.a, "gentle" as an adjective relating to persons: "[h]aving the character appropriate to one of good birth; *noble*, generous, courteous") (italics added). During Shakespeare's time, reflected in that author's occasional usages, "gentle" also started to acquire what was then a secondary meaning (most often in relation to women) and is today the dominant meaning: kind, tender, or mildly disposed. *OED*, v. 6, p. 451 (def. 8: "gentle" as an adjective relating to persons).

As the foregoing suggests, it appears that Shakspere of Stratford (possibly Burbage too) could properly have been described as "gentlemen" by 1603. See, *e.g.*, A. Nelson, "Davies, *Microcosmos*" (2017) (rather unclearly suggesting that reading, while also conceding that as "common players" they did "not risk the stain" of appearing on stage, which would seem to undermine Nelson's own claim that this very passage even refers to them). Regardless, it seems extremely doubtful that either Shakspere or Burbage would ever have been described as having "pure gentle blood," a phrase suggesting aristocratic birth.

[483] Chiljan, p. 260.

[484] See Part V.C.

[485] See note 468 and related text.

conduct "which 'stains' his nobility."[486] She pointed to the evident connection to *Sonnet* 110.[487] Chiljan offered a related argument about the marginal comment by Davies on Roscius, an admired Roman actor. Davies described a "dilemma" facing such actors, whether in Roman or Shakespearean times: The excellence of their acting meant they were well (perhaps best or "only") suited to perform on stage. But the more "honest" (admirable) they were—given the low regard at the time for acting, the theatre business, and the public stage—the "more" they became too "worthy ... to come thereon."[488] A sufficiently great and admirable actor would thus, paradoxically, be too good for the stage.[489]

The related argument about Roscius might not stand too well on its own. Taken in isolation, the comment might merely suggest by analogy that Shakspere of Stratford and Burbage were in some general sense too good for the stage. It might merely be a flowery way for Davies to compliment them, consistent with his own professed "love" for players and the acting profession (in apparent contrast with the attitudes of many at the time), along with a suggestion that they were "generous" to appear on stage and grant audiences the benefit of their theatrical skills.

But Chiljan's Roscius argument does not exist in isolation. It corroborates, and is corroborated by, the suggestion that Shakespeare the author was especially "generous" to appear on stage, not only granting audiences the pleasure of his theatrical gifts but also (as viewed at the time, given then-prevailing social attitudes) risking a "stain" on his high and admirable social status. The

---

[486] Chiljan, p. 260.

[487] See note 468 and related text.

[488] Davies, *Microcosmos* (1603), p. 215 (note "e"), quoted and discussed in Chiljan, p. 260. "Honesty," as used in Shakespeare's time, meant virtue in a general sense as much as truthfulness. See Part IV.2.c & note 46.

[489] One thinks of some prestigious modern stage and film actors (mostly in decades past) who thought of themselves as too good for television, and who perhaps were viewed (by themselves and others) as notably "generous" if they did deign occasionally to act on TV.

overall impression left by this entire passage in *Microcosmos* is in substantial tension with the Stratfordian theory.

Professor Alan Nelson, a respected scholar and well-known Stratfordian partisan, is the author of a very short essay on *Microcosmos* posted on the Folger Shakespeare Library's *Shakespeare Documented* website—an admirable and tremendously useful scholarly resource overall.[490] Nelson missed or ignored most of the foregoing,[491] while making one far-fetched argument and one that is merely doubtful.

Nelson's more tendentious claim was to hype—as many Stratfordian scholars do[492]—a 1613 document recording a payment "to Mr. Shakspeare [*sic*] in gold about my Lord's impreso [*sic*] [and] ... to Richard Burbage for painting and making it, in gold."· The "Lord" was Francis Manners, Sixth Earl of Rutland.[493] An *impresa* is a heraldic device that typically displays a coat-of-arms and the motto of the family in question.[494]

Nelson, noting the praise by Davies for Shakspere's and Burbage's "poetry and painting respectively," asserted they "indeed would practice these skills cooperatively in the Rutland *impresa*."[495] As to Shakspere, that is simply preposterous on its face.

---

[490] A. Nelson, "Davies, *Microcosmos*" (2017).

[491] I would not expect Nelson to embrace or agree with any of the arguments here, but a responsible scholar would at least acknowledge and discuss the issues. His approach is sadly typical of the longstanding response of orthodox Shakespeare scholars to the authorship issue in general. When they do not scornfully mock it, they disdainfully ignore it. That is not how responsible scholars in any field make progress in finding, studying, and understanding facts and phenomena. See also note 498.

[492] For another example, see Part I & note 19, citing Shapiro (2010), p. 244; see also Schoenbaum, *Documentary Life*, p. 272 (discussing some of the questionable aspects of this episode that should have made him doubt why, as he put it, the "leading playwright of the age" would "try his hand at trifling assignments").

[493] Chambers (1930), v. 2, p. 153 (quoting and discussing this document). He was the younger brother and successor of Roger Manners, Fifth Earl of Rutland, who was later seriously touted (though actually a far-fetched possibility) as a Shakespeare authorship candidate. See Part IV.30 & note 800.

[494] See *OED*, v. 7, pp. 738-39; Chambers (1930), v. 2, p. 153.

[495] A. Nelson, "Davies, *Microcosmos*" (2017) (italics in original).

It is remarkable, and really rather disturbing, that an institution like the Folger would endorse such risible nonsense.[496]

As noted above, the text (if any) on an *impresa* would in most cases be merely the family's existing motto. We apparently have no surviving image of the Rutland *impresa* in question. It is speculative at best, and very unlikely (though Nelson stated it flatly as a fact), that any "poetry," or original writing of any kind, would have been needed or involved in its creation.

Nothing in the documentary record suggests anything of the sort. Quite the contrary, while the record describes Burbage "painting and making" the *impresa*, it says nothing about Shakspere "writing" or doing anything, merely that the payment to him was "about" it. The payment might merely have had some connection with Shakspere's overall business relationship with Burbage as a fellow theatrical shareholder. Perhaps he subcontracted some work related to it.

It is not even clear the cited "Mr. Shakspeare" was William of Stratford. No first name is mentioned. The orthodox scholar Sir Edmund Chambers, in his classic 1930 collection of Shakespearean evidence, noted that the *impresa* was for a "tilt," a horseback jousting contest. Chambers cited another orthodox scholar, Charlotte Stopes, who thought the payment might have been to John Shakespeare (no apparent relation to William),[497] the bitmaker for

---

[496] But sadly unsurprising. The Folger, despite disclaimers to the contrary, has long been, and remains at times, a partisan advocate of the Stratfordian theory. See also, *e.g.*, Part 1 & notes 38-41 (discussing the Folger's misleading statements, and omissions of important, relevant, historical facts, during its nationwide 2016 exhibits of the *First Folio*). This is all the more regrettable given what a tremendously important resource the Folger Library is, and its admirable overall work.

[497] As discussed in Part III.A & notes 26-27, orthodox scholars have confirmed that Shakespeare (however spelled) was not an especially rare English surname at the time.

the horses of King James.[498] Chambers curtly dismissed the Stopes conjecture by noting that *"imprese* were not trappings for horses."[499] But that's beside the point. The record, as quoted above, does not indicate that "Mr. Shakspeare" (whoever he was) did any specific work *on* the *impresa*, merely that he was being paid "about" it—that is, on some basis related to it. Since, as Chambers himself noted, it was to be used in a mounted contest, a payment for related "horse trappings" might easily have been recorded as generally "about" the *impresa*. The Stopes conjecture remains very plausible. As Charlton Ogburn Jr. noted, it actually seems more plausible than speculating "what a well-to-do businessman, even if he was also a famous dramatist, would be doing 'about' a painted shield to be used at the tilt."[500]

Further undermining the idea that Shakspere wrote poetry or anything else for the *impresa*, Chambers quoted a record concerning the very tilt for which it was created, which says the devices used were "bare *imprese*, whereof some were so dark, that their meaning is not yet understood, unless perchance that were there

---

[498] Chambers (1930), v. 2, p. 153; see also Ogburn, pp. 32, 806 (discussing the *impresa* far more accurately, sensibly, and illuminatingly than Nelson, and with far greater scholarly respect for the documentary evidence, citing Chambers and Stopes). Yet Nelson, in his own words in his biased 2003 biography of Vere, p. 5, "dismiss[ed] from serious consideration" Ogburn's exhaustively researched and documented 1984 book (misdated by Nelson to 1975), which largely focused on Vere. Nelson did not otherwise discuss, mention, or make even a pretense of engaging Ogburn's scholarly work, which he did not even cite in his bibliography. See also note 491.

[499] Chambers (1930), v. 2, p. 153 (italics in original).

[500] Ogburn, p. 32. By contrast, Burbage's participation as a painter was explicitly described and makes perfect sense. As Chambers noted (1930), v. 2, p. 153, Burbage alone was paid again, in March 1616, "for [a] shelde and ... embleance" (*sic*) for Rutland. Since that was only a month before Shakspere's death in Stratford, his absence from that record is unsurprising and doesn't tell us much in itself. But the 1616 record still suggests (as does common sense) that Burbage alone was needed to create the actual *impresa*, aside from any related "horse trappings." Painting a motto or other text along with a coat-of-arms would hardly have taxed Burbage's skills.

meaning, not to be understood."[501] Such are the pitiful scraps of evidence, dating to his own lifetime, to which Stratfordians are reduced to desperately clinging to support any literary career whatsoever for Shakspere the player.

Less tendentiously, but still dubiously, Nelson asserted that Davies "expresses the opinion that although acting would 'stain' persons of 'gentle' blood, common players not only do not risk the stain, but are capable of being 'generous' in mind and in thought. Here Davies puns on [the] Latin [word] *generosus*, meaning both 'gentleman' and morally elevated."[502]

Let me be clear: This book does not dispute that *Microcosmos* provides some evidence that Shakspere of Stratford might have been the author Shakespeare. On its face it suggests some kind of linkage between "W.S.," "players," and "poesy."[503] But there are several problems with Nelson's analysis.

First of all, Davies did *not* "express," conditionally or hypothetically as Nelson implied, that acting on the stage *"would"* stain gentle blood. He stated flatly that it *"doth."* That's important (not a quibble) because Nelson, aside from trying to nudge that comment in line 8 off-stage as a mere hypothetical, did not even try to explain *why* Davies made it. Nor did Davies "express" anything about "common players" not risking the "stain," nor about them being "generous." That's Nelson's own dubious rephrasing.

---

[501] Quoted in Chambers (1930), v. 2, p. 153, and in Schoenbaum, *Documentary Life*, p. 272.

[502] A. Nelson, "Davies, *Microcosmos*" (2017) (italics in original).

[503] See note 464, acknowledging it as one of at least three arguable items of such evidence during his lifetime. I just wish orthodox scholars, to the extent they cite any of these items (for whatever reason, they don't seem to cite *Microcosmos* much in the context of the authorship debate), would acknowledge and address the *countervailing* evidence they *also* provide of early authorship doubts. See, *e.g.*, Part I, notes 22, 28.

Providing some evidence of something is not, of course, the same as proving it is true or even likely. See Regnier (2015) (explaining how lawyers, like Regnier and myself, are trained to carefully, precisely, and rigorously speak about, write about, weigh, and analyze evidence).

The better reading is that when Davies said "generous ye are" in line 9, he was addressing whoever's "pure gentle blood" *had in fact* been "stain[ed]," as stated in line 8. Why did Davies even include the point about "stain[ing] pure gentle blood"? Evidently, some actual person of "pure gentle blood" had acted on the stage and Davies wanted to write about it. If he was *only* talking about Shakspere and Burbage the players, and if (as Nelson said and I agree) *they* did "not risk the stain," why did Davies make this comment at all?

Nor did Nelson explore why it would be "generous" of Shakspere and Burbage to merely ply their usual trade as actors. I *think* Nelson, with his reference to "gentleman," was trying to suggest that Shakspere and Burbage, while not of high social rank, were at least "gentlemen" by 1603. Shakspere appears to have obtained a coat-of-arms for his father by 1596. Thus, he and Burbage *might* be praised as "too good for the stage" and perhaps "generous" in sharing their theatrical skills with playgoers. I myself articulate this possible argument.[504] But Nelson did not seem to grasp how it undercuts this argument to concede—as he had to—that as professional players they could not really be said to "risk" any "stain" from appearing on stage. Nor would they *likely* be described as "generous" by doing so—nor, *especially*, as having "pure gentle blood."

Chiljan and Nelson also quoted and discussed a somewhat similar poetic reference by Davies of Hereford to the mysterious "W.S." in *Humour's Heaven on Earth* (1609). Here is that key passage (again numbering the lines for convenient reference):

---

[504] See note 482, and text following note 489. I would not quarrel with Nelson's suggestion that Davies, in using the word "generous," was punning on a Latin word to convey a double meaning. That is perfectly consistent with the anti-Stratfordian reading suggested here.

(1) Some [stage players] followed [Lady Fortune[505]]
    by *[1] acting all men's parts,
(2) These on a Stage she raised (in scorn) to fall:
(3) And made them Mirrors, by their acting Arts,
(4) Wherein men saw their *[2] faults, though ne'r so
    small:
(5) Yet some she guerdoned [rewarded[506]] not, to
    their *[3] deserts;
(6) But, othersome, were but ill-Action all:
(7) Who while they acted ill, ill stayed behind,
(8) By custom of their manners in their mind.

[marginal notes in original, linked to superscripted asterisks in
original text above, numbering added here:]

*[1] Stage players.

*[2] Showing the vices of the time.

*[3] W.S.R.B.[507]

---

[505] Referring to chance or luck, often viewed as a goddess or lady. See note
471; *OED*, v. 6, p. 104. The original text says simply "her," but this clearly refers
to Fortune since the preceding stanza refers (in its first line) to "Fortune's followers" and then again to "Fortune" in its last line. Davies, *Humour's Heaven*
(1609), p. 208, stanzas 75-76, excerpted and discussed in A. Nelson, "Davies,
*Humour's Heaven*" (2016).

[506] *OED*, v. 6, pp. 922-23.

[507] Davies, *Humour's Heaven*, p. 208, stanza 76 (bracketed explanations
added here; omitting parentheses around "By custom of their manners"), excerpted and discussed in A. Nelson, "Davies, *Humour's Heaven*" (2016) (dating it to
1609); see also Chambers (1930), v. 2, p. 214 (dating it to 1605). Much of this
stanza is obscure. Here is my best translation into plain modern English:

(1) Some stage actors (the first group) followed Lady Fortune by acting
    all men's parts.
(2) She scornfully elevated those actors (to fame?) but then let them
    fall (into disgrace?).
(3) She made them mirrors, because of their acting skills,
(4) Mirrors in which men (in the audience) could see even their own
    (the audience's) smallest faults, thus revealing the vices of the
    time. (The "faults" seem to be those of the audience, not the actors,
    because the actors are said to be "mirrors" in which audiences see
    something about themselves. The skill of the actors would prevent

(footnote continued on next page)

Two points deserve immediate mention. First, Chiljan and Nelson are surely correct that "W.S." and "R.B." refer ("W.S." at least in part) to William Shakspere and Richard Burbage the players.[508] Second, unlike the similar passage in *Microcosmos*, there is nothing in this passage expressly drawing any linkage between "W.S." and any literary career. On its face it identifies "W.S." only as a "stage player." *Humour's Heaven* thus offers no support whatsoever to the Stratfordian authorship theory. To the extent it bears on the issue, it is purely a source of doubts. That very lack of any express linkage to writing is itself a source of doubt,[509] but there's more.

Nelson appeared to think it best to say as little as possible about what this passage could possibly mean. As to the crucial line 5, he merely paraphrased what it says on its face. After describing the publication of *Humour's Heaven*, quoting the relevant stanza, and noting that it refers to Shakspere and Burbage, he stated: "Evidently these two were not rewarded as highly as they deserved; 'othersome' must refer to less deserving actors."[510]

Chiljan's discussion was also very brief,[511] but she suggested what is truly strange about line 5's reference to Shakspere. If he

---

(footnote continued from previous page)
　　audiences from perceiving the actors' own faults.)
(5) Some actors (a second group, perhaps a subset of the first, notably Shakspere and Burbage) she did not reward as they deserved.
(6) Still other actors (a third group) acted badly all the time,
(7) And while (because?) they acted badly, their bad natures remained
(8) Part of their personalities, judging by their typical behavior.

[508] See Chiljan, p. 260; A. Nelson, "Davies, *Humour's Heaven*" (2016).

[509] Why, in 1609, would Shakespeare (by his initials or any spelling) be referenced solely as an actor with no mention of his well-known literary career? More odd "actor-only" references appear in Ben Jonson's *Works* (1616), see Part III.B & note 38, and in the 1635 answer by Cuthbert Burbage, see Part I & note 8. See also Part IV.26 (discussing Davies, *Scourge of Folly*, c. 1610–11).

[510] A. Nelson, "Davies, *Humour's Heaven*" (2016).

[511] Chiljan, p. 260, quoted only lines 5 and 7 (not line 6), suggesting it was Shakspere and Burbage who "acted ill." But it is pretty clear from line 6 that line 7 does not refer to them (players whom Fortune "guerdoned not"), but rather to a
(footnote continued on next page)

was the author Shakespeare, how on earth could he be said "not" to be rewarded or honored as he deserved? His name was plastered all over numerous admired and hot-selling plays and poems, and he had obtained a coat-of-arms, the coveted status of "gentleman," and great financial success.[512] As a man of common provincial origins, plying the widely despised trade of acting, what more "deserts" could he possibly expect?[513]

*"Evidently,"* to borrow Nelson's word, Davies must have been talking about *someone else,* someone *hidden behind* the initials "W.S." As Chiljan noted, this comment is reminiscent of "others made about Shakespeare, that he could not be openly praised or credited."[514] It echoes the comment in *Microcosmos* that this same goddess Fortune had "refused" something to W.S. It also, yet again, echoes the various suggestions in the *Sonnets* (deeply puzzling under the Stratfordian theory) that Fortune had spited and disgraced the author.[515] Given that *Humour's Heaven* and the *Sonnets* appear to have been published the same year, perhaps the former was in part a comment upon the latter.

These 1603 and 1609 comments by Davies of Hereford, taken in combination, may be read to suggest that the author Shake-

---

(footnote continued from previous page)
separate group ("othersome"). See note 507. In that respect, Nelson's reading is superior and correct. Chiljan did not base any analytical point on her implied (and surely inadvertent) misreading.

[512] See, *e.g.*, note 469 and related text. On the complex and evolving meaning of "gentle" during this time, see note 482.

[513] The comment may make some sense as applied to Burbage, though not a lot, given the admiration and success he also enjoyed, rising far above the typical disrepute of actors. See, *e.g.*, Part IV.16 & note 357. But perhaps Davies meant Burbage deserved more praise, or recompense, or both, for his *painting* (though he did not mention it in *Humour's Heaven*). Painting was viewed at the time as a more refined and respectable pursuit than acting. Chiljan, p. 259, commented (debatably) that Burbage "was not renowned for his painting." See note 465 and related text.

[514] Chiljan, p. 260.

[515] See notes 474-79 and related text; see also Parts IV.4 & note 215; IV.10 & note 287; IV.18 & notes 438-43; IV.23 & notes 578-81; IV.24 & note 605.

speare was an aristocrat hiding behind a pseudonym, whose social status was *"stained"* and who was never honored by his own name as he deserved. As such, they synergize generally with the "many overlooked remarks"[516] surveyed in this book.

The way Davies phrased his comment in line 8 of the key passage in *Microcosmos*, that "the stage doth *stain* pure gentle blood," specifically recalls the 1593 comment by Thomas Edwards, discussed in Part IV.4, that the author was "in purple robes *distained* ... One whose power floweth far, That *should have been* [but somehow was not,] of our rhyme, The only object and the star"—a writer whose "golden art might woo us, To have honored him with bays,"[517] yet who somehow never received such public honor. These early published comments do not sit easily with the Stratfordian theory.

## 21. William Camden, *Remains* (1605) and *Britannia* (1607)

William Camden (1551–1623) was a scholar known for writing several important historical, geographical, and antiquarian books. One of his most famous and highly regarded is *Remains of a Greater Work, Concerning Britain*, a collection of essays first published in 1605. Probably his greatest work is *Britannia*, a geographical and historical survey (chorography) of Great Britain and Ireland. *Britannia* was first published in 1586 and a greatly expanded sixth edition appeared in 1607.[518]

---

[516] Chiljan, p. 260.

[517] Edwards, p. 63 (emphases added); see also, *e.g.*, Stritmatter (2006) (discussing the Edwards poem); Price, pp. 231-32 (same); Chiljan, pp. 253-54 (same).

[518] See, *e.g.*, Jiménez (2013), pp. 46-47; Ogburn, pp. 112-13. *Remains* was published in English; second and third editions appeared in 1614 and 1623. It was actually completed as early as 1596, nine years before publication. See Camden, pp. xxviii, xxxi-xxxvii (introduction to 1984 scholarly edition). The "greater work" was *Britannia*. The first through sixth editions of *Britannia* were in Latin; a revised English translation appeared in 1610.

Camden loved poetry, dabbled in it himself, and was a friend of poet-playwright Michael Drayton (1563–1631), who in turn, like Shakspere of Stratford, was a native of Warwickshire (though not of Stratford).[519] *Remains*, not surprisingly, included a discussion of poetry and a short list of English poets and playwrights including Drayton and "William Shakespeare"—all of whom, according to Camden, "succeeding ages may justly admire."[520]

Nothing in that reference indicates that Camden had any personal acquaintance with or knowledge of the author Shakespeare.[521] For all that appears, he was simply citing the published name on the works. But this passage in *Remains*, and an omission in *Britannia*, arguably generate some authorship doubts when viewed in tandem. We know that Camden *did*, in fact, have *some* specific and personal knowledge about William Shakspere of Stratford, his father John, and the town of Stratford itself. Yet Camden did not connect the town or the player to the author. Ramon Jiménez discussed Camden in his article "Ten Eyewitnesses Who Saw Nothing"—witnesses to Elizabethan and Jacobean life, that is, who saw nothing connecting Shakspere of Stratford with the literary works or career of "Shakespeare."[522]

---

[519] There are good reasons to believe (as many Stratfordian scholars do) that Drayton and Shakspere knew each other. See Jiménez (2013), pp. 47-40.

[520] Camden, p. 294, quoted in Chambers (1930), v. 2, p. 215; see also Jiménez (2013), pp. 46-47. In addition to Shakespeare and Drayton, Camden's list includes Ben Jonson and John Marston, among others. See Part IV.11 (discussing Marston's *Scourge of Villainy*, 1598–99), and Parts III.B & note 38, and IV.28 (discussing some of Jonson's writings).

[521] I do not claim that fact alone has any particular significance. His reference in *Remains* to Drayton also does not betray any personal knowledge, even though we know (from other evidence) that he and Drayton were friends.

[522] Jiménez (2013) (revising and combining his 2002 and 2005 articles); see also Part II & note 2. Jiménez is an Oxfordian scholar. I do not generally view instances of mere silence as items of early doubt warranting prominent treatment as such in this book. Camden's silence in *Britannia* about Shakspere of Stratford seems notable only because of his overt citation of the author "Shakespeare" in *Remains*. However, other early discussions or citations of Shakspere, that fail to connect him to the author "Shakespeare" (or any literary career), are

(footnote continued on next page)

*Britannia* contains a "description of each [county] beginning in the pre-Roman period and extending to contemporary people and events."[523] Camden included a section on Warwickshire. But he never mentioned Shakespeare in either 1607 or any earlier or later edition during his lifetime.[524] With regard to Stratford, Camden "described this 'small market-town' as owing 'all its consequence to two natives of it. They are John de Stratford, later Archbishop of Canterbury, who built the church, and Hugh Clopton, later mayor of London, who built the Clopton bridge across the Avon' [river]."[525] Camden made "no mention of the well-known poet and playwright, William Shakespeare, who had supposedly been born and raised [there], whose family supposedly still lived

---

(footnote continued from previous page)
certainly also interesting, as are people who knew or met Shakspere but likewise failed to draw any such connection. This kind of "evidence from silence" does provide some support for the existence of doubts about the author's identity during and soon after Shakspere's lifetime.

In addition to Camden, for example (and Drayton), Jiménez (2013) identified eight more "eyewitnesses" who knew or met Shakspere, were in a position to know what he was up to, and left significant writings of their own, yet who failed even to hint at any connection between him and the works of "Shakespeare": Thomas Greene, Dr. John Hall (Shakspere's own son-in-law), James Cooke, Sir Fulke Greville, Edward Pudsey, Queen Henrietta Maria (wife of King Charles I), Philip Henslowe, and Edward Alleyn (discussed in Part IV.2.g).

This book has also cited several references to Shakspere *solely as an actor*, with no mention of the well-known literary career of the author. Even apart from *other* ways that some of those references may further express or indicate doubts, such *silences* about any literary career are very significant in themselves. These cited "actor-only" references date to 1609 (Davies of Hereford, *Humour's Heaven*) (Part IV.20 & note 509), *c.* 1610–11 (Davies of Hereford, *Scourge of Folly*) (Part IV.26 & notes 656-57), 1616 (Jonson, *Works*) (Part III.B & note 38), and 1635 (Cuthbert Burbage) (Part I & note 8).

[523] Jiménez (2013), p. 46.

[524] See Jiménez (2013), pp. 46-47; Ogburn, pp. 112-13. As Ogburn noted, p. 113, even the posthumous 1637 (second English) edition, postdating the *First Folio* (and Camden's death) by 14 years, "makes no mention of [Shakespeare]." Not until the *1695* edition was a note added commenting that "William Shakespeare, a native of this place," was a playwright who was buried there. Quoted in Ogburn, p. 113.

[525] Jiménez (2013), pp. 46-47 (quoting *Britannia*).

there, and who by this date had supposedly returned there to live in one of the grandest houses in town."[526]

This was in 1607, fifteen years after Stratfordians assure us that Shakspere of Stratford had become famous in the London theatre scene,[527] years during which bestselling books of poetry and many popular plays appeared under his name. Camden's own *Remains* (1605), along with books like *Palladis Tamia* (1598) by Francis Meres,[528] testify to Shakespeare's fame as an author.

There are additional reasons, aside from Camden's friendship with Drayton (who Stratfordians say knew Shakespeare[529]), why it seems questionable that Camden did not mention the author Shakespeare's supposed connection to Stratford. He certainly knew about the Shakspere family's connections. Camden in 1597 became "one of the two officials in the College of Arms who approved applications for coats of arms."[530] In 1599, William Shakspere's father, John (perhaps with William's help or at his urging), applied to have the family coat-of-arms (which had apparently been approved in 1596) joined with that of John's wife's family (the Ardens), who were from a village close to Stratford. Camden and a colleague at the College of Arms apparently granted the 1599 application, and in a twist that must have made the Shakspere family even more memorable, were later subjected to allegations that they improperly approved 23 applications, including the Shakspere coat-of-arms.[531]

Still more facts suggest that Camden's omission of Shakespeare in *Britannia* may have been because he did not associate the author with Stratford—not, perhaps, because *Britannia* generally disregarded contemporary literary figures. As Jiménez

---

[526] Jiménez (2013), p. 47; see also Ogburn, pp. 112-13.
[527] See Part IV.2 (discussing *Groats-Worth of Wit*, 1592).
[528] See Part IV.12.
[529] See note 519; Jiménez (2013), pp. 47-48.
[530] Jiménez (2013), p. 47.
[531] See Jiménez (2013), p. 47; see also Price, pp. 66-73.

noted, Camden kept a detailed diary in which he recorded the deaths of actor Richard Burbage and poet-playwright Samuel Daniel in March and October 1619. But, reflecting the broader mystery of the Great Silence of 1616,[532] Camden recorded "no such note on [Shakspere's] death ... in April 1616."[533]

Despite the foregoing, Camden's writings, viewed strictly as pre-1616 evidence of authorship doubt, are probably among the weakest indications itemized in this book.[534] The Stratfordian scholar David Kathman has noted that the antiquarian focus of *Britannia*, on historic buildings and the like, may well explain why it ignored Shakespeare when discussing Warwickshire. But still, Camden's writings raise questions.[535]

---

[532] See Part I & note 34.

[533] Jiménez (2013), p. 47; see also p. 56 n. 1; see also Ogburn, p. 113. Burbage is also discussed in Parts IV.16 and 20.

[534] By contrast to his 1605 and 1607 publications, however, his 1616–19 diary entries *following* Shakspere's death are powerful anti-Stratfordian evidence, especially in light of Camden's known personal connections to the Shaksperes. The latter evidence alone justifies Jiménez's inclusion of Camden among his "ten eyewitnesses" and is a key reason this book discusses Camden's writings. Camden's diary entries are not mentioned in Kathman, "Shakespeare's Eulogies" (discussed in note 535), which seeks to debunk Camden's writings as indications of authorship doubt, even though the primary focus of Kathman's article is to attack generally the idea that there was anything unusual about the aftermath of Shakspere's death in 1616. Ogburn, p. 113, noted the diary entries as early as 1984, and Kathman's article (like much else he has written) focuses heavily on criticizing Ogburn. Nor, to my knowledge, have the diary entries ever been discussed by any other Stratfordian scholar since Ogburn pointed them out.

[535] See Kathman, "Shakespeare's Eulogies" (sec. 5). I would note, supporting Kathman's argument, that it also (apparently) failed to mention Camden's friend Drayton. Jiménez (2013), p. 47, commented: "Elsewhere in *Britannia*, Camden noted that the poet Philip Sidney had a home in Kent." But as Kathman observes (sec. 4), Sidney, while best-known today for his poetry, "was much better known [then] as a [knighted] courtier, diplomat, [and] military hero."

Less convincing is Kathman's emphasis (sec. 5) on the facts that *Britannia* was originally written in Latin and first published in 1586 (before Shakespeare's prominence as an author). Why does the language matter? Furthermore, it is not disputed that each new edition was greatly expanded and enriched with new details. It remains at least a bit odd that the editions published in 1607, 1610, and 1637 (the latter two in English) continued to ignore the beloved poet-playwright who (under the Stratfordian theory) must have been by then the town's most renowned personality by far (as he remains to this day).

22. *Sir Thomas Smith's Voyage* (1605) and the Late English Ovid

The Oxfordian scholar Jan Cole, in a stunningly important 2014 article, discussed the anonymous pamphlet, *Sir Thomas Smith's Voyage and Entertainment in Russia*, published in London no later than the fall of 1605. *Voyage's* subtitle refers to "the tragical ends of two Emperors, and one Empress." It describes the tumultuous and violent events surrounding the April 1605 death of Tsar Boris Godunov, during the 1604–05 sojourn in Moscow of England's ambassador Sir Thomas Smith (*c.* 1558–1625). Boris has long been suspected of poisoning his predecessor Ivan the Terrible and arranging the murder of one of Ivan's sons. Boris's own teenage son Feodor was himself murdered in June 1605, just two months after inheriting his father's throne, along with Boris's widow Maria (both said to have been poisoned, but probably strangled), by a usurper known as the False Dmitry.[536]

---

[536] See, *e.g.*, Cole (May 2014), pp. 24-25; Waugh, "My Shakespeare" (2018), p. 73. This Sir Thomas Smith (often spelled "Smythe") is not to be confused with an elder Sir Thomas Smith (1513–77; no apparent relation), the renowned scholar who also served as ambassador (the elder to France; they also both served as Members of Parliament). The elder Smith was an early tutor of Edward de Vere (Earl of Oxford). See Hughes, "Shakespeare's Tutor" (2000); Anderson, pp. 0-0.

We do not seem to have any strong clues about the author of *Voyage*. Could it have been Smith? The title seems to suggest that. Could not *"Smith's Voyage"* be by Smith just as *"Shake-speare's Sonnets"* are (at least implied to be) by "Shakespeare"? I was still a bit unclear on this issue when I gave a conference presentation outlining this book. See Wildenthal, "Early Shakespeare Authorship Doubts" (2017 video, at minute 24) (mistakenly citing *Voyage* as a "letter" by Smith). Cole and Waugh did not offer any opinion on *Voyage's* author, though as Cole noted, p. 26, the author "claims to have had his information from someone in [Smith's] entourage." As a high-ranking official, Smith may have had reasons to maintain at least a polite veneer of anonymity. He was a merchant and politician, not generally known as a writer, but he must have been fairly literate given the many positions he held, not just ambassador but auditor of the City of London and treasurer of St. Bartholomew's Hospital. As Cole noted, p. 25 (quoting *Voyage*; emphasis in original), the author "admits" at one point "that he's no poet himself ... 'no nor any heir to the *Muses*; yet happily a younger brother ....' "

These events at the Russian royal court were operatic enough to inspire *Boris Godunov* (1874) by Mussorgsky, based on the play by Pushkin. Do they also seem, well, Shakespearean? Perhaps remind you of *Hamlet*, with its young prince whose father dies, whose succession is thwarted by a usurper, and who is killed by poison along with his mother? If so, you're not the first. The point is not to suggest these events inspired *Hamlet*—both quartos of that play were published in 1603–04, the second from the same printer as *Voyage*.[537] Rather, it is that *Voyage*'s author was clearly reminded of *Hamlet*. (Pushkin too was inspired by Shakespeare.[538]) As *Voyage* laments:

> His father's Empire and Government [that of Tsar Boris, father of Feodor] was ... but as the Poetical FURY in a Stage-action, complete yet with horrid and woeful Tragedies; a first, but no second to any *Hamlet*; and that now Revenge, just Revenge was coming with his Sword drawn against him [and] his Royal Mother ... to fill up those Murdering Scenes ....[539]

As Cole noted, *Voyage*'s author then muses about which writers might best be suited to dramatize this Russian tragedy, mentioning, for example, Sir Philip Sidney, who had died almost twenty years before in 1586, and Sir Fulke Greville and Ben Jonson, who both, like Shakspere of Stratford, had many years left to live—more than ten in Shakspere's case, 23 for Greville, and 32 for Jonson.[540] The author was obviously a literary insider, being familiar with the fact "that Greville was writing poetic tragedies at a time when they were only circulating privately."[541]

---

[537] Thus further strengthening the connection between the two works. See Cole, pp. 24, 27 (discussing printer James Roberts).

[538] See Cole, p. 28.

[539] Quoted in Cole, p. 25 (emphasis of "FURY" in original; emphasis of "*Hamlet*" and brackets added here).

[540] See Cole, pp. 25-26.

[541] Cole, p. 26.

*Voyage*'s author, as Cole put it rather mildly, "then ... makes an intriguing statement": "I am with the late *English* quick-spirited, clear-sighted *Ovid*: It is to be feared Dreaming, and think I see many strange and cruel actions, but say myself nothing all this while ...."[542] Cole is surely correct that the words following the colon seem to quote or paraphrase "something that 'English Ovid' said or wrote, and with which the author agrees."[543] The author's meaning might be paraphrased as follows: "I agree with the recently deceased English Ovid, a quick-witted and perceptive writer. As he said, and as I have learned, dreaming is to be feared, and one may witness many strange and cruel events yet say nothing about them."

There are three important points to consider: (1) what further connections, if any, this comment has to *Hamlet*, (2) the identity of "English Ovid," and (3) the significance of calling this unnamed writer "the *late* English Ovid." Points 1 and 2 are closely related. Point 3 is the killer.

As for the *Hamlet* connections, we have just seen *Voyage*'s explicit reference to *Hamlet* in the passage preceding the "English Ovid" comment, and the fact that *Voyage* and the 1604 quarto of *Hamlet* shared the same printer. Cole, noting both those connections, digressed for two pages on points 2 and 3 before working her way back to pointing out the similar *Hamlet* echoes of the Ovid comment. I agree strongly with Cole that this comment "reminds us of [the character] Hamlet's own concerns with *fear, dreaming, sleep,* and *silence,*" and with her suggestion that *Voyage*'s author is "echoing Hamlet's speeches."[544]

Cole drew a powerful connection to Hamlet's soliloquy following the arrival and initial demonstration-reading of the players:

---

[542] Quoted in Cole, p. 25 (italics in original; omitting a bracketed "[I]" which Cole inserted before "think I see").

[543] Cole, p. 25.

[544] Cole, p. 27 (emphases added).

O, what a rogue and peasant slave am I!
Is it not monstrous that this player here,
But in a fiction, in a *dream* of passion,
Could force his soul so to his own conceit ...
Tears in his eyes, distraction in his aspect,
A broken voice ... And all for nothing,
For Hecuba! What's Hecuba to him, or he to Hecuba,
That he should weep for her? What would he do
Had he the motive and the cue for passion
That I have? He would drown the stage with tears ...
Yet I, a dull and muddy-mettled rascal, peak
Like John-a-*dreams*, unpregnant of my cause,
And can *say nothing. No, not for a king* ....[545]

As Cole noted, the culmination of Hamlet's lament, that he
"can say nothing," is "almost identical"[546] to the words attributed
to English Ovid: "but say myself nothing." I would add that Hamlet laments he can say nothing despite having *seen strange and
terrible things*—not least the apparition of his royal father's
ghost—just as it is suggested that English Ovid says nothing despite having "*see[n] many strange and cruel actions.*"

Alexander Waugh noted an even more powerful connection to
*Hamlet* in the *first* words attributed by *Voyage* to English Ovid:
"It is to be feared Dreaming, and think I see many strange and
cruel actions ...."[547] Those words link directly to Hamlet's best-
known soliloquy, the most famous speech in the entire Shakespeare canon. Observe again the linkages to the themes Cole
noted—*fear, dreaming, sleep,* and *silence*—as well as to the
"*strange and cruel actions*" that *Voyage*'s author, English Ovid,
and Hamlet have all seen:

---

[545] *Hamlet*, act 2, sc. 2 (my emphases), quoted in part and discussed in Cole,
p. 27.

[546] Cole, p. 27.

[547] See Waugh, "My Shakespeare," p. 74. Waugh focused on the words: "It is
to be feared Dreaming." I build here on Cole's and Waugh's analysis by quoting
more of *Hamlet*, act 3, sc. 1, and drawing additional connections, including to
*Voyage*'s words about "see[ing] many strange and cruel actions."

To be, or *not to be* [to remain *silent?*], that is the
   question:
Whether 'tis nobler in the mind to *suffer*
*The slings and arrows of outrageous fortune*
Or to take arms against *a sea of troubles*
And by opposing end them. To die, *to sleep—*
No more, and *by a sleep* to say we end
*The heartache and the thousand natural shocks*
That flesh is heir to. 'Tis a consummation
Devoutly to be wished. To die, *to sleep—*
*To sleep*, perchance *to dream*—aye, there's the rub,
*For in that sleep of death what dreams may come,*
When we have shuffled off this mortal coil,
*Must give us pause.* ...
For who would bear *the whips and scorns of time* ...
But that *the dread of something after death*
   [*i.c., fear* of the "*sleep* of death"],
The undiscovered country, from whose bourn
No traveler returns, *puzzles the will,*
And makes us rather bear *those ills we have*
Than fly to others that we know not of?
Thus conscience does make *cowards* of us all,
*And thus the native hue of resolution*
*Is sicklied o'er with the pale cast of thought*
   [*i.e.*, out of *fear* we are kept *silent*] ....[548]

As for the second of the three points, the conclusion is almost
irresistible that English Ovid is the author of *Hamlet*—thus,
Shakespeare—even though *Voyage*, oddly (or maybe not so oddly,
as we will see), never mentions him by name. Cole noted it was
quite typical at the time "for an author to be referred to by the
name of a character ... or ... one of his book-titles" and suggested
*Voyage* was "doing the same thing indirectly" by associating English Ovid with the speeches of a memorable character like Hamlet.
She further noted the "implication" that English Ovid "used the

---

[548] *Hamlet*, act 3, sc. 1 (my emphases and brackets).

voice of Hamlet to express his own thoughts—a notion that is oddly [or not so oddly?] identical to the Oxfordian view concerning autobiographical features [of the life of Edward de Vere] in the character of Hamlet."[549]

Supporting this identification, even if none of the compelling linkages to *Hamlet* existed, is the fact that no Elizabethan poet other than Shakespeare fits so well the sobriquet "English Ovid." Francis Meres declared in 1598 that "the sweet witty soul of *Ovid* lives in ... *Shakespeare*."[550] Modern orthodox scholars would be hard-pressed to deny it. Sir Jonathan Bate wrote the leading book and his title says it all: *Shakespeare and Ovid*. Charles and Michelle Martindale even resurrected the same nickname, suggesting that Shakespeare "started his career with a deliberate attempt to present himself as something of an English Ovid."[551]

The third point is the stunning significance of that one little word: "*late*." Cole discussed several other writers of the time who might conceivably have been called English Ovid. But even leaving aside other reasons they are less likely candidates than the author Shakespeare, almost all are eliminated either because they died so long before as to make it unlikely they would be referred to in 1605 as "the late" (suggesting fairly recent death), or they were still alive in 1605.[552]

---

549 Cole, p. 27. On the point that *Voyage* never mentions Shakespeare by name, see Cole, p. 27, and Waugh, "My Shakespeare," p. 73. On authors being known by their characters or titles, Cole, p. 27, cited John Lyly, known as "Euphues," and Thomas Nashe as "Pierce Penniless." On the latter, see also Part IV.3 & notes 129, 188. On the Oxfordian linkages to *Hamlet*, see Part IV.3 & notes 131-34.

550 *Palladis Tamia*, quoted in Chambers (1930), v. 2, p. 194 (italics in original); see also Parts IV.12 & note 295, and IV.16 & notes 359, 370-72.

551 Martindale & Martindale (1990), p. 47, quoted in Cole, pp. 26-27. Cole also, p. 26, cited Bate, *Shakespeare and Ovid* (1993).

552 See Cole, p. 26; see also p. 28 (discussing Thomas Nashe, believed to have died *c.* 1601, and Thomas Churchyard, who died in 1604, but noting other reasons they are unlikely to have been called English Ovid). For example, Cole's analysis, and known death dates, rule out the other writers mentioned in *Voyage*. See, *e.g.*, note 540 and related text on Sidney, Greville, and Jonson. Fur-

(footnote continued on next page)

The problem for the orthodox view of "Shakespeare" is that the timing rules out Shakspere of Stratford too. In the fall of 1605 he had more than a decade still to live, so he could hardly be the *late* English Ovid. That one word, by itself, bids fair to destroy the entire Stratfordian edifice. Whoever the author Shakespeare was, he was dead by 1605. As we will see, *Voyage* is the earliest of *five separate indications* that the author died before 1616.[553]

Yet again, as we have seen, the Shakespearean *doppelgängers* undergo a curious fission. It seems that English Ovid *must* be the author Shakespeare, yet *cannot* be the player Shakspere. As Sherlock Holmes taught us, "when you have eliminated the impossible, whatever remains, however improbable, must be the truth."[554] *Shakspere* cannot be *Shakespeare*.

*Voyage* also points suggestively to Vere as the strongest authorship candidate—yet again corroborating all the other evidence to that effect.[555] The obvious related question is why *Voyage's*

---

(footnote continued from previous page)
thermore, I would note, the structure of the text suggests that English Ovid is someone *different* from the other writers mentioned. *Voyage's* author muses about other writers, but then seems to shift gears, as if leaving them aside, to opt *instead* for alignment with English Ovid.

Cole did not discuss Edmund Spenser, who died in 1599. For various reasons, including the *Hamlet* connections, Spenser seems much less likely than Shakespeare to be *Voyage's* late English Ovid. But Spenser would merit some expert attention in any follow-up studies of this issue.

[553] See also Parts IV.23 (Barksted, *Myrrha, the Mother of Adonis*, 1607), IV.24 (*Shake-speare's Sonnets*, 1609), IV.29 (*Envy's Scourge, and Virtue's Honour*, c. 1605–15), and IV.30 (Brooke, *Ghost of Richard the Third*, 1614, with a discussion of all five items).

[554] Doyle, "The Sign of Four," ch. 6, in *Sherlock Holmes*, p. 111 (emphasis in original).

[555] See Part I, note 4. In keeping with the Preface's comment that this book "is not primarily an Oxfordian tract," I will summarize briefly here: Most simply and compellingly, the timing of Vere's death (on June 24, 1604) fits perfectly for him to be called "the late" in 1605. Cole showed how English Ovid's channeling of *Hamlet* points to Vere. See note 549 and related text. Vere was publicly described as a fine poet-playwright. See Part IV.3 & notes 135-50. According to Waugh, "My Shakespeare," p. 73, the descriptions of English Ovid in *Voyage* as "quick-spirited" and "clear-sighted" match descriptions of Vere by Gabriel Har-

(footnote continued on next page)

author did not explicitly name Shakespeare. As Cole asked, if he "was happy to identify 'English Horace' as 'Benjamin' (Jonson), why did he not identify 'English Ovid' by name?" Cole answered her own question: His "reticence may suggest that he knew the name 'Shakespeare' was a pseudonym."[556]

If *Voyage*'s author had explicitly identified the late English Ovid, that would have risked both a public rejection of the Stratfordian attribution and a clear revelation of the Oxfordian identity. This author, like other writers of the era, clearly did not want to risk that. If telling the truth so blatantly had been viewed at the time as a safe or acceptable option, we would not have the array of curiously veiled doubts and comments surveyed in this book. This author and other writers apparently preferred to avoid both explicit dishonesty and explicit truth-telling about the author Shakespeare. Instead, they opted for the middle course of being politely (even if thinly) veiled, and artfully elliptical.

## 23. William Barksted, *Myrrha, the Mother of Adonis* (1607)

As Stratfordian scholars Terry Ross and David Kathman discuss in a co-authored article, William Barksted (*c.* 1589–?) is an intriguing early modern English poet. He was apparently a boy actor with the Children of the Queen's Revels (sometimes called Children of the Chapel), and is thought to have been only about 18 upon publication of the first of his two known poems, *Myrrha, the Mother of Adonis, or Lust's Prodigies* (1607).[557]

---

(footnote continued from previous page)
vey (no citation given), and Waugh noted other links, including that Shakespeare relied heavily on Vere's uncle Arthur Golding's translation of Ovid's *Metamorphoses*. Waugaman (2018) documented a longstanding Oxfordian suggestion that Vere himself may actually be responsible for the translation credited to Golding.

[556] Cole, p. 27.

[557] See, *e.g.*, Ross & Kathman, "Barksted." Myrrha, in Greek mythology, was the incestuous mother of Adonis. She was turned into a myrrh tree. Barksted's second and only other known significant work, the poem *Hiren, or The*

(footnote continued on next page)

Barksted, as an adult, apparently continued to work as an actor, including at the Whitefriars Theatre which operated *circa* 1608–14. He must have died some time between his 1617 arrest for an altercation with a constable and a 1638 reference to him as deceased.[558] *Myrrha* is very interesting with regard to the SAQ because, despite the strenuous protests of Ross & Kathman, it is the second of five notable indications that the author Shakespeare died before 1616.[559]

Barksted was obviously enamored of Shakespeare's erotic poem *Venus and Adonis*, to which his own poem is in part an homage. He describes in three of the four final stanzas, with seemingly eager sympathy, Venus's pursuit of Adonis: "[N]or Etna now Burns more than her, she roams the wood so wide After her game [Adonis], that to his game doth bow [*i.e.*, he is not interested in her, only in hunting]." In the next stanza: "Oft would she say, and bathe those words in tears, Oh thou fair boy, would God thou lovdst like me, But sure thou art not flesh, it well appears, Thou wert the stubborn issue of a tree, So hard thou art." While Venus desires "this choice flower, clasped in her iron bed," she complains in the next-to-last stanza about the indignity of having to chase him: "Though thou be fair, 'tis I that should be coy."[560]

---

(footnote continued from previous page)
*Fair Greek,* was published in 1611, with a title page identifying him as "one of the servants of his Majesty's Revels." Barksted dedicated *Hiren* to two of the children of Edward de Vere (17th Earl of Oxford): his eldest daughter, Elizabeth Vere Stanley (Countess of Derby), and his son and successor, Henry de Vere (18th Earl of Oxford). See Miller, "Family Affair," pp. 27-28.

[558] See, *e.g.*, Ross & Kathman, "Barksted"; Chambers (1930), v. 2, p. 216 (quoting the crucial final stanza of *Myrrha*).

[559] See also Parts IV.22 (*Sir Thomas Smith's Voyage*, 1605), IV.24 (*Shakespeare's Sonnets*, 1609), IV.29 (*Envy's Scourge, and Virtue's Honour*, c. 1605–15), and IV.30 (Brooke, *Ghost of Richard the Third*, 1614, with a discussion of all five items).

[560] "Etna" refers to Mount Etna, the active volcano in Sicily. Ross & Kathman, "Barksted," helpfully provide a quotation of the four final stanzas of this long poem, on which I gratefully rely here. Brackets and explanations are mine; I
(footnote continued on next page)

It is the final stanza that raises authorship doubts. Barksted shifts gears in conclusion to address his own poetic "Muse." Recall that the Muses, in Greek mythology, are the daughters of gods and live (mythically speaking) on the heights of Mount Helicon— thus, more or less, in heaven. They inspire poets and other artists and scholars.[561]

As Ross & Kathman note, Barksted's poem is mainly devoted to "the tale of Adonis's mother," Myrrha, but in the last four stanzas, as quoted above, he "begins to tell the story of Venus's love for [Adonis]," Myrrha's son. "[T]hen," in the final stanza, he "breaks off, as if realizing that he is encroaching on Shakespeare's poem."[562] Here is the final stanza (numbering the lines for conven- ient reference):

(1) But stay my Muse in thine own confines keep,
(2) And wage not war with so dear loved a neighbor,
(3) But having sung thy day song, rest and sleep,
(4) Preserve thy small fame and his greater favor:
(5) His Song was worthy merit (*Shakspeare* he) [*sic*]
(6) Sung the fair blossom, thou the withered tree,
(7) *Laurel* is due to him, his art and wit
(8) Hath purchased it, *Cypress* thy brow will fit.[563]

The leading anti-Stratfordian arguments about these lines of which I am aware—by Charlton Ogburn Jr., Joseph Sobran, Diana Price, and Katherine Chiljan—have been a mixed bag,

---

(footnote continued from previous page)
silently modernize spellings, and capitalize some words and insert some commas at line beginnings and endings.

[561] Some traditions say they live on Mount Parnassus. Both are actual mountains in Greece, part of the same range. See Parts IV.3 & note 180, and IV.15 & note 333.

[562] Ross & Kathman, "Barksted."

[563] Quoted in Ross & Kathman, "Barksted," and Chambers (1930), v. 2, p. 216 (italics in original as quoted in Chambers). I replace two ampersands with "and" and make some other minor adjustments as described in note 560. I am careful in quoting, however, not to try to correct Barksted's often loose and con- fusing syntax. I save those issues for the follow-up discussion.

though they were all on to something that orthodox scholars have missed. Ross & Kathman criticize, fairly enough, the weak and limited nature of an argument offered by Ogburn and Sobran about the past-tense "was" in line 5. But they utterly fail to comprehend an argument Sobran suggested (but did not develop) about line 8's reference to "*Cypress.*" And they miss the boat completely with regard to lines 1-2, which raise still more doubts.[564] All six scholars miss the significance of another aspect of lines 7-8.

Price and Chiljan both focused on lines 1-2. Price offered a valuable refutation of an especially pernicious orthodox misuse of those lines, but she did not address *Myrrha's* indications that the author Shakespeare was deceased by 1607. Chiljan's treatment is by far the best, though even her argument could use some further development.[565] As usual, the present study attempts a synthesis. It bears emphasis that I could not have accomplished anything here without the insights of all six of these scholars in all five cited studies. It is only from sympathetically reading each other's work that we gain greater understanding.

Ogburn and Sobran focused too briefly on line 5, arguing that because it describes Shakespeare's "song" in the past tense, that indicates he must have died by 1607. As Sobran put it: "Why is [he] ... already being spoken of in the past tense?"[566] Ross & Kathman correctly criticize this as a weak argument, taken by itself. As they spend most of their article belaboring, Shakespeare *himself* is *not* described in the past tense by line 5—only his "song." They show it was quite common then to refer to living writers in the past tense, especially in relation to their past works. They con-

---

[564] See Ogburn, p. 206; Sobran, p. 144; Ross & Kathman, "Barksted."

[565] See Price, p. 146; Chiljan, pp. 260-61.

[566] Sobran, p. 144. Ogburn's analysis, after quoting line 5 ("His Song was worthy merit ..."), was just eight words long: "not his song *is,* but his song *was.*" Ogburn, p. 206 (emphases in original). Sobran, aside from his quoted question, offered only three words of analysis: "*Was* worthy merit?" Sobran, p. 144 (emphasis in original).

clude, plausibly, that "Barksted's use of the past tense [in lines 5-6] is not a sign that Shakespeare had died, but rather that [his] poem *Venus and Adonis* had already become a classic ...."[567]

My brackets acknowledge that Ross & Kathman are attentive to the fact that line 5 is *not the only* past-tense expression relating to Shakespeare in this stanza. Barksted's syntax is a bit confusing, whether from poetic license or youthful exuberance, so it is useful to paraphrase what he seems to say in lines 5-6: "Shakespeare's song (his poem) was worthy and meritorious. He sang about the fair blossom (Adonis)."[568] So we have (so far) not one but *two* past-tense expressions: Shakespeare's "song *was* worthy" and he had "*sung* the fair blossom."

I still agree with Ross & Kathman, so far, that these two expressions (both of which they discuss) do not *prove* Shakespeare was a deceased author, or even make it more likely than not— though they are consistent with that reading and suggest that possibility. If "song" referred to the author's poetic legacy in general, it might better support the Ogburn-Sobran reading. But as Ross & Kathman suggest, given that *Myrrha* says that Shakespeare had "sung" about Adonis, these expressions seem to refer to *Venus and Adonis*, a specific past work published 14 years before in 1593.

There is a *third* past-tense expression to which, surprisingly, none of these six scholars devoted any analytical attention, even though it is the strongest of the three. Line 8 declares that Shakespeare "*hath purchased*" what line 7 calls the "laurel ... due to him," laurels being the traditional honor bestowed on poets. "His

[567] Ross & Kathman, "Barksted."

[568] The "blossom" refers more precisely to the purple flower that springs from Adonis's blood when he is fatally gored by the boar he hunts. See *Venus and Adonis*, lines 1165-88. Barksted's line 6 continues, "thou the withered tree," "thou" referring to Barksted himself (or his own Muse) and "withered tree" referring to Myrrha (see note 557). That is, Barksted's own "song" is mainly about Myrrha, exactly as the title indicates. See text preceding note 562.

art and wit" generally (line 7), not just (it seems[569]) any specific poem, "hath purchased" that honor. This lends a more elegiac tone to the entire stanza. Even so, as Ross & Kathman would surely argue (if they focused on this aspect of lines 7-8), this still does not prove the author Shakespeare was *necessarily* dead. A writer's overall past work could earn him laurels even while still alive.[570]

Going beyond the past-tense references, Sobran hinted too briefly at a very important additional point based on line 8's reference to "cypress." He said simply: "The cypress was a symbol of mourning; is this stanza a salute to a poet whom Barkst[e]d expects his readers to understand is deceased?"[571] Chiljan also suggested this argument, noting that "Barksted said his muse ... is fit to wear cypress, symbolic for mourning."[572]

Ross & Kathman pounce on Sobran's "cypress" argument with careless haste and unseemly glee. This reflects a pervasive weakness of their article, valuable though it is (sympathetic to a poet who deserves more attention). Their analysis seems distorted by

---

[569] I suppose one *might* quibble that Barksted meant *only* Shakespeare's "art and wit" in writing *Venus and Adonis* specifically, but that seems a cramped and less likely reading.

[570] That is suggested by an example offered in Ross & Kathman, "Barksted": Richard Barnfield's 1598 poem, with a notably elegiac title using a word often reserved for deceased persons (emphasis added): "A *Remembrance* of Some English Poets." Barnfield's poem states that *Venus and Adonis* and *The Rape of Lucrece* "have placed" Shakespeare's "name in fame's immortal book." See also Chambers (1930), v. 2, p. 195. As Ross & Kathman note, both Vere and Shakspere were still alive in 1598.

Note further, however, that while Barnfield says Shakespeare's works *"have placed"* (already) his "name in fame's immortal book," Barksted says that such a "laurel *is due* to him" (present tense), implying it has *not previously been conferred* (even though he already "hath purchased it," *i.e.*, earned it). The difference, perhaps, is that Barnfield means merely that the *"name"* ("Shakespeare") has gained "immortal fame," whereas Barksted may suggest that *an author hidden behind a pseudonym* has not yet received due honors *under his own name*. See my discussion in text, citing and building upon Chiljan, p. 261; see also Part IV.24 & notes 600-01 (discussing Ross & Kathman's mistaken use of the Barnfield poem in relation to "ever-living" as used in the *Sonnets* dedication).

[571] Sobran, p. 144.

[572] Chiljan, p. 261 (not citing Sobran).

an obsessive zeal to ridicule and marginalize Oxfordians and authorship doubters as cranks with nothing useful to contribute to Shakespearean studies. As a result, they fail to step back and perceive *Myrrha's* full context and significance. These are weaknesses shared by many Stratfordian contributions to the debate over the SAQ.

Ross & Kathman claim patronizingly that "Sobran has simply misunderstood the lines: clearly it is the laurel ... not the cypress that Shakespeare is due ...."[573] They are obviously correct on the latter point, as I just showed in exploring the other point ("hath purchased") that they and all four cited anti-Stratfordian scholars failed to notice in lines 7-8. As Chiljan suggested, Barksted modestly "fit[s]" the "cypress" to his own "brow" (or that of his Muse), in mourning for Shakespeare. The younger poet both honors and mourns the author Shakespeare by conceding the laurel to his elder while taking only bereaved cypress for himself, a beautifully elegant and graceful way to conclude his long poem.

But wait—Sobran *never said cypress was offered to Shakespeare!* He merely said it "was a symbol of mourning." Granting that he failed to develop the argument (Chiljan could have explained it better too), Sobran has not "misunderstood" anything. There is no basis whatsoever, in fact or logic, to impute to Sobran the misreading *twice* claimed by Ross & Kathman.[574]

Quite the contrary: Sobran's whole point was to argue that the author Shakespeare was *dead* in 1607, *not in mourning.* And if he *was* dead, might that perhaps explain, as both Sobran and

---

[573] Ross & Kathman, "Barksted." They could not similarly pounce on Chiljan, as she stated very clearly, p. 261, that "Shakespeare ... deserves to be wearing laurels." Ross & Kathman do not mention Chiljan in their undated article, apparently having written it prior to her 2011 book and failing to update it since. Failing to bother reading much anti-Stratfordian scholarship would be par for the course for Stratfordians like Ross & Kathman.

[574] As if to make sure readers don't miss it, they first assert that "Sobran misreads Barksted," and then later reiterate that "Sobran has simply misunderstood the lines." Ross & Kathman, "Barksted."

Chiljan suggested, *why Barksted (and his Muse) are apparently in mourning?* After all, Sobran suggested, "this stanza is a salute [by Barksted] to a poet" he thinks "is deceased."[575] That would logically suggest *Barksted* is in mourning for a late poet he admired. People typically mourn others who are deceased. Why do Ross & Kathman somehow think that Sobran somehow meant to suggest that Barksted somehow meant to suggest that Shakespeare should somehow *mourn himself?*

How and why do Ross & Kathman miss all this? Why do they fail to pause and consider *why* Barksted or his Muse *would be in mourning in the first place?* In fact, it's even worse: While conceding (as they must) that Barksted takes the cypress, they *never even acknowledge what that plainly indicates*, that Barksted *is in mourning.* Instead, they grudgingly note only that he "contrasts the low merits of his own muse ... with the poetic greatness of Shakespeare."[576] It is Ross & Kathman, not Sobran (or Chiljan), who have *utterly* "misunderstood" and failed to grasp what this crucial line means.

Ross & Kathman conclude their article with an attempt at sarcastic, self-satisfied humor: "Sobran and other Oxfordians should be warned that Barksted's granting the cypress to his own muse should not be taken as evidence that Barksted himself was dead in 1607."[577] But this lame joke backfires on them. Barksted's

---

[575] Sobran, p. 144 (omitting Sobran's question mark).

[576] With inept pomposity, Ross & Kathman quote lines 3-8 with bracketed explanations "for the benefit of readers who may find Barksted confusing." The closest they come to conceding that Barksted himself might be in mourning is their joke quoted in text (see note 577) about whether "Barksted himself was dead in 1607." Ross & Kathman, "Barksted."

[577] Ross & Kathman, "Barksted." Har har har. Their own cluelessness (see note 576) is much funnier than this pathetic joke. Yet I am clearly being generous in treating them primarily as clueless. They do not bother to contest Sobran's point (which they quote) that cypress symbolizes mourning. Nor could they. See, *e.g., OED*, v. 4, p. 198 (def. 1.c), citing, *e.g.,* Spenser's *Faerie Queen* (1590), book II, canto 1, stanza 60, lines 1-6, p. 220 ("So both agree their bodies to engrave; The great earth's womb they open to the sky, And with sad Cypress seemly it

(footnote continued on next page)

self-conferral of the cypress may well "be taken as evidence that Barksted" thought *Shakespeare* "was dead in 1607." Why else would Barksted be mourning him? Who or what else *would* he be mourning in this context?

As Chiljan perceptively noted, lines 7-8 contain yet a *third* indication of authorship doubt—again completely missed by Ross & Kathman—though this one does not (necessarily) suggest the author Shakespeare was already dead. Chiljan observed what I noted in passing above, that line 7 indicates the author "deserves to be wearing laurels ... but tributes to him are still lacking ('*Laurel* is due to him')."[578]

Chiljan's reading is debatable. It alone, like the past-tense references alone, or all four of those together, would probably not justify devoting a section of this book to *Myrrha*. In the abstract, one *might* already have received something to which one "is due," if it might be conferred repeatedly, as I suppose poetic laurels might be. But the explicit shift from present to past tense in lines 7-8 seems significant—from "laurel is due" to "his art and wit hath purchased it." If the laurels had already been conferred, it would seem Barksted could have said they "*were* due to him." The best reading seems to be that the author Shakespeare, in 1607, has somehow not yet *received* what he has *earned*.[579]

---

(footnote continued from previous page)
embrave, Then covering with a clod their closed eye, They lay therein those corses tenderly, And bid them sleep in everlasting peace."). So what's really going on here? It does not really seem plausible that Ross & Kathman simply missed the point. One may be forgiven for suspecting they kick up all this dust, *twice* falsely accusing Sobran of an obviously nonexistent misreading, in order to divert readers from the obvious authorship doubt (the suggestion that the author Shakespeare must be dead by 1607) conveyed by the reference to cypress.

[578] Chiljan, p. 261 (emphasis in original).

[579] It would have flowed very smoothly, and would seem more consistent with the idea that the author had already both earned *and* received his laurels— *as the name itself clearly had*—if Barksted had simply written: "Laurel was due to him, his art and wit hath purchased it." Compare the 1598 Barnfield poem on which Ross & Kathman rely. See note 570.

(footnote continued on next page)

As Chiljan suggested, this makes no sense whatsoever if Shakspere the player actually wrote the Shakespeare canon under his own name. That *name* had long since received laurels aplenty![580] Barksted may thus be read to imply that some author hidden behind the name was denied due honor. That recalls multiple similar suggestions of denial or disgrace we have seen, in Edwards, *L'Envoy* (1593) ("distained"), Fitzgeoffrey, *Affaniae* (1601) (don't "crucify yourself, O Bard"), Davies of Hereford, *Microcosmos* (1603) ("Fortune ... hath ... [W.S.] refused" and "the stage doth stain pure gentle blood") and *Humour's Heaven* (1609) (Fortune "guerdoned [rewarded W.S.] not"), and in many of the *Sonnets* (1609).[581]

We now come to the strongest expression of authorship doubt in *Myrrha*, in lines 1-2, yet again missed or ignored by Ross & Kathman. In line 1, Barksted explicitly addresses "my Muse," figuratively his own poetic voice. He maintains that self-referential form of address throughout the final stanza, including the last five words noted earlier (line 8, the other strong expression of authorship doubt): "*Cypress* thy brow will fit," thus declaring, in effect, "only cypress is fit for my brow" (in mourning for Shakespeare). In

---

(footnote continued from previous page)

A Strattfordian critic might reply that Barksted may have chosen the present tense because it was more consistent with the overall present tense focus of the final stanza ("stay my Muse," "wage not war," "cypress thy brow will fit," *etc.*). Such a critic might also argue that since "laurel is due" to Shakespeare, the author must still be alive to receive the honor, thus using this indication of authorship doubt to undercut the other indications in *Myrrha* pointing to a deceased author. The problem with the latter argument, however, is that Barksted is clearly comparing Shakespeare to Barksted's own Muse. Read on in the text! Shakespeare, even if mortally deceased, still lives among the Muses (for "ever"— see Part IV.24 & notes 591-602, discussing the *Sonnets* dedication). He would thus remain just as available (figuratively) to receive his laurels as is Barksted's own Muse to receive the "cypress" that his "brow will fit."

[580] See again, *e.g.*, note 570 (discussing the 1598 Barnfield poem).

[581] See Parts IV.4 & note 215 (Edwards), IV.18 & notes 438-43 (Fitzgeoffrey), IV.20 & notes 474-79, 515-17 (both works by Davies of Hereford); see also, *e.g.*, Parts IV.10 & note 287, IV.24 & notes 603-05, and *Sonnets* 25, 29, 37, 72, 81, 90, 111, 112, and 121.

line 2 he describes Shakespeare as "so dear loved a neighbor" of his Muse. He calls upon his Muse—in effect admonishing himself—to "wage not war with" Shakespeare. He states (line 1): "But stay my Muse in thine own confines keep."

As quoted earlier, Ross & Kathman nicely summarize part of what is going on here. Barksted, having devoted most of *Myrrha* to Myrrha herself, begins at the end to retell Shakespeare's version of the tale of *Venus and Adonis*. "[B]ut then [he] breaks off, as if realizing that he is encroaching on Shakespeare's poem."[582] But Ross & Kathman are so focused on knocking down a straw man—the two weakest past-tense references—they miss the far more important point Barksted is making: *The author Shakespeare now lives with the Muses.* He is now a "dear loved ... neighbor" of Barksted's Muse, presumably in their mythical home on the heights of Mount Helicon. *He is deceased and in heaven.*[583]

Ross & Kathman have no good excuse for missing this point. Price noted it.[584] They have long been aware of Price's work, which is cited and criticized on their website.[585] Chiljan discussed it explicitly, noting that Barksted "implies that Shakespeare was no longer mortal, that he was the 'neighbor' of a muse."[586]

---

[582] Ross & Kathman, "Barksted."

[583] See note 561 and related text; see also Part IV.3 & note 180.

[584] See Price, p. 146 (quoting in full and discussing the final stanza of Barksted's *Myrrha*) (pp. 137-38 in Price's 2001 edition). Price mistakenly depicted Barksted's muse in this stanza as interacting "with Shakespeare's Muse." Barksted explicitly identifies the person with whom he admonishes his Muse to "wage not war" (line 2), whose "song was worthy merit" (line 5), *etc.*: "*Shakspeare* he" (line 5, emphasis in original). Poets often address their own Muses, but it would seem a bit odd for a poet to address or comment upon *another poet's Muse*. Barksted's clear purpose here is to honor the author Shakespeare. Both Chiljan, p. 261, and Ross & Kathman, "Barksted," support reading Barksted as addressing Shakespeare directly, not Shakespeare's Muse. In their explanatory bracketed quotation mentioned in note 576, Ross & Kathman identify the two addressees in *Myrrha*'s final stanza as "Barksted's muse" and "Shakespeare."

[585] See Kathman & Ross, *Shakespeare Authorship Page*.

[586] Chiljan, p. 261. But see note 573 (discussing Ross & Kathman's apparent disregard for Chiljan's 2011 book).

Price did not draw the specific connection between *Myrrha* and the author Shakespeare being deceased long before 1616,[587] because it was off-point to the particular focus of her discussion. Price debunked a tradition in which Stratfordian academics have long indulged—distorting impersonal, cryptic, and even satirical *literary* references to the *author* Shakespeare as if they suggested *personal* knowledge of Shakspere of Stratford, often spuriously depicted as "sweet" and well-liked.[588] The most respected modern biographer of Shakspere, for example, treated Barksted's reference to the (apparently deceased) author, as "so dear loved a neighbor" *of his Muse,* as if that meant Barksted and Shakspere were friendly adjoining property owners in London or Stratford![589]

Let us pause and take stock of *Myrrha's* six indications of authorship doubt: We have a total of three past-tense references to Shakespeare's artistic work, in lines 5 ("*was* worthy"), 6 ("*sung* the fair blossom"), and 8 ("*hath* purchased"). Lines 7-8 contain a cluster of three indications: (1) the past-tense reference just mentioned, (2) that Barksted seems to be mourning a deceased Shakespeare ("cypress"), and (3) while Shakespeare "hath purchased" (earned) his wreath of "laurel[s]," it still "is due to him" (he has not yet received it), which makes no sense if he is Shakspere of Stratford writing under his own name. Finally, lines 1-2 indicate that Shakespeare now lives with the Muses.

Grant that the past-tense references suggest the possibility, but do not prove by themselves, that the author Shakespeare was dead by 1607. Grant also that the "laurel is due" reference is an arguably weak indication of doubt, taken by itself, and at best neutral on whether he was dead by then. Still, all six indications

---

[587] She did connect that to the *Sonnets* dedication. See Price, pp. 153-54; Part IV.24 & notes 591-602.

[588] See Price, pp. 144-47.

[589] See Schoenbaum, *Documentary Life,* pp. 255, 353 n. 9; see also Price, pp. 145-46 (debunking that and other Schoenbaum references).

should be weighed together. Two are powerful expressions of doubt: the references to cypress and the Muses. Both are reinforced by the three past-tense references and all five suggest very strongly that the author Shakespeare was deceased.

But Ross & Kathman sarcastically dismiss the idea, considering only the two weakest of *Myrrha*'s five indications to that effect and totally missing the boat on the two *strongest*—failing to grasp the suggestion of mourning despite the availability of Sobran's and Chiljan's commentaries (grossly misconstruing Sobran's), and failing even to notice the relevance of the Muses despite the availability of Price's and Chiljan's commentaries. They also miss the significance of *Myrrha*'s "laurel is due" reference, despite Chiljan's analysis. Here in microcosm we see the obtuse arrogance of much orthodox commentary on the SAQ.

## 24.  Thomas Thorpe (publisher), Dedication and *Shake-speare's Sonnets* (1609)

Shakespeare's famous (or infamous) *Sonnets* were published in 1609 by Thomas Thorpe (*c.* 1569–1625). Here we have authorship doubts of the most compelling nature hiding in plain sight—for 410 years now and counting. I am far from the first to discuss them. Very little in this section is original to me. Yet orthodox academics continue, for the most part, to studiously ignore them.

These doubts were raised in the *Sonnets* themselves by the author himself (whoever that was), and in the prefatory material by Thorpe, a well-known London publisher (or whoever else was involved). Since the *First Folio* of 1623 appears to have been designed, in part, to launch the Stratfordian theory, it seems no wonder that Ben Jonson (or whoever else was involved with the *Folio*) decided to omit the *Sonnets* from that publication.[590] Thorpe is the implied author of the equally infamous dedication of the

---

[590] See, *e.g.*, Part I & notes 36, 38-41.

*Sonnets*, judging by the initials "T.T." at the end. The dedication refers to the author, "Shake-speare,"[591] as:

## "OUR.EVER-LIVING.POET."

The centered, all-capitals, and full-stopped format of these words reflects the original and is in keeping with the stunning importance of this most devastating single expression of authorship doubt before 1616.

What does *"ever-living"* mean? Quite simply, it means the author Shakespeare was dead in 1609, seven years before the death of Shakspere of Stratford. There is very little, if any, reasonable doubt about this. As Diana Price among many has pointed out, this compound "adjective is synonymous with *immortal* and [is] used," almost always, "to describe deities, non-human entities, or dead persons"—almost never (if ever) to describe a living mortal person.[592]

---

[591] Hyphenation in original. One of the almost innumerable oddities of the *Sonnets* is that no full author's name is given on the title page (or elsewhere in the part of the original publication devoted to the *Sonnets*). The author is evident only from the title, "*Shake-speare's Sonnets.*" Very oddly, the title page provides the traditional two parallel lines between which an author's name would normally appear, but with only a blank space between them. Richard Kennedy's 1993 pamphlet, *Between the Lines,* explored this mystery with delightful humor but serious intent and substance. He displayed, for example, the title pages of books by John Day (*Law-Tricks,* 1608) and George Chapman (*May-Day,* 1611), with title-page layouts very similar to the *Sonnets*—and Day's and Chapman's names within parallel lines. Kennedy concluded: "For hundreds of years, a common design, The author's name printed between two lines. A Shakespearean riddle, here's the game: Why put in the lines ... and leave out the name?"

It should be noted that the author's full name, "William Shake-speare" (hyphenated again in original), does appear beneath the title, "A Lover's Complaint," of the poem appended to the 1609 edition of the *Sonnets*. Chiljan, pp. 76-83, discussed a fascinating array of authorship questions raised by "A Lover's Complaint," which could have occupied, perhaps, an entire section of this book. Because this book is already getting too long, however, I merely refer readers here to Chiljan's excellent treatment.

[592] Price, p. 153 (emphasis in original); see generally pp. 153-54; see also Looney, "Was It Oxford" (1923), pp. 197-98; Chiljan, pp. 74-76.

As Price noted, "the *Oxford English Dictionary*'s first illustration of the term 'ever-living,' as applied to a human being,"[593] is drawn from Shakespeare's *Henry VI, Part 1:* "our scarce-cold conqueror, That ever-living man of memory, Henry the Fifth."[594] She noted that Richard Brome's poem, in the 1647 folio of plays by Francis Beaumont and John Fletcher, refers to "the memory of the deceased, but ever-living *Author* ... Fletcher."[595]

Professor Donald Foster, an orthodox Stratfordian, searched early modern literature and did not find *"any instance* of *ever-living* ... to describe a living mortal, including, even, panegyrics on Queen Elizabeth, where one should most expect to find it—though *it does appear sometimes in eulogies for the dead* ...."[596]

---

[593] Price, p. 153.

[594] Act 4, sc. 3, quoted in *OED*, v. 5, p. 464 (def. 1.b).

[595] Quoted in Price, p. 154 (emphasis in original).

[596] Foster (1987), p. 46, quoted in Price, p. 153 (first and third emphases added here; second emphasis by Foster). Foster, p. 46, conceded the usage in *Henry VI.* Despite his helpful empirical finding just cited, Foster made a series of truly preposterous arguments seeking to resolve the mysteries posed by "ever-living" and also the dedication's reference to "Mr. W.H." His arguments were gracefully pulverized in Rollett, "Master F.W.D." (1997). For example, drawing upon references to the religious deity known as "God" as "ever-living," Foster argued that the *Sonnets* dedication, which wished "Mr. W.H. ... that eternity promised by our ever-living poet," *actually meant to refer to God* as "our ever-living poet." Yet again, a Stratfordian is challenged by authorship doubts and common sense flies out the window.

Even leaving aside the obvious point that a reference to a "poet," in a dedication of a book of poetry, might most reasonably be viewed as a reference to the author of said poetry (not the purported "Author of All Things"), Foster's argument was willfully contrary to the actual content and context of the poetry in question, which (as is rather well-known; are citations needed?) includes numerous promises and expressions of hope of eternity and immortality for the fair youth—who, by the way, is generally associated with "Mr. W.H." But not according to Foster, who argued that "W.H." was probably a typographical mistake by the printer and should have appeared as "W.S.," the author of the *Sonnets!* See Rollett, "Master F.W.D." (1997), pp. 8-9 (demolishing these arguments). This would apparently create the laughable prospect (according to Foster, under the Stratfordian theory) that a living author stood by as a book of his own poetry was published which basically wished himself well—though also strongly implying he was already dead, which would seem to put a bit of a damper on "the well-wishing" mentioned in the dedication.

It would be very understandable to find at least a few such flattering usages about the queen or king, since under absolute monarchies it could legally be considered treason even to "imagine" the death of a living royal sovereign.[597] The Oxfordian scholar John Rollett,[598] in what lawyers would call a "statement against interest," corrected Professor Foster by pointing out at least one rare instance in which the term "ever-living" was used in relation to Queen Elizabeth. Rollett noted a passage in Covell's *Polimanteia* (1595) urging that the queen be written about so as to "give immortality to an ever-living Empress."[599]

But even that isolated exception is fully consistent with the general rule. That passage does *not* simply describe the living mortal queen as *already* "ever-living," as the *Sonnets* dedication flatly and simply describes the "poet." Rather, it expresses the *hope* or *desire* that writers *will*, in a suggested *future* sense, "*give immortality*" to Elizabeth and thus, *after her death* (an unpleasant prospect delicately not mentioned), *make* her "ever-living"—at least in a figurative reputational sense. The actual fate of her immortal soul, under the prevailing religious views of the time, would necessarily be left strictly to God.

A religious person might naturally *hope* the queen, or any virtuous person, *will achieve* "ever-living" status in the afterlife. One might similarly *hope*, in a figurative sense, that a writer's works and literary reputation *will* "live forever." But it would simply make no sense in the language of the time—would have been viewed as almost blasphemously presumptuous—to simply and flatly describe a living mortal person as *already* "ever-living."

---

[597] See, *e.g.*, England's Treason Act of 1554.

[598] Rollett later abandoned the Oxfordian theory, instead embracing the theory that the author was William Stanley (Earl of Derby). See Parts I, note 44, and IV.30 & note 798.

[599] Quoted in Rollett, "Master F.W.D." (1997), p. 9; see generally pp. 8-9, cited in Feldman, *Sackville* (2015), pp. 274, 358. For an unrelated discussion of *Polimanteia*, see Part IV.7.

The same distinction explains references in a 1598 poem by Richard Barnfield touted by Stratfordian scholars Terry Ross and David Kathman. Barnfield praised the author Shakespeare and the poet Edmund Spenser, both still living in 1598. His poem states that Shakespeare's *Venus and Adonis* and *Lucrece* "have placed" his "Name in fame's immortal Book." He then expresses a fervent *hope* or *prediction: "Live ever* you, at least in Fame *live ever:* Well may the Body die, but Fame dies never."[600] Ross & Kathman claim this double reference to "live ever" is *"parallel* to the 'ever-living' of the *Sonnets* dedication."[601] But that is precisely *not* the case, for reasons just explained.

The dedication of the *Sonnets* in 1609 thus provides the third and strongest indication we have seen so far—confirming 1605's

---

[600] "A Remembrance of Some English Poets," quoted in Ross & Kathman, "Barksted" (my emphases); see also Part IV.23 & note 570; Chambers (1930), v. 2, p. 195. Ross & Kathman's article is criticized extensively, with regard to Barksted's *Myrrha* (1607), in Part IV.23. Barnfield's poem similarly states: "Live Spenser ever, in thy Fairy Queene Whose like ... was never seen."

[601] Ross & Kathman, "Barksted" (emphasis added). I do fear Ross & Kathman are correct that if Barnfield's poem had "appeared ten years later ... Oxfordians would have brandished it triumphantly, and surely would have made it a centerpiece of their arguments." I confess I might mistakenly have done so myself. But they do not explore the obvious lesson we should all learn. All sides in the authorship debate need to do a better job of reading each other's work respectfully to advance the search for truth, not to score points.

Educated in part by Ross & Kathman's work (which I respect and read very carefully, while criticizing it strongly when warranted), I agree Barnfield's poem does not indicate the subject was dead at the time. For example, Ross & Kathman note a Marlovian might, in theory, cite the Barnfield poem to support Marlowe (thought by most to have died in 1593) as an authorship candidate. (None *has* used it that way to my knowledge. On the Marlovian theory, see, *e.g.*, Part IV.30 & note 799.) I agree that would be mistaken, and if the poem were somehow redated to after 1604, it should not be added to any list of items suggesting the author died before 1616, despite my obvious temptation as an Oxfordian. But the fact that Oxfordians (including me) might well misunderstand or misuse this or that writing is *beside the point*. It does not excuse Ross & Kathman's refusal (or that of other Stratfordians) to concede the obvious meaning of "ever-living" in the *Sonnets* dedication. Nor does it excuse their inattention to the distinctions between that usage and Barnfield's or *Polimanteia's* usages. The point is to figure out the truth: Who really wrote the works of Shakespeare? Whoever did appears to have died by 1609, and probably years earlier.

*Voyage* and 1607's *Myrrha*—that the author Shakespeare was no longer among "the breathers of this world."[602]

Beyond the dedication, the *Sonnets* themselves are an astonishingly explicit and powerful source of authorship doubts. Stratfordians tend to dismiss everything in them as a purely imaginary artistic exercise. Yet the poet seems to speak about himself, laden with authentic pain. The *Sonnets* indicate several times that the author is not known by his true name, is disgraced for some reason, and either desires or perhaps mournfully expects that his true name will never be known.

*Sonnet* 72 states: "My name be buried where my body is, And live no more to shame nor me, nor you"—"you" and "your" referring here to the fair youth praised in many *Sonnets*.[603] *Sonnet* 81, with exquisite sorrow, both celebrates and laments:

From hence your memory death cannot take,
Although in me each part will be forgotten.
Your name from hence immortal life shall have,
Though I, once gone, to all the world must die.
The earth can yield me but a common grave,
When you entombed in men's eyes shall lie.
Your monument shall be my gentle verse,
Which eyes not yet created shall o'er-read ....[604]

---

[602] *Sonnet* 81, line 12; see also Parts IV.22 (discussing *Sir Thomas Smith's Voyage*) and IV.23 (discussing Barksted, *Myrrha, the Mother of Adonis*). There are five indications to that effect altogether. See also Parts IV.29 (*Envy's Scourge, and Virtue's Honour*, c. 1605–15) and IV.30 (Brooke, *Ghost of Richard the Third*, 1614, with a discussion of all five items).

[603] *Sonnet* 72, lines 11-12.

[604] *Sonnet* 81, lines 3-10. The fair youth's name would be "immortal" since he was probably well understood then (as now) to be Henry Wriothesley (Third Earl of Southampton), the famous dedicatee of Shakespeare's *Venus and Adonis* and *The Rape of Lucrece*. See also, *e.g.*, *Sonnets* 25, 29, 37, 90, 111, 112, and 121; Chiljan, pp. 70-76 (providing a superb overview of the authorship doubts and questions raised by the *Sonnets*); Jiménez (2018), pp. 25-26 (summarizing various ways in which the *Sonnets* support the Oxfordian theory).

Yet again, this makes not the slightest bit of sense if Shakspere of Stratford was the author, writing openly under his own name.[605]

Does anything in the *Sonnets* actually *support* the Stratfordian theory? Our orthodox friends cannot be faulted for lack of desperate effort. Some have suggested a hint in *Sonnet* 145: "I hate, from hate away she threw, And saved my life saying not you." Shakspere of Stratford's wife's maiden name was Anne Hathaway. Get it?[606]

More revealing is the reliance of some Stratfordians on the "Will" *Sonnets*.[607] Professor Alan Nelson—apparently with a straight face—declared that they "[e]stablish [Shakspere of Stratford's] identity [as the author] *beyond all question*," quoting that dead giveaway in *Sonnet* 136, "my name is *Will*."[608]

Professor Nelson, meet Professor Digory Kirke in C.S. Lewis's beloved *Narnia Chronicles:* "Logic! Why don't they teach logic at these schools?"[609] We certainly do not need *Sonnet* 136 to tell us

---

[605] See also Parts IV.4 & note 215, IV.18 & notes 438-43, IV.20 & notes 474-79, 515-17, and IV.23 & notes 578-81.

[606] *Sonnet* 145, lines 13-14. Compare, *e.g.*, A. Nelson, "Shakespeare of Stratford" (2018), p. 19 (conceding that this "possible pun" is "[l]ess certain—and less probative" than the "Will" Sonnets discussed in text and notes 607-16), with Chiljan, p. 75 (noting the inconvenient fact that *Sonnet* 145 refers to the poet's lover, not his wife). And to think our orthodox critics attack *doubters* for sometimes straining to find laughably weak linkages to common words? Compare also Part IV.2.d & notes 67-69.

[607] The two main Will *Sonnets* are 135 and 136 (all italics in original). *E.g.*, *Sonnet* 135, lines 1-2 ("Whoever hath her wish, thou hast thy *Will*, And *Will* to boot, and *Will* in over-plus"), lines 5-6 ("Wilt thou whose will is large and spacious, Not once vouchsafe to hide my will in thine?"); *Sonnet* 136, lines 2-3 ("Swear to thy blind soul that I was thy *Will*, And will thy soul knows is admitted there"), lines 13-14 ("Make but my name thy love, and love that still, And then thou lov'st me for my name is *Will*."). See also note 616 and related text.

[608] *Sonnet* 136, line 14 (italics in original), quoted in A. Nelson, "Shakespeare of Stratford" (2018), p. 19 (emphasis added to "beyond all question"); see also, *e.g.*, Waugh & Bate (Sir Jonathan Bate, at minute 56, stating more tentatively that this line "maybe suggests" the author was really named "William").

[609] Lewis, *The Lion, the Witch and the Wardrobe* (1950), p. 48. Digory explains to Peter and Susan, pp. 49-50, why logic suggests Lucy is not lying about the parallel universe she claims to have stumbled into. "But there was no time," Susan objects. "Lucy had no time to have gone anywhere, even if there was such

(footnote continued on next page)

the poet's (nominal) "name is Will." It says so on the title page![610] We already knew this author's works were published, when not anonymously, under the *purported* name of "Will" Shakespeare.

The *Sonnets'* references to "Will" and "will," to the extent they play upon the author's (nominal) name—in addition to sexual punning[611]—do not add *a single iota* of resolving power to the title page attributions, when it comes to the relevant question before us: Is this the author's *real* name or a pseudonym?[612] If it were a pseudonym, then obviously it would be essential, in any open commentary or wordplay on the author's name, to use the pseudonym instead of the real name. Doing anything else would blow the author's cover and defeat the entire purpose of the pseudonym.

Nelson's claim—that these references prove "beyond all question" that the name is not a pseudonym—is precisely equivalent to claiming that a title page attribution alone proves "beyond all

---

(footnote continued from previous page)

a place. ... It was less than a minute, and she pretended to have been away for hours." Digory responds: "That is the very thing that makes her story so likely to be true .... If she had been pretending, she would have hidden for a reasonable time before coming out and telling her story."

[610] Well, O.K., to be technically accurate, it *doesn't* say so on the title page (or the running header throughout the *Sonnets*), which merely refer to his (nominal, and hyphenated) surname "Shake-speare." But the *Sonnets* as published in 1609 give "William" on the first page of the appended poem, "A Lover's Complaint." See note 591. And by presenting "Shake-speare" as the author of the *Sonnets*, the publisher was obviously asserting that this poet was the same widely published author (nominally named "Will" or "William") who wrote *Venus and Adonis, The Rape of Lucrece*, and numerous published plays.

[611] See, *e.g.*, Booth, pp. 466-73 (noting that "will," among several available meanings, refers to both male and female sex organs); see also note 607 (quoting *Sonnet* 135, lines 5-6). Bate suggested agreement with Nelson's argument about "my name is Will." See note 608. Yet Bate himself has also noted that "[t]he combination of *shake* and phallic *speare*, especially in conjunction with the first name Will, has robust bawdy possibilities." Bate, *Soul of the Age*, p. 356 (emphases in original); see also Part IV.16 & note 388 (suggesting that really should cause Bate to take the pseudonym hypothesis more seriously).

[612] See, *e.g.*, Looney, p. 292; Chiljan, p. 75. Looney and Chiljan are among many anti-Stratfordians who have observed these obvious and elementary logical points, upon which I elaborate in the text. Yet they still somehow elude some Stratfordians. One is forced to conclude they do not *want* to understand them.

question" that it cannot be a pseudonym. So what exactly is Nelson claiming here? That pseudonyms did not exist in early modern England? That "Will" Shakspere of Stratford was indeed—"beyond all question"—the actual author of (among other works) *Locrine, The London Prodigal,* and *A Yorkshire Tragedy?*[613]

It gets even worse for Stratfordians. The Will *Sonnets* do tell us something about the authorship question—the exact opposite of what they think. Applying a modicum of Professor Kirke's lost Narnian art of logic, they would seem to be hinting at something very fishy and questionable indeed about this purported authorial name. As Alexander Waugh noted, would we not find it a wee bit odd to find a poem by Marlowe or Spenser belaboring the idea that "my name is Chris" or "my name is Ed"?[614]

So *why is this author* "banging on," as our British friends might put it, about his (nominal) name? (Set aside the naughty puns for a moment.[615]) Waugh perceptively observed that a closer look at that very same *Sonnet* 136, concluding "my name is *Will,*" reveals a powerful resonance with *Sonnets* 72, 81, and others that refer to hidden and disgraced identity and the oblivion of anonymity or pseudonymity:

> *Will,* will fulfill the treasure of thy love,
> Aye fill it full with wills, and *my will one.*
> In things of great receipt with ease we prove,
> Among a number *one is reckoned none.*
> Then in the number *let me pass untold ....*[616]

---

[613] See, *e.g.,* as to pseudonyms, Part III.B & note 33, and as to the plays cited in text (agreed by most orthodox scholars not to have been written by whoever did write the authentic Shakespeare canon), Part III.B & notes 42-45.

[614] See Waugh & Bate (Waugh, at minute 58).

[615] See note 611.

[616] *Sonnet* 136, lines 5-9 (italic emphasis on "Will" in original; other emphases added); see also Waugh, "My Shakespeare" (2018), p. 71; Waugh & Bate (Waugh, at minutes 58-59).

The Will *Sonnets*, if anything, express yet more of the powerful authorship doubts coursing through these enigmatic poems.
There is far, *far* more that may be said, and needs to be said,
about the *Sonnets* in relation to the SAQ. But this book is too long
already. To fully explore them, even from this perspective alone,
would take an entire volume, probably several.

Many great minds, one fears, have gone quietly mad contemplating the almost unfathomable mysteries of the *Sonnets* and
their dedication. Waugh, an acclaimed author and scholar who in
my view remains very much sane, has ventured to explore some of
those mysteries, beyond what has already been cited above. I cannot do justice here to all of his brilliant, complex, and sometimes
controversial work. I am still exploring it myself.[617] If, perhaps, he
turns out to be mistaken on some points, that would only be
because he has not feared to tread where Stratfordians—and
anyone who truly loves and respects the author Shakespeare—

---

[617] I have mostly deferred that until after completing this book, which has a
much more modest scope and goal than Waugh's ambitious work. I merely hope
to establish the existence and general nature of the extensive early Shakespeare
authorship doubts and questions. Waugh aims to provide some ultimate and profound answers to those questions. My Bibliography provides an extensive listing,
but on the *Sonnets* see especially Waugh, "Hidden Truths" (Parts 1-2) (2017), and
his videos "Where Shakespeare Is REALLY Buried" (Parts 1-4) (2017–18).

Waugh has pursued further, for example, the apparent encoded message
discovered in the *Sonnets* dedication by John Rollett, "Dedication" (1997, 1999,
and 2004). See also the separate process whereby Prechter, "*Sonnets* Dedication
Puzzle" (2005) and "Reply" (2015), reported finding several names thought to be
relevant to the *Sonnets* encoded in the dedication.

Rollett's cipher (though he himself later rejected its significance) is elegant-
ly simple and seemingly difficult to explain as a product of random chance. Take
the sixth word in the dedication, then the second word after that (strictly speaking, each word, prefix, or letter set off by periods in the dedication), then the
fourth after that, then again the sixth, the second, and the fourth. The 6-2-4
sequence is suggested by June 24 (Edward de Vere's date of death in 1604); by
the number of letters in his given name, prefix, and family name; and by the
dedication's layout in three distinct segments: six lines, then two, then four. It
yields the following phrase: "these ... insuing ... sonnets ... all ... by ... ever ...."
The last word is a possible anagram suggesting "Vere" or "E. Ver." See Part
IV.25, note 650. For more on anagrams, see also Parts IV.7 and 27.

would do well to follow. The *Sonnets* clearly have a story to tell about the authorship question, and the more we study them, the more it seems they are "still telling what is told."[618]

25. Richard Bonian and Henry Walley (publishers),
Preface to *Troilus and Cressida* (1609)

*Troilus and Cressida* was first published, as "by William Shakespeare," by Richard Bonian and Henry Walley in two quarto editions in 1609. They are generally identical except for the title pages and prefatory matter. Bonian and Walley seem to be known for little else than publishing *Troilus*, though they apparently both had careers as Jacobean publishers. Very scant information about them seems to be available, not even dates of birth or death. It seems plausible, though we'll probably never know for sure, that one or both may have written the anonymous preface to one of the 1609 editions. At any rate, having published it, they are jointly responsible for it.[619]

---

[618] *Sonnet* 76, line 14.

[619] See, *e.g.*, Bevington, pp. 1-3, 398-401 (indicating, p. 401, that Walley was still alive, but Bonian dead, when *Troilus* was included in the 1623 *First Folio*). *Troilus* was apparently a last-minute addition to the *Folio*, not listed in the table of contents and mostly (originally) unpaginated. See *First Folio*, pp. 13, 587-615. Scholars have referred to the 1609 preface as a "publisher's preface," "publicity blurb," or "advertisement." See, *e.g.*, Bevington, pp. 1-2. For convenience, it is cited here as the "Preface," using pagination and lineation in Bevington's standard 1998 Arden edition, pp. 120-22; see also p. 2 (facsimile of first page).

It is quite possible the Preface was originally written *not* by Bonian or Walley in 1608–09, but in 1602–03 (or earlier) by James Roberts, who originally registered *Troilus* for publication in February 1603. Or it might easily have been written at any time before 1609, even years before 1603, by some other person whose name may be lost to history, perhaps someone working with any of the three publishers mentioned. Sir George Greenwood (1908), pp. 495-97, conjectured that Ben Jonson wrote it. See generally pp. 491-97 (discussing the Preface). Roberts never did publish *Troilus*, and following his apparent sale of the rights to Bonian and Walley, they registered it again in January 1609, followed by publication of their two editions. See Bevington, pp. 398-400; "*Troilus and Cressida*, First Edition," and "Second Edition," on *Shakespeare Documented*.

One of the editions has no preface, just a title page indicating it was performed by the King's Men (Shakspere of Stratford's company) at the Globe Theatre. The preface to the other 1609 edition, contradictorily, makes no mention of such a performance and claims that *Troilus* was never publicly performed before. Indeed, it touts that alleged fact.[620] Aside from the conflict between the two 1609 editions on this point, the 1609 Preface's claim is also in conflict with the original registration of the play in 1603.[621]

The title and contents of the 1609 Preface are fairly bursting with authorship doubts, starting with the fact that it nowhere refers to the playwright by name. It sometimes seems to go out of its way to avoid doing so. Consider the bizarrely cryptic title: "A never writer, to an ever reader. News."[622] The "readers" are clear enough: the audience for the sales pitch the Preface generally constitutes. An *"ever"* reader seems a bit odd, but could just mean "faithful." The text similarly begins: "*Eternal* reader, you have here a new play ...."[623]

The "Never Writer" poses a multilayered mystery. First of all, it is not at all clear whether that refers to the writer of the *Preface* or the *play*. (I will pursue below whether they might be the same

---

[620] See Preface, in Bevington, p. 120, lines 1-3. The orthodox scholarly consensus appears to be that the edition of *Troilus* without the Preface appeared first, followed by a second edition with the Preface. See, *e.g.*, "*Troilus and Cressida*, First Edition," and "Second Edition," on *Shakespeare Documented*; Bevington, pp. 1-2, 399-400. The basis for that consensus is not at all clear to me. See Greenwood (1908), p. 493 (suggesting it makes no sense). But it seems to make little if any difference as to the doubts raised by the Preface. Ogburn, pp. 204-05, stated that the Preface appeared in the first edition and was then "quashed" or "dropped" from the second edition. His basis for that assertion is not clear either. Ogburn contradicted his cited source on this point. See p. 822, citing Chambers (1930), v. 2, p. 216 (who stated in turn, without explanation, that the Preface appeared in the "second issue" of *Troilus*).

[621] See note 619 (discussing the 1603 registration); Bevington, p. 398 (quoting Stationer's entry, Feb. 7, 1603, stating that *Troilus* was "acted by my Lo[rd] Chamberlain's Men"); Waugh, "My Shakespeare" (2018), p. 75 (noting this fact).

[622] Preface, p. 2 (facsimile), p. 120 (quoting text).

[623] Preface, p. 120, line 1 (emphasis added). But see note 650!

person.) One would think "writer" would refer to the playwright. But maybe the publisher was trying to say something like: "I'm no writer, faithful reader, but here's some news about this play."

Even if the Never Writer is the playwright, that does not necessarily mean the playwright wrote the Preface. And even if the publisher (or someone else other than the playwright) wrote the Preface, that does not necessarily mean the Preface's author is referring to himself as the Never Writer.[624] The Preface's author might again be a publisher, who might be saying something like: "Here's a play by that Never Writer, for you faithful readers, and I have some news about it."

Perhaps the best way forward is to consider holistically in context the four references in the title and text that appear (at least possibly) to refer or relate to the unnamed playwright:[625]

(1) The title refers to a "never writer."

(2) The text praises "this author's comedies."

(3) It compares *Troilus* to "the best comedy in Terence or Plautus," thus implicitly comparing the playwright to the ancient Roman comedy writers Terence and Plautus.

(4) It says readers should "believe ... that when he is gone" they will have to "scramble" for his plays.[626]

The five overall impressions I receive from those four references, and the Preface as a whole, are that:

(A) All four do refer to the playwright.

(B) The playwright is discussed in the third person; someone else is writing the Preface *about* him.

---

624 Compare Sobran, pp. 144-45 (too quickly assuming that the author of the Preface is the Never Writer—also suggesting, as I happen to think probable, that the author of the Preface is not the playwright).

625 Not counting repeated adjectival references like "his comedies," *e.g.*, Preface, pp. 120-21, lines 13, 20.

626 (1) Preface, p. 120 (title); (2) p. 120, line 9; (3) p. 121, lines 26-27; (4) p. 121, lines 27-28.

(C) Whoever is writing the Preface is carefully (even ostentatiously) *not* naming him, to the point of creating awkward prose.

(D) He and his works are highly praised in a generally elegiac and retrospective way (despite the arguable implication of "when he is gone," suggesting he is currently still around—more on that in a moment).

(E) There may be an intended hint in the reference to Terence, who has been notorious for more than 2,000 years as an alleged frontman for other writers.[627]

For example, as to reference 2 and impression C, it would have flowed so much more smoothly and clearly to say: "especially *[Shakespeare's]* comedies ... so framed to the life ... showing such a dexterity and power of wit," and so forth.[628] Why the stilted reference to "*this author's* comedies"? That connects to reference 1 and reinforces impression A. Since the Preface seems determined not to name this playwright, that makes it more likely that the Never Writer is indeed him—a playwright who is not named and perhaps *never* was publicly identified by his true name.[629]

To be sure, as Stratfordians would doubtless erupt at this point, the playwright *has* been named! The title page of *Troilus*, right before this very Preface, identifies him as "William Shakespeare"! Yes, but ample independent evidence discussed throughout this book had already long suggested by 1609 that "Shakespeare" might well be a pseudonym.

Stratfordians face quite a challenge to explain why their asserted playwright, in the prime of middle age, still active in the literary and theatre worlds (they claim), with several more years of writing ahead of him, would be described in this cryptic, mysterious, and elegiac way. One would think the title and text would

---

[627] See Part IV.26 (including note 670 and related text).

[628] Preface, p. 120, lines 9-12.

[629] See Ogburn, p. 206 (suggesting that the title might mean: "A writer who never was to a constant reader").

go something more like: "Our beloved Mr. Shakespeare: News for
an ever reader. You have here a new play by sweet honey-tongued
Will. You should see those grand censors flock to Shakespeare's
comedies." And so forth.

Is it possible the playwright himself wrote this Preface? Alexander Waugh has so suggested, in the course of arguing that the
Preface, despite being published in 1609, may have originally
been written before 1603. He may be correct on the latter point.[630]
And Waugh and I do happen to agree that Edward de Vere (Earl
of Oxford) very likely wrote the works of "Shakespeare."

But it seems doubtful that Vere also wrote the Preface to this
particular Shakespeare play. In content and tone, as noted above,
the Preface is entirely in the third person with regard to the playwright (while obviously in the second person as to readers). To be
sure, it is *possible* to write about oneself in the third person. But
is it really likely in this case? Was Vere thinking ahead about how
to pitch the sale of one of his plays (not one of his greatest) after
his death? Even while occupied in far grander tasks, like making
the final revisions to *Hamlet*, and concluding his *Sonnets*, lamenting that his name would be buried forever?[631]

That seems both implausible and needlessly complex. We
should always keep Occam's Razor in mind.[632] The better explanation is that the Preface—as orthodox scholars have long believed
and as it appears on its face—is simply a piece of advertising
puffery drafted by one or more of the publishers, or someone working with them.

---

[630] See Waugh, "My Shakespeare," p. 75; see also note 619. Waugh perceptively suggested that the conflict about past public performance between the
1609 Preface (no), and the other 1609 title page and 1603 registration (yes), may
be resolved if the Preface was drafted long enough before 1603 to precede the
performance noted in the 1603 registration.

[631] See, *e.g.*, Part IV.24 (discussing the *Sonnets*).

[632] See Part IV.1 & note 12, Baker, and "Occam's Razor."

What Waugh and other Oxfordians have perceptively noted, however—and orthodox scholars have missed or refused to see—is that the Preface is laden with authorship doubts. Even if not *by* Vere, it seems to be *about* him, or someone very much like him.[633]

One issue is that the Preface arguably refers to the playwright as someone still living who might not be in the near future: "And believe this, that *when he is gone* and his comedies out of sale, you will scramble for them ...."[634] That raises concerns for Oxfordians, since Vere died in 1604. Stratfordians claim the four highlighted words prove the author was still alive in 1609.[635]

But those four words, the only ones in the Preface with any such arguable implication, cannot reasonably be viewed as proof (or much evidence at all) that the author Shakespeare was in fact alive in 1609. For one thing, if "Shakespeare" *were* a pseudonym (the very point in dispute, on which there is ample independent evidence), then using the present tense—at least avoiding any explicit past-tense reference—would be mandated by the need to maintain the pseudonym. "Shakespeare" is credited on *Troilus*'s title page and Shakspere of Stratford was still living in 1609.[636]

Furthermore, as Waugh has argued, there are good reasons to think the Preface may have been written many years before 1609, very possibly before 1604.[637] Unlike Ogburn or Sobran, I do not claim the phrase "when he is gone" somehow affirmatively suggests the author was already dead in 1609.[638] I merely think it does not, in context, prove he was *alive* then. This book cautiously

---

[633] See, *e.g.*, Ogburn, pp. 204-06; Sobran, pp. 144-45; Waugh, "My Shakespeare," p. 75.

[634] Preface, p. 121, lines 27-29 (emphasis added).

[635] See, *e.g.*, Kathman, "Sobran," and "Why I Am Not an Oxfordian."

[636] The broader comment, "when he is gone and his comedies out of sale," taken in context, might also refer generally and impersonally to his literary legacy, *i.e.:* "when his works are gone and sold out."

[637] See notes 619, 630, and related text; Waugh, "My Shakespeare," p. 75.

[638] Compare Ogburn, p. 206; Sobran, p. 144.

avoids claiming that the Preface, overall, is any sort of strong indication the author died before 1609.[639]

The Preface does at least *hint*, however, that this playwright has passed from the scene. As noted earlier, it has an overwhelmingly elegiac and retrospective tone. Sobran perceptively pointed out this "more impalpable" and "subtle" aspect of the Preface:

> [It] talk[s] about "this author" as we always speak of someone who is absent, and absent for good. He is spoken of with respect, but not as if the words could reach his ear. What is said about him belongs to a conversation of which he himself is no longer a part.[640]

The Preface offers still more indications of authorship doubt. As Ogburn noted, it contains comments jarringly at odds with the Stratfordian image of a "playwright of the people" who wrote "for money to meet the demands of performers on the commercial stage."[641] The Preface claims (truthfully or not) that *Troilus* was "never staled with the stage, never clapper-clawed with the palms of the vulgar," and "not ... sullied with the smoky breath of the multitude."[642] That sounds much more consistent with the Oxfordian theory that the author originally wrote for private performances at the royal court or in aristocratic homes.[643]

---

[639] Compare Parts IV.22-24 and 29-30, discussing writings which *do* in my view constitute strong evidence that the author died years before 1616.

[640] Sobran, p. 145.

[641] Ogburn, p. 205.

[642] Preface, p. 120, lines 1-3, and p. 121, lines 31-32.

[643] The Folger Shakespeare Library, in a short essay accompanying the title pages of the two 1609 editions of *Troilus* on the *Shakespeare Documented* website (a wonderful and extremely valuable scholarly resource, overall), notes that orthodox scholars now "speculate" that *Troilus* "was perhaps first written for a private performance." The Folger, however (not to the surprise of authorship skeptics), has not yet chosen to post on *Shakespeare Documented* the actual Preface discussed here that has commanded so much attention in connection with the SAQ (a topic the Folger disdains as much as possible). Instead, the Folger merely comments that what it calls the "second" 1609 edition "adds an epistle to the reader that states that the play has never been performed." As "ever readers"

(footnote continued on next page)

We now come to what may be the Preface's strongest single expression of authorship doubt. In its second-to-last sentence, with regard to the publication of *Troilus*, it informs the "ever readers" that they should "thank fortune for the scape it hath made amongst you, since by the grand possessors' wills I believe you should have prayed for them rather than been prayed."[644] It is generally agreed this means, in plain English: "Thank your lucky stars this play escaped its grand possessors, because if they had their way, you would still be begging them to release it, instead of being begged now by this Preface to buy it."

So who were the "grand possessors" and why, pray tell, were they so "grand"? That has long been a hotly disputed question. Stratfordian scholars have been forced to contend in puzzled desperation that they must be the players and shareholders of Shakespeare's theatre company, in presumed control of his plays.[645] But given the well-known poor repute and low social status of actors during this era, and the widespread disdain for the public theatre business, it is *highly* implausible—really preposterous—to think *they* would be described in this way.[646]

This becomes truly risible when we consider—again, in holistic context—that *this very Preface*, as we just saw, *echoes* the prevailing scornful disdain for the public theatres. The Preface obviously seeks to propitiate a snooty, elite, and well-heeled audience of potential purchasers. (Books were expensive luxuries in those days.) Does it make *any sense whatsoever* that it would knowingly nudge its audience by disparaging the "smoky" and

---

(footnote continued from previous page)
of this book have seen, that is far less than the half of it! See "*Troilus and Cressida*, First Edition," and "Second Edition."

[644] Preface, p. 121, lines 32-35.

[645] See, *e.g.*, Bevington, p. 18.

[646] See, *e.g.*, Parts IV.16 & notes 355-69, and IV.20 & notes 480-89. As Ogburn noted, p. 205, "it would surely never have occurred to an Elizabethan to associate grandeur with a troupe of players." See also Greenwood (1908), p. 494 (dismissing the idea as "absurd").

"clapper-clawed" mob of public playgoers—then turn on a dime and touch the feet of the commercial actors and theatre business-men serving that very market by calling them *"grand"*?

Orthodox scholars cannot dismiss this as an eccentric Oxford-ian argument, though it actually is "Oxfordian" if by that is meant the *Oxford English Dictionary*. The *OED*, citing early modern usages, defines "grand," in regard to "official titles," as: "Chief over others, highest in rank or office."[647] As a "personal designa-tion," says the *OED*, citing two Shakespearean usages and one by Ben Jonson, it conveys the sense of "[p]re-eminent, chief."[648] The *OED* also cites a meaning now obsolete but prevalent in early modern times: "[e]minent; *great in reputation* [or] position."[649]

So, the reference to "grand possessors," the disdain for public theatres, the implied claim that *Troilus* had only been performed (if ever) before elite private audiences—what does all this tell us? The much-maligned Ogburn, whatever other flaws may exist in his analysis, seems to have hit the nail on the head: "[T]he preface appears to be telling the reader ... that the dramatist's plays are held by members of the nobility and that *Troilus and Cressida* was somehow sprung from their control."[650]

---

647 *OED*, v. 6, p. 746 (def. 2.a, citing a usage that *dates precisely from 1609:* "grand-priest").

648 *OED*, v. 6, pp. 746-47 (def. 3.a), citing, *e.g.*, Jonson's 1599 play *Every Man Out of His Humour*, act 1, sc. 2 ("Grand Scourge"), and Shakespeare's *Rich-ard II*, act 5. sc. 6 ("[Henry Percy, 'Hotspur':] The grand conspirator, Abbot of Westminster"), and *Richard III*, act 4, sc. 4 ("[Queen Margaret:] That excellent grand tyrant of the earth").

649 *OED*, v. 6, p. 747 (def. 3.b) (emphasis added) (see also def. 9.b, indicating "high social position," citing usages starting in 1766 but seemingly indistinguish-able from the foregoing definitions supported by usages more contemporary to Shakespeare's time).

650 Ogburn, p. 205; see also, *e.g.*, Sobran, p. 144 ("Certain 'grand possessors' —not the author, not the King's Men—apparently held Shakespeare's manu-scripts."). Ogburn, p. 206, Price, p. 233, and Waugh, "My Shakespeare," p. 75, among others, have also speculated about possible wordplay in the Preface's title. For example, could "A never writer, to an ever reader" be understood as "an E. Ver writer, to an E. Ver reader"? "Ever" might in some instances be an anagram
(footnote continued on next page)

That all resonates well with the Oxfordian conjecture that the "grand possessors" were the aristocratic Herbert brothers—yes, the very same "incomparable pair of brethren" to whom the *First Folio* was dedicated in 1623—and Philip Herbert's wife Susan Vere, who, yes, did just happen to be the youngest and probably favorite of Edward de Vere's three daughters. As with many, many other aspects of Oxford's life, family, and known writings, could this just be *yet another* amazing coincidence?[651]

I contend here, more cautiously, that the Preface to *Troilus and Cressida* should cause us to seriously question the Stratfordian theory. More to the point, it strongly suggests that *many people in 1609*—including the publishers of the Preface and the readers to whom it was directed—either doubted that authorship theory or never entertained it in the first place.

---

(footnote continued from previous page)
of "Vere." "Ver" may be viewed as an alternate spelling of his surname, deriving from the French town Ver in Normandy. See, *e.g.*, Looney, p. 181.

I hesitate to dive down this Oxfordian rabbit-hole—recalling, as my own Preface notes, that this book is not primarily an Oxfordian tract. The Oxfordian scholar Nina Green, "Mytho," Sec. I, p. 51, dismisses as a "myth" the idea that "ever" was *ever* used as an anagram of "Vere." Green quibbles over variant spellings and when the aristocratic prefix "de" was or should be used (on the latter issue see my Preface, note 10). "Vere" was obviously one available and understood spelling of his name. Green herself concedes at least one instance during his lifetime when it clearly *was* played upon by that spelling (though not with an anagram). Thus, it easily *could* have been used in anagrams (though we should be cautious not to look for it *every*where), just as "de Vere" seems to have been anagrammed (sometimes). See Parts IV.7; IV.24, note 617; IV.27. A possible example is *Sonnet* 76, line 7: "That every word [*i.e.*, that word 'every'?] doth almost tell [or 'fell'?] my name." It may, perhaps, "almost" do so because of the "y" in "every." See Part III.A & note 32.

[651] See, *e.g.*, Part I & notes 4, 41. Was Susan the model for *King Lear's* Cordelia? It is known that in 1591, Vere (then a widower not yet remarried) divided up most of his remaining estates, including his ancestral seat of Castle Hedingham, for the benefit of his three daughters, his only legally recognized children at that time. Did he later bequeath to Susan his precious manuscripts? Such are the questions that fascinate Oxfordians. See, *e.g.*, Anderson, pp. 247-49, 354-55, 371-72.

26. John Davies of Hereford, *The Scourge of Folly* (*c.* 1610–11)
and Our English Terence

John Davies of Hereford (*c.* 1565–1618),[652] in addition to his
poetic comments in *Microcosmos* (1603) and *Humour's Heaven on
Earth* (1609), discussed in Part IV.20, wrote a third epigram on
Shakespeare, No. 159 in *The Scourge of Folly*, apparently published by 1611. Here is the full text, some of which is obscure:

*To our English Terence Mr.* Will: Shake-speare [*sic*]

Some say (good *Will*) which I, in sport, do sing[:]
Hadst thou not played some Kingly parts in sport,
Thou hadst been a companion for a *King*;
And, been a King among the meaner sort.
Some others rail [criticize you]; but, rail as they think
    fit [*i.e.*, let them criticize you as they like],
Thou hast no railing, but, a reigning Wit [*i.e.*, you do not
    respond in kind, but rather rule by your sharp intelli-
    gence or humor or both[653]]:
*And* honesty *thou sow'st, which they do reap* [*i.e.*, they
    benefit from your virtue[654]; how seems unclear];
*So, to increase their* Stock *which they do keep.*[655]

---

[652] See Part IV.20 & note 463 (distinguishing Davies of Hereford from the
Davies discussed in Part IV.9, and noting Davies of Hereford's possible connections with family members and associates of Edward de Vere, Earl of Oxford).

[653] On "wit," see Part IV.2.a & note 15, citing *OED*, v. 20, pp. 432-34.

[654] "Honesty" could mean truthfulness, but the broader early modern meaning of overall "virtue" seems more likely here. See Part IV.2.c & note 46, citing
*OED*, v. 7, pp. 349-50; Detobel (2013), pp. 17-18; see also Part IV.20 & note 488.

[655] Davies, *Scourge*, pp. 76-77, Epigram No. 159, on *Shakespeare Documented* (excerpting pp. 76-77, epigrams 158-62, and pp. 231-32; italics in original;
bracketed explanations added here), quoted and discussed in Price, pp. 60-65,
and Chiljan, pp. 264-65; see also Chambers (1930), v. 2, p. 214 (quoting No. 159).
The Folger Shakespeare Library, in Davies, *Scourge*, on *Shakespeare Documented*, describes it as "undated, possibly 1611?" Price, p. 60, dated it to "1610–11,
although its date of composition is not known." It was registered for publication
on October 8, 1610. Chambers, p. 214; Chiljan, p. 264. The quotation in text
(footnote continued on next page)

It must first be noted that this epigram, like *Microcosmos* and *Humour's Heaven*, appears to address and refer to Shakspere the actor, given that it says he "played some ... parts."[656] Second, as with *Humour's Heaven*, nothing in it refers to any literary career, except possibly the title—and as we will see, the title boomerangs *very* badly on the Stratfordian theory.[657] As with *Humour's Heaven*, that very lack of linkage to writing is one source of doubt. And as with *Humour's Heaven*, there's more—much more in this case.

So what about that title? Who was "Terence"? Well, he was an ancient Roman playwright of very modest social origins (born into slavery), possibly of African (Berber) ethnicity.[658] And a long-held traditional belief, prevalent during Elizabethan and Jacobean times, was that he did not actually write the works for which he was credited, but was a frontman for two aristocratic writers.[659]

Davies was more or less directly telling his contemporaries that Shakspere the player was a frontman for an aristocrat. Diana Price discussed this.[660] Price cited, on the aristocratic stigma of print prevailing at the time, an essay by Michel de Montaigne,

---

(footnote continued from previous page)
omits "Epig. 159" beneath the title and replaces with a colon (as indicated) an extraneous closing paren (a printing error?) after "sing" in the first line.

[656] Compare Part IV.20 & notes 464, 481, 507-08.

[657] Compare Part IV.20 & note 509. As Diana Price noted, p. 62 (emphasis in original), "the epigram itself contains no explicit *literary* praise."

[658] Publius Terentius Afer (c. 185–c. 159 BCE).

[659] Scipio Africanus the Younger (c. 185–129 BCE) and Gaius Laelius Sapiens the Younger (c. 188–? BCE). See, *e.g.*, Radice, "Introduction," pp. 13–14, 18, and Suetonius, "The Life of Terence," app. A, pp. 389-94, both in Terence, *Comedies* (Radice ed. 1976); Ogburn, p. 257; Price, pp. 61-62; Chiljan, p. 264. This belief may well be apocryphal and untrue, unfairly denigrating Terence's standing as a playwright, but that's beside the point for present purposes. No less a Roman figure than the philosopher, orator, and statesman Marcus Tullius Cicero (106–43 BCE) was among those who promoted this belief, building on rumors that began during Terence's own time. Terence himself apparently did not discourage the rumors, instead graciously acknowledging that he benefitted from his association with friends like Scipio and Laelius.

[660] See Price, pp. 61-62 (citing a book by Roger Ascham published posthumously in 1570, reprinted in 1579 and 1589, as repeating this belief about Terence; also citing a Montaigne essay translated into English by John Florio in 1603).

who commented that if writing "might bring any glory suitable to a great personage, Scipio and Laelius would never have resigned the honor of their great comedies ... unto an African servant."[661]

The treatment of No. 159 by orthodox scholars has been troubling. Sir Stanley Wells brushed it off in his book on Shakespeare's life and works, stating that the reference to Terence "seems to imply that Davies thinks of [Shakespeare] primarily as a comic playwright, but goes on to speak of him in cryptic terms as an actor[.]" After quoting the first four lines, Wells abruptly concluded that the epigram "is too vague to be helpful."[662] Certainly not helpful to a Stratfordian like Wells!

Wells failed to inform his readers of Terence's well-known reputation as a frontman. He also failed to explore why Davies would compare Shakespeare *only* to a playwright known *only* for writing comedies. Shakespeare was at least equally well-known for writing serious and tragic works, starting with his bestselling poems *Venus and Adonis* and *The Rape of Lucrece* and continuing with many of his greatest plays. As we have seen, other contemporaries—and Ben Jonson's laudatory 1623 *First Folio* poem—compared him to Seneca, the tragic Roman playwright.[663] Jonson's *Folio* poem also compares him to the tragic Greek playwrights Aeschylus, Euripides, and Sophocles.[664]

True, Jonson's *Folio* poem also compares Shakespeare to Terence, among a total of nine comic and tragic ancient writers.[665] But the point is that Terence seems an odd choice if used *alone* as a *general* comparison. As Price observed: "Nothing in the text of the [Davies] poem suggests that 'Terence' was intended to identify

---

661 Quoted in Price, p. 61 (internal quotation marks, italics, and capitalization omitted). On the stigma, see Parts IV.3 & note 149, and IV.20 & note 467.

662 Wells (1995), p. 26, quoted and discussed in Price, p. 62.

663 See, *e.g.*, Part IV.1 & notes 4-6.

664 *First Folio*, p. 9.

665 See *First Folio*, p. 10; for all nine, see pp. 9-10.

Shake-speare as a playwright."[666] Davies probably referred to Terence *precisely and only* because of his reputation as a frontman.

One may speculate whether Jonson's *Folio* citation of Terence—grouped with two other comedy writers, the Greek Aristophanes and the Roman Plautus—was also meant to suggest a frontman. Perhaps not, since Jonson lumped Terence in with other writers. But it deserves consideration. There are ample reasons to think Jonson did not want to be, and could not afford to be, as blatant as Davies. Yet Jonson seemed determined in the *Folio* to drop all kinds of hints that *something* was up.[667]

More intriguing than Jonson's linkage of Terence to Shakespeare, though less arresting than that of Davies, is the linkage to Terence in a 1614 poem by Thomas Freeman. This epigram to Shakespeare praises his versatile literary appeal.[668] Freeman cites Terence to suggest (at least on the surface), not that Shakespeare is a frontman borrowing someone else's work, but that "new" writers are tempted to pass off as their own the works of the author Shakespeare. The epigram states that "in plays thy wit winds like *Meander:* Whence needy new-composers borrow more [t]han *Terence* doth from *Plautus* or *Menander*."[669]

---

[666] Price, pp. 62-63 (hyphenation by Price).

[667] See Part I & note 36; see also Part IV.28 (Jonson's pre-1616 writings).

[668] Freeman, Epigram No. 92, in the second part of his one-volume, two-part collection, *Rub and a Great Cast* and *Run and a Great Cast: The Second Bowl* (1614). Little is known about Freeman (b. 1589), who apparently graduated from Magdalen College, Oxford University, in 1611. His last known poem was apparently written in 1630, so he lived at least until then. The most intriguing fact about him is that, as reported in Miller, "Family Affair," pp. 24-25, his real name was Thomas Vavasour and he was the out-of-wedlock son of Vere's lover Anne Vavasour, by her later lover Sir Henry Lee (she was married at the time to a man who used the alias "Freeman"). Freeman was thus half-brother to Vere's own son by Vavasour, Sir Edward Vere. See Part IV.4, note 218. Nothing in Freeman's poem overtly suggests the author Shakespeare was dead in 1614, but nothing in it suggests he was still living either. Compare Parts IV.22-24, 29-30.

[669] Quoted in Chambers (1930), v. 2, p. 220 (italics in original); also quoted in Miller, "Family Affair," p. 24, and (in part) in Michell, p. 56. Chiljan, p. 266, quoted the last two lines in Freeman's poem, "Then let thine own works thine

(footnote continued on next page)

At the very least, Freeman's epigram reinforces the longstanding *Terence* authorship doubts. It corroborates the inference that he was, at this time, viewed largely as a frontman or plagiarist. While not itself a strong indication of *Shakespeare* authorship doubts, it further strengthens the *Davies* epigram as such. Unlike the Davies epigram, Freeman does not directly imply that Shakspere the player is a frontman, though as with Jonson's *Folio* poem, we may speculate about a possible veiled hint. At the same time, Freeman's poem does nothing to *clear* Shakspere of that suspicion, since it addresses the author in a purely impersonal and literary manner, never suggesting he is also an actor.

Yet a fourth linkage of Terence to Shakespeare appeared in the 1609 Preface to *Troilus and Cressida.* In the course of praising and touting *Troilus*, the Preface suggests that Shakespeare's play is as "deserv[ing] ... as the best comedy in Terence or Plautus."[670] That may in itself mean little more than Jonson's *Folio* reference, since it does not mention Terence's frontman reputation and pairs him with Plautus. Still, again, it is worth considering.

The Folger Shakespeare Library subtitles its posted excerpts of *Scourge* on the *Shakespeare Documented* website as: "John Davies of Hereford *Praises* William Shakespeare."[671] This posting, unlike those in which the Folger provides excerpts of *Microcosmos* and *Humour's Heaven*, is not accompanied by any explanatory essay.[672] But, as suggested by Price's analysis, the subtitle alone is tendentiously misleading—to the point of surrealism.

---

(footnote continued from previous page)
own worth upraise, And help t'adorn thee with deserved Bays." She suggested they may indicate Freeman shared the concerns expressed in some other writings about whether the author Shakespeare had received the honors he was due (*i.e*, poetic laurels or "bays"). Compare, *e.g.*, Part IV.23 & notes 578-81 (discussing Barksted's comment in *Myrrha*, "Laurel is due to him," and other writings).

[670] Quoted in Bevington, p. 121, lines 26-27; see also Part IV.25 & notes 626-27.

[671] See Davies, *Scourge*, on *Shakespeare Documented* (emphasis added).

[672] Compare A. Nelson, "Davies, *Microcosmos*" (2017), and A. Nelson, "Davies, *Humour's Heaven*" (2016), both on *Shakespeare Documented*.

How is it "praise" for Davies to directly imply—in the very title of No. 159—that Shakspere is a fake writer covering for someone else? Or, leaving that aside, not to even *mention* in the epigram (much less "praise") *anything* to do with his supposed literary career? Or to suggest he would have enjoyed more honor if only he had not misbehaved in some obscure ways? True, No. 159 does say he's not prone to "railing" and has "a reigning Wit" and some "honesty." Thank goodness for small favors!

As Price documented, quoting numerous other epigrams in *Scourge*, Davies knew perfectly well how to *really* "praise" people when he wanted to, with entirely lucid and flowery language.[673] As Price put it: "If Davies intended [No. 159] to be complimentary, why did he write cryptic copy?"[674] The whole thing "suggests uncomplimentary satire."[675]

David Kathman and Tom Reedy discuss No. 159 in a way that is both valuable yet also obtuse and deceptive. The valuable part is that they seem to persuasively refute a distracting misreading by Oxfordian scholar Charlton Ogburn Jr., who thought the lines discussing "kings" refer to Edward de Vere (Earl of Oxford) dabbling in acting.[676] The main problem with that reading, Kathman

---

[673] See Price, pp. 62-63.

[674] Price, p. 63.

[675] Price, p. 65.

[676] *I.e.*, only "in sport," with a suggestion that such scandalous behavior cost him some social status at court. See Ogburn, pp. 104-05. Compare Parts IV.5 & note 232, and IV.20 & notes 468, 485-87. Ogburn's reading focused on lines 2-3, was speculative at best, and overshadowed in his book the far more important frontman suggestion. Compare Ogburn, pp. 6, 67, 98, 104-05, 644 (discussing Davies and No. 159 without even mentioning the frontman issue), with p. 257 (finally addressing the latter, once, in the middle of a paragraph beginning on an unrelated point). Ogburn did not address line 4 or what it could possibly have meant to suggest that Vere, if he had *not* dabbled in acting, would have "been a King among the meaner sort."

Chiljan, pp. 264-65, generally followed Ogburn's reading (though not citing him). She did address line 4, but in a puzzling way, arguing that Davies suggested "that had the 'mean' or lower class spectators in the audience known Shakespeare's true identity, he would have been their king, too ...." Chiljan, p.
(footnote continued on next page)

and Reedy note, is that Davies clearly addresses Shakspere *the player* (however spelled). They reason sensibly, in line with Occam's Razor, that the references to "kings" merely play upon the name of Shakspere's theatre company, the King's Men.[677]

The very fact that No. 159's title addresses Shakespeare as "Terence," strongly hinting he was a frontman, shows it does *not* likely address Vere. It would make little sense for Davies to address Vere (or any hidden writer) that way, as if he were in turn a frontman for some *other* writer. Some might suggest a divergent or double meaning in the epigram's text, but that strikes me as too abrupt and awkward a swerve from the title.

That brings us to the troublingly deceptive aspect of Kathman's and Reedy's analyses. Like Wells, they simply ignore Ter-

---

(footnote continued from previous page)

264. But even assuming this were otherwise plausible, Davies did *not* suggest that the addressee of No. 159 would have become like a "king" if his true identity were revealed. Rather, Davies suggested he would have become like a "king" only if he had "*not* played ... Kingly parts in sport." It would seem that such *playing* (rather than *not* playing) would be precisely what would risk revelation of a hidden author's identity.

Waugh, "My Shakespeare" (2018), p. 53, also followed (without citing) the reading proposed by Ogburn. Waugh linked it to a reading of a 1616 Davies of Hereford poem which I have not yet had the opportunity to study (the date of which falls outside the scope of this book), so perhaps there is more to all this. The lines discussing "kings" in No. 159 remain unclear to me, but they would seem to fit better with some aspect of Shakspere's relationship with his fellow players in the King's Men, as Kathman and Reedy suggest. See also Price's suggested reading, pp. 64-65.

[677] See Kathman, "Why I Am Not an Oxfordian," and Reedy & Kathman, both on Kathman & Ross, *Shakespeare Authorship Page*. Kathman's article notes that two other epigrams by Davies in *Scourge*, addressed to other members of the King's Men, also play upon the word "king," which is sufficient in my view to clinch the argument. On Occam's Razor and the principle of simplicity, see Part IV.1 & note 12, Baker, and "Occam's Razor." It is also possible that "play[ing] some Kingly parts in sport" refers to an alleged incident (a tavern joke, most likely) in which Shakspere and Burbage supposedly sought to seduce a female fan by dressing in royal costume. The joke goes that Burbage called upon the lady for a planned assignation dressed as Richard III, but upon arrival was told that William the Conqueror preceded Richard III. See, *e.g.*, Chambers (1930), v. 2, p. 212 (quoting 1602 diary entry by John Manningham); Schoenbaum, *Documentary Life*, pp. 205-06 & n. *; Price, p. 62, citing Brooks, p. 339.

ence's reputation as a frontman in their cited articles—and as far as I can find, on the entire Kathman & Ross *Shakespeare Authorship* website.[678] They ignore it even though it would have helped them refute Ogburn's reading.[679] They implausibly tout the fact

---

[678] This website has been hailed with approval by leading academics. See, *e.g.*, Part II & note 60; Shapiro (2010), p. 281; Wells, "Allusions," p. 259 n. 2.

[679] It also would have assisted that refutation—especially their key point that No. 159 is addressed to Shakspere the player, not to any writer hidden behind him—to point out, as we have seen, that nothing in the text of the epigram contains any literary praise or suggests that Shakspere had any literary career. But, naturally, they studiously avoid mentioning *that*. To do so would have undermined the Stratfordian theory they are desperate to prop up.

Kathman and Reedy accompany their persuasive argument that No. 159 clearly is addressed to Shakspere with the utterly baffling argument that it "is demonstrably *not* addressed to the Earl of Oxford in any kind of disguise, since it is addressed in the present tense to a living person, and Oxford had been dead [since 1604]." Reedy & Kathman (emphasis added); see also Kathman, "Why I Am Not an Oxfordian." They thus fall prey to the pitfall against which I have long warned my law students: the classic mistake of diluting and distracting from a strong argument by throwing in one or more weak or frivolous claims.

First of all, is it really necessary to point out that it was and remains a well-known and perfectly common stylistic choice (both in early modern times and today) to discuss deceased writers in the present tense, especially when impersonally addressing their literary works? Kathman and Reedy may want to check out the Folger Library's subtitle (discussed above) on its website posting of the very writing under discussion: "John Davies of Hereford *Praises [present tense]* William Shakespeare" (emphasis added).

This point goes far, by the way, to negate the claim in Kathman, "Sobran," citing mostly present-tense literary allusions, that "there were many indications [up to 1614] that Shakespeare the author was alive after 1604." In fact, there are *not* any clear indications to that effect. This book specifically refutes Kathman's reliance in that article (in alleged support of his claim) upon No. 159 (here), the 1609 Preface to *Troilus and Cressida* (see Part IV.25 & notes 634-40), and the 1614 Freeman poem (see, in this part, notes 668-69 and related text).

In any event, No. 159's present-tense style, whatever bearing it has on Ogburn's misreading, is totally irrelevant to its direct and powerful expression of authorship doubt and its indirect support for the Oxfordian theory. Kathman asserts in "Why I Am Not an Oxfordian": "Since Oxford had died in 1604, Davies was clearly not addressing him as 'Shakespeare'." But *Shakspere* was obviously still *alive*, and Davies, addressing *him* as a *purported* playwright (like Terence), was directly implying that he was a frontman for a hidden author. Kathman, Reedy, and I thus agree that Davies was not *addressing* any hidden author. But he was strongly and directly implying that *there was a hidden author*, and there is no reason whatsoever why that author would have to still be alive. Vere, though deceased by then, remains by far the strongest candidate.

that Terence "came from humble origins, just like Shakespeare," as if that were the *only* possible explanation for the comparison drawn by Davies.[680]

Kathman and Reedy cannot claim any reasonable excuse of ignorance. Ogburn pointed out the frontman implication in his very book they have caustically sought to dissect in these very articles. They are also fully aware of Price and her work, also attacked on the Kathman & Ross website.[681] They are fully aware that this Davies epigram is one of the key pieces of disputed evidence in the authorship debate, the issue to which their articles and the entire Kathman & Ross website are devoted.

Nor can Kathman and Reedy dispute that Terence has been widely viewed as a frontman (fairly or not) for more than 2,000 years. They simply omit this obviously crucial fact from their arguments urging readers to dismiss (as they do) any doubts about the Stratfordian theory.

We are not quite yet done with Davies of Hereford and his *Scourge of Folly*—perhaps an apt metaphor for the critique of orthodox humbug this entire book has been forced to pursue. Price observed that Epigram No. 159's satirical and questioning nature is strongly corroborated by how it appears in the list of epigrams that precede and follow it. Leading up to No. 159 are gracious and

---

[680] Reedy & Kathman. I view Kathman and Reedy as more actively deceptive on this point than Wells because their articles (unlike Wells's book cited earlier) are specifically focused on the SAQ. As discussed earlier, it is difficult to see why, aside from Terence's reputation as a frontman, he would be singled out for comparison with Shakspere (as the presumed author Shakespeare). It is doubtful, in the first place, that Shakspere would have been viewed as unusually distinctive because of his supposedly "humble origins." Many other early modern English playwrights, including Ben Jonson and Christopher Marlowe, came from backgrounds equally or more modest. Nor would Shakspere's upper-middle-class origins in Stratford really compare that strongly with Terence's background *as a slave*—recalling further that by 1610, Shakspere had attained not only great wealth and success, but also the status of gentleman with a coat-of-arms.

[681] See, again, Ogburn, p. 257, Price, pp. 61-62, and Chiljan, p. 264.

clearly personal epigrams to "my much esteemed" or "my worthy kind friend" and the like.

Then, suddenly, we have the impersonal and collective epigram *"To our English Terence,"* followed by the mocking No. 160, *"To his most constant, though most unknown friend*; No-body," and then No. 161, *"To my near-dear well-known friend*; Somebody."[682] As Alexander Waugh has pointed out, No. 160 calls for especially close scrutiny. He observed that unlike the neighboring epigrams, addressed consistently to *"my"* so-and-so, Nos. 159 and 160 shift gears to say *"our"* and *"his."* And the word "his" seems very significant. It corroborates and amplifies the suggestions of No. 159—and other writings we have seen—that "Shakespeare" is a pseudonym and Shakspere the player was viewed as a plagiarist and frontman for a hidden author.[683]

*Whose* "most constant" and "most unknown friend" was "Nobody"? We have only to look at the previous epigram. This was

---

[682] Davies, *Scourge*, pp. 76-77 (italics, and hyphenation of "No-body" and "Some-body," in original), quoted and discussed in Price, pp. 63-64. Chambers overlooked No. 160 in his 1930 compendium, see, *e.g.*, v. 2, p. 214 (quoting No. 159), even though it constitutes a continuing comment on Shakespeare (referring to "his ... friend") The brief contents of Nos. 160 and 161 seem deliberately cryptic and do not provide much if any additional enlightenment. No. 160 does seem suitable for someone whose true identity remains hidden or not publicly acknowledged in some way, someone who "shall be served with [nothing]." It seems to imply something like "I'll deal with you later," or "I'm not giving you a numbered epigram now," or "I have nothing more to say to you":

> You shall be served; but not with Numbers now:
> You shall be served with nought [*i.e.*, nothing]: that's good for you.

No. 161 states (italics in original; I definitely need help with this one):

> You look that as myself I you should use:
> I will, or else myself I should abuse:
> And yet with Rhymes I but myself undo,
> Yet am I *Some-body* with much ado.

[683] Waugh, "Weever" (2014), pp. 13, 15 n. 9; see also Parts IV.2, 11, 14; IV.15 & notes 337-50; IV.16 & notes 365-69, 386-96; IV.18 & notes 444-47; IV.28.

Shakespeare's friend, the friend of "our English Terence." Terence's own well-known friends were two Roman aristocrats. Was "Nobody" a nobleman who could not be named?

## 27. Henry Peacham, *Minerva Britanna* (1612)

Henry Peacham (1578–*c.* 1644) was a writer perhaps most famous for his book *The Complete Gentleman* (1622). That treatise openly praised the poetry of "Edward Earl of Oxford" in a list of leading Elizabethan poets—while curiously omitting "Shakespeare."[684]

In 1612, Peacham published *Minerva Britanna*, a cryptic collection of images, emblems, anagrams, and other puzzles. The title means "Britain's Minerva," the latter being the Roman goddess of wisdom and warfare, known to the Greeks as Athena (or Pallas). She was also viewed as a patroness of the arts and has always been commonly depicted as brandishing a spear. *Minerva* is complex, obscure, and debatable with regard to the SAQ. Professor Roger Stritmatter explored it in detail in a superb 2000 article. Alexander Waugh has provided a brief recent summary of the early authorship doubts it may express.[685]

The title page of Peacham's *Minerva* depicts what appears to be the arm of a hidden writer emerging from behind a curtain. The hand appears to have just finished writing (upside-down) "MENTE.VIDEBOR"—a Latin phrase that translates: "with the mind I will be seen."[686]

---

[684] The 1622 treatise is a guide to an aspiring young man's literary, artistic, and philosophical development. See, *e.g.*, Ogburn, p. 767. For the best (but still rather desperate and unconvincing) Stratfordian attempt to explain away this puzzling omission, see Ross, "Peacham."

[685] See Stritmatter, "*Minerva*" (2000); Waugh, "My Shakespeare" (2018), pp. 77-78; see also Anderson, pp. 365-67; Part IV.3 & notes 193-97 (discussing the goddess Minerva).

[686] Waugh, "My Shakespeare," p. 78 (capitalization in Peacham's original); see also Magri, "Latin Mottoes," p. 240; Stritmatter, "*Minerva*," pp. 1, 10-13.

As Waugh noted, this may be viewed as "inviting the reader to engage his mind to find [a] hidden letter 'i'."[687] The writer's quill may be viewed as poised to write another letter following "videbor." The shape of the quill looks like a dotted "i"—the "i" the reader may use his "mind" to "see."[688] The word "videbori" would be nonsense, but the additional "i" allows the resulting total of 13 letters (with the period after "mente") to form a perfect anagram:

---

[687] Waugh, "My Shakespeare," p. 78; see also Stritmatter, "*Minerva*," pp. 1, 10-13.

[688] As Noemi Magri, p. 240, and Waugh, p. 78, both noted, the point of the quill, in a literal sense (the plausible surface meaning), is simply marking a dot, or as Magri put it, "an interpoint at the end of the motto." Nina Green, and the late Magri, both Oxfordian scholars who have earned the highest respect, leave a bit to be desired in their treatment of Peacham's *Minerva*. Green, "Myths," Sec. I, p. 52 (citing Magri), calls it a "myth" that the hidden writer "is in the process of completing an unfinished letter." But this seems a pointless quibble, given that, as Green notes, "the quill's point" indeed "*appears to be* an 'i' at the end of the word." Magri likewise noted that it "*seems to be* an 'I' written by the hand." Waugh similarly pointed out that it has "the *strong semblance* of an 'i'." (Pages cited above; all my emphases above.)

*Appearances* and plays upon images and words seem to be the entire *point* of Peacham's book, *n'est-ce pas?* Green also points out, p. 52 (citing Magri), that the word "videbor" is "complete in itself," whereas "videbori" is nonsensical. But that misses another point. The *very fact* that "videbori" is nonsensical may be viewed as a clue inviting the reader to rearrange all the letters (including the suggested "i") to form a *sensible* message.

Magri's essay (very valuable overall) did not address the possibility of an anagram. Green does, but only to note first, p. 52, that "mente videbori" (without the "i") "contains insufficient letters to form the anagram," therefore allegedly violating "Elizabethan rules for anagrams permitt[ing] neither the addition nor the subtraction of letters." But the anagram does not violate this rule since Peacham, as noted above, suggests the needed additional letter—as Stritmatter, "*Minerva*," pp. 10-14, also argued, by a more complex route.

Green also notes, p. 53, that "Peacham's anagrams ... formed from names habitually feature the name alone, with no commentary of any kind." But such a "habit" would not preclude the possibility (likelihood, in fact, as a coincidence seems unlikely) that he created one with commentary *in this case*. It does not support Green's dismissal of this one as a "myth." This anagram, below the central image on the title page, may well be special. Furthermore, this counter-example casts doubt on the accuracy of any such categorical generalization about Peacham's anagrams. Compare Ross, "Oxfordian Myths: *Minerva*" (providing some useful discussion, but also—literally—*missing the point*). For more points that should not be missed, see Part IV.28 & notes 728, 739-41.

"tibi nom. de vere." The Latin phrase *tibi nom(en)* means "your name" or "to you the name." Thus, the anagram suggests: "Your name is de Vere."[689]

The weakness of the *Minerva* title page as an expression of early doubt is that it does not link explicitly to Shakespeare or his works. The picture and apparent anagram, in combination, may be read to imply that Vere was some sort of hidden playwright. That may indirectly corroborate all the other evidence supporting the Oxfordian theory that Vere wrote the works of Shakespeare— especially considering Peacham's inclusion of Vere, and curious omission of "Shakespeare," in his 1622 book, technically outside the pre-1616 period on which this book focuses.

Peacham's *Minerva* does raise questions about the Stratford-ian theory. But taken by itself, it seems suggestive at best, though doubtless intriguing.[690]

## 28. Ben Jonson, "Poet-Ape" and Other Pre-1616 Writings

Ben Jonson (1572–1637) is widely viewed today as perhaps the third-greatest early modern English playwright, after Shake-speare and Marlowe. He was highly regarded in his own time as well—a major literary and cultural figure, not just in the Eliza-bethan era but into the Jacobean and Caroline eras as well. In 1616, some months after Shakspere of Stratford's death, Jonson published a massive folio collecting his own writings, including his plays—which in hindsight marked a major turning point in the

---

[689] See Waugh, "My Shakespeare," p. 78 (crediting early Oxfordian scholar Eva Turner Clark for arriving at this insight in a 1937 book); Stritmatter, *"Minerva,"* pp. 9-15 (providing a much more detailed and extremely useful discussion). For more on anagrams, see Part IV.7 (discussing Covell's *Polimanteia*); see also Parts IV.24, note 617; IV.25, note 650.

[690] Waugh, pp. 78-79, and Magri, "Latin Mottoes," pp. 237-40, pointed out additional Latin phrases on the *Minerva* title page that seem suggestively consis-tent with the Oxfordian theory, but do not provide specific support for it. Com-pare Ross, "Oxfordian Myths: *Minerva*" (providing some useful discussion).

acceptance of theatrical works as literature and paved the way for the "Shakespeare" *First Folio* of 1623.

Jonson contributed two poems to the 1623 *Folio* and probably played a much more extensive role—quite possibly ghostwriting much of the other prefatory material and possibly editing the entire volume. Jonson's own 1616 book and the 1623 *Folio* are both sources of substantial Shakespeare authorship doubts, despite the latter's evident promotion (if not creation) of the Stratfordian theory of authorship.[691] This book has discussed Jonson and his works in connection with the mysteries surrounding the *Parnassus* plays and the Essex Rebellion.[692]

As we have already seen, several writings dating before 1616 suggest that Shakspere, the player from Stratford, was a plagiarist or a frontman for a hidden author.[693] We have seen how "Shakespeare" seems to transmute, mysteriously, into a pair of *doppelgängers*—respected author yet mocked and disreputable actor.[694] Nowhere is this dichotomy more starkly clear—almost schizophrenic—than in Jonson's writings.

There is a deeply felt ring of sincerity in much of Jonson's eloquent encomia for the author Shakespeare, as in the 1623 *Folio:* "Soul of the Age! The applause! delight! the wonder of our Stage! My *Shakespeare*, rise ... to honour thee, I would ... call forth thundering *Aeschylus, Euripides, and Sophocles ... and him of Cordova* dead,"[695] referring to the three great tragic playwrights of ancient Greece, and allusively to the great tragic playwright Seneca, born

---

[691] See Parts I & notes 36-41; II & note 49; III.A & notes 3-6; III.B & notes 36-38; IV.26 & notes 663-67; V & notes 2-3.

[692] Parts IV.15 & note 337; IV.16 & notes 359, 387, 391; IV.17 & note 419.

[693] See Parts IV.2, 11, 14; IV.15 & notes 337-50; IV.16 & notes 365-69, 386-96; IV.18 & notes 444-47; IV.26.

[694] See Parts IV.16 & notes 386-96, and IV.22 & note 554.

[695] Jonson, "To the Memory of My Beloved," in *First Folio*, p. 9 (emphases in original; text mainly in italics with emphases in Roman type, reversed here for clarity); see generally pp. 9-10.

in the ancient Roman province of Hispania.[696] Jonson concludes his passionate paean of praise by imagining the author "in the *Hemisphere* ... and made a Constellation there! Shine forth, thou Star of *Poets* ...."[697]

At the same time, forming a curious bridge across the divide, there is an ostentatious "protesting too much" quality to Jonson's reference, in the very title of this poem in the 1623 *Folio*, "To the memory of my beloved, The AUTHOR" (capitals in original), a shouting banner headline followed in much smaller capitals by "MR. WILLIAM SHAKESPEARE."[698]

On the other side of this divide, even quite a few orthodox scholars have agreed that Jonson seems to scathingly satirize and ridicule Shakespeare—*or perhaps, doubters suggest, only Shakspere of Stratford*—in several references before the latter man's death in 1616. These include the characters "Poet-Ape," targeted by one of Jonson's epigrams, and "Sogliardo" in his play *Every*

---

[696] Seneca the Younger (*c.* 4 B.C.E.–65 C.E.), to be precise. See Part IV.1 & notes 4-6; Chiljan, p. 54; see also *First Folio*, p. 10 ("He was not of an age, but for all time!").

[697] *First Folio*, p. 10 (emphases in original).

[698] *First Folio*, p. 9; *Hamlet*, act 3, sc. 2 ("[Queen Gertrude:] The lady doth protest too much, methinks."). The poem by Leonard Digges, *Folio*, p. 15 (headlining its page in the original, just like Jonson's poem), is—parallel to Jonson's—introduced in *HUGE* capital letters by "TO THE MEMORY," followed below in smaller (but still fairly large) typeface, "of the deceased Authour Maister" (*sic*), followed below that, as with Jonson's poem, in yet smaller capitals: "W. SHAKESPEARE." Why use the word "AUTHOR" AT ALL in these encomia? Was the identity of "Shakespeare" as such not *already obvious* from the attributions on the title page and again above the list of the "Principal Actors" concluding the prefatory materials? If he were "beloved," why not refer simply to "my beloved William (or Will) Shakespeare"? Why suggest the "AUTHOR" ONLY is "beloved," followed by the oddly stiff and formal "Mr. William Shakespeare"? (Readers of this book may note that I dedicate it to "my ever-loving husband Ashish," not "my ever-loving husband, Dr. Ashish Agrawal.") Was Jonson suggesting genuine affection for a hidden "AUTHOR"—see the affectionate (though satirical) portrait of "Puntarvolo" in *Every Man Out of His Humour*, discussed in note 722—but chilly disdain for Shakspere of Stratford? See, *e.g.*, Price, pp. 191-92; Waugh, "My Shakespeare" (2018), p. 79. These comments barely scratch the surface of the *Folio*'s word games. See Part I & note 36.

*Man Out of His Humour.* We cannot be certain these characters satirize Shakespeare. These are points of vigorous debate among Stratfordian and doubting scholars. But they at least raise reasonable doubts about Shakespeare's authorship.[699]

"On Poet-Ape" was first published in Jonson's 1616 folio as Epigram No. 56, but is thought to have been written some time between 1595 and 1612. It is one of only three poems Jonson ever wrote in the form of a Shakespearean sonnet:

> Poor POET-APE, that would be thought our chief,
> Whose works are e'en the frippery of wit,
> From brokage is become so bold a thief,
> As we, the robbed, leave rage, and pity it.
> At first he made low shifts, would pick and glean,
> Buy the reversion of old plays; now grown
> To a little wealth, and credit in the *scene*,
> He takes up all, makes each man's wit his own.
> And, told of this, he slights it. Tut, such crimes
> The sluggish gaping auditor devours;
> He marks not whose 'twas first: and after-times
> May judge it to be his, as well as ours.
> Fool, as if half eyes will not know a fleece
> From locks of wool, or shreds from the whole piece?[700]

---

[699] See, *e.g.*, Chiljan, pp. 122-24 (arguing that Poet-Ape was most likely Edward Alleyn); pp. 204-11, 216 (arguing powerfully, however, that several characters, including Sogliardo, in Jonson's plays *Every Man Out of His Humour*, *Every Man In His Humour*, and *Poetaster*, do satirize Shakspere); notes 715, 718, 726-28, and related text. I happen to agree with Chiljan's powerful argument that Alleyn was the "upstart Crow" ("Shake-scene") in *Groats-Worth of Wit* (1592) (see Part IV.2.g), which could fit with him also being Poet-Ape. But there seem to be better reasons to think Poet-Ape was Shakspere. See, *e.g.*, Price, pp. 87-90; Michell, pp. 70-71. Price, in particular, argued that "Alleyn is not a good candidate," noting: "Jonson's derogatory opinion of this 'Poet-Ape' conflicts with his opinion of Alleyn, to whom he wrote a laudatory epigram .... After Alleyn, Shakspere was the wealthiest actor-shareholder of his day ...." Price, p. 89; see also Jonson, Epigram No. 89, "To Edward Allen" (*sic*), in *Works* (1616), p. 793.

[700] Jonson, *Works* (1616), p. 783 (emphases in original), quoted in full in Price, p. 88; see also Greenwood (1908), pp. 455-57; Greenwood, *Shakespeare Problem?* (1916), pp. 371-75; Michell, p. 70; Anderson, pp. 317-18; Chiljan, pp. 122-23. Jonson's 133 "Epigrams" appear in his *Works* (1616), pp. 765-818, to

(footnote continued on next page)

As John Michell stated: "Jonson's meaning is fairly plain. There is a plagiarizing poet whose works are the ... cast-off items of other writers' wit. He began as a broker of plays ... and now ... passes [them] off as his own."[701] Diana Price noted good reasons to identify Poet-Ape as Shakspere of Stratford. He is described as "an actor and play broker who began by procuring plays" to which legal rights had lapsed ("the reversion of old plays").[702] "He then became 'so bold a thief,' which could mean that he passed off someone else's work as his own or sold plays that were not his to sell." He was "well-known enough to 'be thought our chief,' probably because he [was] a prominent actor-shareholder and paymaster."[703] That might suggest, furthermore, that he enjoyed an undeserved reputation as the greatest playwright of the day.[704]

Katherine Chiljan noted that "ape" could mean an actor and also "one who 'apes' poets, implying he really is not one."[705] Poet-Ape is described as financially successful, "grown [t]o a little

---

(footnote continued from previous page)
which all page citations here refer, if not otherwise identified. On the uncertain (but clearly pre-1616) date of No. 56, see Price, p. 88; see also p. 90 (noting it is one of only three Shakespearean sonnets Jonson ever wrote, which Price suggested is a "clue" to Poet-Ape's identity).

Waugh, "Moniment" (rev. 2015), explored some fascinating resonances between "Poet-Ape" and the "Shakspeare" Monument in Stratford's Holy Trinity Church, before it was altered in later years. Query: Is the name on the monument (spelled as noted) a cleverly cobbled compromise between "Shakspere," the spelling typically used by the player from Stratford and his family, and "Shakespeare," the almost uniform spelling of the author's published name?

[701] Michell, p. 71.

[702] Price, pp. 88-89.

[703] Price, p. 89.

[704] As Price noted, p. 89, even some orthodox scholars have conceded that.

[705] Chiljan, p. 122 (though she argued Poet-Ape was Alleyn; see note 699). Waugh, "Moniment," noted that early modern writers used "ape" to mean "actor" or "player." See also Part IV.16, p. 176 (*Parnassus 3* describing "players" as "mimic apes"). The *OED* fails to note the early modern usage of "ape" as "actor" or "player," but a meaning it does provide, a "mimic" or one who "imitates" ("plays the ape"), is close. The latter usage, during Shakespeare's time (as today), was most often derisive: To "ape" or to be an "ape" is to be a fool, to mimic or imitate in a foolish or silly way. It was used more rarely then (not at all today) in a neutral or positive sense. See *OED*, v. 1, pp. 543-44.

wealth, and credit in the scene."[706] As Price concluded, "[t]he list of successful actor-brokers who could fit this description would be quite short," and Shakspere seems the best candidate.[707]

Price noted that Jonson, in seemingly associated epigrams, mocks similar characters. "Groom Idiot," for example, "is so inept at reading verse that he 'laughs in the wrong place'."[708] More tellingly, Jonson depicts "Person Guilty" as having "no artistic judgment" and "appropriat[ing] some of Jonson's verse." And "Jonson threatens to reveal his identity."[709] Jonson addresses an epigram

---

[706] See Price, p. 89 (quoting the epigram).

[707] Price, p. 89, see also Anderson, pp. 317 18,

[708] Price, p. 90, quoting Jonson, Epigram No. 58, p. 784. Price noted that Jonson accuses an unnamed "Play-wright" (hyphenation in original) of "steal-[ing] Jonson's material." Price, p. 90. Jonson addresses three epigrams to "Play-wright," Nos. 49, 68, and 100, pp. 781, 787, 799. Only No. 100, to my mind, clearly makes this accusation. All of Jonson's epigrams discussed here were apparently first published in his 1616 *Works*, and all (like "Poet-Ape") were presumably written some time before 1616.

[709] Price, p. 90. Price did not further explore the two epigrams addressed "To Person Guilty." No. 30, p. 777, states (emphasis in original):

GUILTY, be wise; and though thou know'st the crimes
Be thine, I tax, yet do not own my rhymes:
'Twere madness in thee, to betray thy fame,
And person to the world; ere I thy name.

No. 38, p. 778, states (emphases in original):

GUILTY, because I bade you late [*i.e.*, recently warned you] be wise,
And to conceal your ulcers, did advise,
You laugh when you are touched, and long before
Any man else, you clap your hands, and roar,
And cry good! good! This quite perverts my sense,
And lies so far from wit [*i.e.*, wisdom or intelligence], 'tis impudence.
Believe it, GUILTY, if you lose your shame,
I'll lose my modesty, and tell your name.

On "wit," see Part IV.2.a & note 15, citing *OED*, v. 20, pp. 432-34. Jonson, in No. 30, seems to say: "Wise up, scoundrel. You and I both know what you're up to in general, but you'd better not steal *my* lines. You're crazy to risk the truth about you and your fame becoming known to the world. Push me further and I might reveal the truth about your name." No. 38 seems to say: "I warned you to wise up

(footnote continued on next page)

"To Proule the Plagiary" that neither Price nor any scholar seems to have yet discussed in relation to the SAQ.[710]

Jonson's epigram "On Don Surly," a pretentious and boorish buffoon, is in some ways as intriguing as "Poet-Ape." It states that Surly "aspire[s] [to] the glorious name [o]f a great man, and to be thought the same ...."[711] As Price noted, this might suggest that he "hopes to be mistaken for someone far above his station, to be recognized *by name* as somebody else."[712]

Another comment about Surly may also hint at some link to a man of high rank, and one suggests a love triangle: "He drinks to no man: that's, too, like a lord. He keeps another man's wife, which is a spice [o]f solemn greatness." Jonson concludes by linking this epigram to his others: Surly "[m]ay hear my *Epigrams*, but like of none. SURLY, use other arts, these only can [s]tyle thee a most great fool, but no great man."[713]

---

(footnote continued from previous page)
and in response you just laughed it off, clapping and roaring 'Good!' This is so messed up and stupid on your part, it's downright impudent. If you continue to act so shamelessly, so will I—by revealing the truth about your name."

[710] No. 81, p. 791 (emphases in original):

> Forbear to tempt me, PROULE, I will not show
> A line unto thee, till the world it know;
> Or that I have by two good sufficient men,
> To be the wealthy witness of my pen:
> For all thou hear'st, thou swear'st thy self didst do.
> Thy wit lives by it, PROULE, and belly too.
> Which, if thou leave not soon (though I am loath)
> I must a libel make, and cosen both.

This seems to convey a message very similar to Nos. 30 and 38 quoted in note 709: "Don't tempt me, you plagiarist. Everything you hear, you swear you wrote. That's the extent of your supposed 'wit' (intelligence—or literary skill or reputation?), and also how you make a living (feed your 'belly'). If you don't stop stealing my lines, I'll have to 'libel' (defame) you (blow your cover?)—though I'd really rather not—and cheat or deprive ('cosen' or cozen) you out of both your 'wit' (reputation?) and your meal ticket."

[711] No. 28, p. 776, quoted in Price, p. 90.
[712] Price, p. 90 (emphasis in original).
[713] No. 28, p. 776 (emphases in original).

We must be very cautious when it comes to drawing any conclusions about all this. Jonson's language is open to various interpretations. Did he target the same person with multiple epigrams
using different satirical names? Or were there multiple pretentious fraudsters in his life with whom he had to contend?

Price pointed out a parallel between Surly's preoccupation
with his name and Sogliardo's with his own name in *Every Man
Out of His Humour*. This Jonson play was performed in 1599 and
published in 1600.[714] The evidence linking Sogliardo to Shakspere
has persuaded even many orthodox scholars, but it remains debatable.[715] Sogliardo asks "Carlo Buffone": "[M]y name, Signior, how
think you? [W]ill it not serve for a gentleman's name[?] ...
[M]ethinks it sounds well."[716] But the joke is on him. "Sogliardo"
was a generic Italian epithet for a boorish and gullible fool.[717]

Price and Chiljan, among others, have traced the connections
between Sogliardo and Shakspere. For example, the play ridicules
Sogliardo for boasting about his new coat-of-arms. Another character comments sardonically that the motto on Sogliardo's coat-of-
arms should be *"not without mustard."* That may, in part, satirize
the Shakspere coat-of-arms—on applications for which appeared

---

[714] See Price, p. 66; Chiljan, p. 204. This play was also published in Jonson,
*Works* (1616), pp. 73-176. For all three Jonson plays discussed here—*Every Man
In His Humour* (1598), *Every Man Out of His Humour* (1599), and *Poetaster*
(1601)—page citations refer to Jonson, *Works* (1616).

[715] See Price, pp. 66-75, 90; Chiljan, p. 204; Morris (2013), pp. 18-22; see
also, *e.g.*, Bate, *Soul of the Age*, p. 356 (endorsing the satire); Parts IV.15 & note
337, and IV.16 & note 391 (discussing Sogliardo in relation to the *Parnassus*
plays). But see, *e.g.*, Donaldson, pp. 159-60 (thoughtfully questioning the satire).

[716] Act 1, sc. 2, p. 91, quoted and discussed in Price, p. 90.

[717] John Florio's 1598 Italian-English dictionary, p. 377 (quoted and discussed in Price, p. 90), defines a "sogliardo" as "a mocker, a scoffer, a quipper, a
flouter, a frumper, a jester. Also slovenly, sluttish, or hoggish. Also a lubbard, a
loggerhead, a gull, a fool, a flatterer ...." Jonson's specific character summary in
the play, p. 79 (original italics omitted), echoes the harsh generic description:
"An essential Clown ... yet so enamored of the name of a Gentleman, that he will
have it, though he buys it. ... He is in his kingdom when he can get himself into
company, where he may be well laughed at."

the French phrase *non sanz droict*, easily misread as *"not without right*."[718] Sogliardo suggests he bribed heraldry officials to get his coat-of-arms. The Shakspere coat-of-arms was also alleged to be improperly granted.[719] Sogliardo's brother Sordido plans to hoard grain, a practice of which Shakspere was also accused.[720]

Chiljan offered intriguing interpretations of two more characters in *Every Man Out*. "Shift," a friend of Sogliardo, posts "bills" (ads) on a church door and when asked about them, responds: "Sir, if I should deny *the manuscripts*, I were worthy to be banished ...." He is observed "expostulating with his rapier," which may be paraphrased as "shaking a sword" (or spear?). He is asked if he would sell it: "My rapier? no, sir: my rapier is my guard, my defence, *my revenue*, my honour."[721]

---

[718] Act 3, sc. 4, p. 124 (emphasis of "not without mustard" in original; other emphases added), quoted and discussed, *e.g.*, in Greenwood (1908), pp. 461-64; Miller, "Jonson and Sogliardo," pp. 44-46; Michell, pp. 72-74; Price, pp. 66-75; Anderson, pp. 318-19; Chiljan, pp. 204-05; see also act 3, sc. 2, p. 121; Hughes, "Not Without Mustard" (2009). This complex issue cannot be fully explored here. As noted, *e.g.*, by Miller, pp. 44-45, quoting Chambers (1930), v. 2, pp. 18-32, by Hughes, and by Price, pp. 69-70 & figs. 1-2, the phrase in the 1596 Shakspere applications more likely indicates initial *rejection* ("no, without right"). It would not accurately translate as "not without right," but could be so read *satirically*. Compare Green, "Myths," Sec. II, pp. 33-37 (criticizing as a "myth" the conjecture that "not without mustard" satirizes, *in part* as argued by Price, pp. 68-69, the phrase in the Shakspere applications); see generally pp. 20-44 (Green's valuable overall discussion of the Shakspere coat-of-arms). Chiljan, p. 205, noted: "Jonson may have learned about these applications from his former schoolmaster and longtime friend, William Camden, an official at the College of Heralds." See also Part IV.21 & notes 530-31 (on Camden and the coat-of-arms); Donaldson, pp. 159-64 (more on Camden; also questioning "not without mustard").

[719] See Price, pp. 69-73; see also Michell, pp. 72-74; Chiljan, p. 204.

[720] Act 1, sc. 3, pp. 95-98, discussed in Chiljan, p. 205; see also p. 204 (Sogliardo, like Shakspere, is ambitious and financially successful but lacks higher education). Jonson's character summary of Sogliardo, p. 79, says "[h]e comes up every Term," consistent with Shakspere's presumed Stratford-London commute.

[721] Act 3, sc. 1, p. 120 ("bills"); sc. 6, p. 126 ("expostulating"), p. 127 ("my rapier"), p. 128 ("manuscripts"), quoted and discussed in Chiljan, pp. 205-06 (Chiljan's emphases). Chiljan observed, p. 206: "The rapier is Shift's 'revenue,' and if denied 'the manuscripts,' he would be out of business." Thus, she argued, Jonson could be read to imply "that Shift is pirating Shakespeare's plays," referenced as "the manuscripts," with the pseudonym "Shakespeare" suggested by

(footnote continued on next page)

"Sir Puntarvolo," nominally presented as a knight, is plainly an aristocratic courtier. He is a fine horseman and jouster who engages in other pastimes of the nobility, like falconry and hunting with dogs. He is "a gentleman of exceeding good humour," well-traveled and known to "brandish" a sword. He has a gigantic ego but also great charm and romantic passion. It is he who mockingly suggests "not without mustard" as Sogliardo's motto. He is said to handle "a staff well at tilt[ing]," referring to the spear used in jousting. In sum, Puntarvolo is described, perhaps in more ways than one, as quite the *spear shaker*.[722]

---

(footnote continued from previous page)
Shift waving his rapier. She suggested Shift might represent printers of Shakespeare plays with Sogliardo as frontman. She developed the argument in several ways that I will not try to reproduce in full here. I again urge readers to buy her excellent book, which is not just eye-opening but mind-opening. The same is true of Price's and Anderson's books. *Buy all three!*

[722] Act 2, sc. 1, p. 102 ("tilt[ing]"), quoted and discussed in Chiljan, p. 206; see also note 718 and related text ("not without mustard"). Jonson's character summary prefacing the play, p. 77 (original italics omitted here; small capitals in following quotations in original), describes Puntarvolo as follows:

A Vain-glorious Knight, over-Englishing his travels, and wholly consecrated to singularity; the very JACOB'S staff of complement: a Sir, that hath lived to see the revolution of time in most of his apparel. Of presence good enough, but so palpably affected to his own praise, that (for want of flatterers) he commends himself, to the floutage of his own family. He deals upon returns, and strange performances, resolving (in despite of public derision) to stick to his own particular fashion, phrase, and gesture.

Those familiar with Edward de Vere's biography may well murmur "hmm!" A "Jacob's staff of complement" might be read as a "measuring stick of perfection," see *OED*, v. 3, p. 609 (defs. I.1-3, "complement" as completion, fulfillment, accomplishment, perfection). But in context here, given comments in act 2, scenes 2-3, it probably means something like "the very measuring stick of courtesy," see p. 610 (def. II.9, "complement"—later spelled "compliment"—as ceremonial courtesy, often with an early modern overtone of insincerity).

There's more in act 2, scene 1. At Puntarvolo's approach, "Fastidius Briske" exclaims: "His hounds! by MINERVA an excellent figure," p. 101; see also note 733; Parts IV.3 & notes 193-97; IV.27 & note 685 (discussing Minerva, *i.e.*, Athena or Pallas, the *spear-shaking* goddess). Fastidius says he is "reported to be a gentleman of exceeding good humour," pp. 101-02. Still more follows, p. 102: Puntarvo-
(footnote continued on next page)

"Jonson was probably hinting," Chiljan inferred, "that [Puntarvolo] represented the great author [Shakespeare] via his pen name."[723] Edward de Vere (Earl of Oxford) was known as a champion jouster and well-traveled *raconteur*. It is thus all the more intriguing that Sogliardo's coat-of-arms depicts a *boar*, also found in Vere's coat-of-arms.[724] Ruth Loyd Miller, Richard Malim, and Mark Anderson, among others, have discussed this connection linking Sogliardo, Puntarvolo, and Vere. Puntarvolo is puzzled by Sogliardo's coat-of-arms and asks him to explain it. Sogliardo res-

---

(footnote continued from previous page)
lo seems to be something of an elusive and sought-after celebrity, as Fastidius gushes that he "ne'er was so favoured of my stars, as to see him yet." Carlo says he "loves dogs, and hawks, and his wife," and "can sit a great horse." He cuts a figure like St. George "when he is mounted," though "instead of a dragon, he will brandish against a tree, and break his sword as confidently upon the knotty bark, as the other did upon the scales of the beast." Fastidius: "They say he has dialogues, and discourses between his horse, himself, and his dog: and that he will court his own lady, as [if] she were a stranger never encountered before." Carlo: "[Aye], that he will, and make fresh love to her every morning ...."

All in all, a quixotic and eccentric figure—reciting "dialogues" to himself and his animals, fond of "strange performances"—one who marches to his own drummer, supremely egotistical but an evergreen romantic with seductive style and panache. If he doesn't sound like the author Shakespeare, who would? Ogburn & Ogburn (1952), pp. 292-94, Morris (2013), and others, have noted very intriguing connections between this play and various works by "Shakespeare," Vere, and other Elizabethan writers.

[723] Chiljan, p. 206.

[724] On Vere's jousting, see, *e.g.*, Anderson, pp. 46-47, 169-72, 199 (describing 1571, 1581, and 1584 tournaments in which he won top honors). Sogliardo's boar is headless. Jonson may play it for laughs in various ways (*e.g.*, "boar" as "boor"). See also note 727. Carlo mocks: "I commend the *Herald's* wit, he has deciphered [Sogliardo] well: A swine without a head, without brain, wit, any thing indeed, ramping to gentility." Act 3, sc. 4, p. 124 (emphasis in original), quoted and discussed in Price, pp. 68-69; Anderson, p. 319; Chiljan, pp. 204-05.

No boar appears in the Shakspere coat-of-arms. Schoenbaum, *Documentary Life*, p. 229, rejected Sogliardo as a satire partly for that reason. See Price, pp. 73-74. But Schoenbaum missed the point by a mile. *A satire typically alters details to serve the satirical goal.* One would not expect a frontman for an aristocrat to be so brazen as to put the latter's emblem on his own coat-of-arms. But a writer offering a veiled send-up might well do so. Schoenbaum and others have noted the Shakspere family never actually used "Not Without Right" as a motto. But Jonson may have mocked the phrase in the applications. See note 718.

ponds: "[S]ir, it is your Boar without a head ...."[725] It may be questioned whether Sogliardo actually connects his boar to Puntarvolo. This may seem surprising to modern readers, but the word "your" in the *early* modern era did not (sometimes) convey the familiar second-person possessive sense it almost always carries today.[726]

---

[725] Act 3, sc. 4, p. 124; see also, *e.g.*, Miller, "Jonson and Sogliardo" (1975), pp. 48-51; Malim, "Oxford's View of Shakespeare" (2004), pp. 247-48; Malim, "Spanish Maze" (2004), p. 284; Malim (2012), pp. 200, 249-50, 292 n. 42; Anderson (2005), p. 319; see also p. 546 (endnote crediting Roger Stritmatter for a related Puntarvolo connection). Related connections were also discussed, *e.g.*, in Ogburn & Ogburn (1952), pp. 292-94, and Morris (2013), pp. 18-22. Greenwood (1908) understandably missed it, writing before the Oxfordian theory was first proposed by Looney in 1920. Looney briefly noted it at the end of a paragraph discussing Vere's boar (focused on other connections). Still others explored it between 1920 and 1975. See Looney, p. 339: "It may be worth mentioning that the character of Puntarvolo ... who, some Baconians believe, was Jonson's representation of Bacon, was also one whose crest was a boar. These things are at any rate interesting if not made too much of." But Looney did not discuss the related Sogliardo-Shakspere connection. Michell, Price, and Chiljan did not discuss the possible Puntarvolo-Vere-boar connection, despite quoting this line. See Michell, p. 73; Price, p. 68; Chiljan, pp. 204-05 (quoting part of Sogliardo's reply but not Puntarvolo's question).

Vere's general attitude toward Shakspere may be guessed from Puntarvolo's comment to Sogliardo at the end of this scene, p. 125: "Sirra, keep close; yet not so close: thy breath will thaw my ruff." As with Shift (see note 721), Chiljan, pp. 206-07, pursued other Puntarvolo connections. She noted he is oddly obsessed with protecting his dog, which she conjectured may represent Shakespeare's literary works. *"[W]hatever you do, Buy"* her book (and Price's and Anderson's too—and Warren's superb, scholarly 2018 reprint of Looney's book and 2019 collection of Looney's articles). See my Preface & note 1.

[726] But it very often did. Compare Green, "Myths," Sec. I, pp. 41-47, with *OED*, v. 20, pp. 771-72. Green insists the entire Sogliardo-Puntarvolo-Vere-boar connection is a "myth" and that Sogliardo's "your" was meant in an indefinite sense—rare today, more common in early modern English—to introduce something merely as a typical example of its kind, *not* suggesting possession by or association with the person addressed (as if Sogliardo merely meant "it's your typical headless boar," just any old boar, with no intended connection to Puntarvolo). But Green's reading is probably mistaken. It seems out of tune with the context of the scene (see note 727) and the primary meaning of "your" (see below). Her dismissal of the possessive reading as a "myth" is untenable.

Green, pp. 42-43, more than amply demonstrates that the non-possessive meaning was available and used at the time, *as a general matter*, citing *OED* and other sources. But *OED*, p. 772, gives that meaning as *secondary* (defs. 5.b, 6), with the possessive or associational sense ("of or belonging to you," with several

(footnote continued on next page)

Careful study of this scene, however, strongly suggests that Jonson was indeed linking Sogliardo's boar to Puntarvolo—and also, debatably to be sure, connecting Puntarvolo to Vere.[727]

---

(footnote continued from previous page)
variations) as the *primary* meaning (defs. 1-5.a), not just today but supported by usages dating back to *Beowulf*—before, during, and after the early modern era.

Green, pp. 42-43, and *OED* and other sources, cite several uses of "your" by Shakespeare and Jonson in the non-possessive sense—and no doubt there are many more in early modern literature. According to Spevack, p. 1568, "your" is used more than 7,000 times in the Shakespeare canon alone. *OED*, p. 772, also cites three uses by Shakespeare and one by Jonson in the *possessive* sense—and surely there are many more of those too. Green herself concedes, p. 42, that the possessive sense was very commonly used during this time. It is quite inexplicable why she insists that Jonson *must* have used it non-possessively here. How can she be so sure? Far from "mythical," the possessive meaning very likely applies in this case. See note 727.

[727] The specific content and context of act 3, scene 4, supports the possessive meaning of "your" in this instance, though not beyond doubt. See note 726. The scene is largely about a coat-of-arms, something Puntarvolo (unlike most of the other characters) would likely have in proper form. It thus seems deliberate, not coincidental, that Sogliardo first explains his boar *to Puntarvolo.*

Sogliardo seems to mean that his boar *resembles* Puntarvolo's—*except that it's headless.* That is another very suggestive aspect of Jonson's multifaceted humor, suggesting a swinish frontman lacking—*literally*—the true author's mind. See, *e.g.*, note 724 (Carlo's mocking comment), and commenters (including Jan Cole), 2009–15, on Hughes, "Not Without Mustard" (2009). As Green notes, "Myths," Sec. II, pp. 35-36, Jonson also deploys an elaborate food joke, which does undermine the connection between "not without mustard" and Shakspere (see note 718). But that seems irrelevant to the Puntarvolo-boar connection.

A total of *twelve* clearly *non*-possessive references by three different characters address the coat-of-arms or its elements, p. 124—*all twelve* using "a" not "your." Most tellingly: Sogliardo, addressing Carlo and all characters present, twice refers to "a Boar's head"; and Puntarvolo replies to Sogliardo: "A Boar without a head, that's very rare!" In the latter context, Puntarvolo would have no reason to link a headless boar, in the coat-of-arms of his social inferior that he and the others are all ridiculing, with anything in his own coat-of-arms. *Sogliardo*, however, would have an obvious incentive to link his coat-of-arms with that of his social superior, Puntarvolo.

*Only Sogliardo*, addressing *Puntarvolo specifically*, calls it *"your* Boar." Could it be mere coincidence that Puntarvolo is depicted as an aristocrat resembling Vere (see note 722) and that Vere had a boar in his own coat-of-arms?

There is only one other instance in this scene when a character uses "your" to refer to any element of the coat-of-arms. That is in an exchange between the *same* two characters, using the *same* form of address ("sir"), which uses "your" *even more clearly in the same possessive sense.* Puntarvolo says to Sogliardo, p. 124: "[Y]our crest is very rare, sir." Yet a *third* possessive use of "your" between

(footnote continued on next page)

The very name "Puntarvolo" demands scrutiny. Like "Sogliardo" it was a generic Italian character type. Jonson very likely took both from his friend John Florio's influential 1598 Italian-English dictionary. But Jonson's portrait *of his own character* Puntarvolo is notably more positive and affectionate than Florio's generic depiction. Sogliardo, by contrast, largely matches Florio's harsh definition of that type. So *why did* Jonson, among the almost limitless options available, choose *this name* for his foolish knight? Perhaps because, in reverse, it comes very close to translating as "Will ... Spear"?[728] Just another coincidence?

---

(footnote continued from previous page)
the same characters (again using "sir") occurs in the very first line of the scene, p. 123. Sogliardo says to Puntarvolo: "[Y]our dog's in health, sir, I see." Jonson's *Poetaster* (discussed below in text), act 3, sc. 1, in *Works* (1616), p. 299, cited in *OED*, v. 20, p. 772 (as still another *possessive* use of "your"), has the character "Horace" address another character as "Sir, your silkiness." There are doubtless some non-possessive uses of "your" by Jonson in both plays as well. There seem to be several in that same scene in *Poetaster*, *e.g.*, p. 295.

Aside from those three apparently possessive uses of "your" in *Every Man Out*, act 3, scene 4, it is instructive to compare *all six other uses* of "your" in that very same scene—*all possessive:* p. 124 (Clove: "your subject"), p. 125 (Fastidius: "Intreat your poor friend," "how does your fair dog?"; Carlo: "change your mood," "stand upon your gentility," "Spread your self"). It may be added that Macilente (p. 123) says "here be a couple of fine parrots" (not "a couple of *your* fine parrots"), Fastidius (p. 124, emphasis in original) says "yonder's the knight Puntarvolo" (not "yonder's *your* knight"), and Sogliardo (p. 125) says "I am to walk with a knight, here" (not "with *your* knight").

It seems that when Jonson (at least in this scene) wanted to identify something in the second-person possessive sense, he used "your." When he did not, he avoided "your" and used "a" or "the" instead.

728 On Jonson's friendship with Florio, see, *e.g.*, Donaldson, p. 12. On the consistent descriptions of Sogliardo, see note 717 and related text. On Jonson's portrait of Puntarvolo, see note 722 and related text.

Florio, p. 302, defines a "puntarvolo" as "a nice, coy, affected, scrupulous, self-conceited fellow," as "a man that stands upon points, a carper, a find-fault." Modern readers must be cautioned that "nice" did not then carry its current primary meaning (agreeable or kind), which dates from the 18th century. The *early* modern meaning was partly positive, overlapping with the secondary current sense of "nice" as precise, accurate, careful, or attentive (a "nice distinction"). But the early modern senses were mostly very negative, though in some cases grudgingly complimentary: *e.g.*, foolish, stupid, wanton, lascivious; extravagant and flaunting (as to dress); strange, rare; refined or over-refined in taste;

(footnote continued on next page)

(footnote continued from previous page)

cultured, luxurious, fastidious, delicate, tender; shy or modest, but in an affected way—and (more rarely): lazy; trim, elegant, or smart; effeminate or unmanly. See *OED*, v. 10, pp. 386-87.

Even Oxfordian admirers of Vere must concede that many of these adjectives apply rather well to much of what we know about him. Indeed, much of Florio's definition (mostly negative though it is) fits quite well with Vere's apparent image, in some eyes, as an effete "Italianate" courtier. See, *e.g.*, Anderson, pp. 140-41. In any event (again, see note 722), Jonson drew his own portrait more affectionately, though it is still (to be sure) satirical.

To my knowledge, Malim (2012), p. 292 n. 42, is the only previous scholar to suggest the name "Puntarvolo" may be viewed as a play upon "William Shakespeare." Jonson did not invent the name and Malim was probably mistaken to infer that the Greek word *tarasso* ("shake") was involved. A friend fluent in Greek (who studied ancient Greek) tells me that "tar" has never been a standard abbreviation or root of *tarasso*. The syllable "ar" appears very frequently in Italian words, as even a cursory perusal of Florio's (or any) dictionary confirms. Jonson obviously used an existing Italian word. We cannot, however, rule out the possibility that Jonson noticed a linkage to *tar(asso)* and found that serendipitously felicitous to his possible purpose.

In any event, Malim was certainly on to something and deserves credit for this very important insight. As he suggested, *volo* is well-known Latin for "will," the ultimate source for English "voluntary" (it also means "to fly"). As Malim also suggested, "punt" may resonate with Latin *punctum* (a puncture), noun form of the verb *pungo* meaning to puncture, prick, stab, or penetrate. See *Cassell's Latin Dictionary*, pp. 488-89, 647-48. *Cassell's* does not cite "spear," but the linkage is obvious and telling.

Let us now develop Malim's insight using Florio and the *OED*. In early modern Italian (at least), *vólo* meant "flight" and *volontà* meant "*will*, good *will*, affection, mind, heart, meaning, consent, desire." Florio, p. 455 (emphases added). *Punta* meant "a point, a sting, a sharpness, a prick," or a "*thrust with any weapon*." *Punto* meant "pricked, pointed, stung ... or *thrust at*," also "a point, a prick with a pin or *any sharp thing ... a thrust*." Florio, p. 302 (emphases added). "Punt*ura*"—so now we have not just "punt" and "punt*a*," but even the "r" in "punt*ar*"—meant "a prick, or *a thrust, a stoccado*." Florio, p. 303 (emphases added). "Stoccado," in turn, is an English word meaning a "thrust or stab with a *pointed weapon*." *OED*, v. 16, p. 730 (emphasis added), citing, *e.g.*, *The Merry Wives of Windsor*, act 2, sc. 1.

In English, "punt" did not have any clear early modern usages, but the later sporting sense, "to kick," *OED*, v. 12, p. 850 (verb form 3), has an "obscure" dialect history, a variation on "bunt," meaning to push, strike, or butt with the head, horns, or feet (possible nasalized variations on "butt" or "put").

The English word "punto" (no surprise), derives from Italian (or Spanish) *punto* and Latin *punctum*, see *OED*, p. 850, also obviously related to the English words "punctilio," "punctilious," and "punctuate." *OED*, pp. 850-51 (emphasis added), gives four early modern meanings for "punto": (1) a small point, detail, or moment, citing, *e.g.*, Jonson, *Every Man In His Humour*, act 4, sc. 7; (2) a small

(footnote continued on next page)

Chiljan also explored doubts expressed in Jonson's earlier play *Every Man In His Humour*, performed in 1598. The characters "Master Stephen" and "Master Matthew" are described as the "country gull" and the "town gull."[729] Chiljan suggested this was "to emphasize they were to be viewed as one entity. [Shakspere] lived in both the country and the city."[730]

Chiljan, following Sir George Greenwood's analysis, pursued still more doubts expressed in Jonson's play *Poetaster, or His Arraignment*, performed in 1601 and published in 1602. A "poetaster" is one who merely has pretensions to poetry. Jonson's title character is "Crispinus," a gauche would-be gentleman. Like Sogliardo, he is inordinately proud of a laughable coat-of-arms.[731]

---

(footnote continued from previous page)
point of behavior or dress, citing, *e.g.*, Jonson, *The Devil Is an Ass*, act 4, sc. 4; (3) *in fencing*, a "*stroke or thrust with the point of the sword or foil*," again citing *Merry Wives*, act 2, sc. 3, and *Every Man In*, act 4, sc. 7; and (4) a pricking pain— as, one might add, we might (to put it mildly) feel upon being *speared*. These are all telling *points* indeed, *n'est-ce pas?*

In sum, "Puntarvolo" strongly suggests (in reverse): "Will ... Spear." And if Jonson (who knew Greek) possibly thought of *tar(asso)*, it might even (conceivably) be viewed as hinting that he chose the name (among almost limitless options) to suggest in *precise reverse order:* "Will ... Shake ... Spear." Could this all be mere "coincidence" or "myth"? At what point does an extraordinary cascade of "coincidental" details and linkages start to mean something?

As another gentleman by the name of Mark Anderson has noted (not to be confused with the Oxfordian author Mark Anderson, nothing in the cited essay explicitly indicates Shakespeare authorship doubt): "[T]he Italian names in *Every Man Out* are, like hieroglyphics, signs with hidden truths accessible through reason and learning." Anderson, "Defining Society" (1981), p. 184.

[729] This play was also published in Jonson, *Works* (1616), pp. 1-72 (and earlier, in 1601). See p. 4 ("The Persons of the Play," describing Master Stephen and Master Matthew); see also Chiljan, pp. 207-09.

[730] Chiljan, p. 207 (she developed the argument much further; see pp. 207-09); see also pp. 330-31 (discussing possible authorship doubts raised by *Eastward Ho*, a 1605 play co-authored by Jonson with George Chapman and John Marston). On Marston, see Part IV.11. As with Chiljan's arguments on Shift and Puntarvolo in *Every Man Out* (see notes 721, 725), I must again urge readers to "look ... on ... h[er] book." See note 725, and Part IV.2.g & note 114.

[731] See Chiljan, pp. 210-11, 424 nn. 9-10, citing Greenwood (1908) and Greenwood, *Shakespeare Problem?* (1916); see also Greenwood (1908), pp. 456-61; Michell, p. 72. This play was also published in Jonson, *Works* (1616), pp. 271-
(footnote continued on next page)

Most strikingly, Jonson makes a point of spelling his name (at least once) with an awkward hyphen: "[M]y name is CRISPINUS, or CRI-SPINAS indeed."[732] Later he is described as "CRISPINUS, alias CRISPINAS, *Poetaster*, and *plagiary*."[733] These references suggest a comparison to the occasional hyphenation of the published name of the author Shakespeare, and its different spelling compared to the versions of the surname typically used by the Stratford player

---

(footnote continued from previous page)

354. The orthodox view is that *Poetaster* only satirizes John Marston and Thomas Dekker. See, *e.g.*, Part IV.11 (Marston); Part IV.16 & notes 386-87 ("poets' war" or *poetomachia* as to Jonson's *Poetaster* and Dekker's *Satiromastix*); Greenwood (1908), pp. 459 & n. 3, 460 & n. 1; Chiljan, pp. 210-11; Donaldson, p. 169. But Greenwood and Chiljan soundly disputed any such *exclusive* interpretation.

[732] Act 2, sc. 1, p. 288 (emphases in original), quoted and discussed in Greenwood (1908), pp. 459-61; Michell, p. 72; Chiljan, p. 210. Crispinus himself explains the hyphenated "Cri-" (with "spinas" referring to spines or thorns—and possibly suggesting "spear" as discussed below in text?), by noting that his absurd coat-of-arms consists of "a Face crying *in chief*; and beneath it a bloody Toe, between three Thorns *pungent*," p. 288 (emphases in original). But that is obviously, as Greenwood noted, p. 460, a contrived and "absurd explanation." It cannot plausibly explain why Jonson *actually* deployed this ostentatiously hyphenated and differently spelled name.

[733] Act 5, sc. 3, p. 339, quoted and discussed in Chiljan, p. 210 (small-capitals emphases in original; remainder of original text in italics, emphases in Roman type, reversed here for clarity). The act 5 reference to "Crispinas" is not hyphenated in Jonson's *Works* (1616) (quoted here). Chiljan hyphenated it in reliance upon the original 1602 quarto publication. Whether it is hyphenated both times or only in act 2 is of little importance anyway.

Crispinus is named in the act 5 reference as part of a criminal indictment of him and co-defendant Demetrius, alleging they did "maliciously ... calumniate the person and writings of QUINTUS HORACIUS FLACCUS ... *poet*, and *priest* to the *Muses*," p. 339 (same note as above on emphases); see also Chiljan, p. 210 (suggesting that here Jonson "split the identity of Crispinus between [Shakspere] and writer John Marston"—see note 731—and that "Horacius" might stand for Jonson himself, a victim of Marston's defamation); Donaldson, pp. 168-71. The prosecutors show Crispinus a writing and demand he confess: "[D]ost thou stand upon it, pimp? Do not deny thine own MINERVA, thy PALLAS, the issue of thy brain," p. 340 (emphases in original); see also note 722; Parts IV.3 & notes 193-97; IV.27 & note 685 (discussing Minerva, *i.e.*, Athena or Pallas, the *spear-shaking* goddess). Crispinus confesses, p. 340: "Yes, it is mine." It is revealed that Demetrius's calumny contains the following lines (among other aspects of *Poetaster* meriting further exploration): "Our *Muse* is in mind for th'untrussing a *poet:* I slip by his name; for most men do know it," p. 341 (original text in italics, emphases in Roman type, reversed here for clarity).

and his family.[734] As Chiljan observed, it seems especially notable that *Poetaster* openly describes Crispinus as using an "alias"—that too, an almost identical hyphenated version of his name.[735]

Stratfordians often try to laugh off authorship doubts with the common joke that the works of Shakespeare may have been written "by another gentleman of the same name." They dismiss the differences in the spelling of that name as meaningless. They typically ignore, and sometimes falsely deny, the very consistent spelling of the author's published name as "Shakespeare" or "Shake-speare," in contrast to the spelling "Shakspere"—or variants thereof, typically without the medial "e" or second "a" and rarely if ever hyphonated—often used by the Stratford player himself and his family.[736]

But Jonson's alias for Crispinus hints that such differences could have been viewed as significant by writers and readers of the time.[737] Linking Crispinus (Cri-spinas) to Shakspere (Shake-speare) is still more justified by the meaning of the Latin verb *crispo*—to "brandish" or "move rapidly," that is, to *shake*. Greenwood noted that *crispo* was a word "frequently used by Virgil, and other writers," in relation to "*spear*."[738] The play is set in ancient Rome. As Greenwood hinted, but did not quite explicitly clarify, *spina* and *spinus* (both Latin for "thorn") are easily read to

---

[734] See Parts III.A-B (especially notes 33-38 and related text).

[735] Chiljan, p. 210: "Crispinus and Cri-spinas are names so similar it is as if Jonson was pointing out the name similarity between Shakspere (the Stratford Man) and Shake-speare (the great author)."

[736] See Part III.A (especially notes 10-13 and related text). There is no hyphenated spelling of the name in Kathman, "Non-Literary Spelling List" (see also Kathman, "Spelling"), with the sole exception of the curious spelling "Shake-Speare" in one of *Jonson's own* cast lists in his 1616 *Works*. See Part III.B & note 38. It is doubtful that the latter properly counts as a "non-literary" usage. It was not a usage by Shakspere (being posthumous) or his family.

[737] On Jonson's meticulous attention to the precise spelling of his own name, see Part III.A & notes 3-6.

[738] Greenwood (1908), p. 460 (emphasis added); see also *Cassell's Latin Dictionary*, p. 158; Chiljan, p. 210.

suggest "spear."[739] The Latin *spica*, "from [the] same root" as *spina*, "literally" means "*a spike*."[740] A spine, a thorn, a *spike*, a *spear*, all similar *pointed* things, I hear? And Jonson's games with words and names, all equally pointed clues—to Vere?[741]

It is difficult to resist speculating that Jonson pointedly chose the name "Crispinus" (or "Cri-spinas") in *Poetaster*, like the name "Puntarvolo" in *Every Man Out of His Humour*, to point to "William Shakespeare"—author, player, or some play upon both.[742] As one scholar has noted, "Jonson's historical characters in *Poetaster*, like the allegorical characters of *Every Man Out* ... are the foundation for the artistic truths of the[se] play[s]," "experiment[al]" dramas which this scholar observed "have been frequently misunderstood and underrated."[743]

---

[739] See Greenwood (1908), p. 460: "I think, therefore, that 'Cry-thorns' here probably stands for 'Shake-speare'." For clarifying context, readers should at this point review note 732. But Greenwood proceeded only to note the meaning of Latin *crispo*. He either overlooked or did not think it necessary to mention that *spina* and *spinus* are both Latin words for types of thorn. *Cassell's Latin Dictionary*, p. 566. The specific Latin word for "spear" is *hasta*. *Cassell's*, pp. 272, 836; see also Part IV.3 & notes 171-73.

The English word "spine" derives (no surprise) from Latin *spina*, *OED*, v. 16, pp. 236-37, and had two early modern meanings (both still familiar), p. 237 (emphasis added): a thorn or any other "*sharp-pointed*" plant growth (def. I.1) and the backbone of any vertebrate (def. II.6.a), citing (as to the former) the Shakespeare-Fletcher play *The Two Noble Kinsmen*, act 1, sc. 1 (referring to the "sharp spines," *i.e.*, thorns, of "roses"). Greenwood did not explore the English word "spine," nor (see note 740) the Latin word *spica*.

[740] *Cassell's Latin Dictionary*, p. 566 (italics in original); see also p. xii (defining "special terms" used in the definitions, *e.g.*, "lit." for "literal"). Spica is also, *Cassell's* reminds us, p. 566 (italics in original), "*the brightest star in the constellation Virgo*." Hmm ... "Thou *Star* of Poets?" *Just joking!* One can take these perceived connections too far.

[741] On *points* generally, and on extraordinary cascades of "coincidental" details and linkages, see notes 728 and 739, and Part IV.27, note 688.

[742] Any *conclusion* in this regard certainly *should* be resisted, in the sense of subjecting it to rigorous scrutiny—as I would urge readers and other scholars to do. But the conjecture should not be dismissed out-of-hand. See H. Smith (1986), p. 151 (presumably an orthodox scholar, noting "the punning habits of the time").

[743] Anderson (no, not *that* Anderson), "Defining Society" (1981), pp. 191-92. So far as appears, the cited Anderson may well be an orthodox Stratfordian who did not intend any comment on the SAQ. See the final paragraph of note 728.

As Sir George himself—the first major post-Stratfordian scholar—wrote more than a century ago:

> The strength of the Stratfordian faith undoubtedly lies in certain utterances of Ben Jonson .... It is all-important, therefore, to examine [his] testimony carefully, as a whole, and no matter which side we take in this vexed controversy, I think it will be admitted that the various Jonsonian utterances with regard to "Shakespeare" are by no means easy to reconcile one with the other, and that, considered all together, they provide us with an extremely hard nut to crack. Old Ben in this matter appears as a Sphinx, and if, like his prototype, he could have devoured all those who gave erroneous answers to his riddle, great would have been the mortality among the critics and commentators.[744]

In brief, we would do well in studying everything Jonson wrote to pay heed to the very first epigram, "To the Reader," in his collected *Works* of 1616: "Pray thee, take care, that tak'st my book in hand, To read it well: that is, to understand."[745]

## 29. *Envy's Scourge, and Virtue's Honour* (c. 1605–15)

The heading above is the title of a long poem of entrancing beauty, by an unknown author with the initials "M.L." The mystery surrounding it is deepened by the fact that only a single copy is known to survive—a printed pamphlet from which the title page is missing along with the date of publication and the poet's full name (if it appeared there). The publication can therefore be dated only approximately: some time from 1605 to 1615. This sole

---

[744] Greenwood (1908), p. 453; see generally pp. 453-88; Greenwood, *Shakespeare Problem?* (1916), chs. 11-12, pp. 371-453; Greenwood, *Jonson* (1921); see also Part IV.2.d & notes 52-59 (discussing Greenwood's pioneering role).

[745] Epigram No. 1, in Jonson, *Works* (1616), p. 769.

surviving version was discovered more than 365 years later, when sold in 1982 by a rare-book dealer.[746]

The leading scholar of this poem, Professor Richard Peterson, concluded it must have been written no earlier than 1599, the year Edmund Spenser died. As Peterson noted, stanzas 20-23 lament the death of some great but unnamed poet—who Peterson inferred was Spenser.[747] As Peterson also noted, the next three stanzas (24-26) offer a heartfelt apology to a "sweet" and "reverend wit," for some "poem or work in which M.L. has unjustly disparaged" some (other?) great but unnamed poet.[748]

*Aye, there's the rub:* Peterson, and apparently other orthodox scholars, have concluded that the poet to whom M.L. apologizes is *not* Spenser but very likely the author *Shakespeare*. Since M.L. does not mention any names, the latter inference rests largely on the slender but telling reed of *one word* among all 408 lines of this 68-stanza poem: "Let worthless lines be scattered here and there, But verses live supported by a *spear*."[749]

---

[746] See Roche (1986); Peterson (2010), pp. 288, 307 n. 3; see also pp. 311-25 (providing the full text of the poem—my quotations herein rely on this edition). The author's purported initials "M.L." appear twice in a dedicatory epistle to Master Thomas Paget, Esquire, of the Middle Temple (a lawyer at one of the four Inns of Court). M.L. identifies himself as Paget's "poor kinsman." Roche, p. 147. Nothing more has been discovered about him.

[747] Peterson (2010), p. 298; see also Peterson (1986), p. 166.

[748] Peterson (2010), p. 299; accord Peterson (1986), p. 167; see also Chiljan, p. 261 (quoting *Envy's Scourge*, stanza 24, line 5, "reverend wit," and stanza 25, line 1, "sweet wit").

[749] Stanza 25, lines 5-6 (emphasis added), quoted and discussed in Peterson (1986), pp. 167-68 ("possibly Shakespeare"), and in Peterson (2010), p. 299 ("almost certainly ... Shakespeare"). It is reasonable to assume that Peterson is a Stratfordian (like the vast majority of English professors), though I don't actually know. Chiljan (an Oxfordian), pp. 262, 426 n. 23, also supported the Shakespearean identification, citing a 1984 article by R.C. Horne (presumably a Stratfordian). Kernan (1986), p. 154, another presumed Stratfordian, also endorsed this identification, though more hesitantly. See also H. Smith (1986), p. 151, who conceded that the "spear" line "will make any reader familiar with the punning habits of the time wonder if there is a pun here," after first suggesting, however, that "[t]he most obvious candidate for the 'reverend wit' is Joseph Hall ...." See also Part IV.10 (discussing Hall). The latter suggestion seems far-fetched in any

(footnote continued on next page)

Professor Peterson's 1986 and 2010 articles are beautifully perceptive and illuminating, surely written without any concern for the SAQ. I see no reason to doubt his central finding that the poem is deeply influenced and inspired by Spenser, often echoing his poetic language.[750] Yet a poem written in the *style* of Spenser would not necessarily be *about* Spenser, in whole or in part. Peterson himself (and others) think the apology stanzas (24-26) are *not* about Spenser—and surely they are not.[751] But, as we will see, Peterson may well be correct that at least one key passage is, most likely, about Spenser. The poem demands careful textual analysis.

Peterson did not explore how M.L. might previously have "stained" Shakespeare's public image, so as to prompt his apology. Katherine Chiljan pursued the issue in a thoughtful discussion.[752]

---

(footnote continued from previous page)
event. Hall is unlikely to have been viewed or honored as so great a poet. He also lived until 1656.

[750] See Peterson (1986), especially, *e.g.*, p. 158 (M.L. appears "to have meditated upon, assimilated, and creatively transformed a major predecessor [Spenser] in a surprisingly complete act of homage and inventive good stewardship," also noting that the poem's "vocabulary ... is thoroughly Spenserian"); p. 160 (it "opens out into more encompassing Spenserian themes"); p. 162 (its "title ... is equally Spenserian"); accord, *e.g.*, Peterson (2010), p. 288-90. Such parallels should not be overstated. Peterson acknowledged one case, for example, where M.L. "spins *his own variation* on Spenserian themes," noting "Spenser's *quite different* use of Ovid's account" of one legend. Peterson (2010), pp. 297, 308 n. 11 (emphases added) (discussing stanza 19); accord Peterson (1986), p. 165 & n. 9.

[751] See note 749 and related text. Kernan (1986), p. 154 (emphasis added), wisely identified, as *distinct issues*, whether *Envy's Scourge* "sounds like Spenser" (Kernan, like Peterson, felt it does, and I agree), and whether it "*may* refer to [Spenser] as a poet." Peterson suggested that when M.L. in stanzas 16-17 discusses "Alcydes" (Hercules), stating "by a learned pen [he] is made alive" (stanza 17, line 6), the "learned pen" was Spenser's. But as Peterson's own discussion suggested, the "learned pen" could just as well be the ancient Roman poet Ovid's. See Peterson (2010), pp. 297, 308 n. 14. If Ovid is associated most strongly with any early modern English poet, that would be *Shakespeare*. See Part IV.22.

[752] Chiljan, pp. 261-63. I do not mean to suggest any criticism of Peterson for not focusing on that issue. It would have been tangential, at best, to the focus of his article. See stanza 25, line 4 ("giddy rage so clear a spring did stain"), briefly discussed in Peterson (2010), p. 299.

She noted one publication that seems an obvious candidate to have done so: the scandalous verse-novel *Avisa* (1594), discussed in Part IV.5, supposedly written by "Henry Willobie." *Avisa* satirizes an "old player," "W.S.," and his "friend," "H.W."—widely construed as Henry Wriothesley (Earl of Southampton), to whom "William Shakespeare" (W.S.) dedicated *Venus and Adonis* and *The Rape of Lucrece.* Chiljan thus inferred that the author of *Envy's Scourge*, the mysterious "M.L.," may have been whoever hid behind the rather obvious pseudonym "Willobie." This seems plausible, though probably not crucial to the significance of *Envy's Scourge* as an expression of early authorship doubt.

The dilemma that *Envy's Scourge* raises in the context of the SAQ is how—and *why*—to separate its discussions of the deceased poet it laments and the poet to whom it remorsefully apologizes. Occam's Razor would suggest the overall discussion (at least most of it) might be about the same poet.[753]

As Peterson and others have recognized, it would be very difficult to maintain that the poem's relevant discussion is *entirely* about Spenser, even if some parts of it may be.[754] The problem is not just the evident focus of stanzas 24-26 on Shakespeare, reflected (as we have seen) in the reference to "verses ... supported by a spear." M.L. *twice* suggests even in *earlier* stanzas—the ones Peterson and others think are focused on Spenser—that the lamented poet suffered some "disgrace."[755]

These references are a puzzlingly poor fit with Spenser, who is not known to have suffered any serious reputational "stain" at the hands of another writer such as might account for the deeply remorseful apology in stanzas 24-26. By contrast, they fit perfectly with the author Shakespeare, who repeatedly laments his "dis-

---

[753] See Part IV.1 & note 12, Baker, and "Occam's Razor."

[754] See notes 749, 751, and related text.

[755] See stanza 15, lines 1-2 ("delicious Poets lie despised, disgraced, as worthy of defame"); stanza 23, lines 3-4 ("Let thy beams shine as far as farthest Inde [India], that it may vanquish every black disgrace").

grace" and "shame" in the *Sonnets*, and about whom we have seen multiple additional suggestions of shame, disgrace, and denial of due honor—all strangely at variance with the known career of Shakspere of Stratford.[756]

It is even more difficult for any scholar imprisoned by the Stratfordian paradigm to consider that all these passages in *Envy's Scourge* might be entirely (or largely) about Shakespeare, given that Shakspere of Stratford did not die until 1616.[757] Yet if we had to choose, the most specific identifying testimony is the line about "a spear." And the apology stanzas, as we will see, echo and extend the theme in the earlier stanzas of death, lament, yet celebration of continued life—*only* through the poet's art.

Peterson was led to propose a puzzling and awkward discontinuity. A whole series of stanzas culminates in what Peterson aptly called the "central lament" for a deceased poet in stanzas 20-23.[758] Yet we are told that in the immediately ensuing apology stanzas (24-26), M.L. suddenly veers off into a digression about an entirely *different* poet—though also great, admired, and unnamed.

Peterson briefly sought to explain the supposed digression: "The apology ... serves an important strategic purpose ... establishing M.L.'s credentials as one personally embattled with envy and guilty of a 'giddy rage' ...."[759] But isn't M.L.'s battle with envy and guilt more powerfully conveyed if he apologizes to the very same poet whose death he laments? It is worth quoting much of these gorgeous stanzas, to convey how they echo and reinforce these themes of *death, disgrace*, yet celebration of continued *life:*

---

[756] See, *e.g.*, *Sonnets* 29 (line 1, "disgrace"), 72 (lines 12-13, "shame"), and 25, 37, 81, 90, 111, 112, and 121; Parts IV.10 & note 287, and IV.24 & notes 603-05 (discussing the *Sonnets*); see also Parts IV.4 & note 215; IV.18 & notes 438-43; IV.20 & notes 474-79, 515-17; IV.23 & notes 578-81.

[757] As Part IV.2.b observes, orthodox scholars have long been constrained by an invisible electronic fence of assumptions within which they have worked.

[758] Peterson (2010), p. 298; see also Peterson (1986), p. 166.

[759] Peterson (1986), p. 168; accord Peterson (2010), p. 299.

(15, lines 1-3) But (ah the while) delicious *Poets* lie
     *despised, disgraced,* as worthy of *defame*
When *hellbred ignorance* doth mount on high ....

(19, lines 1-2) I know lines steeped in dew of Castalie[760]
     have power *to bring to life a buried man* ....

(20) Heavenly Astraea show thy mighty force
          upon Ignosco's utter overthrow;
     That *would all praise from learned wits divorce*
          and *shut them in obscurest vaults below,*
     Let his stigmatic lump be made a scorn
     To *all that live* and all that shall be born.

(21) Issue of hateful Herebus and night
          hard-hearted Atropos the knife of fate
     *Why so untimely* didst thou *dim the light*
          of him that sweetest lays *did chant of late*
     The dear bemoaner of his honoured friend
     Which got much honour *when his life did end.*

(22) He 'gan to chase from out the utmost parts
          of fairest Albion that professed foe,
     Placing ripe knowledge in their brutish hearts,
          which steps of hellish darkness wont to go,
     Though *grave contain thy trunk* (on earth desired)
     *Thy fame yet lives* of all the earth admired.

(23) Let the divine perfection of thy mind,
          *as it was chief* so have the chiefest place,
     Let thy beams shine as far as farthest Inde,
          that it may vanquish every *black disgrace:*

---

[760] "Castalie" (Castalia) refers in Greek mythology to a spring at Delphi on Mount Parnassus (home of the Muses), a source of poetic inspiration. See Part IV.15 & note 333; Peterson (2010), p. 323 (note to line 109; see also notes to lines 115, 116-19, 121, 122, 135, 139, and 141; *i.e.*, stanza 20, lines 1 and 2-5; stanza 21, lines 1 and 2; stanza 23, line 3; stanza 24, lines 1 and 3), explaining references to "Astraea," "Ignosco's ... stigmatic lump," "Herebus," "Atropos," "Inde," "Nurslings of Parnassus," *i.e.*, the Muses, and "Calendar," *i.e.*, a record). "Albion" is an ancient term for Britain. "Inde" is French for India.

Let Reason censure of thy virtue's beauty,
And cause all hearts to honour thee of duty.

(24) Dear Nurslings of Parnassus [the Muses] be not won
     by rash credulity to leave to time
A *shameful* Calendar of *deeds misdone*
     by those which never yet committed crime;
Myself instead a reverend wit have *blamed*
*Without desert*,[761] whereof I am *ashamed*.

(25) Pardon sweet wit (which hast a liberal part
     of pure infusion in thy happy brain)
My sorrowing sobs have bloodless left my heart,
     that *giddy rage* so clear a spring did *stain*.
Let worthless lines be scattered here and there,
But *verses live supported by a spear*.

(26, lines 1-2) Now I do praise what I *dispraised of late*,
     and hold thy favorites in high admire ....[762]

An obvious ambiguity in stanza 21, lines 5-6, requires special attention. Does the phrase "his life did end" refer to the death of the lamented poet or the death of his "bemoane[d]" and "honoured friend"? Chiljan read it as the former,[763] which makes some sense. The poet's death is otherwise the clear and dominant focus of stanzas 21-22. Yet the "bemoan[ing]" of the poet's friend also suggests the *friend's* possible death. If this passage refers to the poet's death, it suggests at first blush a very odd scenario. Why would a friend receive honor, not when he himself dies, but only when the poet who bemoans him dies? Chiljan sought to explain this by arguing that it correlates with known historical facts about Henry Wriothesley (Earl of Southampton), the likely "friend" (H.W.) in Willobie's *Avisa*, and Edward de Vere (Earl of

---

[761] *I.e.*, without his deserving it.
[762] Quoted in Peterson (2010), pp. 313-15 (my emphases).
[763] See Chiljan, p. 263.

Oxford), the likely "old player" (W.S.) in *Avisa*—thus suggesting the lamented poet is neither Spenser, nor Shakspere of Stratford, but rather Vere, the likely true author "Shakespeare."[764]

Peterson's reading, however, that this passage refers to the *friend's* death, seems more natural and convincing. People often die in ways that honor them, as Sir Philip Sidney did in 1586. Peterson viewed these lines as reflecting "Spenser's own lament[s] ... for Sidney, who got much honor through his noble death in battle,"[765] at the tragically young age of 31. This would in turn support the inference that all of stanza 21 (at least), and probably stanza 22 as well, refer to Spenser, not the author Shakespeare. Leaving aside for the moment that Shakspere of Stratford lived until 1616 and assuming Vere was "Shakespeare," stanza 21, line 3—referring to the lamented poet's "untimely" death ("dim[ming]" his "light")—still seems to fit better with Spenser, who died in

---

[764] See Chiljan, pp. 262-63 (she avoided, however, mentioning Vere's name). On *Avisa*, see discussion above in this part and in Part IV.5. Wriothesley was imprisoned as a convicted traitor after the Essex Rebellion (see Part IV.17), but was released and pardoned by King James, and his title and "honours" restored by the king and parliament during 1603–04, which was also the "end" of "life" for Vere, who died in June 1604.

Chiljan, p. 262, also noted that *Avisa* was printed repeatedly, "for the fifth time in 1609." That could help explain the urgency and intensity of M.L.'s (inferred) apology for a 1594 publication (a decade or more in the past), even though (as Chiljan and I agree) the recipient was no longer alive to receive it. We think it was a public *mea culpa*, not a personal apology. The author Shakespeare famously bemoaned a great deal in relation to his dear beloved "friend," the fair youth of the *Sonnets* (widely linked with Wriothesley), whom he "honoured" with his famous poetic dedications of 1593–94. Chiljan therefore suggested, pp. 262-63, that *Envy's Scourge* may have been published in 1609, perhaps prompted by the publication of the *Sonnets* that same year. For more discussion of the *Sonnets*, see note 756 and related text, and Parts IV.18 and 24.

[765] Peterson (2010), p. 299; accord Peterson (1986), p. 167. Hallett Smith (1986), p. 151 (emphasis added), questioning Peterson's confident conclusion that it must be Spenser whom M.L. laments in stanzas 20-23, stated hesitantly that stanza 21, lines 5-6, "could *possibly* refer to Spenser, who died in 1599 and who had mourned the [1586] death of [Sir Philip] Sidney in [Spenser's] *Astrophel* (1595)." Accord Kernan (1986), p. 154 (emphasis added) (this passage "*may* refer to [Spenser] as a poet"). In any event, Smith supported Peterson's reading that these lines refer to the *friend's* death, *not* that of the lamented *poet* (whoever that was). If so, the friend could not be Wriothesley, who died in 1624.

1599 at age 46. It could fit with Vere, who died in 1604 at age 54. But combined with the apparent echo of Spenser's well-known lament for Sidney (in Spenser's "Astrophel"), it seems much more likely that M.L. refers to Spenser in stanza 21. Peterson offered additional reasons why stanza 22 probably also refers to Spenser,[766] consistently with its description of what "[h]e" then "[be-]gan" to do—pretty clearly meaning the same poet as in stanza 21, not the friend (who under this reading predeceased the poet, not vice versa as Chiljan suggested).

Yet Peterson's inference that Spenser is the poet in *all* the lament stanzas ends up producing the abrupt discontinuity mentioned earlier. It also drains urgency from M.L.'s self-lacerating remorse in the apology stanzas—obviously much more intense if the poet he defamed is now *dead*. As noted earlier, it makes little sense to think M.L. somehow defamed Spenser, but it is very plausible to infer he defamed Shakespeare (perhaps in *Avisa*).

Furthermore, the text of *Envy's Scourge* does not provide much support for a sharp transition between stanzas 23 and 24. On the contrary, there are multiple indications of continuity. The apology stanzas (24-26), by consensus relating to Shakespeare, continue to resonate with the laments of the preceding stanzas about a deceased poet who yet still lives *only* through his art and the fame it has rightfully earned him. M.L. states suggestively in stanza 26, line 1, that he is now "prais[ing]" a poet that he "dispraised *of late*."

Even taking stanza 25, line 6, entirely by itself, it conveys a sense of the poet's art outliving his mortal life: "*verses* live"—not the poet, just his poetry. And his writing lives because it is "supported by a spear"—published and perpetuated under the pseudo-

---

[766] See Peterson (2010), pp. 299, 309 n. 19, 323 (note to lines 124-32, *i.e.*, stanza 21, lines 4-6, and stanza 22).

nym "Shakespeare"?[767] It is difficult to miss the echo between that line—"*verses live* supported by a spear"—and stanza 22, line 6: "Thy *fame yet lives* of all the earth admired."

Peterson himself highlighted that very connection, perhaps unintentionally. In his concluding summary in both his leading articles on *Envy's Scourge*, he declared: "Bathed in the balm of his own words and phrases, Spenser *lives again.*"[768] Doubtless he had in mind the phrase just quoted from the lament stanzas: "Thy *fame yet lives* ...." Perhaps he also thought of stanza 20, line 6: "To *all that live* ...." "*But,*" M.L. declares, "*verses live*" as well, in the very line that Peterson himself said points "almost certainly" to Shakespeare.[769]

Just as the apology stanzas extend the theme of death and lamentation, the lament stanzas preview—indeed *forcefully inaugurate*—the theme of "*disgrace.*" Perhaps suggesting we should not strain too hard to identify any specific poet as excluding allusions to any other in this poem, M.L. refers in the plural to "Poets" in stanza 15, line 1, and to "learned wits" in stanza 20, line 3. He declares (15, line 2) that poets have been "*despised, disgraced,*" and "*defame[d].*" He says (20, line 3) that "wits" have been "*divorce[d]*" from "all praise."

Most powerfully, evoking a searchlight of literary brilliance spanning the globe—"as far as farthest Ind[ia]"—M.L. pleads that the lamented poet's art may "vanquish every *black disgrace*" (stanza 23, lines 3-4). By comparison, the references to shame or disgrace in the apology stanzas themselves—"blamed [w]ithout desert," "ashamed," "stain," "dispraised"[770]—seem almost tame. It may be noted, as Chiljan did, that the word "stain" links specifi-

---

[767] Chiljan similarly suggested, p. 262: "M.L. was not just making a pun—he was openly saying that Shakespeare's verses exist because they are 'supported' by a pen name."

[768] Peterson (2010), p. 306 (emphasis added); accord Peterson (1986), p. 174.

[769] Peterson (2010), p. 299.

[770] Stanza 24, lines 5-6; stanza 25, line 4; stanza 26, line 1.

cally to two earlier expressions of authorship doubt we have seen: *L'Envoy* to *Narcissus* by Edwards (1593), "purple robes distained" (Part IV.4), and *Microcosmos* by Davies of Hereford (1603), "the stage doth stain pure gentle blood" (Part IV.20).[771]

In sum, *Envy's Scourge* is the *fourth* separate indication we have seen that the author Shakespeare died before 1616.[772] Almost eerily, its estimated date-range (1605–15) fits with perfect symmetry between Vere's death in 1604 and that of Shakspere of Stratford in 1616—and also encompasses the dates of all four of the other indications (1605, 1607, 1609, and 1614).

Still, this memorable poem—a unique letter in a bottle, salvaged from the ocean of time—must count by itself as relatively weak evidence of early authorship doubts. The connection to Shakespeare rests on a single and fairly common word: "spear." And there are good reasons to associate some (possibly all) of the stanzas most clearly indicating the death of a great unnamed poet with Spenser, not Shakespeare. This item is a matter of reasonably debatable interpretation. But it should not be ignored.

### 30. Christopher Brooke, *The Ghost of Richard the Third* (1614): With an Overview of Five Indications That the Author "Shakespeare" Died Years Before 1616

*The Ghost of Richard the Third*, an epic poem by Christopher Brooke (c. 1566–1628), has that notorious king address the reader directly and vividly in his own voice. Published in 1614, it is the *fifth* suggestion that the author Shakespeare died before 1616. Shakspere of Stratford still had two years to live. The long-dead tyrant makes quite a *rentrée:*

---

[771] See Chiljan, p. 262.

[772] See also Parts IV.22 (*Sir Thomas Smith's Voyage*, 1605), IV.23 (Barksted, *Myrrha, the Mother of Adonis*, 1607), IV.24 (*Shake-speare's Sonnets*, 1609), and IV.30 (Brooke, *Ghost of Richard the Third*, 1614).

What magic, or what fiend's infernal hand,
Rears my tormented ghost from Orcus' flame?
And lights my conscience, with her burning brand,
Through death and hell to view the world's fair frame?
Must I again regreet my native land,
Whose graves resound the horror of my name?[773]

Twenty pages later Brooke's Richard praises—while curiously never *naming*—the author whose indelible depiction of this king, in the play *Richard III*, has left him forever imprinted in our collective memory:

To him that impt [added to] my fame with Clio's quill,
Whose magic raised me from oblivion's den;
That writ my story on the Muses' hill,
And with my actions dignified his pen:
He that from Helicon sends many a rill,
Whose nectared veins, are drunk by thirsty men;
Crowned be his style with fame, his head with bays;
And none detract, but gratulate his praise.

Yet if his scenes have not engrost all grace,
The much-famed action could extend on stage:
If time, or memory, have left a place
For me to fill; t'inform this ignorant age;
To that intent I show my horrid face,
Imprest with fear, and characters of rage:

---

[773] Brooke, *Ghost*, Part 1 ("Character"), p. 59. Brooke was a lawyer at Lincoln's Inn and Member of Parliament as well as a poet. *Ghost* takes up more than 80 pages in Alexander Grosart's 1872 scholarly edition—120 if you count the dedication, prefatory epistles, and notes—and is divided into three parts: "His Character," "His Legend," and "His Tragedy." While its authorship does not seem to be in much doubt, Brooke is identified only as "C.B." See Brooke, *Complete Poems*, pp. 13-14, 25-32 (Grosart's "Memorial-Introduction"), pp. 59-143 (text of poem); see also Chambers (1930), v. 2, pp. 219-20 (quoting excerpt and confirming Brooke's authorship); Chiljan, pp. 265-66; Cole (Letter).

The other four indications that the author died before 1616 are discussed in Parts IV.22-24 and 29. See also Sobran, pp. 143-48 (discussing some but not all of these).

Nor wits, nor chronicles could ere contain,
The hell-deep reaches, of my soundless brain.[774]

"Helicon" refers to Mount Helicon, lofty home of the Muses in Greek mythology (heaven, more or less)—the Muses being the daughters of gods (Zeus and Mnemosyne) who inspire poets and other artists and scholars. "Clio" refers specifically to the Muse of historians (*Richard III* being a history play).[775]

I think most readers would concede this passage gives at least the *impression* that this unnamed playwright is deceased. He now seems to live with the Muses, echoing Barksted's *Myrrha* (see Part IV.23). He "sends" down "rills," "*from Helicon*"—whenever we read his work or watch his plays? "Sends" is in the present tense; "impt," "raised," "writ," and "dignified," in the four preceding lines, all in the past tense. His "veins" are now "nectared" (sounds rather divine).[776] He is (or should be) "crowned" with bays (a poet's

---

[774] Brooke, *Ghost*, Part 2 ("Legend"), p. 79. As Grosart explained in a footnote, "soundless" here does not mean "silent" but rather evokes the nautical sense of "not to be sounded or fathomed." For explanations of other words, see note 775 and related text. There is no serious doubt, as orthodox scholars seem to agree, that Brooke refers to Shakespeare and his play *King Richard III*. See, *e.g.*, Brooke, *Complete Poems* (Grosart's "Memorial-Introduction"), p. 31; Chiljan, pp. 265, 426 n. 28 (noting that phrases from the play appear in other parts of *Ghost*); Cole (Letter).

[775] See Parts IV.3 & note 100, IV.15 & note 333; IV.23 & note 561. Cole (Letter) read "impt" to mean "snatched." One might, I suppose, view the playwright as somehow stealing Richard's "fame" (or infamy), to enhance the playwright's own fame. But any such depiction would also, necessarily, enhance the subject's own fame (or infamy). So has it really been "snatched" *from* Richard? Seems more like a "win-win" for both subject and playwright. In any event, *OED* does not provide "snatched" or "stolen" as a meaning (early modern or otherwise) for "imped" (or verb "imp"), though one might well think of theft as a likely action of *an imp* (noun: a mischievous or devilish child). See *OED*, v. 7, pp. 693-94. Chiljan, p. 265, read "impt" as "implanted," doubtless relying on *OED*, p. 694 (verb "imp," defs. 1-4, to engraft or implant), or p. 704 ("imped" as engrafted or implanted). But the most relevant meaning here, I think, would be to "extend ... enlarge, add to" (verb "imp," def. 5).

[776] Cole (Letter) suggested that "nectared veins" stands out as a sufficiently unusual phrase to invite analysis as a possible anagram. And indeed, as she noted, it contains the letters for "de Vere." But this seems too far a stretch. It is

(footnote continued on next page)

laurels). We do (or should) "gratulate his praise." The elegiac mood is reinforced by the reference to "time, or memory." This poet has joined the immortals.

Admittedly, that is all debatable interpretation. As evidence for the author Shakespeare dying before 1616, this particular item is both stronger and weaker than the similarly debatable evidence provided by *Envy's Scourge* (see Part IV.29). Stronger in the sense that there is no reasonable doubt (as there is with *Envy's Scourge*) that the poet described is Shakespeare.[777] Weaker, in that the lamentations of death in *Envy's Scourge* (if they apply to Shakespeare) are very direct and explicit, whereas Brooke's *Ghost* is, again, debatable in this regard.

Still, if the author was alive and kicking in Stratford-upon-Avon in 1614, why is he not only honored by Brooke as an immortal, but also *not named?* Does that suggest a common awareness at the time that the name was a pseudonym?[778]

Keep in mind that however weak *Envy's Scourge* and *Ghost* may arguably be (each taken by itself), as evidence the author died before 1616, we have stronger evidence pointing to that conclusion in *Sir Thomas Smith's Voyage* (1605), Barksted's *Myrrha* (1607), and the *Sonnets* (1609). What we have here is a classic example of a hypothesis, first suggested by one very compelling data point—*"ever-living"* in the dedication of the *Sonnets*—being confirmed, strengthened, and reinforced, *four times over*, by mutually corroborating evidence.[779]

---

(footnote continued from previous page)
very far from a perfect anagram, in contrast to the genuinely powerful and compelling anagram, "courte-deare-verse" as "our de vere a secret," in Covell's *Polimanteia*, discussed in Part IV.7. "De Vere" has six letters but "nectared veins" has more than twice as many (13). The risk of cherry-picking and confirmation bias, of seeing what we are looking for, is thus too great. See, *e.g.*, discussions of anagrams in Part IV.7 and Friedman & Friedman, chs. 2, 7-8, pp. 15-26, 92-113.

[777] See note 774.

[778] See Cole (Letter) (suggesting it does, and I agree).

[779] See Parts IV.22-24.

Katherine Chiljan pointed out the odd comment (or command?) that *"none detract"* this great writer. Under the Stratfordian theory, for heaven's sake, why would anyone be "detracting" good sweet Will in 1614? Why would anyone feel the need to comment on the (obvious) lack of detraction of such a popular, successful, and socially ascendant writer[780]—or admonish readers not to detract him?[781]

Yet again, the Oxfordian theory comes to the rescue with much-needed clarification and explanatory power. As Chiljan noted, the obvious inference is "that people *were* disparaging" the *real* author.[782] "Was the true author, a nobleman, getting disparaging remarks because he wrote plays that appeared on the public stage, and because he also acted in them?"[783]

Edward de Vere (Earl of Oxford) came of age with the brightest prospects in the kingdom, but eventually lost most of his inherited wealth and suffered repeated, battering blows to his reputation during the final decades of his life.[784] As Chiljan suggested, Brooke's comment in *Ghost* resonates with others indicating that the author Shakespeare "was not adequately praised or recognized because doing so in his real name would 'stain' him."[785] This

---

[780] See, *e.g.*, Part IV.18 & note 440. He had it all in his comfortable Stratford retirement in 1614, or so we are told—about all a common boy from the provinces (whose father at one time faced destitution) might reasonably hope for: a successful career in the big city behind him, great fame, great wealth, the biggest house in town, and the status of "gentleman" with a coat-of-arms. Contrast that relative trajectory with Vere's, as summarized in the text.

[781] It seems to be an imperious royal command by Richard's fearsome ghost. In effect: "Let him be crowned with bays, and let none detract him, but sing his praise." Yeah, O.K. But how much more praise does he need? Wasn't he already getting plenty? Who was "detracting" him, and why?

[782] Chiljan, p. 265 (emphasis added).

[783] Chiljan, p. 266.

[784] See Part IV.18 & notes 441-43; see generally Moore, "Order of the Garter" (1996), in Moore (2009), p. 263; A. Nelson (2003); Anderson (2005).

[785] Chiljan, p. 266; see also pp. 266-67 (Chiljan's superb summary of the early doubts discussed in her book, which once again I can only urge my readers to *("whatever you do")* *"Buy"*—same for Price's and Anderson's books).

comment reinforces the repeated suggestions we have seen that the *author* suffered some kind of shame, disgrace, and denial of honor—all puzzlingly discordant with the known career of the *player* from Stratford.[786]

One or two veiled references like those we have seen might be unremarkable. But we have seen suggestions like this again and again and again—pointing to pseudonymity, to plagiarism, to a frontman, to an aristocratic author, to an author "stained" somehow by mysterious disgrace, to an author denied due honor, to an author who laments that his "name" will "be buried" forever, "forgotten," and that he, "once gone, to all the world must die."[787]

The early references to the author "Shakespeare" are riven by a deep conflict. Some commentators, including leading literary lights—not least Ben Jonson—felt profound admiration, even love, for this talented but tortured artist. Some offer praise for this writer and seem to protest or try to counterbalance aspersions cast upon him. Yet much of this praise was curiously veiled. Some did not even recite a name. Clearly he inspired passionately divergent views—then as today.

---

[786] See Parts IV.4 & note 215; IV.10 & note 287; IV.18 & notes 438-43; IV.20 & notes 474-79, 515-17; IV.23 & notes 578-81; IV.24 & notes 603-05. On suggestions that Vere may have dabbled with acting, see Parts IV.5 & note 232; IV.20 & notes 468, 485-87; IV.26 & notes 676-77; Malim, "Oxford the Actor" (2004); Waugh, "My Shakespeare" (2018), pp. 52-53; see also Anderson, pp. 3-4, 187-88.

Furthermore, all the evidence we have seen of early (pre-1616) authorship doubts must be considered in relation to the remarkable paucity of pre-1616 (or even pre-1623) evidence *affirmatively supporting* the Stratfordian theory, as even one of the most prestigious Stratfordian scholars in the world (Sir Stanley Wells) has conceded on at least one occasion. See Part I & notes 6, 9, citing, *e.g.*, Wells, "Allusions," p. 81. Stratfordians sometimes tout as supporting evidence a poem addressed to Ben Jonson by "F.B." (thought to be Francis Beaumont), which both orthodox and skeptical scholars have discussed. See, *e.g.*, Chambers (1930), v. 2, pp. 222-25; Ogburn, pp. 22, 108-10. Its date is uncertain (*c.* 1615 according to Chambers). As Ogburn showed, the F.B. poem is curiously ambiguous and it is unclear what bearing it has on the SAQ. It does not seem to me to have any particular bearing on the issue of early authorship doubts.

[787] *Sonnets* 72 and 81, quoted and discussed in Part IV.24 & notes 603-04.

In any event, we now have *five separate indications* during the decade 1605–15, all following Vere's death in 1604, that the author Shakespeare was by then deceased—years before the Stratford player died. These indications resonate powerfully, we can now see, with the Great Silence of 1616: the virtual absence of literary reactions upon the Stratford man's death. That deafening silence now becomes far less mysterious—but even more damaging to the Stratfordian theory.[788]

These indications go far to explain the 1623 *Folio*'s otherwise baffling comment that the author was "by death" deprived of the opportunity "to have set forth, and overseen his own writings."[789] These indications remind us why the Oxfordian theory does not in fact suffer from any "1604 problem," and why by contrast—so ironically—it is the *Stratfordian* theory that labors under a far more puzzling and multifaceted set of 1604 and 1616 problems.[790]

When evidence like this begins to accumulate, over and over, more and more, year after year, reason and logic begin to suggest an inference—and at some point compel the conclusion—that *"something is rotten in the state of Denmark."*[791]

Some may attack or dismiss the significance of the early doubts discussed throughout Part IV, perhaps by focusing on the arguable weakness of one or more specific items, taken individually. But that would suggest a basic lack of understanding of the related concepts of corroboration and cumulative evidence.

Skepticism is always important and generally wise. Authorship skepticism should itself be skeptically examined, as I would be first to agree. But if a skeptic were to impatiently dismiss a vast array of evidence based merely on the possible weakness of

---

[788] See Part I & note 34.

[789] "To the great Variety of Readers," *First Folio*, p. 7, quoted and discussed in Part I, note 17.

[790] See Part III.B & notes 49-53.

[791] *Hamlet*, act 1, sc. 4 (Marcellus) (emphasis added).

some pieces of it, that would not deserve much respect as a serious approach to the issue.

Skeptics who dismiss the SAQ would do well to study the treatment of evidence by detectives, lawyers, and others involved in the investigation and prosecution of crime—a context where the stakes are very high indeed. Serious criminal investigative work, in turn, follows the approach used by scientists researching any number of fields. As one venerable criminal justice textbook has noted, an "investigator, faced with a complex crime, may be compared to a research scientist, employing the same resources of reason ...."[792]

Cumulative and corroborative evidence is very often circumstantial in nature. "Circumstantial evidence" has a bad reputation in popular parlance and is very often misunderstood by casual critics or the uninformed layperson. But as any good scientist, detective, or lawyer knows, circumstantial evidence is often preferable, more powerful, and more reliable than "direct" testimony or eyewitness evidence.[793] Witnesses may lie. Even honest eyewitness testimony is often tainted and rendered unreliable by unconscious biases and misperceptions. This is a subject of great concern and much study in our criminal justice systems.

But facts don't lie. An accumulation of observed circumstantial facts, mutually corroborating and reinforcing a given inference, speaks very loudly indeed. Such cumulative and corroborative evidence—even though many individual items may seem weak or insignificant by themselves—may acquire tremendous force in the aggregate.

Any evidence, however, must always be subjected to careful scrutiny. There is always that possible, ever-present, alternative explanation: "*It's just a coincidence.*" The plausibility of that alter-

---

[792] O'Hara & O'Hara, pp. 19-20.
[793] See Part I & notes 23-24, citing Regnier (2015) (an experienced attorney providing an excellent overview of evidentiary principles as applied to the SAQ).

native will often depend on an expert calculation of probabilities and statistical odds, an area beyond my expertise.

The pioneering Oxfordian scholar, J. Thomas Looney, despite his easily mocked surname, provided a very sane and thoughtful discourse on these issues in his landmark 1920 book. As the present book has noted, if only more people would simply read Looney's book—now approaching its centennial—Shakespeare authorship doubts, and the Oxfordian theory specifically, would be far more widely embraced.[794] As Looney noted,

> what is called circumstantial evidence [is] mistakenly supposed by some to be evidence of an inferior order, but [is] in practice the most reliable form of proof we have. ... [A]s we proceed in the work of gathering together facts and reducing them to order, as we hazard our guesses and weigh probabilities, as we subject our theories to all available tests, we find that the case at last either breaks down or becomes confirmed by such an accumulation of support that doubt is no longer possible.[795]

I pause here to note that the present book's goal is not to eliminate "doubt" but rather to surmount a much lower bar. It merely seeks to show that there *were* significant published doubts during Shakspere of Stratford's lifetime about the authorship of the literary works of "Shakespeare." Looney continued:

> The predominating element in what we call circumstantial evidence is that of coincidences. A few coincidences we may treat as simply interesting; a number ... we regard as remarkable; a vast accumulation ... we accept as conclusive proof. ...
>
> ... [A] critic may disagree with one or other of the points on which we have insisted; he may regard this or

---

[794] See Part I & notes 4 and 43, especially text related to note 43.
[795] Looney, p. 80.

that argument as trifling or insufficient in itself, and it is possible we should agree with many of the several objections he might raise. It may even transpire that, notwithstanding all our efforts to ensure accuracy, we have fallen into serious mistakes not only in minor details but even upon important points: a danger to which the wanderer into unwonted fields is specially liable. It is not, however, upon any point separately, but upon the manner in which all fit in with one another, and form a coherent whole, that the case rests; and it is this that we desire should be kept in mind.[796]

While the present book is not an Oxfordian tract, I have noted how the evidence relating to these early doubts often supports the Oxfordian theory that Edward de Vere was the actual author hiding behind the name "Shakespeare." It is thus useful to briefly survey the eight alternative candidates, aside from Vere, for whom the most serious and significant claims to Shakespeare authorship have been made.

Four candidates were seriously proposed before the Oxfordian theory was published. Sir Francis Bacon (1561–1626), made Baron Verulam in 1618 and Viscount St. Alban in 1621, was the first alternative candidate to be set forth—in 1856—launching the modern era of Shakespeare authorship doubts.[797]

William Stanley, Sixth Earl of Derby (1561–1642), was proposed in 1891.[798] Christopher Marlowe (1564–93?) was proposed

---

[796] Looney, pp. 80-81.

[797] See, *e.g.*, Part I & notes 42, 44; D. Bacon (1857); W. Smith (1857); Michell, ch. 5, pp. 113-60; Clarke, in Leahy (2018), ch. 7, p. 163; compare Hope & Holston, chs. 1-5, pp. 7-63. The Baconian theory was proposed independently in an article by Delia Bacon (an American scholar, no relation), and a pamphlet by British scholar William Henry Smith, both published in 1856. Looney (1920), pp. 332-33, suggested reasons why the Baconian theory (despite its long and storied history) remains fundamentally implausible. See also Friedman & Friedman (1957) (debunking supposed ciphers or cryptograms allegedly supporting it).

[798] See, *e.g.*, Lefranc (1918–19, rep. 1988); Raithel (2009); Rollett (2015); compare Hope & Holston, pp. 66-67 (criticizing this theory, which originated with British antiquarian James Greenstreet in 1891 and American writer Robert

(footnote continued on next page)

in 1895.[799] A third aristocratic candidate, Roger Manners, Fifth Earl of Rutland (1576–1612), along with a fourth aristocrat, Vere, 17th Earl of Oxford (1550–1604), round out this initial group of five. Manners was proposed in 1906, followed by Vere in 1920.[800]

Following those first five candidates, no others of any serious significance emerged for almost a century.[801] But since 2000, at

---

(footnote continued from previous page)
Frazer in 1915); Looney, "Derby" (1922) (going far to refute it); Hughes, "Oxfordian Response" (2009), pp. 99-102 (same).

[799] See, *e.g.*, Part III.B & note 43; Part V & note 37; Hoffman (1955); Wraight (1994); Blumenfeld (2008); Pinksen (2008); Farey (2009); Barber, "Marlowe," in Leahy (2018), ch. 4, p. 85; compare Hope & Holston, pp. 64-66 (criticizing this theory, which apparently originated in a novel by American writer Wilbur Gleason Zeigler in 1895).

Marlovians propose that Marlowe did not die in 1593, a conjecture contradicting specific documentary (and compelling circumstantial) evidence that he did, despite concededly serious doubts about the details of his death and the post-mortem investigation. See, *e.g.*, Anderson, p. 274 (Occam's Razor "would suggest a simpler explanation" for the "dodgy inquiry" into his death: that it "was a hit job"); see also Part IV.1 & note 12, Baker, and "Occam's Razor."

The conjecture that Marlowe lived past 1593 is not ultimately based on any solid affirmative evidence, but mainly on the desire to facilitate the Marlovian theory. Without it, the entire theory collapses. Hughes, "Oxfordian Response," pp. 105-07, showed the theory's implausibility even though she accepted the possibility that Marlowe survived 1593. See also Hughes, "Great Reckoning." Stritmatter & Wildenthal, "Oxford's Poems," pp. 8-9, noted reasons to question whether linguistic parallels, upon which Hoffman relied heavily, support the theory. In any event, Marlowe was born too late. See note 802.

[800] On Manners, see, *e.g.*, Porohovshikov (1940); Sykes (1947); compare Hope & Holston, p. 66 (criticizing the Manners theory, which apparently originated with several German writers starting in 1906, and was developed by Belgian writer Célestin Demblon in 1912). On Vere, see Part I & note 4.

[801] Two arguable exceptions are John Florio (1553–1625) and Sir Edward Dyer (1543–1607). Florio was proposed by several writers starting in 1927 and most recently, in 2008, by Lamberto Tassinari. See, *e.g.*, Tassinari (2011). Alden Brooks proposed Dyer in his 1943 book. See Hope & Holston, p. 67 (briefly mentioning Florio as a candidate), pp. 166-67 (briefly summarizing Brooks's book, but not independently discussing Dyer's candidacy); see also Part IV.13 (discussing Gabriel Harvey's marginalia mentioning Dyer, *c.* 1598–1600). Dyer seems a very weak candidate. I am not aware of anyone in recent times who has endorsed him.

Florio is a fascinating figure in his own right, with a known literary career more than ample to fill up his time—a brilliant linguistic scholar famous for his Italian-English dictionary *A World of Words* (first published in 1598; cited in

(footnote continued on next page)

least four interesting new claimants have been proposed, including Sir Henry Neville (1562–1615) in 2005,[802] and, in 2011, Sir Thomas Sackville (1536–1608), made Baron Buckhurst in 1567 and First Earl of Dorset in 1604.[803]

This latest batch of candidates also includes two women. Mary Sidney Herbert, Countess of Pembroke (1561–1621), is the first serious female nominee, set forth as the possible author in 2006.[804]

---

(footnote continued from previous page)

Part IV.28 & notes 717, 728), and for translating the French philosopher Michel de Montaigne. He was a friend of Ben Jonson, see, *e.g.*, Donaldson, p. 12, and many suspect he may have had connections to the author Shakespeare. But the argument that he *was* that author is, in a word, implausible.

[802] See James & Rubinstein (2005, rep. 2006); Casson & Rubinstein (2016); Casson, Rubinstein & Ewald, "Neville," in Leahy (2018), ch. 5, p. 113; compare Hope & Holston, pp. 128-29 (criticizing the Nevillean theory). Green, "Neville Myths" (2019), has criticized numerous additional problems with the Nevillean theory's alleged supporting evidence—much of which appears to evaporate under scrutiny. The theory relies heavily on unproven and extremely dubious handwriting claims, and the two leading books contain many factual mistakes, as Green documents at devastating length.

Another problem with the Nevillean theory is that, even while it rejects the Stratfordian theory, it paradoxically "depends in part upon the orthodox [Stratfordian] dating of the plays." Casson & Rubinstein (2016), p. 8. But as widely discussed over the years and conceded in moments of candor even by Stratfordian scholars, that chronology (always largely speculative and hotly disputed) is an essentially circular construct based on the *assumption* that Shakspere of Stratford was the author (an assumption that Nevilleans obviously reject).

For reasons discussed in this part and Parts IV.22-24 and 29, and also in Part III.B & note 55 (discussing Jiménez's findings on early plays and the likely dating of *Henry V* to 1584), the overall chronological evidence is a *huge* problem for the Stratfordian theory—and equally so for any alternative candidates (like Neville or Marlowe for example) who have either birth or death dates that are close to Shakspere's (Neville has both).

[803] See Feldman, *Sackville* (2015); see also Feldman, *Apocryphal* (2011); Hess, "Literary Mentor" (2011) (arguing that Sackville was more likely the author's literary mentor); Feldman, "Response" (2011). Sackville, like Vere, was acknowledged at the time as a writer in his own right, listed by Meres in 1598 as among "our best for tragedy." See Part IV.12 & note 298.

[804] See Williams (2006, 2d ed. 2012); Williams, "Herbert," in Leahy (2018), ch. 6, p. 139; compare Hope & Holston, p. 129 (criticizing this theory). Mary Sidney married Henry Herbert (Second Earl of Pembroke) in 1577, and he died in 1601. Their children included William Herbert (Third Earl of Pembroke) and Philip Herbert (First Earl of Montgomery and Fourth Earl of Pembroke), the "in-
(footnote continued on next page)

Amelia Bassano Lanier (1569–1645) was in turn proposed as the real "Shakespeare" in 2009.[805]

---

(footnote continued from previous page)
comparable pair of brethren" to whom the *First Folio* was dedicated in 1623. See Part I & note 41; see also note 805 below on female candidates generally.

[805] See Hudson (2009, 2014); compare Hughes, "Oxfordian Response," pp. 102-05 (criticizing this theory); see also Winkler (2019). In reality, it is unlikely for many reasons that the author was either of these women, or any woman. Mary Sidney and Bassano deserve more recognition and celebration *in their own right* as important early modern writers and cultural figures. Bassano's life story and accomplishments are truly fascinating. See, *e.g.*, Hughes, "New Light on the Dark Lady" (2000). Those who suggest a female "Shakespeare" typically emphasize the author's deep (seemingly uncanny) insights into female psychology. But as my friend Bill Glaser has suggested, if the author were indeed a woman, her deep (if not deeper) insights into *male* psychology would seem equally (if not more) uncanny. This author had an uncanny understanding of all *humanity*.

Queen Elizabeth I (1533–1603) has herself been suggested as a possible authorship candidate—likewise King James I (1566–1625). But I am not aware of anyone who actually views either monarch as a serious candidate. The latter was a speculation of Malcolm X. See Part V.C & note 33. Not a single book or even short article, to my knowledge, has ever developed a case for either.

Stratfordians often belabor the fact that perhaps 70 or more individuals have been mentioned (at least passingly) as possible candidates. They use this to ridicule the entire SAQ, perhaps hoping the sheer number of names will obscure and distract from the powerful support for Vere (by far the strongest candidate). See, *e.g.*, Waugh & Bate (2017) (Sir Jonathan Bate, at minute 19, regrettably deploying this tactic). This is an exceptionally stupid argument. The large number of alternative candidates suggested over the years testifies to the extreme dissatisfaction with the Stratfordian theory that so many thoughtful people have felt for centuries. The overwhelming majority of all these candidates have never been serious and may safely be dismissed from consideration. Only Vere, and the other eight alternatives mentioned in the text, currently merit serious consideration—and that's being generous to some of the non-Oxfordian alternatives.

It must be added, however, that the highly regarded author and scholar Dennis McCarthy self-published a book in 2011 suggesting that Sir Thomas North (1535–1604) was the author or at least played some substantial role. North was a well-known translator and has been hailed as a master of early modern English prose. He was an aristocrat, but as the second son of a baron did not inherit any title himself. His year of death (the same as Vere's) is certainly intriguing in light of the discussion in this part.

But McCarthy does not currently appear to be promoting this theory. A note on the 2011 book's Amazon page (presumably drafted by McCarthy) states that "access" to it "has been temporarily halted ... to make way for ... McCarthy's latest book on [North]," which it states was to be published by 2016. No such book has yet appeared and no new copies of the 2011 book are available for sale—only a single used copy with an asking price of more than $2,000! (I
(footnote continued on next page)

All of the non-Oxfordian alternative candidates appear very weak in comparison to Vere. None appears to be supported by evidence even remotely comparable to that supporting the Oxfordian theory. It is, in fact, rather generous to describe some of these candidates as "serious" and "significant."[806] For one thing, all except Vere and Sackville were—like Shakspere of Stratford—born too late.[807] Manners was born far too late, absurdly so. He was only 13 when the author of *Hamlet* was knowingly alluded to as "English Seneca," only 16 when the "Shake-scene" reference was published, and merely eight (at most) when *Henry V* was probably first performed.[808] Marlowe was not only born too late, he died too soon.[809]

In fact, the five indications we have seen, that the author died many years before 1616, appear inconsistent with every candidate other than Vere. This evidence indicates the author probably died before 1605, even more likely before 1607, and *very likely indeed*

---

(footnote continued from previous page)
purchased a new copy at cover price in 2012.) McCarthy's argument in the 2011 book is difficult to follow and needs more development. The Amazon page states it "was published ... to establish priority on the Thomas North discovery."

McCarthy has authored or co-authored several well-received books from prestigious publishers. See, *e.g.*, McCarthy (2009) (Oxford UP); McCarthy & Schlueter (2018) (D.S. Brewer & British Library). The latter, an exciting development in Shakespeare studies, discusses a manuscript by George North (a possible relative of Sir Thomas; they apparently both lived for a time in the baronial house of Sir Thomas's elder brother), which appears to be a significant and previously unexplored source used by the author Shakespeare. See, *e.g.*, McCarthy & Schlueter (2018), pp. 1, 8. Oxfordians have noted in online discussions that Vere would seem to have had more likely opportunities to gain access to it than Shakspere of Stratford. The flyleaf of the 2018 book states that McCarthy "is at work on a book tentatively entitled *The Earlier Playwright: Sir Thomas North and the Shakespeare Canon*." To quote Mr. Spock of *Star Trek* fame: "Fascinating!" We shall see what we shall see.

[806] Compare the discussions and sources cited in notes 797-805 with those in Part I, notes 4 and 33.

[807] See note 802, and Parts III.B & note 55, and IV.17 & note 407 (discussing Jiménez's findings, especially as to the likely dating of *Henry V* to 1584).

[808] See note 807 (1584: *Henry V* as dated by Jiménez); Part IV.1 (1589: "English Seneca"); Part IV.2.a (1592: "Shake-scene").

[809] See notes 799, 802, and 807.

before 1609. Yet Manners lived until 1612, Neville to 1615, Shakspere of Stratford to 1616, Sidney to 1621, Bacon to 1626, Stanley to 1642, and Bassano to 1645.

Only Sackville, who died in 1608, would seem to pose a somewhat close call with regard to that evidence. As noted above, he was born early enough as well. Sackville's date of death is consistent with the 1609 *Sonnets*, Brooke's *Ghost* in 1614, and possibly *Envy's Scourge*. But it appears difficult to reconcile with the reference to the late English Ovid in *Sir Thomas Smith's Voyage* (1605), and the mourning for Shakespeare, seen as living with the Muses, in Barksted's *Myrrha* (1607).[810]

In sum, the evidence of the author's likely date of death, as with so much of the evidence we have seen in Part IV, is inconsis-

---

[810] Sir Edward Dyer (1543) and John Florio (1553) were also born early enough (see note 801). But Florio died too late (1625) and is not a plausible candidate in any event. Dyer's death in May 1607 is consistent (at least) with the 1609 *Sonnets* and Brooke's *Ghost* in 1614, and possibly with *Envy's Scourge* and Barksted's *Myrrha*—but not with *Voyage* (1605). We do not know, as far as I am aware, exactly when during 1607 *Myrrha* was published. Dyer seems a very weak candidate anyway.

Feldman, *Sackville* (2015), pp. 274-76, 291, cognizant of the evidence in the *Sonnets* that the author was deceased by 1609, argued that the timing of the *Sonnets* (at least) is consistent with Sackville's authorship. But she did not discuss (was presumably unaware when she wrote) that *Voyage* and *Myrrha*, in 1605 and 1607, indicate the author died before 1608.

Feldman, p. 291, also argued that "Sackville's death in 1608 is consistent with his possible authorship of *King Lear* and *Macbeth*, which contain clear topical allusions to events that occurred in 1605 and 1606 ... [which] pose a major challenge to the candidacy of ... Vere, who died in 1604." See also Feldman, pp. 237-42. *Au contraire*—there is *no* evidence clearly proving that *Macbeth* or *King Lear* (or any Shakespearean works) were written after Vere's death. It is unfortunate that Feldman—a generally brilliant and thoughtful scholar, see Part IV.12 & note 298—categorically endorsed this debunked myth promoted by some (not even all) Stratfordians. Even many orthodox scholars vigorously debate the dating of such plays, which has never been established with any clarity at all. Feldman, p. 237, was mistaken to claim a "wide scholarly consensus." See, *e.g.*, Part III.B & notes 49-53 (discussing the nonexistent Oxfordian "1604 problem" in comparison to the very real and profound 1604 and 1616 problems afflicting the Stratfordian theory); Anderson, Waugh & McNeil (2016) (debunking much the same argument by Shapiro in his 2015 book, *The Year of Lear*).

tent with the Stratfordian theory but perfectly consistent with the Oxfordian theory. This evidence also indicates the implausibility of all eight of the other major authorship candidates (in order of first proposal): Bacon, Stanley, Marlowe, Manners, Neville, Sidney, Bassano, and Sackville.

More to the point, in relation to the primary thesis of this book, this date-of-death evidence strongly reinforces and corroborates the many other early indications of doubt we have seen about the Stratfordian theory, expressed before the death of Shakspere of Stratford in April 1616.

In short, as suggested at the end of the Introduction, doubts about the authorship of the works of "William Shakespeare" were an authentic, integral, and persistent part of the very time and culture that gave rise to those works.

## V. Conclusion

### A. *A New Paradigm*

This book asked, at the end of Part I, what it would mean if the reality and scope of early Shakespeare authorship doubts were fully recognized. If you have continued to read this far, the answer should be clear. The Shakespeare Authorship Question (SAQ) can no longer be quarantined in time, no longer marginalized as a contingent product of modern culture. Doubts and questions about who wrote these poems and plays were an authentic and integral product of Elizabethan and Jacobean culture. They were present at the creation.

The evidence surveyed in Part IV is more than enough to prove that the SAQ must at least, and at long last, be taken seriously by academics and the mainstream media. It is extremely unlikely that all this evidence of early doubts could somehow be explained away. The point is not what any particular piece of it may prove but that, overall, *questions* were raised. *Doubts* were entertained. They were expressed by many different writers during the very time these works were written and published.

Parts I to IV barely begin to survey all the reasons now known to doubt that Shakspere of Stratford wrote the works of Shakespeare. Modern studies have uncovered many reasons why that is deeply implausible, given the profound mismatch between the known facts of his life and the timing, content, and perspectives of these literary works. This book has not even attempted to explore that broader subject in any depth. But these early doubts certainly reinforce the fact that the true authorship of Shakespeare remains not just in "reasonable doubt" today but in very grave doubt.[1]

Concededly, mere doubts (then or now) do not necessarily disprove the Stratfordian theory or prove any alternative theory. But one cannot avoid noticing that some of the evidence discussed in this book does suggest who (or what type of person) the true author must have been. These documented early doubts profoundly undermine the Stratfordian theory. Some of this evidence also supports the Oxfordian theory, though this book has likewise not even attempted to survey in depth the full and powerful scope of the evidence supporting Edward de Vere as the author. Whether any or all of the evidence surveyed in Part IV actually proves or disproves the case for any specific author remains a complicated question beyond the scope of this book.

As noted in the Preface, scholars have interpreted and evaluated this evidence, and will continue to do so, in many different ways. This book makes no claim that this survey is comprehensive, though it aims to be reasonably thorough. Doubtless many scholars will question whether this or that item actually indicates early doubts, and some may question all of them. It would not be at all surprising if it were shown that one or more should be stricken from the list. I suspect other items will be added over time. I welcome such scholarly scrutiny. That would be exactly what has been largely and sadly lacking when it comes to the issue of early Shakespeare authorship doubts. As mentioned in a footnote to Part IV.24, all sides in this debate, both Stratfordians and those of us who question and criticize that theory, need to do a better job of reading each other's scholarly work respectfully—to

---

[1] See Shahan, "Declaration of Reasonable Doubt" and "Beyond Reasonable Doubt" (Parts 1-3); see also Part I & note 33.

advance the search for truth, not to score points. The point is to figure out who truly did write the works of Shakespeare.

Let us step back and consider the big picture, which in my view suggests a new paradigm. These doubts were entertained and expressed during the lifetime of the conventionally credited author. Doubts began arising before, during, and soon after the time the first works were published using the author's name (or pseudonym) in 1593–94.

By contrast, the first documentation linking those works to Stratford-upon-Avon did not appear—and even then, only ambiguously in scattered hints and implications—until the 1623 *First Folio*, a work loaded with evasive double meanings whose *very first page* explicitly instructs readers to ignore ("look not on") the purported author's "picture" and instead focus only on his writings (his "book"). There lies an irony! When orthodox scholars insist, as they almost frantically do sometimes, that we must not "look" for the author in his works,[2] they are precisely and directly defying what Ben Jonson told us to do! Yet otherwise, so often, they treat Jonson as an infallible oracle to be taken literally.[3]

Pause and think about it. Doubts and questions about who this author was began arising *more than thirty years before any link to Stratford was first suggested*. Here we have yet another irony, perhaps the greatest of all the many ironies lurking in the SAQ. For well over a century now, defenders of Stratfordian orthodoxy have denigrated authorship doubts as belated and anachronistic. But we now see, in proper perspective, that the *Stratfordian* theory is the true johnny come-lately (or should we say "willy-come-lately"?), not proposed until seven years after the purported author died. *Authorship doubts predate the Stratfordian theory itself—by at least three decades!*

---

[2] See, *e.g.*, Shapiro (2010), pp. 263-80; Shapiro (2013), pp. 238-40.
[3] See, *e.g.*, Wells, "Allusions," p. 84. For more on Jonson, see Part IV.28.

This suggests a new way of framing the history of Shakespeare studies. The Early Authorship Doubt Era may be defined as the period leading up to 1623. It began no later than 1592, possibly earlier.[4] It is the focus of this book, though I mainly consider only the pre-1616 period.[5] During that era, hardly any references (very few at most) linked the works of Shakespeare to an actor (presumably from Stratford, though that was never stated) with the same (or a similar) name. However, those very same scraps of evidence also, in and of themselves, indicate early authorship doubts. Furthermore, they are part of a larger body of evidence raising early doubts, as detailed in Part IV.

The Stratfordian Era, launched by the *First Folio*, came next. It lasted 233 years, from 1623 to 1856. Doubts about authorship were raised by the *Folio* itself and by the Stratford Monument.[6] In fact, the early posthumous doubts—which began in 1616, the year Shakspere died—persisted well into the Stratfordian Era. There are some striking examples up to 1645. But they seem to be fewer and more scattered from the mid-17th to mid-19th centuries.[7]

The Baconian Era then debuted in 1856 and ran for 64 years.[8] To be sure, the Stratfordian theory continued to dominate that era, as it has to the present day. But authorship doubts blossomed and ran riot. Other candidates emerged. No matter how hard orthodox Stratfordians pushed back, they largely lost control of the conversation and have never regained it to this day.

Finally, the Oxfordian Era was launched in 1920 by an earnest schoolteacher with a funny name. We will soon celebrate the centennial of his landmark study.[9]

---

[4] See Parts IV.1-3.

[5] See Part I & note 37.

[6] See Part I & notes 35-36.

[7] See Part I, note 37.

[8] See Part I & note 42.

[9] See Part I & note 4. Based on the discussion in Part IV.30 & notes 797-805, we may assemble the following list of all serious (or quasi-serious) proposed authorship candidates. Based on all the evidence explored in this book and

(footnote continued on next page)

Authorship doubts certainly *seem* to have become far more widespread in the 19th, 20th, and 21st centuries, as compared to the Early Authorship Doubt Era. But then again, are they just better *recorded* and *circulated* with our modern technologies and freedoms? Our sense of exactly how widespread the early doubts were depends on various unknowable factors, including how many such doubts were ever committed to writing in the first place. And to the extent they were, how many survived to the present day?

Perhaps many people then not only doubted but *knew* the author was not Shakspere of Stratford. But if there was any systematic effort to hide or obscure the true author's identity, it would stand to reason that at least some of whatever was put in writing may have been destroyed. The doubts documented by the surviving records discussed in Part IV represent a core minimum, a starting point.

People during the Early Authorship Doubt Era, and well into the Stratfordian Era, may have been reluctant for various reasons to record in writing whatever facts (or gossip) they heard about the issue—if they even cared about it, as most probably did not.

---

(footnote continued from previous page)
sources cited herein, it would appear the *least* serious (when actually first proposed, by those who first proposed him) was Shakspere of Stratford!

1. 1623: William Shakspere of Stratford-upon-Avon (1564–1616)
2. 1856: Sir Francis Bacon (1561–1626) (made Baron Verulam in 1618 and Viscount St. Alban in 1621)
3. 1891: William Stanley, Sixth Earl of Derby (1561–1642)
4. 1895: Christopher Marlowe (1564–93?)
5. 1906: Roger Manners, Fifth Earl of Rutland (1576–1612)
6. 1920: Edward de Vere, 17th Earl of Oxford (1550–1604)
7. 1927: John Florio (1553–1625)
8. 1943: Sir Edward Dyer (1543–1607)
9. 2005: Sir Henry Neville (1562–1615)
10. 2006: Mary Sidney Herbert, Countess of Pembroke (1561–1621)
11. 2009: Amelia Bassano Lanier (1569–1645)
12. 2011: Sir Thomas Sackville (1536–1608) (made Baron Buckhurst in 1567 and First Earl of Dorset in 1604)
13. 2011: Sir Thomas North (1535–1604)

England in those days was a highly repressive police state in which arbitrary arrest, censorship, torture, and the death penalty were routine.

Stratfordians themselves often fall back on the argument that much written evidence has been lost over the centuries of wars, plagues, and fires that wracked England. That is a standard excuse offered for the glaring paucity of contemporaneous (pre-1623) documentary evidence supporting the Stratfordian theory.

Yet orthodox scholars dismiss even the possibility of an alternative author unless and until some undeniably explicit evidence is found—the very same kind of contemporaneous "smoking gun" *that has never been found in support of the Stratfordian claim.*[10] If there was an intentionally hidden author, however well-kept a secret (or not) at the time, it stands to reason that much less evidence would have been put to paper in the first place about that and even less would survive today.

The early doubts we have seen were not extensively explored until much later. But there is nothing strange about that. Most people at the time, very understandably, probably accepted without question the Stratfordian attribution artfully and elliptically conveyed by the *First Folio.* Even before 1623, most readers and playgoers probably felt no particular motivation to inquire or wonder what real person was behind the name "Shakespeare" on a printed page or playbill. Why would they give a damn?[11] Life

---

[10] If Stratfordians are serious about smoking guns, they should carefully examine the parallels between Edward de Vere's known early poems and the Shakespeare canon. See Part III.B, note 45; "Twenty Poems" (2018); Stritmatter, *Poems of Edward de Vere* (2019).

[11] Some ask the same question of doubters today. My Preface and this Conclusion answer to the best of my ability. We have direct contemporary testimony, from Ben Jonson no less, that as Price put it, p. 88, "most readers or playgoers [at that time] were too indiscriminate to care much about authorship attribution." Jonson's epigram "On Poet-Ape" (*c.* 1595–1612) states: "The sluggish gaping auditor [*i.e.*, the typical audience of the day] ... marks not whose 'twas first: and after-times may judge it to be his, as well as ours." Jonson, *Works* (1616), p. 783, quoted and discussed in Part IV.28 & notes 699-707.

was more difficult in those days. Most people, including most who enjoyed play performances, were illiterate. Few had the luxury of pursuing historical, artistic, or cultural studies.

The fact that far more has been *published and openly discussed* about authorship doubt since 1856 is probably due mostly to modern literacy rates, freedom of the press and intellectual inquiry, and the rise of a much larger educated middle class. Some significant number of people during Shakespeare's time, especially in the literary and aristocratic elites, surely knew or had some idea who the true author was. But the general public, on the whole, may neither have known nor cared.

B. *The Conspiracy Issue*

The foregoing discussion goes far to refute the common derision of the SAQ as just another "conspiracy theory." It is often suggested that concealing a secret author would have required some impossibly vast yet tightly controlled plot. Well, first of all, conspiracies do happen. And they often succeed, at least for many years. The possibility of a conspiracy, even in a strong sense, should not be ridiculed or dismissed out of hand. History testifies that many important (even sensational) secrets have successfully been kept for long periods of time. Part III.D notes the hypocrisy of criticizing anti-Stratfordians on this ground, since Stratfordians themselves concede and even contend for the existence of long-hidden authors and co-authors of works published as by "Shakespeare."

But authorship doubts do not really depend on any strong notion of conspiracy. Consider this comparison: Until not long ago, the idea that President Thomas Jefferson had a sexual relationship with one of his African American slaves, Sally Hemings, and fathered children with her, was widely viewed as an unsavory and sensationalist fringe theory. Mainstream historians scornfully rejected the idea out of hand for almost 200 years. Today, most historians accept it as very likely true. How was it kept secret all that time? Was there some impossibly widespread conspiracy to hush it up? No—nothing like that was required. More to the point, it was *not* completely hushed up—just like doubts about the true identity of "Shakespeare" were not. Rumors about the Jefferson-Hemings relationship circulated even at the time, long before DNA testing made it impossible to ignore.[12]

In the same way, the early doubts that were in fact expressed and published about Shakespeare's authorship—as this book shows—demonstrate that whatever conspiracy, deception, or secrecy may have been attempted was actually not that successful, even at the time. The truth may well have been an open secret, the pseudonym a polite fiction—possibly well-known to some, suspected by others, and a matter of indifference to most.

Oxfordians say we pretty much figured out the truth almost a century ago, 297 years after the Stratfordian theory was first promulgated—not too far out of line with how long it took to blow the cover off Jefferson's relationship with Hemings. Peter Moore has pointed out, using a closer historical parallel, that it took exactly a century after the publication of Sir Philip Sidney's "Astrophel and Stella" before anyone mentioned in print that Sidney's beloved "Stella" was based on Lady Penelope Rich.[13] She scandalized Elizabethans and Jacobeans by abandoning her hus-

---

[12] See, *e.g.*, Gordon-Reed, especially pp. vii-xiii (1999 Author's Note).

[13] As Moore described, in an article that should be required reading before anyone speaks above a whisper about "conspiracies," this connection was widely known in literary circles after Sidney's sonnet sequence was published in 1591—but no one dared publish it explicitly for fear of tarnishing the reputation of the admired Sidney, who died a war hero in 1586. Only in 1691 was it briefly mentioned in print—and then mostly ignored for another 243 years. A book published in 1934 sought to disprove the long-rumored connection, but in 1935 a definitive article by Hoyt Hudson forced the literary establishment (at long last) to openly acknowledge the truth. See Moore, "Stella" (1993), in Moore (2009), p. 312; see also, *e.g.*, Sobran, pp. 209-11. On Oxford, see Looney (1920) and other sources cited in Part I, note 4.

band to live openly with her lover Charles Blount, Baron Mount-joy, bearing him several children. Then, even worse in the eyes of that hypocritical and misogynistic society, she freely confessed her adultery, divorced her husband, and married her lover in defiance of church law. It was not until 1935—*344 years after publication*—that the truth of the Penelope-Stella connection came to be widely accepted by literary scholars.

Diana Price has drawn an insightful analogy to the polite code of silence observed among American journalists and govern-ment officials about such matters as President Franklin D. Roose-velt's polio disability and the sexual escapades of President John F. Kennedy. As she noted, the general public was mostly unaware of those secrets at the time, even though hundreds and maybe thousands of people were "in the know."[14] We eventually learned those presidential secrets within a few decades, but that is because we—unlike the subjects of Queen Elizabeth I—live in a democracy with almost universal literacy and a free press, in a culture that affords many people the opportunity to pursue such questions.

By contrast, just 19 years after the 1623 *First Folio* sought to paper over the issue of Shakespeare's authorship, Britain descen-ded into civil war. That same year, 1642, the theatres were closed for an entire generation as Christian fundamentalists (the Puri-tans) rose to power. By the time the monarchy was restored and the theatres reopened, after years of war, the generations with firsthand knowledge of Shakespeare's time were mostly gone.

Price noted that with a large number of people in on a secret, whether in Elizabethan England or 20th-century America, a true "conspiracy" of silence, in the strict sense, is impossible:

---

[14] See Price, pp. 230-33.

Then why didn't all these people talk about it? Amongst themselves, they probably did talk about it. They just didn't *write* about it, at least not in plain English. When contemporaries wrote about the dramatist Shakespeare, they did one of two things: they confined their remarks to comment on his literary output, or they encrypted their allusions.[15]

As Price stated:

These writers were not part of a conspiracy. They were products of their time, schooled in the art of ambiguity. While it is commonplace to find poetry, prose passages, and dialogue that defy deciphering, it is highly unusual, if not unique, to find one particular writer for whom *all* the literary allusions with some hint of personal information are ambiguous or cryptic.[16]

She continued: "Any other writer of consequence from Shakespeare's day can be clearly and personally identified in some of his literary paper trails. Yet all that remains in Shakespeare's file are allusions that read as though everyone avoided explicit identification of the man."[17]

---

[15] Price, p. 231 (emphasis in original).

[16] Price, p. 233 (emphasis in original).

[17] Price, p. 233. For reasons noted in Parts V.A-B, I respectfully disagree with Sabrina Feldman's suggestion that "[t]he only way to argue that another [person] wrote the Bard's works is to postulate that ... [a] deliberate authorship deception was known only to [a] small circle of people who closely guarded the secret." Feldman, *Sackville* (2015), p. ix.

The widely published early doubts explored in this book indicate that any "secret" was *not* that "closely guarded." As Joseph Sobran suggested (1997), p. 176, "we need not assume that there was any great conspiracy to conceal Shakespeare's identity. It was probably one of those open secrets that elites share among themselves and even discuss in coded language."

It is also puzzling that Feldman (a brilliant and generally perceptive authorship skeptic, see Part IV.12, note 298) stated, p. ix, that "[t]here can be no real doubt that William Shakespeare [of Stratford] was widely accepted by his peers as the author of the Shakespeare canon," that "[h]e is memorialized as the great author in a monument erected in the Stratford church, as well as in the 1623

(footnote continued on next page)

When we consider all this carefully, it is not at all surprising that doubts about Shakespeare fully blossomed only during the 19th-century Victorian era. It was only then that really substantial numbers of people were finally able to look beyond the demands of daily survival. Only then did large numbers of people, not just the privileged elite but the broad middle classes as well, start acquiring the resources to pursue literary, artistic, cultural, and historical interests.

J. Thomas Looney in 1920 responded to the understandable objection many have raised, that if the Stratfordian attribution is mistaken, then the true author "should have been discovered long before." And if we have not been able to reach a consensus by now, perhaps "the necessary data do not exist, and his identity must remain for ever a mystery."[18] Looney pointed out that it was not until the 19th century that Shakespearean scholarship got seriously underway, "and this was essential to the mere raising of the problem." He quoted Ralph Waldo Emerson's comment: "Not until two centuries had passed after [this author's] death did any criticism which we think adequate begin to appear."[19]

What is surprising is how many distinguished and otherwise well-informed Shakespeare scholars have overlooked the evidence

---

(footnote continued from previous page)
First Folio," and that "there is clear evidence that William was generally known to his contemporaries as both a writer and an actor." *Au contraire!* As this book has discussed, as many studies have shown, *and as even Stratfordians like Sir Stanley Wells sometimes concede in moments of candor* (see Part I & note 6), there is a stunning *dearth* of evidence that "contemporaries" during Shakspere's lifetime thought he was a writer of any sort.

Even the posthumous evidence is surprisingly weak, as Part I summarizes (though not my focus here). The peculiar Stratford Monument seems deliberately cryptic about Shakspere's alleged status as a writer. It does not provide any specific indications that he was a playwright or that relate to anything in the Shakespeare canon. See Part I & note 35; see also sources cited in Part I, note 36 (discussing the many ambiguities and doubts lurking in the *First Folio*).

[18] Looney, p. 77.

[19] Quoted in Looney, p. 78 (from Emerson's *Representative Men*, as noted in Warren's 2018 annotated edition of Looney).

of early doubts—or if noticing the facts, have not appreciated their implications and have never explored them.[20] It is not a matter of conscious dishonesty or suppression, which I do not think could explain this oversight. I think most academics, like others marinated in the Stratfordian faith, simply and honestly do not *see* these facts or their implications.

Most academics, it seems, have not felt motivated to explore or challenge this "mythography," which appears quasi-religious. Not only is there little incentive to question this myth, there are significant social sanctions *against* doing so, as anyone who pursues the SAQ soon becomes well aware. Some Stratfordians view their theory as inerrant gospel truth—an infallible and unquestionable premise—and they do not take kindly to those who question it. To do so, in their eyes, is not merely foolish but heresy. Mark Anderson, in his 2005 biography of Edward de Vere, recalled "encounters with otherwise reasonable people who became irrational and red-faced with anger when the words 'earl of Oxford' were uttered."[21]

C. *The Snobbery Slander and Its Ironies*

The Stratfordian Shakespeare, the provincial commoner who became the jewel in the crown of English literature, is a revered icon in Britain, the national poet. It is not just Britons, of course, who feel an emotional connection to Shakespeare. I do myself, though I have a different view of his identity. Indeed, it sometimes seems like Americans and people of many other nationalities are even more obsessed with Shakespeare than the British. For many Britons, however, the Stratfordian theory is a matter of

---

[20] See Part II.

[21] He also noted that the SAQ is "considered a heresy in the church of English letters." Anderson, p. 411 (Author's Note). On "mythography," see the 1998 article by Erne (a Stratfordian) with that very word in its title.

patriotism and national pride. You mess with their small-town hero at your peril.

The charge of snobbery often leveled against those who doubt the Stratfordian theory, especially Oxfordians, is a tiresome old chestnut—a classic *ad hominem* cheap shot, grossly inaccurate and unfair as applied to the overwhelming majority of Oxfordians and other doubters, past and present. But this snobbery slander is deeply revealing and merits careful attention. Class-based feelings play a very important role in the SAQ.

While it is possible that some people have been drawn to Vere or other authorship candidates by some elitist preference, a theory is not disproven just because some (even many) may embrace it for the wrong reasons. Charles Darwin's insights into biological evolution, for example, cannot rationally be rejected simply because they became entangled (and remain so to some extent) in spurious associations with rightwing and often racist "social Darwinist" ideas.

Sauce for the goose is sauce for the gander. Scholars in glass houses should not throw stones. The obvious ideological and emotional appeal of the Stratfordian story—a poet who rose from the common people in a small provincial town to take London by storm and become England's greatest writer—is likewise a spurious and invalid basis for any views about authorship, one way or the other. Either preference could, in principle, become a source of bias.

Even some Stratfordian scholars have admitted that this has, in fact, generated troubling distortions in orthodox scholarship. Professor Lukas Erne has observed that "it seems impossible to approach [Shakespeare's] life from a neutral and disinterested point of view."[22] Quoting another Stratfordian scholar, he noted

---

[22] Erne, "Mythography," p. 439.

that this has created constant pressure to interpret and embellish the known facts with "guesswork, legend and sentiment."[23]

There are ample grounds for the late Supreme Court Justice Antonin Scalia's suggestion that Stratfordians may be "more ... affected by a democratic bias than the Oxfordians are ... by an aristocratic bias."[24] Very revealing is a statement by Sir Jonathan Bate: "I actually think it's terrific that someone from an ordinary background can get to be a great writer, just as it's terrific that someone from an ordinary background can get to be president of the United States."[25] Was Bate perhaps projecting the mirror image of his own bias when he accused Alexander Waugh of embracing the Oxfordian theory in part because Waugh and other members of his family allegedly *"love* an aristocrat"?[26]

Bate notwithstanding, most orthodox scholars are now too polite—or too politic—to fling the snobbery canard around as freely as it used to be. They realize, perhaps, that it does not come across well to rudely and falsely slander large numbers of sincere and thoughtful people (however mistaken we, as anyone, may be), as snobs besotted with the British elite.[27]

---

[23] Erne, "Mythography," p. 439 & nn. 34, 37, quoting Dutton, pp. 1-2 (internal quotation marks omitted).

[24] Quoted in Bravin (reporting that Scalia's own wife needled him with the old snobbery chestnut, charging that Oxfordians just "can't believe that a commoner" wrote the works of Shakespeare); see also Wildenthal, "Oxfordian Era," p. 6. On the Oxfordian theory, see Part I, note 4.

[25] Wilson & Wilson, *Last Will. & Testament* (2012) (at minute 2).

[26] Waugh & Bate (2017) (at minute 18) (Bate's mocking emphasis on "love" is pretty clear in the video; he also referred to Oxfordians, at minute 17, as "cultists"). Waugh, a successful author in his own right, is a grandson of Evelyn Waugh (1903–66) (author of the beloved classic *Brideshead Revisited* and other novels) and son of Auberon Waugh (1939–2001) (a prominent writer and columnist). With this smoothly vicious comment, Bate united the snobbery slander with a charge of inherited guilt by association. Nice! Bate's extreme early-doubt denialism during this same debate is quoted at the end of Part II. For a thorough critique of his performance, see Steinburg (2018).

[27] All right, all right! I confess! I enjoyed *Downton Abbey*! (Well, mildly. I felt afterward like I had eaten too much English trifle.) At least one staunchly Stratfordian scholar, Professor Steven May (who has produced valuable studies

(footnote continued on next page)

But Professor James Marino of Cleveland State University, who has published valuable Shakespearean scholarship,[28] has vigorously promoted the snobbery slander. He gives it a hip contemporary spin, linking it to the struggle against income inequality. "Occupy Wall Street" meets the Bard?

Marino asserted in a blog post—writing under his own thinly veiled pseudonym—that Oxfordians "desire to claim that Shakespeare was in the 1%. Only an aristocrat, the conspiracy theorists say ... on top of the social and economic pyramid, could have created such art. The stakes here," he suggested, involve some kind of plot to claim the works of Shakespeare as "the property of the inherited elite." (Wow, talk about a conspiracy theory!) "The Oxfordian argument is ... [a] crazier version of a process ... in which the small elite of the super-wealthy are given credit for the achievements of the rest of society."[29]

---

(footnote continued from previous page)

of Vere's known early poetry), has more reasonably conceded that Oxfordians have "made worthwhile contributions to our understanding of the Elizabethan age" and "are educated men and women ... sincerely interested in Renaissance English culture," whose "arguments ... are entertained as at least plausible by hosts of intellectually respectable persons ...." May, "Poems" (1980), p. 10, quoted in Stritmatter & Wildenthal, "Methodological," p. 189 n 12.

[28] See, *e.g.*, Marino, *Owning William Shakespeare* (2011). This is a brilliant and important book, which implicitly (if surely unintentionally) provides some support for authorship doubts. See Part III.B & notes 50-54.

[29] Marino (*Dagblog*, Nov. 3, 2011); see also Part III.B, note 33 (discussing another example of Marino's mockery of Oxfordian views); Part I, note 28 (discussing his exaggerations of Stratfordian evidence). Writing under his own name, Marino accused Oxfordians of "a deep-seated need to believe that Shakespeare was an aristocrat." Marino (*Penn Press Log*, Nov. 1, 2011); see also Marino (*Dagblog*, Dec. 31, 2014) (revealing his authorship of the foregoing).

Marino also provided more examples of the extreme early-doubt denialism surveyed in Part II. His 2014 post asserted that the SAQ "didn't start until the 19th century .... No one in the 16th, 17th, or 18th centuries expressed any doubts." The online echo chamber of denialism mentioned at the outset of Part I is well illustrated by Marino's 2011 *Dagblog* post, which claimed that *"[n]o one from the time shows any doubt* about" the Stratfordian theory, followed by a dittohead commenter who chimed in that *"no person ever questioned* Shakespeare's authorship in his lifetime" and "[f]or the next two centuries *no one* raised a *hint* of doubt" (emphases added).

Marino's screed is entertaining, to be sure. It is also a caricature utterly detached from the reality of true-life Oxfordians, few
if any of whom he seems to have actually met.[30]

Yet Marino, thou art more temperate compared to Amanda
Marcotte, a political blogger who described authorship doubts as
"Shakespeare trutherism" motivated by "unsavory classism,"
which she ranted is "quite a bit like Obama birtherism." (How
could anyone have missed that?) She asserted that both "serve [a]
belief that the person in question, by virtue of his supposedly low
birth, does not deserve his fame and authority," and that both
allegedly "express unsavory ideas—that black men cannot be
Presidents, [and] common men cannot be great poets ...."[31]

Marcotte conceded "surprise" that Mark Twain was a doubter,
but that barely slowed her down from falsely dismissing his views

---

[30] As an Oxfordian myself who has gotten to know many others quite well, I
speak from direct personal knowledge. Quite irrelevant, strictly speaking, is my
personal sympathy for Marino's left-leaning concerns about economic inequality.
But I do not think my own political and economic views have any rational bearing on who wrote the patently aristocratic-leaning works of Shakespeare, a point
Marino should pause to consider.

[31] Marcotte (*Rawstory*, 2014). Marino's 2014 *Dagblog* post linked approv-
ingly to Marcotte's, calling it a "smart takedown" of authorship doubts. So
perhaps he's not more temperate (sigh). I wearily relegate to this footnote the
irrelevant fact that former President Obama enjoys many impassioned (now very
nostalgic) supporters among Oxfordians, including me. Not that it should matter,
but Oxfordians encompass a vastly diverse range of political, religious, and social
views. I find it refreshing how our movement brings together so many thoughtful
people of good will across such divisions, united only by our love of Shakespeare
and our fascination with the history of his era.

It is telling that the leading conservative voice for many years on the U.S.
Supreme Court (the late Justice Scalia) was an Oxfordian, just like his retired
long-serving colleague widely viewed as a leader of the Court's liberals (Justice
Stevens). Another liberal (the late Justice Blackmun, also an Oxfordian) and two
centrist "swing voters" (the late Justice Powell and the retired Justice O'Connor)
round out the ranks of known authorship doubters on the Court during the past
half-century. Justice Ruth Bader Ginsburg, currently the senior liberal on the
Court, has also expressed some interest in the SAQ, perhaps influenced by her
friend Scalia. See Part I, note 4; Wildenthal, "Oxfordian Era."

as dating only from "his cranky old rich man years."[32] Would she diss Walt Whitman with a similar *ad hominem* smear? Given her playing of the race card, one wonders what she would make of the fact that Malcolm X was also a doubter. Just another snob? Whitman foreshadowed the Oxfordian theory in 1888, suggesting that "only one of the 'wolfish earls' so plenteous in the plays themselves, or some born descendant and knower, might seem to be the true author of those amazing works."[33]

Whitman arose from a famously modest social background. Passionate tribune of democracy and the common man that he was, he actually expressed distaste for Shakespeare's own elitist attitudes.[34] But I suppose Marcotte would still backhand him as being, by 1888, just another "cranky old rich man." Oxfordians, I suppose, should feel honored to be lumped together with some of America's finest writers as objects of such mindless bile.

It's hard to choose, but perhaps most unhinged is Ron Rosenbaum's essay, with a title that pretty much says it all: "10 Things I Hate About *Anonymous* and the Stupid Shakespearean Birther Cult Behind It." While Rosenbaum, an otherwise rational and respected journalist and author, allowed that "Oxfordianism is *not exactly* the literary equivalent of Holocaust denial," he declared: "I

---

[32] Marcotte (*Rawstory*, 2014). Actually, as Marcotte could have learned with a modicum of research before spewing venom on the internet, Twain's fascination with the SAQ dates to his youth as an apprentice boat pilot on the Mississippi River, as he himself stated near the beginning of his widely available book on the subject (which, typically for Twain, is highly entertaining; Marcotte might enjoy reading it). See Twain (1909), p. 4 (noting "my fifty years' interest in" the issue).

[33] Whitman, p. 52 (referring to the English history plays). Malcolm, during his famous self-education in prison, began to think the true "Shakespeare," based on the evidence of the works, must be not merely aristocratic, but royal. He speculated that the true author might have been King James I. Unlike Marino and Marcotte, Malcolm was able to separate his own normative ideological views from evidentiary questions of literary history. He obviously did not favor aristocrats or royalty. He thought the King James Bible had "enslaved the world." Malcolm X, *Autobiography*, p. 185 (see generally ch. 11).

[34] See, *e.g.*, Sobran, p. 167.

really *hate* what these people do, the Oxfordians. Their titanic smugness, their snobbishness. ... Most of all, I hate the way they pride themselves on the vain, mendacious conceit that they're in on a grand historical secret deception that only they have the superior intelligence to understand."[35] Oh my. And we doubters are often told *we* are too humorless and weirdly obsessed? Can we all just relax, get along, and debate this issue in a friendly and constructive way?[36]

Bate, Marino, Marcotte, Rosenbaum, and others notwithstanding, I have never met a *single* Oxfordian, or any Shakespeare authorship doubter, who would not cheerfully agree that many common men (and women) have become great writers. Whitman and Christopher Marlowe are just two examples. Some Stratfordians may have a hard time wrapping their heads around it, but quite a few Oxfordians (like me) are distinctly left-liberal in our politics. As much as we love the works of Shakespeare and admire whoever wrote them, many of us (like Whitman) are actually troubled by the degree to which they are pervaded by aristocratic prejudice—among other biases. But then, life and art are often messy and do not conform to prim and pristine notions of virtue.

To recognize Oxford as the likely author is not something we "*desire*." It's a matter of facing up to reality based on compelling circumstantial evidence. Personally, I would far rather find evidence that Marlowe, the gay commoner and atheist rebel, was the true author. Certainly no one could accuse Marlovians of snob-

---

[35] Rosenbaum (*Slate*, 2011) (first emphasis added; the second emphasis, on "*hate*," is in the original). *Anonymous* (2011) is a largely speculative costume drama film of debatable quality, which flopped at the box office and about which most Oxfordians (at least privately) have very mixed feelings. I found it flawed but entertaining.

[36] Memo to the hyperventilating Rosenbaum: Yes, Oxfordians do think we have figured out the real author, not because we claim any special "intelligence" but because the circumstantial evidence is quite compelling. You might try reading up on it. Honestly, we're not snobs and we certainly don't "hate" anyone over it (awfully sorry you do). We just want to explore a fascinating historical mystery. Is that really so bad?

bery! He came from a more modest background than Shakspere, who after all was a product of the upper middle class.[37]

As Joseph Sobran pointed out in his insightful 1997 book,[38] it is "strange that an author whose biases are so obviously aristocratic,"[39] indeed, whose "philosophy is thoroughly feudal,"[40] has become "an icon and test of democratic faith."[41] That's a pretty big irony—on top of the irony, discussed above, that many Stratfordians accuse doubters of being biased by snobbery when in fact they seem far more biased by their own preference for a humble author.

Sobran grasped the nettle that many Stratfordians seem to find too painful: This author has "little interest in the sort of self-made man his [Stratfordian] champions suppose him to have

---

[37] Granted, Marlowe's sexuality and views on religion will probably always remain matters of debate, as will the circumstances of his death. I wish I had more time and space to discuss him. But as fond as I am of our Marlovian friends and allies in the authorship struggle, and as much as Marlowe intrigues me in his own right as a great literary artist, honesty compels me to say I find implausible the proposition that he was the primary author of the Shakespeare canon. See Parts III.B & note 43; IV.30 & note 799.

[38] Given the tendency of some Stratfordians to go *ad hominem*, it seems best to preemptively concede that Sobran (1946–2010) was a troubling character, a prominent rightwing columnist whose views on some issues (anathema to mine to begin with) became more reckless and extreme with time (he was eventually fired by William F. Buckley Jr.'s *National Review*). See, *e.g.*, Grimes (2010). But his book on the SAQ is deeply thoughtful and gracefully written. There seems no basis whatsoever to link his views or writings on the SAQ with his unrelated ideological views. For example, Sobran was viciously antigay. I still shudder with anger to recall some of his homophobic columns during the 1990s when I was coming out as a young gay man. Yet he followed what he saw as the evidence to argue that the author Shakespeare may have been gay or at least bisexual—a conclusion that must have troubled him. See Sobran, pp. 124-26, 197-204. Stratfordians have furiously attacked Sobran's book, *e.g.*, Kathman, "Sobran," seizing on various alleged minor errors, while grudgingly conceding how accessibly and persuasively he wrote. Kathman, as I have noted before, should recall the saying about glass houses. See Part IV.2.d & notes 76-77, and, *e.g.*, Parts II & note 60, III.A & note 9, IV.16 & notes 380-84, IV.23, and IV.26 & notes 676-81.

[39] Sobran, p. 13.

[40] Sobran, p. 169.

[41] Sobran, p. 13.

been."[42] To the extent he shows any interest in commoners, it is most often to ridicule their speech, which he treats as a class trait.[43] As Sobran perceptively noted, such mockery of speech patterns is a classic marker of stereotyping against "those we perceive as 'others.' If Shakespeare laughs at the illiterate speech of the lower classes, he also lampoons the affected speech of upwardly mobile commoners like Malvolio and Osric who, in trying to talk like their betters, overdo it to comic effect."[44]

Shakspere was an ambitious commoner, as reflected in his coat-of-arms.[45] The author seems to view such people across a wide and deep class divide. By contrast, he portrays members of the social elite as nuanced individuals—"because he is one of them," Sobran suggested.[46] Sobran documented his "habitual language [in] the idiom of the courtier," matching that to Vere's surviving letters.[47] Judging from the works, this author seems not to have the smug bourgeois attitudes of a commercially successful middle-class *arriviste*, but rather exactly the kind of tortured ambivalence and preoccupations one might expect to find in a decadent, disgraced, and disillusioned aristocrat.

---

[42] Sobran, p. 13. Sobran did not contend, nor would I, that the author lacks all empathy for commoners. See Sobran, p. 164. I agree with Harold Bloom, p. 148, for example, that Nick Bottom the Weaver may be seen as the intriguing heart of *A Midsummer Night's Dream*, perhaps "Shakespeare's most engaging character before Falstaff," though I think Bloom gets a bit carried away. See generally Bloom, ch. 11, pp. 148-70. The infamous and beloved Falstaff is often and rightly cited as Shakespeare's greatest "everyman" character, an earthy volcano of lustful humanity. But Falstaff, though not a nobleman, is a knight who hobnobs with a prince and thus very much part of the courtly elite—as brought home in the comic recruitment scene which (very typically) ridicules commoners of lower social class. See *Henry IV, Part 2*, act 3, sc. 2; see generally Bloom, ch. 17, pp. 271-314. Falstaff seems exactly the kind of louche retainer a decadent aristocrat like Vere would interact with (some Oxfordians see elements of self-parody as well), but whom it seems more difficult to connect with the successful (and likely more disciplined) businessman Shakspere.

[43] See Sobran, pp. 164-65, and generally pp. 163-72.

[44] Sobran, p. 165.

[45] See, *e.g.*, Wildenthal, "Rollett and Shapiro," pp. 1-2; Wolfe & Witmore.

[46] Sobran, p. 165. But see also note 42.

[47] Sobran, p. 170, and see generally pp. 167-72.

We should hesitate to psychoanalyze Stratfordians as they so freely indulge in psychoanalyzing doubters. But one has to wonder if the fervor and even fury with which some of them fling the snobbery charge—and recoil from the evidence pointing to the real author—may for some be a way of projecting (unconsciously?) their own discomfort and dissonant feelings about the painfully obvious class and other biases in these works we all love so much. It almost seems like an effort to cancel that out by building up the author, however implausibly, as some sort of working-class hero— which Shakspere never was in any event.

Like so many Shakespeare lovers past and present, Stratfordian and skeptical alike, I veer close to "idolatry" of this writer.[48] Whatever privileges he inherited, whatever personal demons possessed him, he was a supremely gifted artist with profound psychological insight—brilliantly perceptive, capable of transcending himself and empathizing with a stunning range of characters, and self-aware enough to grasp the cruel random truths and ironies of his unjust society and his own place in it.

But no one who truly loves Shakespeare, who respects the depth and complexity of this artist and his work, should flinch from confronting his many disturbing facets.[49] Many Stratfordians

---

[48] See Ben Jonson's famously ambivalent comment (clearly referring to the *author* "Shakespeare," whoever that was) that "I loved [him] ... this side idolatry" (*i.e.*, pointedly stopping short of idolatry). Quoted in Crider, p. 19. We should follow Jonson's cautious private example, even while thrilling (as below, cited note 67) to his more exuberant public encomium in the *First Folio*, pp. 9-10. The "idolatry" line is from Jonson's private remembrance "De Shakespeare Nostrati," unpublished during his lifetime but found in his notebooks and published posthumously in *Timber, or Discoveries* (1641). Crider, p. 19; see generally pp. 19-22. Jonson's title may translate literally as "About Shakespeare Our Native Son," though its essential meaning seems to be simply "Our Shakespeare." See *Cassell's Latin Dictionary*, pp. 166-67 (*de*, sense 3.a), p. 396 (*nostras* or *nostratis*); *OED*, v. 10, p. 536 ("Nostratic").

[49] I suspect the author wrestles with his own conscience when he has Queen Gertrude beg: "O Hamlet, speak no more. Thou turnst mine eyes into my very soul, And there I see such black and grained spots As will not leave their tinct." *Hamlet*, act 3, sc. 4. In a pervasively racist time and milieu, this author dares to

(footnote continued on next page)

seem to want to celebrate a more politically correct and palatable author—good sweet Will, man of the people, hale fellow well met. But in doing so, they take the easy way out.

It is not snobbery but simply realistic to observe that the works of Shakespeare "suggest an author of privileged background—one who not only received the best education available, but who also knew court life, traveled widely, and enjoyed other advantages beyond the reach of a man of rustic origins, however intelligent."[50] Nor is it snobbery to admit the glaringly obvious mismatch between the known facts of Shakspere's life and the content and ambience of the Shakespeare canon.

No one doubts ingenious artists of modest origins may achieve supreme artistry—many have. But the issue is what *sort* of art any given genius may create. As Sobran noted: "*A Streetcar Named Desire* may not be as great a play as *Hamlet*, but the author of *Hamlet* couldn't have written it and Tennessee Williams could. This is a matter not of genius but of individuality."[51]

---

(footnote continued from previous page)
depict a dark-skinned hero in *Othello*—flawed, but noble *personally* (not by birth or title)—who defiantly marries a privileged white woman (the ultimate taboo in any white-supremacist society), portraying their passionate love with heart-rending authenticity. Yet he embraces racist and anti-Semitic stereotypes readily enough on other occasions, as in *Titus Andronicus* (Aaron), *The Tempest* (Caliban), and most infamously *The Merchant of Venice*, where yet he cannot resist turning Shylock (his most controversial character) into a compellingly three-dimensional and memorable person.

One hesitates even to broach the author's wildly conflicted attitudes toward women: the comedic (satirical?) celebration of patriarchy in *The Taming of the Shrew*; the bitter venting of misogyny in *Hamlet* (see the aforementioned Gertrude), contrasting with his agonized grieving for Ophelia; and the luminous adoration of richly imagined female characters in (just to give a few examples) *The Rape of Lucrece* (perhaps the first, and a profoundly empathetic, major literary depiction of sexual violence from a woman's perspective—this long-neglected poem richly repays a fresh reading, as I recently found), *Much Ado About Nothing* (Beatrice is an articulate proto-feminist), *As You Like It* (Rosalind), *King Lear* (Cordelia), and *The Winter's Tale* (Hermione and Paulina). See, *e.g.*, note 66; Packer (2015); Winkler (2019).

[50] Sobran, p. 9.
[51] Sobran, p. 9.

The snobbery slander, in the final analysis, is just another diversionary tactic for those Stratfordians who seem unwilling to confront the implausibility of their own theory. For far too long when it comes to the SAQ, orthodox academics, whatever their motives, have largely avoided the simple duty that any serious scholar has: to engage forthrightly with the evidence.

Such scholars, when they deign to mention the SAQ at all, have focused almost entirely on trying to denigrate or psychoanalyze authorship doubters. In its most insulting and ridiculous forms, this has involved suggestions not just of snobbery but outright mental illness and even (as by Rosenbaum above) comparisons to Holocaust denial.[52] The milder version—almost more maddeningly smug and condescending—has been to retreat behind a fog of fashionable academic jargon, analyzing authorship doubt as a purely contingent product of time and culture.[53]

---

[52] See Preface & notes 3, 12; Wildenthal, "Rollett and Shapiro," pp. 7-9, Shahan, "SAC Letters to SBT and RSC re: Wells' False and Libelous Claims About Authorship Doubters"; Edmondson & Wells (2011). On the outrageous comparisons to Holocaust denial, see especially note 56 below.

Samuel Schoenbaum, one of the most respected Shakespeare scholars of the 20th century, penned the classic attack on the mental stability of doubters. He asserted "a pattern of psychopathology ... paranoid structures of thought ... hallucinatory phenomena" and "descent, in a few cases, into actual madness." He argued that such "manifestations of the uneasy psyche" indicate a need "not so much for the expertise of the literary historian as for the insight of the psychiatrist. Dr. Freud beckons us." Schoenbaum, *Shakespeare's Lives*, p. 440, quoted in Sobran, p. 13. This began a chapter, pp. 440-44, in which Schoenbaum patronizingly purported to psychoanalyze Sigmund Freud's own Oxfordian persuasion. Was Schoenbaum suggesting the great psychoanalyst was himself just another nutcase? No, just that "psychoanalytic theory explain[s] the unconscious origins of anti-Stratfordian polemics." Schoenbaum, p. 444. Really? If only someone could figure out what might explain the unhinged polemics of many Stratfordians. See above in text for my own tentative and amateur suggestion.

[53] Typical examples of the latter are Shapiro (2010) and many of the essays in Edmondson & Wells (2013).

## D.  *Beyond Name-Calling: Why Authorship Matters*

Somehow, from the orthodox perspective, the SAQ is never about the simple factual and historical issue at its heart: Does the available evidence, fully considered in context, raise reasonable questions about who actually wrote these particular works of literature? Professor James Shapiro, as so often,[54] illustrates the problem all too well. He spoke at length about the SAQ in a 2016 interview with Brooke Gladstone on the radio show *On the Media*. One cannot begrudge Shapiro his strongly held opinions, but one might have hoped Gladstone, a respected journalist, would try to be a bit more fair.

Sadly, while Gladstone claimed "we won't fix on resolving that [authorship] question," she joined Shapiro in dismissing skeptics with the offensive and nonsensical epithet "Shakespeare deniers" (once by Gladstone, three times by Shapiro).[55] This epithet suggests a comparison to Holocaust deniers.[56] Both Shapiro

---

[54] See the criticisms of his scholarship on the SAQ in Part I & notes 16-17, 28-31, 44; Part II & notes 3, 39-51; Part III.A & notes 11-13.

[55] Gladstone & Shapiro (2016). *On the Media* is produced by New York City's WNYC and syndicated on numerous public radio stations nationwide.

[56] See Preface & note 12 (discussing the contested naming of the disputants in the SAQ and why "denier" is an especially tendentious epithet in this context). My essay "Rollett and Shapiro," pp. 7-9, discussed the crude comparisons of the SAQ to Holocaust denial by Professors Stephen Greenblatt of Harvard University and Gary Taylor of Florida State University. Such comparisons are repeated *ad nauseum* online by internet trolls. Leading academics do set a tone.

Professor Shapiro of Columbia University has claimed to eschew such comparisons as a "mistake." Yet he could not really resist. He piously disclaimed any intention of "draw[ing] a *naive* comparison between the Shakespeare controversy" and various "other issues"—among which he listed Holocaust denial—"except insofar as [the SAQ] too turns on underlying assumptions and notions of evidence that cannot be reconciled." Shapiro (2010), p. 8 (emphasis added). So he actually was invoking a Holocaust denial comparison—just not (so he claimed) a "naive" one. His was more subtle, more cleverly cloaked in plausible deniability.

Does it not occur to these tenured pooh-bahs just how arrogant, reckless, and harmful such comparisons truly are? Leave aside how nasty and unwarranted. Little wonder that arguments about the SAQ have so often, so sadly, become

(footnote continued on next page)

and Gladstone embraced the false meme debunked by this book—that authorship doubts did not arise before the mid-19th century.[57] While they briefly acknowledged a few anti-Stratfordian arguments, both made clear they were "far more interested," "*not* [in] *what* people thought, but *why* they thought it."[58]

And why *do* doubters doubt, in Shapiro's condescending psychoanalytical imagination? First, he suggested it is a mere

---

(footnote continued from previous page)
so strangely and needlessly bitter, given such outrageous overkill. Does it not occur to these professors—who really should know better—how much the comparison insults and disrespects the victims of the Holocaust by linking denial to a legitimate debate about literary history? Does it not occur to them that this enhances the credibility of those who deny or question the reality of the Holocaust by linking them to those with incomparably more reasonable, well-founded, and morally responsible questions about Shakespeare authorship?

Is it even minimally responsible or reasonable (let alone "naive") to compare extensively documented events within living memory—and uncountable thousands of contemporaneous, detailed, written and oral testimonials—with far more obscure and murky aspects of 16th and 17th century literary history, as to which all witnesses died hundreds of years ago, surviving documentation is scarce, and what there is, difficult to interpret?

Holocaust denial is a disturbing subject meriting careful study. This book can hardly do justice to it or the broader problem of irrational denialism. Both offer cautionary lessons for authorship doubters—and for any skeptic venturing to question a dominant mainstream view in a rational and responsible way. The literature on Holocaust denial is vast, but excellent overviews are provided in Professor Deborah Lipstadt's indispensable book, and, *e.g.*, Shermer, *Why People Believe Weird Things*, ch. 13, pp. 188-210.

Anyone who seriously studies and compares Holocaust denial and the SAQ will be struck far more by their profound differences, not similarities. Modern authorship doubters, for more than 150 years, have included thousands of distinguished scholars, judges, and other highly educated, thoughtful, well-informed, and decent people (including many Jews, not least Sigmund Freud as discussed in the text)—some of whom lost family members or other loved ones to the Holocaust. We do not deserve to be linked to Holocaust deniers. More importantly, *they do not deserve to be linked to us.*

[57] Hearing them repeat this canard when I listened to the interview in December 2016 was the last straw that made me realize I *had* to write this book.

[58] Gladstone & Shapiro (2016) (first quotation by Gladstone, second by Shapiro) (emphases added). Gladstone led into Shapiro's statement by saying: "[W]e won't fix on resolving that [authorship] question. We're far more interested in the way that war has been waged across centuries." This was consistent with the primary focus of Shapiro's 2010 book, in which he mainly analyzed the SAQ as a cultural phenomenon, making hardly any serious effort to engage its merits.

infantile obsession, mockingly imitating the childish voice of a fourth-grader—apparently an impressively well-informed young student—who dared to ask him an authorship question. Shapiro suggested he felt inhibited from bullying that innocent young questioner into silence, "like I do in my Columbia classrooms, and say, that's rubbish and I'll fail you if you ask that question again."

We must assume, I suppose, giving Shapiro the benefit of the doubt, that this was sarcastic humor. But his offhand comment, even if a joke, is revealing about the level of orthodox conformity that chills any discussion of the SAQ in academia. Would even an adult student hearing this, who perhaps hoped to obtain Shapiro's coveted support as a mentor, or his supervision of a thesis, feel free to openly express authorship doubts?

Threats of ridicule, leave aside a failing grade, are a very effective social sanction. In fact, like name-calling, they constitute a form of psychological bullying. Most authorship doubters among Shapiro's students probably stay fearfully closeted. Does he truly feel comfortable about that? What is it about the SAQ that reduces even leading public intellectuals, even professors at our finest universities, to this kind of irrational fever? As a career teacher myself, I find it deeply troubling.

Shapiro then mentioned what he conceded were "some of the smartest people" in the history of authorship doubt: "Mark Twain, Sigmund Freud, Henry James, Helen Keller, it's a long list." Indeed it is. And yes, speaking of infantile obsessions, Shapiro the amateur shrink went on to psychoanalyze Freud.[59] How do you spell *chutzpah* again?

But why—*why*—did this long line of brilliant, diverse, and thoughtful people join what Shapiro called "this company of Shakespeare deniers"? Well, according to Shapiro, "for really complicated and very interesting and sometimes sad reasons" they apparently somehow just "had to deny his authorship."

---

[59] Following unwisely in Schoenbaum's footsteps. See note 52.

At this point, Gladstone interrupted to ask whether the SAQ might "start with the fact [that] there's very little documentary evidence" for the Stratfordian theory. By gosh, she might be on to something there. Could it be that people of this caliber might actually be swayed by a reasoned assessment of facts?

But Gladstone promptly backed off, as Shapiro's own students perhaps often feel compelled to do, when he kept talking right over her, recycling the stock Stratfordian claim that we allegedly have more relevant evidence about Shakespeare than about most of his peers. We don't.[60] And so it goes.

Instead of scorning the SAQ, academics like Professor Shapiro, Professor Marino, Sir Stanley Wells, and Sir Jonathan Bate should be grateful for the intellectual challenge it poses. They should heed Carl Sagan, the great astronomer and exponent of science and rational inquiry, who pointed out that "reasoned criticism of a prevailing belief is a service to the proponents of that belief; if they are incapable of defending it, they are well advised to abandon it." Sagan's most telling point: "*It does not matter what reason the proponent has for advancing his ideas or what prompts his opponents to criticize them: all that matters is whether the ideas are right or wrong, promising or retrogressive.*"[61]

---

[60] See Part I (citing and discussing Price's demolition of that false meme).

[61] Sagan, pp. 82-83 (pp. 90-97, pap. ed. 1980), quoted in Danner, p. 143 (emphasis added here). I am a longtime admirer of Sagan and grateful to be alerted to this quotation by Danner (a Stratfordian scholar). See also Part II & note 37 (quoting another Sagan insight). Sagan's comments began a lengthy chapter in which he chided his fellow astronomers for failing to patiently engage on the merits (as he proceeded to do) with the scientifically unsound ideas (as he patiently showed) of Immanuel Velikovsky. Shakespeare authorship doubts (and the Oxfordian theory) are incomparably far better grounded in evidence and logic than Velikovsky's theories, but Sagan's point was that even if a theory seems highly suspect, it is best to stick to a reasoned response on the merits. Ridicule and *ad hominem* attacks are generally wrong and counterproductive.

Danner's essay is a thoughtful critique of the prevailing orthodox academic attitude to the SAQ. The fact that Danner, p. 144 n. 4, apparently thought the anti-Stratfordian view was refuted by Irvin Matus (1994), and the Oxfordian theory by Professor Alan Nelson (2003) (in fact, Nelson barely even pretended to

(footnote continued on next page)

We authorship doubters find it very frustrating that most Shakespeare scholars do not take the SAQ seriously. But we do enjoy the satisfaction of knowing their frustration when the first question they are often asked, again and again and again, around the great globe itself—by taxi drivers, by schoolchildren (as Shapiro found), by strangers at parties—is whether Shakspere of Stratford really was the true author.[62] Orthodox scholars need to focus their minds on why this question has persisted more than 425 years and is clearly not going away. Here's a clue: It's real and it's important. Authorship matters.

We doubters do not dispute that one can enjoy the plays and poems without worrying about who wrote them. We do not expect most people to share our unusual degree of fascination with the issue. We ourselves often put it aside to just revel in the art. Nor do we expect Stratfordians to abruptly alter or discard their long-held views. But there is plainly—at a bare minimum—a serious, reasonable, and interesting issue to be debated here.

The suggestion often heard that "it doesn't matter who the author was, we have the works and that's enough," is singularly unpersuasive. It is also deeply puzzling. As noted in the Preface, should not the brilliance of these works *heighten* (not *reduce*) our interest in their true author? Orthodox scholars can hardly disclaim interest in the authorship question when they are constantly churning out fascinating (if dubious) new (co-)authorship theories of their own, as discussed in Part III.B.

In any event, the issue is ultimately one of historical *truth*— which has an absolute, intrinsic, and unchanging value of its own.

---

(footnote continued from previous page)
engage its merits), merely shows that Danner needs to read more on the subject, including the ample groundbreaking scholarship published in just the last 16 years since Nelson's biased biography.

[62] See, *e.g.*, Bate, *Genius*, p. 65 ("It is the first question which the professional Shakespearean is always asked in casual conversation outside the walls of the academy—who wrote the plays?"); Bate & Reid (2017 video interview) (Bate, at the outset, noting taxi drivers asking such questions).

As Edward de Vere wrote near the end of his life—one of many lines in his letters and known early poetry that resonate power-fully with the Shakespeare canon—"truth is truth though never so old, and time cannot make that false which was once true."[63] It is a matter not merely of truth but of basic justice to be sure we are honoring the actual artist.

Leave aside that most lovers of literature find that learning more about a writer's life and social context deepens and enriches our appreciation of the writings. And how can we understand the social context of the artist if we remain deeply unsure who that artist was? No wonder literary biography is an enduringly popular genre. Why should Shakespeare, arguably the greatest writer in human history, be an exception?

As Katherine Chiljan aptly summed up: "If the true biography of one of the greatest minds of Western civilization does not matter, then whose does?"[64]

Behind all the derision and dismissal of the SAQ lurks a troubling implied message: Just pipe down, move along, stop worrying about it, and accept the official story. "Quit these pretentious things." Well—no. We doubters refuse to "just punch the clock."[65]

---

[63] Quoted in Fowler, p 771 (letter to Robert Cecil, May 7, 1603); see also "Twenty Poems" (2018); Stritmatter, *Poems of Edward de Vere* (2019).
   As Waugh put it, "From the Pulpit" (2015), p. 4:

> History needs to be true and accurate if it is to serve any purpose at all. To plead that Shakespearean biography does not matter since it does not affect one's personal enjoyment of his works displays not only a gross disregard for the concept and purpose of biography, but a myopic and wholly self-centered confusion of history and private, personal responses to aesthetic stimuli.

[64] Chiljan, p. 340.
[65] The quotations are from lyrics sung by Régine Chassagne in Arcade Fire's haunting song, "Sprawl II (Mountains Beyond Mountains)," in their 2010 album *The Suburbs:* "They heard me singing and they told me to stop. Quit these pretentious things and just punch the clock."

To be sure, our troubled world will always have more pressing problems that demand most of our attention, most of the time. But the mystery of art and its creation will always be profoundly important to the human condition. Tina Packer, a Stratfordian whose *Women of Will* is an often-perceptive meditation, notes the enduring fascination with "*who* [this author] is; and why he has lived and is living and will live, as long as human beings are on this planet."[66] It will be a lamentable day if we ever cease to care about the true identity and life of this artist—one who, as Ben Jonson put it so well, "was not of an age, but for all time!"[67]

The evidence surveyed in this book shows that many people during Elizabethan and Jacobean times, in the age when the works of Shakespeare were actually written and published, had doubts and questions about their authorship. The questions they raised in their time continue to merit our study in our time.

---

[66] Packer (2015), p. xii (emphasis added). Though insightful, Packer's book is also a classic example of the distorting effects of Stratfordian assumptions, as she constantly and awkwardly tries to shoehorn her analysis of the author's vision of women into Shakspere's ill-fitting and unpromising biography. It is sad to contemplate the synergy Packer might have gained from considering the biography of Edward de Vere, which *overflows* with far more suggestive information about *his* relationships with women, including the female sovereign with whom we know he interacted extensively (see Cleopatra among other characters), his mother (who during his adolescence remarried not long after his father's death—sound familiar?), two wives (the first of whom, who died young, he accused of infidelity before later reconciling—sound familiar?), three daughters among whom he split his ancestral inheritance (sound familiar?), and at least one headstrong lover (Anne Vavasour) of whom we know for sure, with ample grounds to suspect others of both sexes. See note 49, and Part I, note 4.

[67] *First Folio*, p. 10.

# BIBLIOGRAPHY

Readers may wish to consult the pdf of this Bibliography, part of the excerpts of this book freely available online (https://ssrn.com/abstract=3007393), in order to click directly on the hotlinks available for many of the sources below.

Anonymous works (even if commonly attributed), collective works with no primary designated author(s) or editor(s), and standard reference works with multiple authors and editors, are alphabetized by title (disregarding "A," "The," *etc.*). Modern editions of works credited to "Shakespeare" or Edward de Vere are alphabetized by editor(s) (if designated), as well as under "Shakespeare" or "Vere." All other works are alphabetized by designated author (whether pseudonymous or not), or by editor if no overall author is designated, or by co-author(s) or co-editor(s). Works by the same author or editor are generally listed in order of date of original publication. For internet sources, the dates when they were last updated are provided only where relevant, as in the discussion of SAQ-related internet articles in Part II. Otherwise, it should be understood that all citations to internet sources are to the versions available on May 10, 2019, when the manuscript of this book was finalized.

Ackroyd, Peter, *Shakespeare: The Biography* (2005).

Akrigg, G.P.V., *Shakespeare and the Earl of Southampton* (1968).

Alexander, Mark André, "Shakespeare's Knowledge of Law: A Journey Through the History of the Argument," *Oxfordian* 4 (2001), p. 51 (https://shakespeareoxfordfellowship.org/wp-content/uploads/Oxfordian2001_Alexander_Shx_Law.pdf).

_____, ed., *Shakespeare Authorship Sourcebook* (https://sourcetext.com/sourcebook).

_____, ed. See Greenwood, *Shakespeare's Law and Latin* (1916, rep. 2013).

Allen, Don Cameron, ed. See Meres, *Palladis Tamia* (1598, rep. 1933).

Anderson, Mark, "Revisiting 'Apis Lapis'," *Shakespeare Oxford Newsletter* 34:4 (Winter 1999), p. 19 (https://shakespeareoxfordfellowship.org/wp-content/uploads/2014/03/SOSNL_1998_4.pdf).

_____, *"Shakespeare" By Another Name: The Life of Edward de Vere, Earl of Oxford, the Man Who Was Shakespeare* (2005) (cited as Anderson) (third, latest, and best comprehensive scholarly biography of Vere). See also Ward (1928), A. Nelson (2003), and Green's concise biography on Green, *Oxford Authorship Site*.

Anderson, Mark & Roger Stritmatter (in *Shakespeare Matters*), "The Potent Testimony of Gabriel Harvey," 1:2 (Winter 2002), p. 26 (https://shakespeareoxfordfellowship.org/wp-content/uploads/2013/08/SM1.2.pdf), "Ross's Supererogation," 1:3 (Spring 2002), p. 28 (https://shakespeareoxfordfellowship.org/wp-content/uploads/2013/08/SM1.3.pdf) (online reprint with endnote citations, on *Shakespeare Oxford Fellowship*, https://shakespeareoxfordfellowship.org/terry-ross-supererogation), and "More on Pierce Penniless," 2:2 (Winter 2003), p. 26 (https://shakespeareoxfordfellowship.org/wp-content/uploads/2013/08/SM2.2.pdf) (first article credited to Anderson & Stritmatter; second article to Anderson with contributions by Stritmatter; final 2003 article to Anderson alone) (cited collectively as Anderson & Stritmatter, "Harvey").

Anderson, Mark, Alexander Waugh & Alex McNeil, eds., *Contested Year: Errors, Omissions and Unsupported Statements in James Shapiro's "The Year of Lear: Shakespeare in 1606"* (Amazon Kindle, 2016) (https://amazon.com/Contested-Year-Unsupported-Statements-Shakespeare-ebook/dp/B01BGAMI9S).

Anderson, Mark (*a different author*, not known to be a Shakespeare authorship doubter and not to be confused with "Mark Anderson" above), "Defining Society: The Function of Character Names in Ben Jonson's Early Comedies," *Literary Onomastics Studies* 8 (1981), art. 19, p. 180 (https://digitalcommons.brockport.edu/los/vol8/iss1/19).

Angell, Pauline K., "Light on the Dark Lady: A Study of Some Elizabethan Libels," *Papers of the Modern Language Society* 53 (1937), p. 652.

Appleton van Dreunen, Elizabeth, *An Anatomy of the Marprelate Controversy, 1588–1596* (2001). See also Stritmatter's review (2002).

Arber, Edward, ed. See *Art of English Poesy* (1589, rep. 1869); Greene, *Menaphon* (1589, rep. 1895); *Tottel's Miscellany* (1557, rep. 1870).

*The Art of English Poesy* (anonymous; widely attributed to George Puttenham) (London: Richard Field, 1589, rep. Edward Arber ed. 1869, https://books.google.com/books?id=ThEJAAAAQAAJ, and as *The Art of English Poesy by George Puttenham: A Critical Edition*, Frank Whigham & Wayne A. Rebhorn eds. 2007) (citations to 2007 edition).

Baca, Nathan, "Wilmot Did Not: The 'First' Authorship Story Called Possible Baconian Hoax," *Shakespeare Matters* 2:4 (Summer 2003), p. 1 (https://shakespeareoxfordfellowship.org/wp-content/uploads/2013/08/SM2.4.pdf).

Bacon, Delia, *The Philosophy of the Plays of Shakspere Unfolded* (Boston: Ticknor & Fields, 1857) (https://books.google.com/books?id=wTI_AAAAYAAJ) (cited as D. Bacon).

Bains, Yashdip S., *The Contention and the True Tragedy: William Shakespeare's First Versions of 2 and 3 Henry VI* (Shimla [Himachal Pradesh, India]: Indian Institute of Advanced Study, Rashtrapati Nivas, 1996).

Baker, Alan, "Simplicity" (2004, rev. 2016) (https://plato.stanford.edu/entries/simplicity), in Zalta, *Stanford Encyclopedia of Philosophy*. See also "Occam's Razor."

Barber, Rosalind, "Shakespeare Authorship Doubt in 1593," *Critical Survey* 21:2 (2009), p. 83.

_____, "Shakespeare and Warwickshire Dialect," *Journal of Early Modern Studies* 5 (2016), p. 91 (http://dx.doi.org/10.13128/JEMS-2279-7149-18084).

_____, "My Shakespeare: Christopher Marlowe," in Leahy (2018), ch. 4, p. 85.

Baron, Dennis, *"Penniless, Groatsworth*, and Shakespeare," *Shakespeare Oxford Newsletter* 55:1 (Winter 2019), p. 16.

Barrell, Charles Wisner, "New Milestone in Shakespearean Research: Contemporary Proof That the Poet Earl of Oxford's Literary Nickname Was 'Gentle Master William'," *Shakespeare Fellowship Quarterly* (U.S.) 5:4 (Oct. 1944), p. 49 (https://shakespeareoxfordfellowship.org/wp-content/uploads/Vol.-V-No.-4-1944-Oct..pdf [*sic*]).

Bate, Jonathan, *Shakespeare and Ovid* (1993).

_____, *The Genius of Shakespeare* (U.K.: Picador, 1997; rev. ed., Oxford UP, 2008) (citations to 2008 edition).

_____, *Soul of the Age: A Biography of the Mind of William Shakespeare* (U.S.: Random House, 2009) (orig. pub. as *Soul of the Age: The Life, Mind and World of William Shakespeare*, U.K.: Viking, 2008) (citations to 2009 U.S. edition).

Bate, Jonathan & Jennifer Reid (interview), Shakespeare Birthplace Trust, "The Shakespeare Authorship Question" (March 21, 2017) (https://youtu.be/JXUg0cbEzaE).

Bate, Jonathan & Alexander Waugh. See Waugh & Bate.

Bedingfield, Thomas, trans. See Cardano, *Comfort*.

Bevington, David, ed., *Troilus and Cressida* (1998, rep. 2012).

Bianchi, Julie Sandys, "Brevity and the Soul of Witlessness," *Shakespeare Oxford Newsletter* 53:4 (Fall 2017), p. 13 (https://shakespearcoxfordfellowship.org/wp-content/uploads/SO-Newsletter-Fall-2017.pdf).

Blayney, Peter W.M., ed. See Shakespeare, *Comedies, Histories, and Tragedies [First Folio]*.

Bloom, Harold, *Shakespeare: The Invention of the Human* (1998).

Blumenfeld, Samuel L., *The Marlowe-Shakespeare Connection: A New Study of the Authorship Question* (2008).

Booth, Stephen, ed., *Shakespeare's Sonnets* (1977, rev. 1978). See also Shakespeare, *Shakespeare's Sonnets* (1609).

Boyle, Bill, "Wikipedia Wars: Is Coverage of the Authorship Question 'Fair and Balanced'?" *Shakespeare Matters* 10:3 (Summer 2011), p. 1 (https://shakespeareoxfordfellowship.org/wp-content/uploads/2013/08/SM10.3.pdf).

_____, ed., *Shakespeare Online Authorship Resources* (SOAR) (https://opac.libraryworld.com/opac/home.php).

Brady, Jennifer & W.H. Herendeen, eds., *Ben Jonson's 1616 Folio* (1991).

Bravin, Jess, "Justice Stevens Renders an Opinion on Who Wrote Shakespeare's Plays," *Wall Street Journal* (April 18, 2009), p. A1 (https://wsj.com/articles/SB123998633934729551).

Brooke, Christopher, *The Ghost of Richard the Third* (1614), rep. in Brooke, *Complete Poems* (Grosart ed. 1872), pp. 37-156 (citations to 1872 edition).

_____, *The Complete Poems of Christopher Brooke* (Alexander B. Grosart ed. 1872), in Grosart, *Miscellanies* (1876), v. 4, pp. 9-238.

Brooks, Alden, *Will Shakspere and the Dyer's Hand* (1943).

Buckley, William E., ed. See Edwards, *"Cephalus and Procris" & "Narcissus"*.

Bull, George, ed. See Castiglione, *Courtier*.

Camden, William, *Remains of a Greater Work, Concerning Britain* (London: Simon Waterson, 1605, rep. as *Remains Concerning Britain*, Robert D. Dunn ed. 1984) (citations to 1984 edition).

Campbell, Harry, "Shakspere's Will and (Missing) Inventory," *Shakespeare Oxford Newsletter* 53:4 (Fall 2017), p. 16 (https://shakespeareoxfordfellowship.org/wp-content/uploads/SO-Newsletter-Fall-2017.pdf).

Cardano (Cardanus), Girolamo, *De Consolatione [Comfort]* (orig. pub. in Latin, Venice, 1542, rep. Thomas Bedingfield trans., London: Thomas Marsh, 1573, https://books.google.com/books?id=T2MgAQAAMAAJ; rev. London: Thomas Marsh, 1576) (citations to 1573 edition as Cardano, *Comfort*).

Carroll, D. Allen, "Reading the 1592 *Groatsworth* Attack on Shakespeare," *Tennessee Law Review* 72:1 (2004), p. 277.

_____, ed. See Greene, *Groats-Worth of Wit* (1592, rep. 1994).

*Cassell's Latin Dictionary* (5th ed. 1968) (rev. & ed. by Donald P. Simpson).

Casson, John & William D. Rubinstein, *Sir Henry Neville Was Shakespeare: The Evidence* (2016). See also James & Rubinstein (2005, rep. 2006); Casson, Rubinstein & Ewald (2018); Green, "Neville Myths" (2019).

Casson, John, William D. Rubinstein & David Ewald, "Our Shakespeare: Henry Neville, 1562–1615," in Leahy (2018), ch. 5, p. 113. See also James & Rubinstein (2005, rep. 2006); Casson & Rubinstein (2016); Green, "Neville Myths" (2019).

Castiglione, Baldassare, *Il Cortegiano [The Courtier]* (orig. pub. in Italian, Venice: Aldine Press, 1528, rep. Thomas Hoby trans. [English] 1561, Bartholomew Clerke trans. [Latin] 1572, and as *The Book of the Courtier*, George Bull ed. & trans. [English] 1967, rev. 1976, rep. Penguin, 2003) (citations to 2003 edition as Castiglione, *Courtier*).

Chambers, Edmund K., ed., *The Tragedy of Hamlet, Prince of Denmark* (Boston: Heath, 1895) (https://books.google.com/books?id=low9AAAAYAAJ).

_____, *William Shakespeare: A Study of Facts and Problems* (2 vols., 1930).

Chettle, Henry, *Kind-Heart's Dream: Containing Five Apparitions With Their Invectives Against Abuses Reigning* (London: William Wright, 1592, rep. Edward F. Rimbault ed., in *Early English Poetry, Ballads, and Popular Literature of the Middle Ages*, 1841, v. 5, https://books.google.com/books?id=v24JAAAAQAAJ) (citations to 1841 edition).

_____, *England's Mourning Garment* (London: Thomas Millington, 1603, rep. Robert Detobel ed. n.d., on Kreiler, *Anonymous Shake-speare*, http://www.anonymous-shakespeare.com/cms/index.293.0.1.html) (citations to Detobel edition).

_____. See also Greene, *Groats-Worth of Wit* (1592) (of which Chettle was transcriber, printer, and possible ghostwriter).

Chiljan, Katherine, *Shakespeare Suppressed: The Uncensored Truth About Shakespeare and His Works* (2011, rev. 2016) (cited as Chiljan to 2016 edition).

_____, "Origins of the Pen Name 'William Shakespeare' " (Shakespeare Oxford Fellowship Conference Presentation, Sept. 26, 2015) (posted on YouTube Dec. 13, 2015, https://youtu.be/ezk1B-airWI) (cited as Chiljan, "Origins").

Chow, Winston. See Hess, "Shakespeare Cipher Systems."

Churchill, R.C. (Reginald Charles), *Shakespeare and His Betters: A History and a Criticism of the Attempts Which Have Been Made to Prove That Shakespeare's Works Were Written by Others* (1958).

Clarke, Barry, "My Shakespeare—Francis Bacon," in Leahy (2018), ch. 7, p. 163.

Cleave, Julia, "Seeing Double: Early Doubters of Shakespeare's Identity," *De Vere Society Newsletter* 21:2 (May 2014), p. 32 (http://deveresociety.co.uk/articles/NL-2014may.pdf).

Clerke, Bartholomew, trans. See Castiglione, *Courtier*.

Cole, Jan, Letter (on *The Ghost of Richard the Third* by Christopher Brooke), *De Vere Society Newsletter* 21:1 (Jan. 2014), p. 19 (https://deveresociety.co.uk/articles/NL-2014jan.pdf) (cited as Cole, Letter).

_____, "Who Was 'the Late English Ovid'?" *De Vere Society Newsletter* 21:2 (May 2014), p. 24 (http://deveresociety.co.uk/articles/NL-2014may.pdf) (cited as Cole).

Cook, Hardy M., "A Selected Reading List," in Edmondson & Wells (2013), p. 241.

Cott, Jonathan (interview), "Sam Shepard on Working With Dylan, Why Jim Morrison Has No Sense of Humor," *Rolling Stone* (Dec. 18, 1986) (https://www.rollingstone.com/culture/features/sam-shepard-the-rolling-stone-interview).

Cragg, Cecil, ed. See Lefranc, *Under the Mask of William Shakespeare* (1918–19, rep. 1988).

Crider, Andrew, "Is Ben Jonson's *De Shakespeare Nostrati* a Depiction of Edward de Vere?" *Shakespeare Oxford Newsletter* 51:3 (Summer 2015), p. 19 (https://shakespeareoxfordfellowship.org/wp-content/uploads/SO-Newsletter-Summer-2015.pdf).

Crosse, Henry, *Virtue's Commonwealth, or The Highway to Honor* (London: John Newbery, 1603, rep. Alexander B. Grosart ed. 1878, https://books.google.com/books?id=TKo-AQAAMAAJ) (citations to 1878 edition).

Cutting, Bonner Miller, "Shakespeare's Will ... Considered Too Curiously," *Brief Chronicles* 1 (2009), p. 169 (https://shakespeareoxfordfellowship.org/wp-content/uploads/Cutting-Will.pdf), rep. in Shahan & Waugh (2013), ch. 5, p. 58; Cutting (2018), ch. 2, p. 27.

_____, "A Contest of Wills: Reviewing Shapiro's Reviewers," *Shakespeare Matters* 9:3 (Fall 2010), p. 12 (https://shakespeareoxfordfellowship.org/wp-content/uploads/2013/08/SM9.3.pdf), reviewing Shapiro (2010), rep. in Cutting (2018), ch. 1, p. 17.

_____, "Alas, Poor Anne: Shakespeare's 'Second-Best Bed' in Historical Perspective," *Oxfordian* 13 (2011), p. 76 (https://shakespeareoxfordfellowship.org/wp-content/uploads/Oxfordian2011_cutting_poor_anne.pdf), rep. in Cutting (2018), ch. 3, p. 59.

_____, Book Review, *Brief Chronicles* 3 (2011), p. 272 (print version) (online version, p. 267, https://shakespeareoxfordfellowship.org/wp-content/uploads/Detobel-Review.pdf), reviewing Detobel, *Concealed Poet* (2010).

_____, "Evermore in Subjection: Edward de Vere and Wardship in Early Modern England," *Oxfordian* 18 (2016), p. 65 (https://shakespeareoxfordfellowship.org/wp-content/uploads/TOX18_Bonner_Cutting_Wardship.pdf), rep. in Cutting (2018), ch. 5, p. 105, and ch. 6, p. 119.

_____, "A Sufficient Warrant: Censorship, Punishment, and Shakespeare in Early Modern England," *Oxfordian* 19 (2017), p. 69 (https://shakespeareoxfordfellowship.org/wp-content/uploads/TOX19_Cutting_Sufficient_Warrant.pdf), rep. in Cutting (2018), ch. 7, p. 133.

_____, "Edward de Vere's Tin Letters" (Shakespeare Oxford Fellowship Conference Presentation, Oct. 14, 2017) (posted on YouTube Jan. 22, 2018, https://youtu.be/M_heshWne8o).

_____, *Necessary Mischief: Exploring the Shakespeare Authorship Question* (2018).

Danner, Bruce, "The Anonymous Shakespeare: Heresy, Authorship, and the Anxiety of Orthodoxy," in Starner & Traister (2011), ch. 7, p. 143.

Davies, John (of Hereford), *Microcosmos: The Discovery of the Little World, With the Government Thereof* (Oxford: Joseph Barnes, 1603), excerpted in A. Nelson, "Davies, *Microcosmos*" (2017) (https://shakespearedocumented.folger.edu/exhibition/document/microcosmos-john-davies-hereford-alludes-shakespeare), on *Shakespeare Documented*.

_____, *Humour's Heaven on Earth: With the Civil Wars of Death and Fortune, as Also the Triumph of Death* (1609), excerpted in A. Nelson, "Davies, *Humour's Heaven*" (2016) (https://shakespearedocumented.folger.edu/exhibition/document/civil-wars-death-and-fortune-john-davies-hereford-alludes-shakespeare), on *Shakespeare Documented*.

_____, *The Scourge of Folly* (London: Richard Redmer, *c.* 1610–11), excerpted in "*The Scourge of Folly:* John Davies of Hereford Praises William Shakespeare" (updated 2017) (https://shakespearedocumented.folger.edu/exhibition/document/scourge-folly-john-davies-hereford-praises-william-shakespeare), on *Shakespeare Documented*.

Davis, Frank M., "Shakespeare's Medical Knowledge: How Did He Acquire It?" *Oxfordian* 3 (2000), p. 45 (https://shakespeareoxfordfellowship.org/wp-content/uploads/Oxfordian2000_Davis_Medical_Knowledge.pdf).

_____, "Greene's *Groats-worth of Witte:* Shakespere's Biography?" *Oxfordian* 11 (2009), p. 137 (https://shakespeareoxfordfellowship.org/wp-content/uploads/Oxfordian2009_Davis_Groatsworth.pdf).

_____, "Shakspere's Six Accepted Signatures," in Shahan & Waugh (2013), ch. 2, p. 29.

De Grazia, Margreta, "The Scandal of Shakespeare's Sonnets," in Schiffer (1999), p. 89 (orig. pub. *Shakespeare Survey* 46, 1994, p. 35) (citations to 1999 reprint).

De Luna, Barbara N., *The Queen Declined: An Interpretation of* Willobie His Avisa (1970).

De Vere, Edward. See Vere, Edward de.

*De Vere Society* (https://deveresociety.co.uk/public).

Detobel, Robert, "Melicertus," in Malim (2004), ch. 25, p. 223.

_____, *Shakespeare: The Concealed Poet* (privately printed, Germany, April 2010) (assisted by K.C. Ligon), reviewed by Cutting (2011). See my own book, Part IV.2.g, p. 101 n. 108, noting Stritmatter's apparent reliance on this book by Detobel. By the great kindness of my Oxfordian colleague Jan Scheffer in the Netherlands, I have just obtained a copy of this book by Detobel, after the manuscript of my own book was finalized (thus too late to discuss herein). It remains awkward to cite in any event, since not widely available, a situation that hopefully may be remedied soon. This book appears, among other things, to provide important additional details and discussion of Thomas Nashe's hints (in pamphlets published in 1592–96) that "Shakespeare" was indeed Edward de Vere (Earl of Oxford). See Part IV.3; Detobel, *Concealed Poet*, pt. 3, chs. 2-4, pp. 133-77.

_____, "Henry Chettle's Apology Revisited," *Shakespeare Matters* 12:3 (Summer 2013), p. 14 (https://shakespeareoxfordfellowship.org/wp-content/uploads/Detobel.Henry-Chettle-Apology-Revisited.pdf).

_____, ed. See Chettle, *England's Mourning Garment* (1603); Greene, *Menaphon* (1589).

"Detobel, Robert: In Memoriam" (Sept. 26, 2018) (https://shakespeareoxfordfellowship.org/in-memoriam-robert-detobel).

Detobel, Robert & K.C. Ligon, "Francis Meres and the Earl of Oxford," *Brief Chronicles* 1 (2009), p. 97 (https://shakespeareoxfordfellowship.org/wp-content/uploads/MeresOxford.DetobelLigon.pdf).

Donaldson, Ian, *Ben Jonson: A Life* (2011).

Doyle, Arthur Conan, *The Complete Sherlock Holmes* (Doubleday, 1930, rep. 1988) (citations to 1988 edition).

Dudley, Michael, Gary Goldstein & Shelly Maycock, "All That Is Shakespeare Melts Into Air," *Oxfordian* 19 (2017), p. 195 (https://shakespeareoxfordfellowship.org/wp-content/uploads/TOX19_Dudley_Goldstein_Maycock_Review.pdf), reviewing Taylor & Egan (2017).

Duncan-Jones, Katherine, *Ungentle Shakespeare: Scenes From His Life* (2001).

Dunn, Robert D., ed. See Camden, *Remains* (1605, rep. 1984).

Dutton, Richard, *William Shakespeare: A Literary Life* (1989).

Eagan-Donovan, Cheryl (director, writer & producer), *Nothing Is Truer Than Truth* (2018) (documentary film) (https://vimeo.com/201559620).

Edmondson, Paul, " 'The Shakespeare Establishment' and the Shakespeare Authorship Discussion," in Edmondson & Wells (2013), ch. 19, p. 225.

Edmondson, Paul & Stanley Wells, *Shakespeare Bites Back: Not So Anonymous* (ebook, 2011) (http://bloggingshakespeare.com/shakespeare-bites-back-the-book).

_____, eds., *Shakespeare Beyond Doubt: Evidence, Argument, Controversy* (2013).

Edwards, Richard, ed. See *Paradise of Dainty Devices*.

Edwards, Thomas, *"Cephalus and Procris" & "Narcissus"* (William E. Buckley ed., London: Nichols, 1882) (https://archive.org/details/cu31924013121045).

Egan, Gabriel & Gary Taylor. See Taylor & Egan.

Ellis, David, *The Truth About William Shakespeare: Fact, Fiction and Modern Biographies* (2012).

*Envy's Scourge, and Virtue's Honour* (by "M.L.") (London: Thomas East or Thomas Snodham [?], *c.* 1605–15) (unique known copy held by Princeton University Library, https://catalog.princeton.edu/catalog/3853886), rep. in Peterson (2010), pp. 311-25. See also Kernan (1986); Peterson (1986); Roche (1986); Smith (1986).

Erne, Lukas, "Biography and Mythography: Rereading Chettle's Alleged Apology to Shakespeare," *English Studies* 79:5 (1998), p. 430.

_____, *Shakespeare as Literary Dramatist* (2003, 2d ed. 2013) (citations to 2013 edition).

Ewald, David. See Casson, Rubinstein & Ewald (2018).

Eyre, Hermione. See Waugh & Bate (2017 debate).

Fagone, Jason, *The Woman Who Smashed Codes: A True Story of Love, Spies, and the Unlikely Heroine Who Outwitted America's Enemies* (2017) (biography of Elizebeth [*sic*] Friedman). See also Friedman & Friedman.

Farina, William, *De Vere as Shakespeare: An Oxfordian Reading of the Canon* (2006).

Farey, Peter, "Playing Dead: An Updated Review of the Case for Christopher Marlowe," *Oxfordian* 11 (2009), p. 83 (https://shakespeareoxfordfellowship.org/wp-content/uploads/Oxfordian2009_Farey_Marlow.pdf).

Feldman, Sabrina, *The Apocryphal William Shakespeare: Book One of A "Third Way" Shakespeare Authorship Scenario* (2011).

_____, "A Response to W. Ron Hess, 'Did Shakespeare Have a Literary Mentor?',," *Oxfordian* 13 (2011), p. 153 (https://shakespeareoxfordfellowship.org/wp-content/uploads/Oxfordian2011_feldman_response.pdf). See also Hess, "Literary Mentor" (2011).

_____, *Thomas Sackville and the Shakespearean Glass Slipper: Book Two of A "Third Way" Shakespeare Authorship Scenario* (2015).

*First Folio.* See Shakespeare, *Comedies, Histories, and Tragedies* (1623).

Fitzgeoffrey, Charles, *Affaniae: Sive Epigrammatum Libri Tres* (orig. pub. in Latin, Oxford: Joseph Barnes, 1601, rep. Dana F. Sutton ed. & trans. 1999, rev. 2006, Philological Museum, University of Birmingham, http://www.philological.bham.ac.uk/affaniae).

Fleay, Frederick G., *A Chronicle History of the Life and Work of William Shakespeare: Player, Poet, and Playmaker* (London: Nimmo, 1886) (https://books.google.com/books?id=FG0JAAAAQAAJ).

Florio, John, *A World of Words* (Italian-English Dictionary) (London: Edward Blount, 1598, rep. Georg Olms Verlag, 1972) (http://www.pbm.com/~lindahl/florio1598/) (rev. & rep. as *Queen Anna's New World of Words*, 1611, https://books.google.com/books?id=5MlKAAAAcAAJ) (citations to 1598 edition).

Folger Shakespeare Library. See *Shakespeare Documented.*

Foster, Donald W., "Master W.H., R.I.P.," *Publications of the Modern Language Association (PMLA)* 102:1 (Jan. 1987), p. 42.

Fowler, William Plumer, *Shakespeare Revealed in Oxford's Letters* (1986).

Fox, Robin, *Shakespeare's Education: Schools, Lawsuits, Theater and the Tudor Miracle* (Gary Goldstein ed. 2012).

Frazier, Kendrick, "From the Editor: From Shakespeare to American Archaeology," *Skeptical Inquirer* 35:6 (Nov.-Dec. 2011), p. 4.

Friedman, William F. & Elizebeth [*sic*] S. Friedman, *The Shakespearean Ciphers Examined* (1957). For a recent biography of Elizebeth Friedman, see Fagone.

"George Greenwood." See "Greenwood, George" (*Wikipedia*).

Gilvary, Kevin, ed., *Dating Shakespeare's Plays: A Critical Review of the Evidence* (2010).

Gilvary, Kevin, *The Fictional Lives of Shakespeare* (2018).

Gladstone, Brooke & James Shapiro (interview), "Our Shakespeare, Ourselves," *On the Media* (WNYC Radio, Dec. 29, 2016) (https://www.wnyc.org/story/our-shakespeare-ourselves-1).

Goldstein, Gary, *Reflections on the True Shakespeare* (2016).

_____, ed. See Moore (2009), Fox (2012), and Magri (2014).

Goldstein, Gary, Michael Dudley & Shelly Maycock. See Dudley, Goldstein & Maycock.

Goldstone, Jack A., "The Latin Inscription on the Stratford Shakespeare Monument Unraveled," *Shakespeare Matters* 11:2 (Spring 2012), p. 1 (https://shakespeareoxfordfellowship.org/wp-content/uploads/2013/08/SM11.2.pdf).

Gordon-Reed, Annette, *Thomas Jefferson and Sally Hemings: An American Controversy* (1997, rev. 1999).

Green, Nina, *The Oxford Authorship Site* (http://www.oxford-shakespeare.com) (including her valuable and concisely documented biography of Edward de Vere, http://www.oxford-shakespeare.com/oxfordsbio.html).

_____, "An Earl in Bondage," *Shakespeare Oxford Newsletter* 40:3 (Summer 2004), p. 1 (https://shakespeareoxfordfellowship.org/wp-content/uploads/2014/03/SOSNL_2004_3.pdf).

_____, "The Fall of the House of Oxford," *Brief Chronicles* 1 (2009), p. 41 (https://shakespeareoxfordfellowship.org/wp-content/uploads/Green.Fall_.of_.House_.Oxford.pdf).

_____, "*Gratulationes Valdinenses*" (n.d.) (http://www.oxford-shakespeare.com/Nashe/Gratulationes_Valdinenses.pdf) (on Gabriel Harvey's 1578 addresses to Queen Elizabeth and various courtiers), on Green, *Oxford Authorship Site* (cited as Green, "Harvey's *Gratulationes*").

_____, "Myths Concerning Sir Henry Neville" (version posted on May 10, 2019) ("Oxmyths and Stratmyths," Section VI, http://www.oxford-shakespeare.com/Oxmyths/MythsSirHenryNeville.pdf), on Green, *Oxford Authorship Site* (cited as Green, "Neville Myths").

_____, "Oxmyths and Stratmyths" (versions posted on May 10, 2019), on Green, *Oxford Authorship Site* (cited as Green, "Myths"):

Section I (http://www.oxford-shakespeare.com/Oxmyths/OxmythsOxford.pdf);

Section II (http://www.oxford-shakespeare.com/Oxmyths/OxmythsShaksper.pdf);

Section III (http://www.oxford-shakespeare.com/Oxmyths/OxmythsOtherindividuals.pdf);

Section IV (http://www.oxford-shakespeare.com/Oxmyths/OxmythsPennameAndPlays.pdf);

Section V (http://www.oxford-shakespeare.com/Oxmyths/MythsHandD.pdf).

Greenblatt, Stephen, *Will in the World: How Shakespeare Became Shakespeare* (2004).

Greene, Robert, *Menaphon* (London: Sampson Clarke, 1589, rep. Edward Arber ed., London: Constable, 1895, https://books.google.com/books?id=Tl4LAAAAIAAJ, and Robert Detobel ed., n.d., without Nashe's preface, on Kreiler, *Anonymous Shakespeare*, http://www.anonymous-shakespeare.com/cms/front_content.php?idart=832).

_____, *Groats-Worth of Wit, Bought With a Million of Repentance* (London: William Wright, 1592 [transcribed, printed, and possibly ghostwritten by Henry Chettle], rep. London: John Lane & New York: Dutton, Bodley Head Quartos, 1923; D. Allen Carroll ed. 1994) (citations to 1923 edition).

"Greenwood, George" (n.d.), *Wikipedia* (https://en.wikipedia.org/wiki/George_Greenwood).

Greenwood, (Granville) George, *The Shakespeare Problem Restated* (London & New York: John Lane, 1908) (https://books.google.com/books?id=h1I4AAAAYAAJ).

_____, *Is There a Shakespeare Problem?* (London & New York: John Lane, 1916) (https://books.google.com/books?id=qBgMAQAAIAAJ).

_____, *Shakespeare's Law and Latin* (London: Watts, 1916, https://www.archive.org/details/shakespeareslaw100gree, rep. Mark André Alexander ed., Amazon Kindle, 2013, https://www.amazon.com/Shakespeares-Law-Latin-Exposed-Robertson-ebook/dp/B0070PFPJE).

_____, *Shakespeare's Law* (London: Cecil Palmer, 1920) (https://books.google.com/books?id=C1UPAAAAQAAJ).

\_\_\_\_\_, *Ben Jonson and Shakespeare* (London: Cecil Palmer, 1921) (https://books.google.com/books?id=D8A8AAAAYAAJ).

\_\_\_\_\_, *The Shakspere Signatures and "Sir Thomas More"* (London: Cecil Palmer, 1924, facsimile rep. Kessinger).

\_\_\_\_\_, *The Stratford Bust and the Droeshout Engraving* (London: Cecil Palmer, 1925, facsimile rep. Kessinger).

Greg, Walter W., *The Shakespeare First Folio: Its Bibliographical and Textual History* (1955).

Grimes, William, "Joseph Sobran, Writer Whom Buckley Mentored, Dies at 64," *New York Times* (Oct. 1, 2010) (https://www.nytimes.com/2010/10/02/books/02sobran.html) (in print, Oct. 2, 2010, p. A17).

Grosart, Alexander B., ed., *Miscellanies of the Fuller Worthies' Library, Vol. 4* (1876) (https://books.google.com/books?id=dHxLAQAAMAAJ).

\_\_\_\_\_. See also Brooke, *Complete Poems* (1872); Crosse, *Virtue's Commonwealth* (1603, rep. 1878); Vere, *Poems of Edward de Vere, Earl of Oxford* (1872).

*GW*. See Greene, *Groats-Worth of Wit* (1592).

Haley, Alex. See Malcolm X, *Autobiography*.

Hamill, John, "The Dark Lady and Her Bastard: An Alternative Scenario," *Shakespeare Oxford Newsletter* 41:3 (Summer 2005), p. 1 (https://shakespeareoxfordfellowship.org/wp-content/uploads/2014/03/SOSNL_2005_3.pdf).

\_\_\_\_\_, "New Light on Willobie His Avisa and the Authorship Question," *Oxfordian* 14 (2012), p. 130 (https://shakespeareoxfordfellowship.org/wp-content/uploads/Oxfordian2012_Hamill_Willobie.pdf).

\_\_\_\_\_, "Antonio Pérez, Penelope Rich, and Avisa" (Shakespeare Oxford Fellowship Conference Presentation, Oct. 13, 2017) (posted on YouTube Jan. 5, 2018, https://youtu.be/cI1IINp4KU2Q).

Hannas, Andrew, "Gabriel Harvey and the Genesis of 'William Shakespeare'," *Shakespeare Oxford Newsletter* 29:1B (Winter 1993), p. 1 (https://shakespeareoxfordfellowship.org/gabriel-harvey-genesis-of-shakespeare).

\_\_\_\_\_, " 'The Rest' Is Not Silence: On Grammar and Oxford in *The Art of English Poesie*," *Ever Reader* 3 (Spring-Summer 1996) (https://shakespeareoxfordfellowship.org/the-rest-not-silence).

Hayes, Donald P., "Social Network Theory and the Claim That Shakespeare of Stratford Was the Famous Dramatist," in Shahan & Waugh (2013), app. C, p. 237.

Herendeen, W.H. & Jennifer Brady. See Brady & Herendeen.

Hess, W. Ron, "Robert Greene's Wit Re-evaluated," *Elizabethan Review* 4:2 (Autumn 1996), p. 41.

\_\_\_\_\_, *The Dark Side of Shakespeare* (http://home.earthlink.net/~beornshall/index.html).

\_\_\_\_\_ (with assistance of Winston Chow), "Stabbing at 'Shakespeare Cipher Systems' and Other Parasites" (2009, rev. 2011) (http://home.earthlink.net/~beornshall/index.html/id26.html), on Hess, *Dark Side of Shakespeare*.

\_\_\_\_\_, "Did Shakespeare Have a Literary Mentor?" *Oxfordian* 13 (2011), p. 146 (https://shakespeareoxfordfellowship.org/wp-content/uploads/Oxfordian2011_Hess_Mentor.pdf). See also Feldman, "Response" (2011), and Feldman, *Sackville* (2015).

Hinman, Charlton, ed. See Shakespeare, *Comedies, Histories, and Tragedies [First Folio]*.

"History of the Shakespeare Authorship Question." See "Shakespeare Authorship Question, History of the" (*Wikipedia*).

Hoby, Thomas, trans. See Castiglione, *Courtier.*

Hoffman, Calvin, *The Murder of the Man Who Was "Shakespeare"* (1955) (citations to Grosset & Dunlap rep. 1960).

Holston, Kim & Warren Hope. See Hope & Holston.

Hope, Warren, Book Review, *Brief Chronicles* 2 (2010), p. 211 (https://shakespeareoxfordfellowship.org/wp-content/uploads/Hope.ContestedWill1.pdf), reviewing Shapiro (2010).

Hope, Warren & Kim Holston, *The Shakespeare Controversy: An Analysis of the Authorship Theories* (2d ed. 2009).

Hoster, Jay, *Tiger's Heart: What Really Happened in the Groats-Worth of Wit Controversy of 1592* (1993).

Hudson, Hoyt H., "Penelope Devereux as Sidney's Stella," *Huntington Library Bulletin*, No. 7 (April 1935).

Hudson, John, "Amelia Bassano Lanier: A New Paradigm," *Oxfordian* 11 (2009), p. 65 (https://shakespeareoxfordfellowship.org/wp-content/uploads/Oxfordian2009_Hudson_Bassano.pdf).

_____, *Shakespeare's Dark Lady—Amelia Bassano Lanier: The Woman Behind Shakespeare's Plays?* (2014).

Hughes, Stephanie Hopkins, *Politicworm: Shakespeare Authorship* (https://politicworm.com).

_____, "The Great Reckoning: Who Killed Christopher Marlowe, and Why?" (1997, rev. 2004) (https://politicworm.files.wordpress.com/2010/07/hughes-the-great-reckoning.pdf), on Hughes, *Politicworm*, rep. in *Oxfordian* 18 (2016), p. 101 (https://shakespeareoxfordfellowship.org/wp-content/uploads/TOX18_Stephainie-Hughes_Reckoning.pdf).

_____, "Robert Greene: King of the Paper Stage" (1997, rev. 2009) (https://politicworm.files.wordpress.com/2009/04/hughes-king-of-the-paper-stage.pdf), on Hughes, *Politicworm*.

_____, " 'Shakespeare's' Tutor: Sir Thomas Smith (1513–1577)," *Oxfordian* 3 (2000), p. 19 (https://shakespeareoxfordfellowship.org/wp-content/uploads/Oxfordian2000_Hughes_Shxs_Tutor.pdf).

_____, "New Light on the Dark Lady," *Shakespeare Oxford Newsletter* 36:3 (Fall 2000), p. 1 (https://shakespeareoxfordfellowship.org/wp-content/uploads/2014/03/SOSNL_2000_4.pdf).

_____, Book Review, *Shakespeare Oxford Newsletter* 41:3 (Summer 2005), p. 2 (https://shakespeareoxfordfellowship.org/wp-content/uploads/2014/03/SOSNL_2005_3.pdf), reviewing Anderson (2005).

_____, "An Oxfordian Response" (to other authorship candidates), *Oxfordian* 11 (2009), p. 99 (https://shakespeareoxfordfellowship.org/wp-content/uploads/Oxfordian2009_Hopkins_Response.pdf).

_____, "Not Without Mustard: Ben Jonson's Clue" (2009) (https://politicworm.com/oxford-shakespeare/to-be-or-not-to-be-shakespeare/why-not-william/the-authorship-question-2/not-without-mustard), on Hughes, *Politicworm*.

Hunter, Thomas, Book Review, *Shakespeare Oxford Newsletter* 46:1 (May 2010), p. 12 (https://shakespeareoxfordfellowship.org/wp-content/uploads/2014/03/SOSNL_2010_1.pdf), reviewing Shapiro (2010).

James, Brenda & William D. Rubinstein, *The Truth Will Out: Unmasking the Real Shakespeare* (U.S.: Regan [HarperCollins], 2006; orig. pub. U.K.: Pearson, 2005) (citations to 2006 U.S. edition). See also Casson & Rubinstein (2016); Casson, Rubinstein & Ewald (2018); Green, "Neville Myths" (2019).

Jiménez, Ramon, "Camden, Drayton, Greene, Hall, and Cooke: Five Eyewitnesses Who Saw Nothing," *Shakespeare Oxford Newsletter* 38:4 (Fall 2002), p. 1 (https://shakespeareoxfordfellowship.org/wp-content/uploads/2014/03/SOSNL_2002_4.pdf), rev. & rep. as Jiménez (2013).

_____, "Shakespeare in Stratford and London: Five More Eyewitnesses Who Saw Nothing," *Shakespeare Oxford Newsletter* 41:1 (Winter 2005), p. 3 (https://shakespeareoxfordfellowship.org/wp-content/uploads/2014/03/SOSNL_2005_1.pdf), rev. & rep. as Jiménez (2013).

_____, "The Case for Oxford Revisited," *Oxfordian* 11 (2009), p. 45 (https://shakespeareoxfordfellowship.org/wp-content/uploads/Oxfordian2009_Jimenez_Revisited.pdf).

_____, "Shakspere in Stratford and London: Ten Eyewitnesses Who Saw Nothing," in Shahan & Waugh (2013), ch. 4, p. 46. See also Jiménez (2002) and Jiménez (2005).

_____, "An Evening at the Cockpit: Further Evidence of an Early Date for *Henry V*," *Oxfordian* 18 (2016), p. 9 (https://shakespeareoxfordfellowship.org/wp-content/uploads/TOX18_Ramon_Jimenez_Cockpit.pdf).

_____, *Shakespeare's Apprenticeship: Identifying the Real Playwright's Earliest Works* (2018).

Jolly, Eddi [Margrethe], "Sc(e)acan, Shack, and Shakespeare," *Oxfordian* 18 (2016), p. 41 (https://shakespeareoxfordfellowship.org/wp-content/uploads/TOX18_Eddi_Jolly_Sceacan.pdf).

Johnson, Paul, *The Birth of the Modern: World Society, 1815-1830* (1991).

Jonson, Ben, *The Works of Benjamin Jonson* (1616) (facsimile available at University of Pennsylvania Libraries' Schoenberg Center for Electronic Text and Image) (SCETI) (http://sceti.library.upenn.edu/index.cfm) (go to "Search Page" and enter "Jonson" and "Works" into author and title fields).

Jowett, John, "Johannes Factotum: Henry Chettle and *Greene's Groatsworth of Wit*," *Papers of the Bibliographical Society of America* 87:4 (Dec. 1993), p. 453.

_____, "Shakespeare as Collaborator," in Edmondson & Wells (2013), ch. 8, p. 88.

Kathman, David, "Shakespeare Wrote Shakespeare," *Oxfordian* 11 (2009), p. 13 (https://shakespeareoxfordfellowship.org/wp-content/uploads/Oxfordian2009_Kathman_Shak_Wrote.pdf).

_____, "Shakespeare and Warwickshire," in Edmondson & Wells (2013), ch. 11, p. 121.

_____, "Chronological List [etc.]" and "List of Non-Literary [etc.]." See below following "The Spelling and Pronunciation of Shakespeare's Name."

_____, "Joseph Sobran's *Alias Shakespeare*: A Selective Critique" (n.d.) (https://shakespeareauthorship.com/sobran.html), on Kathman & Ross, *Shakespeare Authorship Page*.

_____, "Seventeenth-Century References to Shakespeare's Stratford Monument" (n.d.) (http://shakespeareauthorship.com/monrefs.html), on Kathman & Ross, *Shakespeare Authorship Page*.

_____, "Shakespeare's Eulogies" (n.d.) (http://shakespeareauthorship.com/eulogies.html), on Kathman & Ross, *Shakespeare Authorship Page*.

_____, "Shakespeare's Will" (n.d.) (http://shakespeareauthorship.com/shaxwill.html), on Kathman & Ross, *Shakespeare Authorship Page*.

_____, "The Spelling and Pronunciation of Shakespeare's Name" (n.d.) (http://shakespeareauthorship.com/name1.html), on Kathman & Ross, *Shakespeare Authorship Page* (cited as Kathman, "Spelling").

_____, "Chronological List of References to Shakespeare as Author/Poet/Playwright" (n.d.) (http://shakespeareauthorship.com/name3.html), on Kathman & Ross, *Shakespeare Authorship Page* (cited as Kathman, "Literary Spelling List").

_____, "List of Non-Literary References to William Shakespeare of Stratford-upon-Avon" (n.d.) (https://shakespeareauthorship.com/name2.html), on Kathman & Ross, *Shakespeare Authorship Page* (cited as Kathman, "Non-Literary Spelling List").

_____, "Why I Am Not an Oxfordian" (n.d.) (http://shakespeareauthorship.com/whynot.html), on Kathman & Ross, *Shakespeare Authorship Page* (also pub. *Elizabethan Review* 5:1, 1997, p. 32).

Kathman, David & Tom Reedy. See Reedy & Kathman.

Kathman, David & Terry Ross. See Ross & Kathman.

_____, eds., *The Shakespeare Authorship Page* (http://shakespeareauthorship.com).

Kennedy, Richard, *Between the Lines* (Oxenford Press, 1993) (unpaginated pamphlet).

Kernan, Alvin, *"Enuies Scourge, and Vertues Honour:* A Literary Mystery—The Kindly Satyr," *Princeton University Library Chronicle* 47:2 (Winter 1986), p. 152 (https://www.jstor.org/stable/26404272). See also *Envy's Scourge.*

Kositsky, Lynne & Roger Stritmatter, "A Rebuttal to Tom Reedy and David Kathman's 'How We Know That Shakespeare Wrote Shakespeare'" (Sept. 12, 2004) (https://shakespeareoxfordfellowship.org/rebuttal-to-reedy-and-kathman), on *Shakespeare Oxford Fellowship.*

_____. See also Stritmatter & Kositsky.

Kreiler, Kurt, ed., *Anonymous Shake-speare* (http://www.anonymous-shakespeare.com/cms).

*Last Will. & Testament* (2012). See Wilson & Wilson.

Leahy, William, "Introduction: The Life of the Author," in Leahy, ed., *Shakespeare and His Authors: Critical Perspectives on the Authorship Question* (2010), p. 1.

_____, ed., *My Shakespeare: The Authorship Controversy* (2018).

Lee, Sidney, "Hayward, Sir John (1564?–1627)," in *Dictionary of National Biography*, v. 25, p. 311 (Leslie Stephen & Sidney Lee eds. 1891) (https://books.google.com/books?id=DLscAQAAIAAJ).

_____, ed., *Venus and Adonis, The Rape of Lucrece, The Passionate Pilgrim, Shake-speare's Sonnets, and Pericles, Prince of Tyre* (Oxford UP, 1905) (https://books.google.com/books?id=9Go3AAAAIAAJ) (apparently a one-volume collection, identified on Google Books only as *Venus and Adonis*, but in fact containing facsimile reprints of each of the five named works, including "A Lover's Complaint" with the *Sonnets*, with extensive introductory editorial notes on each, separately and not sequentially paginated).

Lefranc, Abel, *Under the Mask of William Shakespeare* (orig. pub. in French, *Sous le masque de William Shakespeare*, Paris: Payot, 2 vols., 1918–19, rep. Cecil Cragg ed. & trans. 1988).

Lewis, C.S., *The Lion, the Witch and the Wardrobe* (Pauline Baynes illus. 1950, rep. Harper Trophy, 2000) (Book Two, *The Chronicles of Narnia*) (citations to 2000 edition).

Ligon, K.C. & Robert Detobel. See Detobel & Ligon.

Lipstadt, Deborah E., *Denying the Holocaust: The Growing Assault on Truth and Memory* (1993, pap. ed. 1994).

Looney, J. (John) Thomas, *"Shakespeare" Identified in Edward de Vere the Seventeenth Earl of Oxford* (London: Cecil Palmer, 1920, rep. New York: Stokes, 1920, https://books.google.com/books?id=B004AAAAIAAJ; 2d ed., New York: Duell, Sloan & Pearce, 1948; 3d ed., Ruth Loyd Miller ed., Port Washington, N.Y.: Kennikat Press & Jennings, La.: Minos Publishing, 2 vols., 1975; 4th ed., James A. Warren ed., Forever Press, 2018) (cited as Looney to 1920 New York edition; pagination of the annotated and highly recommended 2018 edition is virtually identical).

\_\_\_\_\_, Letter to the Editor, *Bookman's Journal and Print Collector* 2:30 (May 21, 1920), p. 58, rep. in Warren, "Looney in *Bookman's Journal*: Five Letters" (2018), p. 148; Looney, *Collected Articles*, p. 17.

\_\_\_\_\_, " 'Shakespeare': Lord Oxford or Lord Derby?" *National Review* (U.K.) 78 (Feb. 1922), p. 801, rep. in *Shakespeare Oxford Newsletter* 53:2 (Spring 2017), p. 1 (https://shakespeareoxfordfellowship.org/wp-content/uploads/SO-Newsletter-Spring-2017.pdf); Looney, *Collected Articles*, p. 107 (cited as Looney, "Derby").

\_\_\_\_\_, " 'Shakespeare': Was It Oxford, Bacon, or Derby?" *Freethinker* (U.K.) 43:26 (July 1, 1923), p. 412, rep. in Looney, *Collected Articles*, p. 195 (cited as Looney, "Was It Oxford").

\_\_\_\_\_, *"Shakespeare" Revealed: The Collected Articles and Published Letters of J. Thomas Looney* (James A. Warren ed. 2019) (cited as Looney, *Collected Articles*).

\_\_\_\_\_, ed. See Vere, *Poems of Edward de Vere* (1921).

M.L. See *Envy's Scourge, and Virtue's Honour*.

Macray, William D., ed., *The Pilgrimage to Parnassus With the Two Parts of the Return From Parnassus* (Oxford UP, 1886) (https://books.google.com/books?id=khAMAQAAIAAJ). See *Parnassus* plays.

Magri, Noemi, "The Latin Mottoes in Peacham's *Minerva Britanna*," *Elizabethan Review* 7:1 (Spring 1999), p. 65, rep. *De Vere Society Newsletter* (May 1999), p. 3, and in Magri (2014), p. 237 (citations to 2014 reprint).

\_\_\_\_\_, *Such Fruits Out of Italy: The Italian Renaissance in Shakespeare's Plays and Poems* (Gary Goldstein ed. 2014).

Malcolm X & Alex Haley, *The Autobiography of Malcolm X* (1965) (citations to Ballantine rep. 1973).

Malim, Richard, "Oxford the Actor," in Malim (2004), ch. 24, p. 212.

\_\_\_\_\_, "Oxford's View of Shakespeare," in Malim (2004), ch. 27, p. 247.

\_\_\_\_\_, "The Spanish Maze," in Malim (2004), ch. 31, p. 284.

\_\_\_\_\_, *The Earl of Oxford and the Making of "Shakespeare": The Literary Life of Edward de Vere in Context* (2012).

\_\_\_\_\_, et al., eds., *Great Oxford: Essays on the Life and Work of Edward de Vere, 17th Earl of Oxford, 1550-1604* (2004).

Marcotte, Amanda, "The Unsavory Motivations of the Shakespeare Truthers" (Dec. 29, 2014), *Rawstory* (http://www.rawstory.com/2014/12/the-unsavory-motivations-of-the-shakespeare-truthers).

Marino, James J., *Owning William Shakespeare: The King's Men and Their Intellectual Property* (2011).

\_\_\_\_\_, *"Anonymous* Is Terrible, But We're to Blame" (Nov. 1, 2011), *Penn Press Log* (https://pennpress.typepad.com/pennpresslog/2011/11/anonymous-is-terrible-but-were-to-blame-says-shakespearan-scholar-james-marino.html).

\_\_\_\_\_ (as "Doctor Cleveland"), "Shakespeare, Oxford, and the 1%" (Nov. 3, 2011), *Dagblog* (https://dagblog.com/arts-entertainment/shakespeare-oxford-and-1-12098).

\_\_\_\_\_ (as "Doctor Cleveland"), "Shakespeare 'Authorship Debates' and Amateur Scholarship" (Dec. 31, 2014), *Dagblog* (https://dagblog.com/personal/shakespeare-authorship-debates-and-amateur-scholarship-19167).

Martindale, Charles & Michelle Martindale, *Shakespeare and the Uses of Antiquity: An Introductory Essay* (1990).

Matus, Irvin Leigh, *Shakespeare, In Fact* (1994).

May, Steven W., "The Authorship of 'My Mind to Me a Kingdom Is'," *Review of English Studies* 26:104 (1975), p. 385.

_____, "The Poems of Edward de Vere, Seventeenth Earl of Oxford and of Robert Devereux, Second Earl of Essex," *Studies in Philology* 77:5 (1980), p. 5.

_____, "Tudor Aristocrats and the Mythical 'Stigma of Print'," *Renaissance Papers* (1980), on Kathman & Ross, *Shakespeare Authorship Page*, (https://shakespeareauthorship.com/stigma.html).

_____, *The Elizabethan Courtier Poets: The Poems and Their Contexts* (Missouri UP, 1991, rep. Pegasus Press, University of North Carolina at Asheville, 1999) (citations to 1991 edition; 1999 reprint appears identical).

Maycock, Shelly, "Branding the Author: Feigned Authorship Neutrality and the Folger Folio Tour," in Stritmatter, *First Folio Minority Report* (2016), p. 5 (https://shakespeareoxfordfellowship.org/wp-content/uploads/BC_FF_Maycock_Branding-the-Author.pdf).

Maycock, Shelly, Michael Dudley & Gary Goldstein. See Dudley, Goldstein & Maycock.

McCabe, Richard A., ed. See Spenser, *Shorter Poems*.

McCarthy, Dennis, *Here Be Dragons: How the Study of Animal and Plant Distributions Revolutionized Our Views of Life and Earth* (2009).

_____, *North of Shakespeare: The True Story of the Secret Genius Who Wrote the World's Greatest Body of Literature* (2011).

McCarthy, Dennis & June Schlueter, *"A Brief Discourse of Rebellion & Rebels" by George North: A Newly Uncovered Manuscript Source for Shakespeare's Plays* (2018).

McCrea, Scott, *The Case for Shakespeare: The End of the Authorship Question* (2005).

McCrum, Robert, "Who Really Wrote Shakespeare?" *Guardian [Observer]* (March 13, 2010) (https://www.theguardian.com/culture/2010/mar/14/who-wrote-shakespeare-james-shapiro).

McNeil, Alex, Mark Anderson & Alexander Waugh. See Anderson, Waugh & McNeil.

Meres, Francis, *Palladis Tamia* (London: Cuthbert Burby, 1598, rep. Don Cameron Allen ed. 1933, University of Illinois Studies in Language and Literature, vol. 16).

Michell, John, *Who Wrote Shakespeare?* (1996).

Miller, Ruth Loyd, "Ben Jonson and the Arms of Sogliardo," in "Oxfordian Vistas," ch. 3, p. 44, in Looney (Miller ed., 3d ed. 1975), v. 2.

_____, "The First Folio: A Family Affair," in "Oxfordian Vistas," ch. 1, p. 1, in Looney (Miller ed., 3d ed. 1975), v. 2.

_____, ed. See Looney (1920, 3d ed. 1975).

Moore, Peter R., "The Rival Poet of Shakespeare's Sonnets," *Shakespeare Oxford Society Newsletter* 25:4 (Fall 1989), p. 8 (https://shakespeareoxfordfellowship.org/wp-content/uploads/SOSNL-1989.compressed.pdf [pdf p. 69]), rep. in Moore (2009), p. 2, and as "Essex, the Rival Poet of Shakespeare's Sonnets" in *Oxfordian* 18 (2016), p. 133 (https://shakespeareoxfordfellowship.org/wp-content/uploads/TOX18_Peter_Moore_Essex.pdf).

_____, "The Stella Cover-Up," *Shakespeare Oxford Society Newsletter* 29:1A (Winter 1993), p. 12 (https://shakespeareoxfordfellowship.org/wp-content/uploads/SOSNL-1993.compressed.pdf [pdf p. 13]), rep. in Moore (2009), p. 312.

_____, "Oxford, the Order of the Garter, and Shame," *Shakespeare Oxford Newsletter* 32:2 (Spring 1996), p. 1 (https://shakespeareoxfordfellowship.org/wp-content/uploads/2014/03/SOSNL_1996_2.pdf), rep. as "The Earl of Oxford and the Order of the Garter" in Moore (2009), p. 263.

_____, "Recent Developments in the Case for Oxford as Shakespeare" (Shakespeare Oxford Society Conference Presentation, Oct. 1996) (https://www.shakespeareoxfordfellowship.org/developments-in-case), on *Shakespeare Oxford Fellowship*.

_____, *The Lame Storyteller, Poor and Despised: Studies in Shakespeare* (Gary Goldstein ed. 2009).

Mooten, Michael, "*Willobie His Avisa* Decoded" (2010) (https://willobiehisavisadecoded.webs.com).

Morris, Carolyn, "Did Joseph Hall and Ben Jonson Identify Oxford as Shakespeare?" *Oxfordian* 15 (2013), p. 5 (https://shakespeareoxfordfellowship.org/wp-content/uploads/Oxfordian2013_Morris-Oxford-Identified.pdf).

_____, "An Arrogant Joseph Hall and an Angry Edward de Vere in *Virgidemiarum* (1599)," *Brief Chronicles* 7 (2016), p. 33 (https://shakespeareoxfordfellowship.org/wp-content/uploads/BC7_Morris_Virgidemiarum.pdf).

Nashe, Thomas, "To the Gentlemen Students of Both Universities" (preface), in Greene, *Menaphon* (1589, Arber ed. 1895), p. 5.

Nelson, Alan H., *Monstrous Adversary: The Life of Edward de Vere, 17th Earl of Oxford* (2003) (second biography of Vere) (cited as A. Nelson). See also Ward (1928), Anderson (2005), and Green's concise biography on Green, *Oxford Authorship Site*.

_____, "The Civile Wars of Death and Fortune [Humour's Heaven on Earth]: John Davies of Hereford Alludes to Shakespeare" (updated 2016) (https://shakespearedocumented.folger.edu/exhibition/document/civile-wars-death-and-fortune-john-davies-hereford-alludes-shakespeare) (cited as A. Nelson, "Davies, Humour's Heaven"), on *Shakespeare Documented*.

_____, "*Microcosmos:* John Davies of Hereford Alludes to Shakespeare" (updated 2017) (https://shakespearedocumented.folger.edu/exhibition/document/microcosmos-john-davies-hereford-alludes-shakespeare) (cited as A. Nelson, "Davies, *Microcosmos*"), on *Shakespeare Documented*.

_____, "William Shakespeare of Stratford-upon-Avon and London," in Leahy (2018), ch. 1, p. 1 (cited as A. Nelson, "Shakespeare of Stratford").

Nelson, Donald Frederick, "Schurink's Discovery of a Century," *Shakespeare Oxford Newsletter* 44:2 (Spring 2008; issue number misprinted as "1"), p. 10 (https://shakespeareoxfordfellowship.org/wp-content/uploads/2014/03/SOSNL_2008_2.pdf) (cited as D. Nelson).

Nickell, Joe, "Did Shakespeare Write 'Shakespeare'? Much Ado About Nothing," *Skeptical Inquirer* 35:6 (Nov.-Dec. 2011), p. 38.

_____, "Joe Nickell Responds," *Skeptical Inquirer* 36:2 (March-April 2012), p. 63.

Niederkorn, William S., "Absolute Will," *Brooklyn Rail: Critical Perspectives on Arts, Politics, and Culture* (April 2, 2010) (https://brooklynrail.org/2010/04/books/absolute-will), reviewing Shapiro (2010).

_____, "Shake-Speare Fission," *Brooklyn Rail: Critical Perspectives on Arts, Politics, and Culture* (Feb. 5, 2013) (https://brooklynrail.org/2013/02/books/shake-speare-fission).

North, George. See McCarthy & Schlueter.

*Nothing Is Truer Than Truth* (2018). See Eagan-Donovan.

O'Brien, Patrick, "De Vere, Shakespeare and Queens' College Cambridge," *De Vere Society Newsletter* 21:2 (May 2014), p. 8 (http://deveresociety.co.uk/articles/NL-2014may.pdf).

"Occam's Razor" (n.d.), *Wikipedia* (https://en.wikipedia.org/wiki/Occam%27s_razor). See also Baker, "Simplicity."

O'Donnell, C. Patrick, Jr., ed. See Spenser, *Faerie Queen* (1590, rep. 1978).

*OED*. See *Oxford English Dictionary*.

Ogburn, Charlton (Jr.), *The Mysterious William Shakespeare: The Myth and the Reality* (1984, rev. 1992) (cited as Ogburn to 1992 edition).

Ogburn, Charlton (Sr.). See Ogburn & Ogburn (1952).

Ogburn, Dorothy & Charlton Ogburn (Sr.), *This Star of England: "William Shake-speare" Man of the Renaissance* (1952) (cited as Ogburn & Ogburn).

O'Hara, Charles F. & Gregory L. O'Hara, *Fundamentals of Criminal Investigation* (5th ed. 1980).

Oreskes, Naomi, *The Rejection of Continental Drift: Theory and Method in American Earth Sciences* (1999).

Orwell, George, *1984* (1949, rep. Steven Devine illus., Folio Society, 2001) (citations to 2001 edition).

*The Oxford English Dictionary* (20 vols., 2d ed. 1989) (cited as *OED*).

Oxford, 17th Earl of. See Vere, Edward de.

Packer, Tina, *Women of Will: Following the Feminine in Shakespeare's Plays* (2015).

*The Paradise of Dainty Devices* (Richard Edwards ed., London: Henry Disle, 1576, rep. Hyder Edward Rollins ed. 1927).

*Parnassus* plays (anonymous):

　　*Parnassus 1*. See *Pilgrimage to Parnassus* (c. 1598–99).

　　*Parnassus 2*. See *Return From Parnassus [Part 1 of Return]* (c. 1599–1600).

　　*Parnassus 3*. See *Return From Parnassus [Part 2 of Return]* (c. 1601).

Peterson, Richard S., "*Enuies Scourge, and Vertues Honour:* A Literary Mystery—Spenser Redivivus," *Princeton University Library Chronicle* 47:2 (Winter 1986), p. 155 (https://www.jstor.org/stable/26404273). See also *Envy's Scourge*.

_____, "*Enuies Scourge, and Vertues Honour:* A Rare Elegy for Spenser," *Spenser Studies: A Renaissance Poetry Annual* 25 (2010), p. 287. See also *Envy's Scourge*.

Phillips, Gerald W., *Lord Burghley in Shakespeare* (1936).

*The Pilgrimage to Parnassus* (anonymous) (c. 1598–99), rep. in Macray (1886), p. 1 (citations to 1886 edition as *Parnassus 1*).

Pinksen, Daryl, *Marlowe's Ghost: The Blacklisting of the Man Who Was Shakespeare* (2008).

_____, "Was Robert Greene's 'Upstart Crow' the Actor Edward Alleyn?" *Marlowe Society Research Journal* 6 (2009).

Pollack-Pelzner, Daniel, "The Radical Argument of the New Oxford Shakespeare," *New Yorker* (Feb. 19, 2017) (https://www.newyorker.com/books/page-turner/the-radical-argument-of-the-new-oxford-shakespeare), reviewing Taylor & Egan (2017).

Pointon, Anthony J., *The Man Who Was Never Shakespeare: The Theft of William Shakspere's Identity* (2011).

_____, "The Man Who Was Never Shakespeare: The Spelling of William Shakspere's Name," in Shahan & Waugh (2013), ch. 1, p. 14.

_____, "The Rest Is Silence: The Absence of Tributes to Shakespeare at the Time of Mr. Shakspere's Death," in Shahan & Waugh (2013), ch. 6, p. 69.

Porohovshikov, Pierre S., *Shakespeare Unmasked* (1940).

Prechter, Robert R., Jr., "Veres and de Vere: The Privilege of the Prefix," *Shakespeare Oxford Newsletter* 38:1 (Winter 2002), p. 1 (https://shakespeareoxfordfellowship.org/wp-content/uploads/2014/03/SOSNL_2002_1.pdf).

_____, "The *Sonnets* Dedication Puzzle" (Parts I & II), *Shakespeare Matters* 4:3 (Spring 2005), p. 1 (https://shakespeareoxfordfellowship.org/wp-content/uploads/2013/08/SM4.3.pdf), and 4:4 (Summer 2005), p. 1 (https://shakespeareoxfordfellowship.org/wp-content/uploads/2013/08/SM4.4.pdf). See also Prechter, "Reply" (2015).

_____, "On the Authorship of *Willobie His Avisa*," *Brief Chronicles* 3 (2011), p. 135 (https://shakespeareoxfordfellowship.org/wp-content/uploads/Prechter.Willobie.pdf).

_____, "Reply to Morse's Critique of the *Sonnets* Dedication Puzzle," *Shakespeare Oxford Newsletter* 51:1 (2015), p. 19 (https://shakespeareoxfordfellowship.org/wp-content/uploads/SO-Newsletter-Winter-2015.pdf). See also Prechter (2005).

_____, "Is Greene's *Groats-worth of Wit* About Shakespeare, or by Him?" *Oxfordian* 17 (2015), p. 95 (https://shakespeareoxfordfellowship.org/wp-content/uploads/TOX17_Prechter_Groatsworth-1.pdf).

Price, Diana, *Shakespeare's Unorthodox Biography: New Evidence of an Authorship Problem* (2001, rev. 2012) (cited as Price to 2012 edition) (*Shakespeare's Unorthodox Biography* is also the title of Price's website, with updates to her book and additional scholarly work and commentary, http://www.shakespeare-authorship.com).

_____, "The Mythical 'Myth' of the Stigma of Print" (2002) (http://www.shakespeare-authorship.com/?page=stigma), on Price, *Shakespeare's Unorthodox Biography* (website).

_____, "Hand D and Shakespeare's Unorthodox Literary Paper Trail," *Journal of Early Modern Studies* 5 (2016), p. 329 (http://dx.doi.org/10.13128/JEMS-2279-7149-18095).

Puttenham, George. See *Art of English Poesy*.

Radcliffe, Debbie. See Rollett, "Doublet" Video (2015).

Radice, Betty, ed. See Terence.

Raithel, John, "The Other W.S., William Stanley, Sixth Earl of Derby," *Oxfordian* 11 (2009), p. 20 (https://shakespeareoxfordfellowship.org/wp-content/uploads/Oxfordian2009_Raithel_Stanley.pdf).

Ramsey, Paul, *The Fickle Glass: A Study of Shakespeare's Sonnets* (1979).

"RationalWiki" (n.d.), *RationalWiki* (https://rationalwiki.org/wiki/RationalWiki) (as updated April 30, 2019, and current on May 10, 2019).

"RationalWiki: What Is a RationalWiki Article?" (n.d.), *RationalWiki* (https://rationalwiki.org/wiki/RationalWiki:What_is_a_RationalWiki_article%3F) (as updated June 21, 2018, and current on May 10, 2019).

Ray, William, "Two Years After *Contested Will* or, How Are the Stratfordians Doing?" *Shakespeare Matters* 10;4 (Fall 2011), p. 24 (https://shakespeareoxfordfellowship.org/wp-content/uploads/2013/08/SM10_4.pdf), reviewing Shapiro (2010).

Rebhorn, Wayne A., ed. See *Art of English Poesy*.

Reedy, Tom & David Kathman, "How We Know That Shakespeare Wrote Shakespeare" (n.d.) (http://shakespeareauthorship.com/howdowe.html), on Kathman & Ross, *Shakespeare Authorship Page*.

Regnier, Thomas, "Could Shakespeare Think Like a Lawyer?" in Shahan & Waugh (2013), ch. 8, p. 86.

_____, "The Law of Evidence and the Shakespeare Authorship Question" (Shakespeare Oxford Fellowship Conference Presentation, Sept. 27, 2015) (posted on YouTube Dec. 7, 2015, https://youtu.be/qRAQMQPkcS4).

Reid, Jennifer & Jonathan Bate. See Bate & Reid.

*The Return From Parnassus [Part 1 of Return]* (anonymous) (c. 1599–1600), rep. in Macray (1886), p. 25 (citations to 1886 edition as *Parnassus 2*).

*The Return From Parnassus, or The Scourge of Simony [Part 2 of Return]* (anonymous) (c. 1601; orig. pub. London: John Wright, 1606), rep. in Macray (1886), p. 76 (citations to 1886 edition as *Parnassus 3*).

Riggs, David, *Ben Jonson: A Life* (1989).

Rimbault, Edward F., ed. See Chettle, *Kind-Heart's Dream* (1589, rep. 1841).

Roche, Thomas P., Jr., *"Enuies Scourge, and Vertues Honour:* A Literary Mystery—Poor Relations, or, The Case of M.L.," *Princeton University Library Chronicle* 47:2 (Winter 1986), p. 147 (https://www.jstor.org/stable/26404270). See also *Envy's Scourge*.

_____, ed. See Spenser, *Faerie Queen* (1590, rep. 1978).

Roe, Richard Paul, *The Shakespeare Guide to Italy: Retracing the Bard's Unknown Travels* (2011).

Rollett, John M., "The Dedication to Shakespeare's Sonnets," *Elizabethan Review* 5:2 (1997), p. 93, rev. & rep. in *Oxfordian* 2 (1999), p. 60 (https://shakespeareoxfordfellowship.org/wp-content/uploads/Oxfordian1999_Rollett_Dedication.pdf), and in Malim (2004), ch. 28, p. 253 (with new Postscript, p. 265) (cited as Rollett, "Dedication," and by date).

_____, "Master F.W.D., R.I.P." (1997), *Shakespeare Oxford Newsletter* 33:3-4 (Fall 1997–Winter 1998), p. 8 (https://shakespeareoxfordfellowship.org/wp-content/uploads/SOSNL_1997_4.compressed.pdf) (cited as Rollett, "Master F.W.D.").

_____, "Shakespeare's Impossible Doublet: Droeshout's Engraving Anatomized," *Brief Chronicles* 2 (2010), p. 9 (https://shakespeareoxfordfellowship.org/wp-content/uploads/Rollett.Doublet.pdf), rev. & rep. in Shahan & Waugh (2013), ch. 10, p. 113 (citations to 2013 reprint as Rollett, "Doublet").

_____, *William Stanley as Shakespeare: Evidence of Authorship by the Sixth Earl of Derby* (2015) (cited as Rollett).

_____, "The 'Impossible Doublet' in the Droeshout Engraving of William Shakespeare" (video posted by Shakespeare Authorship Coalition, narrated by Debbie Radcliffe, summarizing and based upon Rollett's work) (Nov. 22, 2015) (https://youtu.be/gCQt4pOMUqc) (cited as Rollett, "Doublet" Video).

Rollins, Hyder Edward, ed. See *Paradise of Dainty Devices*.

Rosenbaum, Ron, "10 Things I Hate About *Anonymous* and the Stupid Shakespearean Birther Cult Behind It" (Oct. 27, 2011), *Slate* (https://www.slate.com/articles/arts/the_spectator/2011/10/anonymous_a_witless_movie_from_the_stupid_shakespearean_birther_.html).

Ross, Terry, "Oxford's Literary Reputation" (n.d.) (https://shakespeareauthorship.com/rep.html), on Kathman & Ross, *Shakespeare Authorship Page*.

_____, "Oxfordian Myths: 'First Heir of My Invention' " (n.d.) (https://shakespeareauthorship.com/heir.html), on Kathman & Ross, *Shakespeare Authorship Page* (cited as Ross, "Oxfordian Myths: First Heir").

_____, "Oxfordian Myths: The Oxford Anagram in [Peacham's] *Minerva Britanna*" (n.d.) (https://shakespeareauthorship.com/peachmb.html), on Kathman & Ross, *Shakespeare Authorship Page* (cited as Ross, "Oxfordian Myths: *Minerva*").

_____, "Oxfordian Myths: Was Burghley Called 'Polus'?" (n.d.) (https://shakespeareauthorship.com/polus.html), on Kathman & Ross, *Shakespeare Authorship Page* (cited as Ross, "Oxfordian Myths: Burghley").

_____, "Peacham's Silence About Shakespeare" (n.d.) (https://shakespeareauthorship.com/peachcg.html), on Kathman & Ross, *Shakespeare Authorship Page* (cited as Ross, "Peacham").

_____, "What Did George Puttenham Really Say About Oxford and Why Does It Matter?" (n.d.) (https://shakespeareauthorship.com/putt1.html), on Kathman & Ross, *Shakespeare Authorship Page*.

Ross, Terry & David Kathman, "Barksted and Shakespeare" (n.d.) (https://shakespeareauthorship.com/barksted.html), on Kathman & Ross, *Shakespeare Authorship Page*.

_____. See also Kathman & Ross, *Shakespeare Authorship Page*.

Rubinstein, William D. See James & Rubinstein (2005, rep. 2006); Casson & Rubinstein (2016); Casson, Rubinstein & Ewald (2018); see also Green, "Neville Myths" (2019).

Sagan, Carl, *Broca's Brain: Reflections on the Romance of Science* (1979, pap. ed. 1980).

Schiffer, James, ed., *Shakespeare's Sonnets: Critical Essays* (1999).

Schlueter, June. See McCarthy & Schlueter.

Schoenbaum, Samuel, *Shakespeare's Lives* (1970, rev. 1991) (citations to 1991 edition).

_____, *William Shakespeare: A Compact Documentary Life* (1975, rev. & abridged 1987) (citations to 1987 edition).

Schuessler, Jennifer, "Shakespeare: Actor. Playwright. Social Climber." *New York Times* (June 29, 2016) (https://www.nytimes.com/2016/06/30/theater/shakespeare-coat-of-arms.html) (in print June 30, 2016, p. C1, as "Shakespeare, Hungering For Status").

Schurink, Fred, "An Unnoticed Early Reference to Shakespeare," *Notes and Queries* (March 2006), p. 72.

Shahan, John M., Shakespeare Authorship Coalition (SAC), "Declaration of Reasonable Doubt" (2007, rev. 2015) (https://doubtaboutwill.org).

_____, "Shahan's Letter to [Michael] Shermer, the Skeptic" (Aug. 2, 2009) (https://shakespeareoxfordfellowship.org/shahans-letter-to-shermer-the-skeptic).

_____, SAC, "SAC Letters to [Shakespeare] Birthplace Trust [SBT] and RSC [Royal Shakespeare Company] re: Removal of Stanley Wells' False and Libelous Claims About Authorship Doubters" (April 5, 2010, June 17, 2014, and Jan. 20, 2015) (https://doubtaboutwill.org/letters_to_sbt_and_rsc/1).

_____, SAC, "Beyond Reasonable Doubt: New Evidence and Arguments Since the Declaration of Reasonable Doubt, Part 1: Additional Reasons to Doubt Shakspere Wrote the Works" (2016) (https://doubtaboutwill.org).

_____, SAC, "Beyond Reasonable Doubt: New Evidence and Arguments Since the Declaration of Reasonable Doubt, Part 2: Major Discoveries: First Folio and Stratford Monument" (2016) (https://doubtaboutwill.org).

_____, SAC, "Beyond Reasonable Doubt: New Evidence and Arguments Since the Declaration of Reasonable Doubt, Part 3: The Stratfordian Response: Stanley Wells and James Shapiro" (2016) (https://doubtaboutwill.org).

Shahan, John M. & Alexander Waugh, eds., *Shakespeare Beyond Doubt? Exposing an Industry in Denial* (2013).

"Shakespeare Authorship" (n.d.), *RationalWiki* (https://rationalwiki.org/wiki/Shakespeare_authorship) (as updated Sept. 19, 2018, and current on May 10, 2019). See also "Talk: Shakespeare Authorship" (*RationalWiki*).

Shakespeare Authorship Coalition (SAC). See Shahan (several works) and Rollett, "Doublet" Video (2015).

"Shakespeare Authorship Question" (n.d.), *Wikipedia* (https://en.wikipedia.org/wiki/Shakespeare_authorship_question) (as updated Jan. 28, 2019, and current on May 10, 2019).

"Shakespeare Authorship Question, History of the" (n.d.), *Wikipedia* (https://en.wikipedia.org/wiki/History_of_the_Shakespeare_authorship_question) (as updated Dec. 5, 2018, and current on May 10, 2019).

*Shakespeare Documented: An Online Exhibition Documenting Shakespeare in His Own Time* (Folger Shakespeare Library, https://shakespearedocumented.folger.edu).

*Shakespeare Oxford Fellowship* (https://shakespeareoxfordfellowship.org).

Shakespeare, William, *Venus and Adonis* (author designated not on title page but only following dedication) (London: Richard Field, 1593, facsimile rep. Lee ed. 1905).

_____, *The Rape of Lucrece* (author designated not on title page but only following dedication) (London: Richard Field, 1594, facsimile rep. Lee ed. 1905).

_____, *Hamlet, Prince of Denmark* (1603–04; rev. & rep. *First Folio*, 1623; rep. Chambers ed. 1895, https://books.google.com/books?id=low9AAAAYAAJ).

_____, *Shake-speare's Sonnets* (author of *Sonnets* designated only in title, by surname, with blank space between two lines on title page where author's name would normally appear; "William Shake-speare" designated as author of appended poem "A Lover's Complaint") (London: George Eld for Thomas Thorpe, 1609, facsimile rep. Lee ed. 1905, and Booth ed. 1977) (cited as *Sonnet(s)*, relying on Booth's excellent facsimile and critical edition unless indicated otherwise; beware other modern editions which obscure, alter, or eliminate the original italics, punctuation, dedication format, *etc.*).

_____, *Pericles, Prince of Tyre* (London: Henry Gosson, 1609, facsimile rep. Lee ed. 1905).

_____, *Troilus and Cressida* (London: Richard Bonian & Henry Walley, 1609, rev. & rep. *First Folio*, 1623, rep. Bevington ed. 1998). See also Bevington, and "*Troilus and Cressida*, First Edition," and "*Troilus and Cressida*, Second Edition," on *Shakespeare Documented*.

_____, *William Shakespeare's Comedies, Histories, and Tragedies* (London: Isaac Jaggard & Edward Blount, 1623, facsimile rep. as *The First Folio of Shakespeare: The Norton Facsimile*, Charlton Hinman & Peter W.M. Blayney eds., 2d ed. 1996) (cited as *First Folio* to pagination of 1996 edition).

_____. See also Vere, Edward de (17th Earl of Oxford) (works by and relating to likely author behind the "Shakespeare" pseudonym).

"Shakespeare, William" (n.d.), *Wikipedia* (https://en.wikipedia.org/wiki/William_Shakespeare) (as updated Nov. 27, 2018).

Shapiro, James, *Shakespeare and the Jews* (1996).

_____, *Contested Will: Who Wrote Shakespeare?* (2010).

_____, "Hollywood Dishonors the Bard," *New York Times* (Oct. 16, 2011) (https://nytimes.com/2011/10/17/opinion/hollywood-dishonors-the-bard.html) (in print Oct. 17, 2011, p. A25).

_____, "Afterword," in Edmondson & Wells (2013), p. 236.

_____, *The Year of Lear: Shakespeare in 1606* (2015).

Shapiro, James & Brooke Gladstone. See Gladstone & Shapiro.

Shermer, Michael, *Why People Believe Weird Things: Pseudoscience, Superstition, and Other Confusions of Our Time* (1997, rev. 2002).

_____, "Skeptic's Take on the Life and Argued Works of Shakespeare," *Scientific American* (Aug. 2009) (https://www.scientificamerican.com/article/skeptics-take-on-the-life).

Showerman, Earl, "How Did Shakespeare Learn the Art of Medicine?" in Shahan & Waugh (2013), ch. 9, p. 99.

_____, "The Rediscovery of Shakespeare's Greater Greek," *Oxfordian* 17 (2015), p. 163 (https://shakespeareoxfordfellowship.org/wp-content/uploads/TOX17_Showerman_Greater-Greek-1.pdf).

Simpson, Donald P., ed. See *Cassell's Latin Dictionary*.

Smith, Hallett, "*Enuies Scourge, and Vertues Honour*: A Literary Mystery—Preliminary Evidence," *Princeton University Library Chronicle* 47:2 (Winter 1986), p. 150 (https://www.jstor.org/stable/26404271) (cited as H. Smith). See also *Envy's Scourge*.

Smith, William Henry, *Bacon and Shakespeare: An Inquiry Touching Players, Playhouses, and Play-Writers in the Days of Elizabeth* (London: John Russell Smith, 1857) (https://books.google.com/books?id=TgZKAAAAIAAJ) (cited as W. Smith).

Sobran, Joseph, *Alias Shakespeare: Solving the Greatest Literary Mystery of All Time* (1997).

*Sonnet(s).* See Shakespeare, *Shake-speare's Sonnets* (1609).

Spenser, Edmund, *The Faerie Queen* (orig. pub. 1590) (Thomas P. Roche Jr. & C. Patrick O'Donnell Jr. eds. 1978) (citations to 1978 edition).

_____, *The Shorter Poems* (Richard A. McCabe ed. 1999).

Spevack, Marvin, *The Harvard Concordance to Shakespeare* (1973).

Spielmann, Marion H., *The Title-Page of the First Folio of Shakespeare's Plays: A Comparative Study of the Droeshout Portrait and the Stratford Monument* (1924).

Starner, Janet Wright & Barbara Howard Traister, eds., *Anonymity in Early Modern England: "What's in a Name?"* (2011).

Steinburg, Steven, "The 'Post-Truth World' of Sir Jonathan Bate" (Jan. 30, 2018) (https://shakespeareoxfordfellowship.org/post-truth-world-sir-jonathan-bate), reviewing Waugh & Bate (2017), on *Shakespeare Oxford Fellowship*.

Stritmatter, Roger, *The Marginalia of Edward de Vere's Geneva Bible: Providential Discovery, Literary Reasoning, and Historical Consequence* (2001, 4th ed. 2015) (Ph.D. dissertation, University of Massachusetts, Amherst).

_____, "A Matter of Small Consequence," *Ever Reader* 3 (Spring-Summer 1996) (https://shakespeareoxfordfellowship.org/small-consequence).

_____, "The Not-Too-Hidden Key to [Peacham's] *Minerva Britanna*," *Shakespeare Oxford Newsletter* 36:2 (Summer 2000), p. 1 (https://shakespeareoxfordfellowship.org/wp-content/uploads/2014/03/SOSNL_2000_3.pdf) (cited as Stritmatter, "*Minerva*").

_____, Book Review, *Shakespeare Matters* 1:3 (Spring 2002), p. 25 (https://shakespeareoxfordfellowship.org/wp-content/uploads/2013/08/SM1.3.pdf), reviewing Appleton van Dreunen (2001).

_____, " 'Tilting Under Frieries': *Narcissus* (1595) and the Affair at Blackfriars," *Cahiers Élisabéthains: A Journal of English Renaissance Studies* 70:1 (Autumn 2006), p. 37, rep. in *Shakespeare Matters* 6:2 (Winter 2007), p. 1 (https://shakespeareoxfordfellowship.org/wp-content/uploads/2013/08/SM6.2.pdf).

_____, book reviews of Shapiro, *Contested Will* (2010), on *Amazon.com* (Feb. 19, 2011, https://amazon.com/review/R30CSX3RT5GSBT, and April 5, 2013, https://amazon.com/review/RERTJ0A73ONJA).

_____, "Leveraging the Shakespeare Allusion Book" (Shakespeare Oxford Fellowship Conference Presentation, Oct. 15, 2017) (posted on YouTube Dec. 14, 2017, https://youtu.be/xcxXrHKNKWY).

_____, ed., *The 1623 Shakespeare First Folio: A Minority Report* (2016) (*Brief Chronicles* special issue) (https://shakespeareoxfordfellowship.org/wp-content/uploads/BC_FF_2016_Full.pdf).

_____, ed., *The Poems of Edward de Vere, 17th Earl of Oxford ... and the Shakespeare Question* (2 vols.): v. 1, *He That Takes the Pain to Pen the Book* (2019); v. 2, *My Mind to Me a Kingdom Is* (forthcoming 2019). See also "Twenty Poems" (2018).

Stritmatter, Roger & Mark Anderson. See Anderson & Stritmatter.

Stritmatter, Roger & Lynne Kositsky, *On the Date, Sources and Design of Shakespeare's The Tempest* (2013).

_____. See also Kositsky & Stritmatter.

Stritmatter, Roger & Alexander Waugh. See Waugh & Stritmatter.

Stritmatter, Roger & Bryan H. Wildenthal, "Oxford's Poems and the Authorship Question," in Stritmatter, *Poems of Edward de Vere* (2019), v. 1, p. 1.

_____, "A Methodological Afterword," in Stritmatter, *Poems of Edward de Vere* (2019), v. 1, p. 175.

Suetonius (Gaius Suetonius Tranquillus), "The Life of Terence," in Terence, *Comedies* (Radice ed. 1976), app. A, p. 389.

Sutton, Dana F., "Introduction," in Fitzgeoffrey, *Affaniae* (Sutton ed.) (1999, rev. 2006) (http://www.philological.bham.ac.uk/affaniae/intro.html).

Sykes, Claude W., *Alias William Shakespeare?* (1947).

"Talk: Shakespeare Authorship" (n.d.), *RationalWiki* (https://rationalwiki.org/wiki/Talk:Shakespeare_authorship) (as updated May 14, 2018, and current on May 10, 2019).

Tannenbaum, Samuel A., *Problems in Shakespeare's Penmanship* (1927).

Tassinari, Lamberto, "John Florio: The Anglified Italian Who Invented Shakespeare," *Oxfordian* 13 (2011), p. 135 (https://shakespeareoxfordfellowship.org/wp-content/uploads/Oxfordian2011_Tassinari_Florio.pdf).

Taylor, Gary & Gabriel Egan *et al.*, eds., *The New Oxford Shakespeare: Authorship Companion* (2017).

Terence (Publius Terentius Afer), *The Comedies* (Betty Radice ed. 1976).

*Tottel's Miscellany (Songs and Sonnets)* (1557, rep. Edward Arber ed. 1870, https://archive.org/details/tottelsmiscellan00tottuoft/page/n9) (citations to 1870 edition).

Traister, Barbara Howard & Janet Wright Starner. See Starner & Traister.

"*Troilus and Cressida*, First Edition" (title page only) (updated 2017) (https://shakespearedocumented.folger.edu/exhibition/document/troilus-and-cressida-first-edition), on *Shakespeare Documented*.

"*Troilus and Cressida*, Second Edition" (title page only) (updated 2017) (https://shakespearedocumented.folger.edu/exhibition/document/troilus-and-cressida-second-edition), on *Shakespeare Documented*.

Twain, Mark, *Is Shakespeare Dead? From My Autobiography* (New York & London: Harper, 1909) (https://books.google.com/books?id=fK4NAAAAYAAJ).

"Twenty Poems of Edward de Vere Echo in the Works of Shakespeare" (Preliminary Website Presentation, June 22, 2018) (https://shakespeareoxfordfellowship.org/wp-content/uploads/DeVerePoemsJune2018.pdf). See also "Poetic Justice for the True Shakespeare?" (June 22, 2018) (https://shakespeareoxfordfellowship.org/poetic-justice), linking to html and paginated pdf versions of the website presentation, on *Shakespeare Oxford Fellowship*. The website presentation, though published anonymously, was primarily written and edited by Professor Roger Stritmatter, with editorial and research assistance by Professor Bryan H. Wildenthal. Professor Stritmatter builds upon the website presentation in his scholarly edition, *Poems of Edward de Vere* (2019).

Van Dreunen, Elizabeth Appleton. See Appleton van Dreunen, Elizabeth.

Vere, Edward de (17th Earl of Oxford). See generally Shakespeare, William (poems and plays attributed to "William Shakespeare," Vere's likely pseudonym).

_____, *The Poems of Edward de Vere, Earl of Oxford* (Alexander B. Grosart ed. 1872), in Grosart, *Miscellanies* (1876), v. 4, pp. 349-51, 359, 394-429.

_____, *The Poems of Edward de Vere* (London: Cecil Palmer, J. Thomas Looney ed. 1921), rep. in Looney (Miller, 3d ed. 1975), v. 1, app. 3, pp. 537-644.

_____. See also Stritmatter, *Poems of Edward de Vere* (2019); "Twenty Poems" (2018).

_____. See generally Anderson (2005) (best and most recent full scholarly biography); Fowler (1986) (selected letters); Green, Nina (concise documented biography and extensive and valuable additional materials on *Oxford Authorship Site*); Hughes, *Politicworm* website (numerous valuable articles and discussions); May (1975, 1980, and 1991) (selected poems); *Paradise of Dainty Devices* (1576, rep. 1927) (selected poems); Stritmatter, *Poems of Edward de Vere* (2019), "Twenty Poems" (2018), and Sobran (1997), apps. 2-4, pp. 231-86 (latter three sources contain selected poems, some discussion of letters, and extensive overall analysis); see also *De Vere Society* and *Shakespeare Oxford Fellowship* websites.

Vickers, Brian, *Shakespeare, Co-Author: A Historical Study of Five Collaborative Plays* (2002).

Ward, Bernard M., *The Seventeenth Earl of Oxford: 1550–1604* (1928) (first biography of Vere). See also A. Nelson (2003), Anderson (2005), and Green's concise biography on Green, *Oxford Authorship Site*.

Warren, James A., "Oxfordian Theory, Continental Drift, and the Importance of Methodology," *Oxfordian* 17 (2015), p. 193 (https://shakespeareoxfordfellowship.org/wp-content/uploads/TOX17_Warren_Continental_Drift-1.pdf).

_____, "J. Thomas Looney in *The Bookman's Journal*: Five Letters (1920–1921)," *Oxfordian* 20 (2018), p. 131.

_____, ed., *An Index to Oxfordian Publications* (4th ed. 2017).

_____, ed. See also Looney, *"Shakespeare" Identified* (1920, 4th ed. 2018), and Looney, *Collected Articles* (2019).

Waugaman, Richard M., "Did Edward de Vere Translate Ovid's *Metamorphoses*?" *Oxfordian* 20 (2018), p. 7 (https://shakespeareoxfordfellowship.org/wp-content/uploads/TOX20_Waugaman_Ovid.pdf).

Waugh, Alexander, "Keeping Shakespeare Out of Italy," in Shahan & Waugh (2013), ch. 7, p. 72.

_____, "A Secret Revealed: William Covell and His *Polimanteia* (1595)," *De Vere Society Newsletter* 20:3 (Oct. 2013), p. 7 (revised version available at http://deveresociety.co.uk/articles/AW-2013Oct-Shakespeare.pdf) (citations to revised version).

_____, "Shakespeare Was a Nom de Plume—Get Over It," *Spectator* (Nov. 2, 2013) (https://www.spectator.co.uk/2013/11/diary-636). See also *De Vere Society Newsletter* 21:1 (Jan. 2014), pp. 4, 18-19 (http://deveresociety.co.uk/articles/NL-2014jan.pdf).

_____, *Shakespeare in Court* (ebook, Amazon Kindle, 2014) (https://amazon.com/Shakespeare-Court-Kindle-Single-Alexander-ebook/dp/B00O4V4V9W) (reissued as two audio CDs with printed liner pamphlet, De Vere Society, 2016). See also "Shakespeare Birthplace Trust EXPOSED!" on *Alexander Waugh* (YouTube).

_____, " 'Shakespeare,' 'Birthplace,' and 'Trust': Three Words to Think About," in Waugh, *Shakespeare in Court* (2014, rep. De Vere Society, 2016, audio CD liner pamphlet, p. 7) (citations to 2016 reprint). See also "Shakespeare Birthplace Trust EXPOSED!" on *Alexander Waugh* (YouTube).

_____, "John Weever—Another Anti-Stratfordian," *De Vere Society Newsletter* 21:2 (May 2014), p. 12 (http://deveresociety.co.uk/articles/NL-2014may.pdf).

_____, "Jonson's 'Sweet Swan of Avon'," *Oxfordian* 16 (2014), p. 97 (https://shakespeareoxfordfellowship.org/wp-content/uploads/Waugh.Swan-of-Avon.pdf). See also "Sweet Swan of Avon" on *Alexander Waugh* (YouTube).

_____, " 'Thy Stratford Moniment'—Revisited," *De Vere Society Newsletter* 21:3 (Oct. 2014), p. 28 (rev. 2015, available at https://www.shakespeareoxfordfellowship.org/thy-stratford-moniment-revisited) (citations to revised 2015 version as Waugh, "Moniment"). See also "Monkey Business at Stratford-upon-Avon" on *Alexander Waugh* (YouTube).

_____, "From the Pulpit: A Few Home Truths—A British Introduction," *Brief Chronicles* 6 (2015), p. 1 (https://shakespeareoxfordfellowship.org/wp-content/uploads/Waugh.FromPulpit.Intro_.pdf).

_____, "Shakespeare's 'Vulgar Scandal' [Mentioned in the Sonnets]: Oxford, Southampton, and the 'First Heire' of Their Invention" (Shakespeare Oxford Fellowship Conference Presentation, Sept. 25, 2015) (posted on YouTube May 15, 2016, https://youtu.be/Q6l70pqgQEY).

_____, "A Grave Problem" (Part 1) (Shakespearean Authorship Trust Conference Presentation, Nov. 20, 2016) (posted on YouTube Feb. 13, 2017, https://youtu.be/wzseIwez8YA). See also revised version, "Where Shakespeare Is REALLY Buried" (Parts 1-4), on *Alexander Waugh* (YouTube).

_____, "A Grave Problem" (Part 2) (Shakespearean Authorship Trust Conference Presentation, Oct. 29, 2017) (posted on YouTube Nov. 6, 2017, https://youtu.be/zGiq_u48Rec). See also revised version, "Where Shakespeare Is REALLY Buried" (Parts 1-4), on *Alexander Waugh* (YouTube).

_____, "Hidden Truths in Written and Pictoral Notes" ["Hidden Truths, Part 1"], *De Vere Society Newsletter* 24:2 (April 2017), p. 14. See also "Where Shakespeare Is REALLY Buried" (Parts 1-4), on *Alexander Waugh* (YouTube).

_____, "Hidden Truths (Part II)" ["Hidden Truths, Part 2"], *De Vere Society Newsletter* 24:4 (Oct. 2017), p. 22. See also "Where Shakespeare Is REALLY Buried" (Parts 1-4), on *Alexander Waugh* (YouTube).

_____, "Hidden Truths" ["Hidden Truths, SOF Presentation"] (Shakespeare Oxford Fellowship Conference Presentation, Chicago, Oct. 13, 2017). See also "Where Shakespeare Is REALLY Buried" (Parts 1-4), on *Alexander Waugh* (YouTube).

_____, "My Shakespeare Rise!" in Leahy (2018), ch. 3, p. 47.

_____, *Alexander Waugh* (YouTube channel launched 2017) (https://www.youtube.com/channel/UCHN7SCKlsa9lPYJmqqQ2uIg), *e.g.*:

"Ben Jonson Knew ..." (Jan. 6, 2018) (https://youtu.be/iQThnv8c2uI).

"A Fair Youth, a Dark Lady and Shakespeare—The Scandal Exposed!" (Dec. 8, 2018) (https://youtu.be/IN3ZOOnJQqk).

"Francis Meres Knew ..." (Oct. 19, 2018) (https://youtu.be/fFaGybgFs9M).

"Henry Peacham Knew ..." (Jan. 8, 2018) (https://youtu.be/3bhb6SCXlDQ).

"John Warren Knew ..." (Jan. 16, 2018) (https://youtu.be/DB9_xC_upRs).

"John Weever Knew ... (Part 1)" (Dec. 23, 2018) (https://youtu.be/oCGN6K1LkUg).

"John Weever Knew ... (Part 2)" (Jan. 11, 2019) (https://youtu.be/wu4FD4Zii8c).

"Monkey Business at Stratford-upon-Avon" (Feb. 3, 2018) (https://youtu.be/TRDX5wIx_8I).

"Shakespeare and the Case of the Missing Playwright" (Sept. 11, 2017) (https://youtu.be/2oxzvxHdDrw).

"Shakespeare Birthplace Trust EXPOSED!" (May 7, 2018) (https://youtu.be/ERJS-NWZ7Ns).

"Sweet Swan of Avon" (March 27, 2018) (https://youtu.be/GpHT3LzvcjM).

"What the Eye Cannot See ..." (March 9, 2018) (https://youtu.be/ljM11ib4Apk).

"Where Shakespeare Is REALLY Buried (A Grave Problem)" (Part 1) (Dec. 25, 2017) (https://youtu.be/XqV44taFNUc).

"Where Shakespeare Is REALLY Buried (A Grave Problem)" (Part 2) (Dec. 25, 2017) (https://youtu.be/38dk0ctTUNM).

"Where Shakespeare Is REALLY Buried (A Grave Problem)" (Part 3) (March 1, 2018) (https://youtu.be/u2aw0mez19I).

"Where Shakespeare Is REALLY Buried (A Grave Problem)" (Part 4) (Aug. 20, 2018) (https://youtu.be/W3P3HKJtwWY).

"William Covell Knew ..." (Sept. 11, 2017) (https://youtu.be/SxVdLiAX4Es).

Waugh, Alexander, Mark Anderson & Alex McNeil. See Anderson, Waugh & McNeil.

Waugh, Alexander & Jonathan Bate, "Who Wrote Shakespeare?" (debate moderated by Hermione Eyre, Sept. 21, 2017) (posted on YouTube Sept. 26, 2017, https://youtu.be/HgImgdJ5L6o).

Waugh, Alexander & John M. Shahan. See Shahan & Waugh.

Waugh, Alexander & Roger Stritmatter, *The New Shakespeare Allusion Book: Literary Allusions to Shakespeare, 1584–1786, on Historical Principles* (forthcoming 2020).

Wells, Stanley, *Shakespeare: A Life in Drama* (1995).

_____, "Allusions to Shakespeare to 1642," in Edmondson & Wells (2013), ch. 7, p. 73.

Wells, Stanley & Paul Edmondson. See Edmondson & Wells.

Werth, Andrew, "Shakespeare's 'Lesse Greek'," *Oxfordian* 5 (2002), p. 11 (https://shakespeareoxfordfellowship.org/wp-content/uploads/Oxfordian2002_werth_greek.pdf).

Whalen, Richard F., *Shakespeare—Who Was He? The Oxford Challenge to the Bard of Avon* (1994).

_____, "A Dozen Shakespeare Plays Written After Oxford Died? *Not Proven!*" *Oxfordian* 10 (2007), p. 75.

_____, Book Review, *Shakespeare Oxford Newsletter* 46:1 (May 2010), p. 7 (https://shakespeareoxfordfellowship.org/wp-content/uploads/2014/03/SOSNL_2010_1.pdf), reviewing Shapiro (2010).

_____, " 'Look Not on This Picture': Ambiguity in the Shakespeare First Folio Preface," *Shakespeare Matters* 10:3 (Summer 2011), p. 1 (https://shakespeareoxfordfellowship.org/wp-content/uploads/2013/08/SM10.3.pdf).

_____, "The Ambiguous Ben Jonson: Implications for Assessing the Validity of the First Folio Testimony," in Shahan & Waugh (2013), ch. 11, p. 126.

_____, "The Stratford Bust: A Monumental Fraud," in Shahan & Waugh (2013), ch. 12, p. 136 (orig. pub. *Oxfordian* 8, 2005, p. 7, https://shakespeareoxfordfellowship.org/wp-content/uploads/Oxfordian2005_Whalen_Fraud.compressed.pdf).

_____, "Was 'Shakspere' Also a Spelling of 'Shakespeare'? Strat Stats Fail to Prove It," *Brief Chronicles* 6 (2015), p. 33 (https://shakespeareoxfordfellowship.org/wp-content/uploads/Whalen.Shakspere.Spelling.pdf).

Whigham, Frank, ed. See *Art of English Poesy.*

Whitman, Walt, "What Lurks Behind Shakspere's Historical Plays?" in Whitman, *November Boughs* (Philadelphia: McKay, 1888) (https://books.google.com/books?id=k6IbzuvvhXcC), p. 52.

Whittemore, Hank, *100 Reasons Shake-speare Was the Earl of Oxford* (2016).

_____, *Hank Whittemore's Shakespeare Blog* (https://hankwhittemore.com).

"Wikipedia: Policies and Guidelines" (n.d.), *Wikipedia* (https://en.wikipedia.org/wiki/Wikipedia:Policies_and_guidelines) (as updated April 22, 2019, and current on May 10, 2019).

Wildenthal, Bryan H., *Native American Sovereignty on Trial: A Handbook With Cases, Laws, and Documents* (2003).

_____, "Nationalizing the Bill of Rights: Revisiting the Original Understanding of the Fourteenth Amendment in 1866–67," *Ohio State Law Journal* 68:6 (2007), p. 1509 (https://ssrn.com/abstract=963487).

_____, "Federal Labor Law, Indian Sovereignty, and the Canons of Construction," *Oregon Law Review* 86:2 (2007), p. 413 (https://ssrn.com/abstract=970590).

_____, Letter to the Editor, *Skeptical Inquirer* 36:2 (March-April 2012), p. 63 (responding to Frazier 2011 and Nickell 2011).

_____, "Remembering Rollett and Debunking Shapiro (Again)" (2016, rev. 2017) (https://ssrn.com/abstract=2899575) (orig. pub. *Shakespeare Oxford Fellowship*, July 13, 2016).

_____, "End of an Oxfordian Era on the Supreme Court? Remembering Justice Antonin Scalia (1936-2016)" (2016, rev. 2017) (https://ssrn.com/abstract=2834349) (orig. pub. *Shakespeare Oxford Newsletter* 52:3, Summer 2016, p. 9).

\_\_\_\_\_, "Early Shakespeare Authorship Doubts: Debunking the Central Stratfordian Claim" (Shakespeare Oxford Fellowship Conference Presentation, Oct. 14, 2017) (posted on YouTube Dec. 8, 2017, https://youtu.be/oefmNJ6_suc).

\_\_\_\_\_, "Indian Sovereignty, General Federal Laws, and the Canons of Construction: An Overview and Update," *American Indian Law Journal* (Seattle University School of Law) 6:1 (2017), art. 3, p. 98 (https://ssrn.com/abstract=2987620).

\_\_\_\_\_, "How I Became an Oxfordian" (Feb. 27, 2018) (https://shakespeareoxfordfellowship.org/bryan-h-wildenthal-became-oxfordian), on *Shakespeare Oxford Fellowship*.

Wildenthal, Bryan H. & Roger Stritmatter. See Stritmatter & Wildenthal, "Oxford's Poems and the Authorship Question," in Stritmatter, *Poems of Edward de Vere* (2019), v. 1, p. 1; Stritmatter & Wildenthal, "A Methodological Afterword," in Stritmatter, *Poems of Edward de Vere* (2019), v. 1, p. 175. See also "Twenty Poems" (2018) (edited by Stritmatter with assistance by Wildenthal, though published anonymously).

"William Shakespeare." See "Shakespeare, William" (*Wikipedia*).

Williams, Robin P., *Sweet Swan of Avon: Did a Woman Write Shakespeare?* (2006, 2d ed. 2012).

\_\_\_\_\_, "Mary Sidney Herbert, the Countess of Pembroke," in Leahy (2018), ch. 6, p. 139.

Willobie, Henry (probably a pseudonym), *Avisa* (London: John Windet, 1594, rep. Charles Hughes ed. 1904, https://books.google.com/books?id=sJNBAAAAYAAJ) (often cited as given on title page, *Willobie His Avisa*; cited herein as *Avisa* to 1904 edition).

Wilson, Ian, *Black Jenny* (1992) (rep. as *Shakespeare's Dark Lady*, http://www.shakespearesdarklady.com).

Wilson, Laura & Lisa Wilson (directors & producers), *Last Will. & Testament* (2012) (documentary film) (https://youtu.be/Mp3gF9f-Ns4).

Winkler, Elizabeth, "Was Shakespeare a Woman?" *Atlantic* (online May 2019, in print June 2019) (https://www.theatlantic.com/magazine/archive/2019/06/who-is-shakespeare-emilia-bassano/588076).

Witmore, Michael & Heather Wolfe. See Wolfe & Witmore.

Wolfe, Heather & Michael Witmore, "William Shakespeare, Poet and Gentleman" (Jan. 18, 2017), *The Collation: Research and Exploration at the Folger* (https://collation.folger.edu/2017/01/william-shakespeare-post-gentleman).

Wraight, A.D., *The Story That the Sonnets Tell* (1994).

Zalta, Edward N., *et al.*, eds., *Stanford Encyclopedia of Philosophy* (https://plato.stanford.edu/info.html).

# INDEX

Persons, places, literary works, topics, *etc.*, are indexed here in a single alphabetical list. The Index generally covers only references in the main text, but material in the footnotes is sometimes indexed where it seems useful. Page references in the Index do not distinguish between items in the main text and footnotes (to the extent the latter are indexed), so when consulting any indexed page, be sure to check not only the main text but also any footnote on that page. It is advisable to check the Bibliography for a comprehensive listing of all cited authors and editors and their works.

# ABOUT THIS AUTHOR

(Now if only *that* author had provided a convenient note like *this* one ... ?)

Bryan H. Wildenthal was born in 1964 in Houston, Texas. While his family has deep roots in Texas (including Alpine, a small town west of the Pecos where his parents met in high school and acted together in a college production of *A Midsummer Night's Dream*), he grew up mainly in the suburbs of Lansing, Michigan, graduating from Okemos High School in 1982. He would like to credit his wonderful public high school English teachers, including Ms. Tanner, Ms. Albert, Mr. Parkinson, Ms. Haner, and Mr. Collar, for teaching him the fundamentals of writing and nurturing his interest in Shakespeare and literature. He would also like to thank the two central heroes and role models of his life, his mother Joyce and his father Hobson (Shakespeare lovers both), who have taught and continue to teach him about unconditional love, along with so much else, including history, literature, science, and critical thinking.

He earned his A.B. from Stanford University in 1986 (political science, with honors), taking mostly courses on history and international relations, inspired by many wonderful professors. He earned his J.D. from Stanford Law School in 1989 (with distinction), where he served as an editor of the *Stanford Law Review* and was inspired by more outstanding professors, motivating him to pursue teaching himself. He served as a law clerk for the Honorable Frank M. Johnson Jr., Circuit Judge, U.S. Court of Appeals, 11th Circuit (Montgomery, Alabama) (1989–90), and for the Honorable Michael F. Cavanagh, Chief Justice of the Supreme Court of Michigan (1990–92).

He is now Professor of Law Emeritus. He served for 22 years (1996–2018) as a member of the faculty of Thomas Jefferson School of Law (San Diego, California), and has continued to teach as a Visiting Professor since 2018. He also taught as a Visiting Professor at Chicago-Kent College of Law (1994–96) and in Thomas Jefferson School of Law's International and Comparative Law Summer Program (2011) in Nice, France (co-hosted by the University of Nice Faculty of Law). He practiced law with Wilmer, Cutler & Pickering (now WilmerHale) in Washington, D.C. (1992–94), and is an attorney licensed to practice by the State Bar of Michigan and the Bar of the Supreme Court of the United States.

His main scholarly and teaching specialties are American constitutional law, comparative constitutional law, civil procedure, federal court jurisdiction, legal history (with a particular focus on the American Civil War and Reconstruction), American Indian law (rights and sovereignty of Native Americans and

Indian Nations), and sexual identity law (rights of gay, lesbian, bisexual, and transgender people). Most of his writings relating to law or Shakespeare (some relate to both) are available online (https://ssrn.com/author=181791). He has published a textbook on Native American sovereignty and numerous law review articles.

His 2007 *Ohio State Law Journal* article, examining the historical basis for enforcing the Bill of Rights against state and local governments pursuant to the Fourteenth Amendment of the U.S. Constitution, was cited by the Supreme Court of the United States in *McDonald v. Chicago*, 561 U.S. 742, 763 n. 10 (2010) (also cited in a concurring opinion, pp. 829 n. 10, 830 n. 12, 841), and *Timbs v. Indiana*, 586 U.S. ___, 139 S. Ct. 682, 691 (Feb. 20, 2019) (unanimous decision) (cited in a concurring opinion).

His 2007 *Oregon Law Review* article on the sovereignty of Indian Nations and the Indian law "canons of construction" has likewise been cited as a major contribution to that field. See, *e.g.*, *Cohen's Handbook of Federal Indian Law* (Nell Jessup Newton *et al.* eds. 2012), § 2.03, p. 123 n. 2 (influencing major revisions of § 2.03). In 2017, he published a major follow-up article in Seattle University School of Law's *American Indian Law Journal*.

Bryan has loved the plays and poems of "Shakespeare" since his teenage years. He became interested in the Shakespeare Authorship Question (SAQ) in 2000, and started getting more actively involved as an Oxfordian in 2012. He has published several articles on the SAQ, and has served since 2016 as a member of the Board of Trustees—and since 2018 as First Vice-President—of the Shakespeare Oxford Fellowship (SOF) (https://shakespeareoxfordfellowship.org). He lives in San Diego with his husband, Ashish Agrawal, M.D. (a critical care physician), and his mother-in-law, Pushpa Lala.

Those curious about the word "Zindabad" in the name of the author's self-publishing entity—a salutation of Persian origin used in Hindi, Urdu, and other South Asian languages—may wish to look it up on *Wikipedia* and ponder its relevance to the SAQ. For a usage very well-known to Indians of a certain age, see the classic Bollywood epic film, *Mughal-e-Azam* (1960), two hours and 29 minutes into the subtitled and colorized version freely available on YouTube (see https://youtu.be/rq8MktR_Ctc).